Alastair
Sawday's
Special Places
to Stay
French Châteaux
& Hotels
"Sawday unearths the
most beguiling châteaux,
auberges and hotels."
The Daily Telegraph
D0835322
"Indispensable."
Evening Standard

Alastair
Sawday's
Special Places
to Stay
Portugal
"The best if you're seeking
an unusual or spectacular bed
for the night."
The Times

Alastair
Sawday's
Special Places
to Stay
Dog-friendly
Breaks in Britain
Foreword by
Ben Fogle

Alastair
Sawday's
Special Places to Stay

Seventh edition

Published in 2012
ISBN-13: 978-1-906136-56-7

Alastair Sawday Publishing Co. Ltd,
The Old Farmyard, Yanley Lane,
Long Ashton, Bristol BS41 9LR, UK
Tel: +44 (0)1275 395430
Email: info@sawdays.co.uk
Web: www.sawdays.co.uk

The Globe Pequot Press,
P. O. Box 480, Guilford,
Connecticut 06437, USA
Tel: +1 203 458 4500
Email: info@globepequot.com
Web: www.globepequot.com

Series Editor Alastair Sawday
Editor Florence Fortnam
Editorial Director Annie Shillito
Content & Publishing Manager
Jackie King
Senior Editor Jo Boissevain
Production Coordinator Alex Skinner
Writing Alex Baker, Jo Boissevain, Sarah Bolton, Annaliza Davis, Florence Fortnam, Monica Guy, Matthew Hilton-Dennis
Inspections Richard & Linda Armspach, Kate Ball, Lois Ferguson, Heidi Flores, Florence Fortnam, Abbi Greetham, Jill Greetham, Tessa Phipps, Katrina & Mike Power, Janine Raedts, Pamela Romano, Clare Roskill, Jennifer Telfeyan
Thanks to those people who did an inspection or write-up or two.
Marketing & PR 01275 395433

A catalogue record for this book is available from the British Library. This publication is not included under licences issued by the Copyright Agency. No part of this publication may be used in any form of advertising, sales promotion or publicity.

We have made every effort to ensure the accuracy of the information in this book at the time of going to press. However, we cannot accept any responsibility for any loss, injury or inconvenience resulting from the use of information contained therein.

Maps: Maidenhead Cartographic Services
Printing: Butler, Tanner & Dennis, Frome
UK distribution: Penguin UK, London
Production: The Content Works

1. Agriturismo Ramuse, entry 270 2. Mark Bolton, www.markboltonphotography.co.uk, entry 161
3. Loupe Images/Chris Tubbs

Alastair Sawday's

Special Places to Stay

Italy

Contents

'It may be said of men,' declared Machiavelli, 'that they are ungrateful, voluble, dissembling, and covetous of gain'. This isn't our experience with Special Places!

For those of us who can ignore such pessimism and love Italy – and the innumerable little lessons she has to teach us about how to live, eat, love, play and just be – the events of the last year have been dispiriting to watch. We winced as their former leader's outlandish behaviour was revealed, and we have seen how the financial chaos that has overtaken most of Europe has been worse, somehow, in Italy – because of the dreamy view of Italy many of us have.

So what is our role here at Sawday's 'Special Places'? It is to focus on the hundreds of families in this book and on our website, in the hope that the extra visitors will help them out, at least. They deserve it; they are out on a limb, doing their own thing in their own way and without slavishly following trends. They are authentic, good, kind and creative people – setting examples and breaking new ground. They have chosen their paths and invite us in.

Given the recession it is a delight to report that we have more special places in Italy than ever before, with scores waiting in the wings for us to inspect them. We seem, too, finally, to have cracked the difficulty of finding special places in towns and cities: we have many in Venice, Florence and Rome. Florence Fortnam, our leading Italy lady, made a special effort to track down fine places in Sicily, and it has paid off handsomely. Puglia, too, has revealed more places to us – as has Sardinia.

Part of the fun of putting this book together is the breathtaking variety of houses that you can stay in. At one end is the Palazzo Lantieri near the Slovenian border – a 15th-century house of ravishing beauty. It is a treat to stay there, and to wander the estate at will. It is also a treat to descend the social ladder and sleep, perhaps, in a simple farmhouse – or a B&B tucked into the 'centro storico' of Florence.

If you are a sensitive traveller, wonder at the Florentine philosopher Ficino's assertion in 1492: 'It is a golden age which has restored to the light the liberal arts that were almost destroyed: grammar, poetry, eloquence, painting, sculpture, architecture and music.' Bring on another golden age – launched by the rediscovered Italian arts of cooking and wine growing. You can discover them for yourself at these Special Places.

Alastair Sawday

Photo: Tom Germain

It's simple. There are no rules, no boxes to tick. We choose places that we like and are fiercely subjective in our choices. We also recognise that one person's idea of special is not necessarily someone else's so there is a huge variety of places, and prices, in this book. Those who are familiar with our Special Places series know that we look for comfort, originality, authenticity, and reject the insincere, the anonymous and the banal. The way guests are treated comes as high on our list as the setting, the architecture, the atmosphere and the food.

We have selected the widest range of places, and prices, for you to choose from – castles, villas, city apartments, farmhouses, country inns, even a monastery or two. It might be breakfast under the frescoed ceiling of a Renaissance villa that is special, or a large and boisterous dinner in a farmhouse kitchen, or a life-enhancing view. We have not necessarily chosen the most opulent places to stay, but the most interesting and satisfying. But because Italy has, to quote Lord Byron, 'the fatal gift of beauty' it is easy to forget that it hasn't all been built with aesthetics in mind. Don't be put off when you discover that there are swathes of industrial plant (yes, even in Tuscany). These things can't be airbrushed out, but acknowledge that they exist and they won't spoil your fun.

Inspections

We visit every place in the guide to get a feel for how both house and owner tick. We don't take a clipboard and we don't have a list of what is acceptable and what is not. Instead, we chat for an hour or so with the owner or manager and look round. It's all very informal, but it gives us an excellent idea of who would enjoy staying there. If the visit happens to be the last of the day, we may stay the night. Once in the book, properties are re-inspected every few years, so that we can keep things fresh and accurate.

Feedback

In between inspections we rely on feedback from our army of readers, as well as from staff members who are encouraged to visit properties across the series. This feedback is invaluable to us and we always follow up on comments.

So do tell us whether your stay has been a joy or not, if the atmosphere was great or stuffy, the owners and staff cheery or

Photo: Casa Serena, entry 362

bored. The accuracy of the book depends on what you, and our inspectors, tell us. A lot of the new entries in each edition are recommended by our readers, so keep telling us about new places you've discovered too. You will find the forms on our website at www.sawdays.co.uk.

However, please do not tell us if your starter was cold, or the bedside light broken. Tell the owner, immediately, and get them to do something about it. Most owners, or staff, are more than happy to correct problems and will bend over backwards to help. Far better than bottling it up and then writing to us a week later!

Subscriptions

Owners pay to appear in this guide. Their fee goes towards the high costs of inspecting, maintaining our website and producing an all-colour book. We only include places that we find special for one reason or another, so it is not possible for anyone to buy their way onto these pages. Nor is it possible for the owner to write their own description. We will say if the bedrooms are small, or if a main road is near. We do our best to avoid misleading people.

Disclaimer

We make no claims to pure objectivity in choosing these places. They are here simply because we like them. Our opinions and tastes are ours alone and this book is a statement of them; we hope you will share them. We have done our utmost to get our facts right but apologise unreservedly for any mistakes that may have crept in. The latest information we have about each place can be found on our website, www.sawdays.co.uk.

You should know that we don't check such things as fire alarms, swimming pool security or any other regulation with which owners should comply. This is the responsibility of the owners.

Photo: Poderi Firenze, entry 176

Finding the right place for you

All these places are special in one way or another. All have been visited and then written about honestly so that you can take what you want and leave the rest. Those of you who swear by the Sawday's books trust our write-ups precisely because we don't have a blanket standard; we include places simply because we like them. But we all have different priorities, so do read the descriptions carefully and pick out the places where you will be comfortable. If something is particularly important to you then check when you book: a simple question or two can avoid misunderstandings.

Maps

Each property is flagged with its entry number on the maps at the front. These maps are a great starting point for planning your trip, but please don't use them as anything other than a general guide – use a decent road map for real navigation. Most places will send you detailed instructions once you have booked your stay. Self-catering places are marked in blue on the maps; others are marked in red.

Ethical Collection

We're always keen to draw attention to owners who are striving to have a positive impact on the world, so you'll notice that some entries are flagged as being part of our 'Ethical Collection'. These places are working hard to reduce their environmental footprint, making

Photo: Nada Matti

significant contributions to their local community, or are passionate about serving local or organic food. Owners have had to fill in a very detailed questionnaire before becoming part of this Collection – read more at the end of the book. This doesn't mean that other places in the guide are not taking similar initiatives – many are – but we may not yet know about them. (See page 419.)

Symbols

Below each entry you will see some symbols, which are explained at the very back of the book. They are based on the information given to us by the owners. However, things do change: bikes may be under repair or a new pool may have been put in. Please use the symbols as a guide rather than an absolute statement of fact and double-check anything that is important to you – owners occasionally bend their own rules, so it's worth asking if you may take your child or dog even if they don't have the symbol.

Wheelchair access – The symbol shows those places that are keen to accept wheelchair users and have made provision for them. However, this does not mean that wheelchair users will always be met with a perfect landscape, nor does it indicate that they have been officially assessed for such a status. You may encounter ramps, a shallow step, gravelled paths, alternative routes into some rooms, a bathroom (not a wet room), perhaps even a lift. In short, there may be the odd hindrance and we urge you to call and make sure you will get what you need.

Limited mobility – The limited mobility symbol shows those places where at least one bedroom and bathroom is accessible without using stairs. The symbol is designed to satisfy those who walk slowly, with difficulty, or with the aid of a stick. A wheelchair may be able to navigate some areas, but these places are not fully wheelchair friendly. If you use a chair for longer distances, but are not too bad over shorter distances, you'll probably be OK; again, please ring and ask. There may be a step or two, a bath or a shower with a tray in a cubicle, a good distance between the car park and your room, slippery flagstones or a tight turn.

Photo: Villa Le Piazzole, entry 152

Children – The symbol shows places which are happy to accept children of all ages. This does not mean that they will necessarily have cots, high chairs, etc. If an owner welcomes children but only those above a certain age, we have put these details at the end of their write-up. These houses do not have the child symbol, but even these folk may accept your younger child at quiet times. If you want to get out and about in the evenings, check when you book whether there are any babysitting services. Even very small places can sometimes organise this for you.

Pets – Our symbol shows places which are happy to accept pets. It means they can sleep in the bedroom with you, but not on the bed. It's really important to get this one right before you arrive, as many places make you keep dogs in the car. Check carefully: Spot's emotional wellbeing may depend on it.

Owners' pets – The symbol is given when the owners have their own pet on the premises. It may not be a cat! But it is there to warn you that you may be greeted by a dog, serenaded by a parrot, or indeed sat upon by a cat.

Types of places

Each entry is simply labelled (B&B, hotel, self-catering) to guide you, but the write-ups reveal several descriptive terms. This list serves as a rough guide to what you might expect to find.

Agriturismo: farm or estate with B&B rooms or apartments; Albergo: Italian word for an inn, more personal than a hotel; Azienda agrituristica: literally, 'agricultural business'; Casa (Cà in Venetian dialect): house; Cascina: farmhouse; Castello: castle; Corte: courtyard; Country house: a new concept in Italian hospitality, usually family-run and akin to a villa; Dimora: dwelling; Fattoria: farm; Locanda: means 'inn', but sometimes used to describe a restaurant only; Podere: farm or smallholding; Palazzo: literally a 'palace' but more usually a mansion; Relais: an imported French term meaning 'inn'; Residenza: an apartment or house with rooms for guests; Tenuta: farm holding, or 'tenancy'; Villa: country residence.

Photo: Monteluce Country House, entry 345

Rooms

Bedrooms – We tell you about the range of accommodation in singles, doubles, twins, family rooms and suites, as well as apartments and whole houses. A 'family' room is a loose term because, in Italy, triples and quadruples often sleep more than the heading suggests; extra beds can often be added for children, usually with a charge, so check when booking.

Where an entry reads '4 + 2' this means 4 B&B rooms plus 2 self-catering apartments/villas/cottages.

Bathrooms – Assume that bathrooms are en suite unless we say otherwise. Italian bathrooms often have a shower only.

Meals

Eating in Italy is one of life's great pleasures. There is plenty of variety, and each region has its own specialities and surprises. Many owners use organic, local or home-grown ingredients, and more often than not will have produced some part of your meal themselves.

Vegetarians – Although fresh, seasonal vegetables are readily available in Italy, most Italian dishes contain meat and some Italians still find the concept of vegetarianism quite bizarre. Our owners who offer a good range of vegetarian options have a special symbol – but don't be surprised if those without it struggle to understand a meal without meat.

Breakfast – What constitutes breakfast varies hugely from place to place. Many hotels don't offer it at all, especially in towns, where it is normal to walk to the nearest bar for your first espresso. (Prices double or triple as soon as you sit down, so if you want to save money, join the locals at the bar.) If you are confronted with a vacuum-packed breakfast it's because B&Bs are only allowed to serve fresh ingredients if they meet certain strict regulations. On farms, however, you are likely to find homemade jams and cakes as well as home-produced cheeses and fruit.

Dinner – Hotels and other places with restaurants usually offer the widest à la carte choice. Smaller places may offer a set dinner (at a set time) and you will need to book in advance. Many of our owners are excellent cooks so, if you fancy an evening sitting two steps from your bedroom on your host's terrace overlooking Tuscan hills or Umbrian valleys, be sure to ask your hosts – on booking or on arrival – if they are able to share their culinary skills and serve up a sumptuous dinner on site. Sometimes you will eat with the family; sometimes you will be eating in a separate dining room, served by a member of the family. Small farms and inns often offer dinners which are excellent value and delicious, so keep an open mind. Nonetheless, be aware that laws in some regions of Italy do not allow B&Bs to serve dinner to their guests.

Prices

The prices we quote are the prices per night per room unless otherwise stated, breakfast included. For self-catering, we specify if the price is per week. For half-board, it may be per person (p.p.). Meal prices are always given per person; we try to give you an approximate price and say if wine is included. Prices quoted are those given to us for 2012 but be aware they may change; treat them as a guideline rather than as infallible. We try to list any extra hidden costs – e.g. linen, towels, heating – but always check on booking.

Booking and cancellation

Hotels will usually ask you for a credit card number at the time of booking, for confirmation. Remember to let smaller places know if you are likely to be arriving late, and if you want dinner. Some of the major cities get very full (and often double in price) around the time of trade fairs (e.g. fashion fairs in Milan, the Biennale in Venice). And book well ahead if you plan to visit Italy during school holidays.

Some cancellation policies are more stringent than others. It is also worth noting that some owners will take the money directly from your credit/debit card without contacting you to discuss it. So ask them to explain their cancellation policy clearly before booking so you understand exactly where you stand; it may well avoid a nasty surprise. And consider taking out travel insurance (with a cancellation clause) if you're concerned.

Photo left: Auberge de la Maison, entry 1
Photo right: Alberghetto La Marianna, entry 23

Payment

The most commonly accepted credit cards are Visa, Eurocard, MasterCard and Amex. Many places in this book don't take plastic because of high bank charges. Check the symbols at the bottom of each entry before you arrive, in case you are a long way from a cash dispenser!

Tipping

In bars you are given your change on a small saucer, and it is usual to leave a couple of small coins there. A cover charge on restaurant meals is standard. A small tip ('mancia') in family-run establishments is also welcome, so leave one if you wish.

Closed

When given in months this means for the whole of the month stated. So, 'Closed: November to March' means closed from 1 November to 31 March.

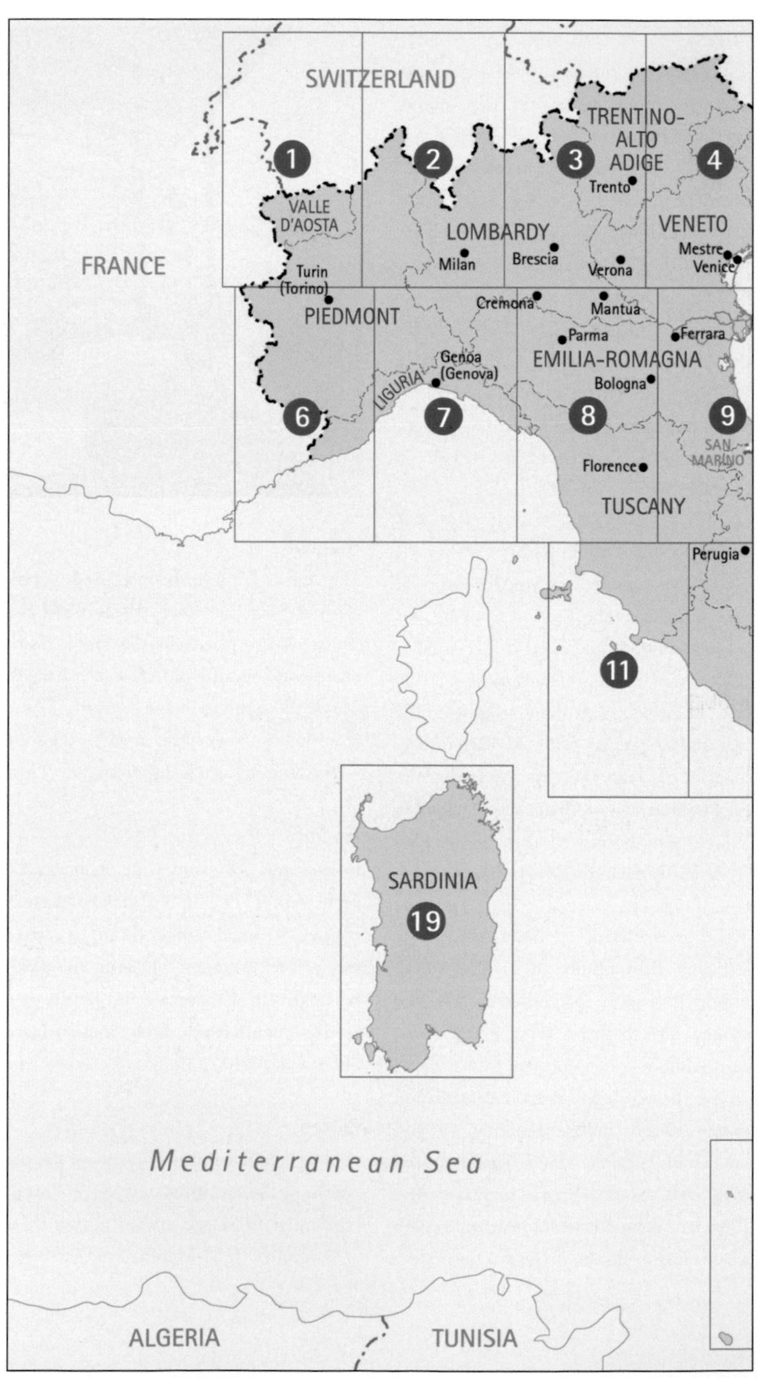
SWITZERLAND
TRENTINO-ALTO ADIGE
1
2
3
4
Trento
VALLE D'AOSTA
LOMBARDY
VENETO
FRANCE
Milan
Brescia
Verona
Mestre
Venice
Turin (Torino)
Cremona
Mantua
PIEDMONT
Parma
Ferrara
Genoa (Genova)
EMILIA-ROMAGNA
LIGURIA
Bologna
6
7
8
9
SAN MARINO
Florence
TUSCANY
Perugia
11
SARDINIA
19
Mediterranean Sea
ALGERIA
TUNISIA

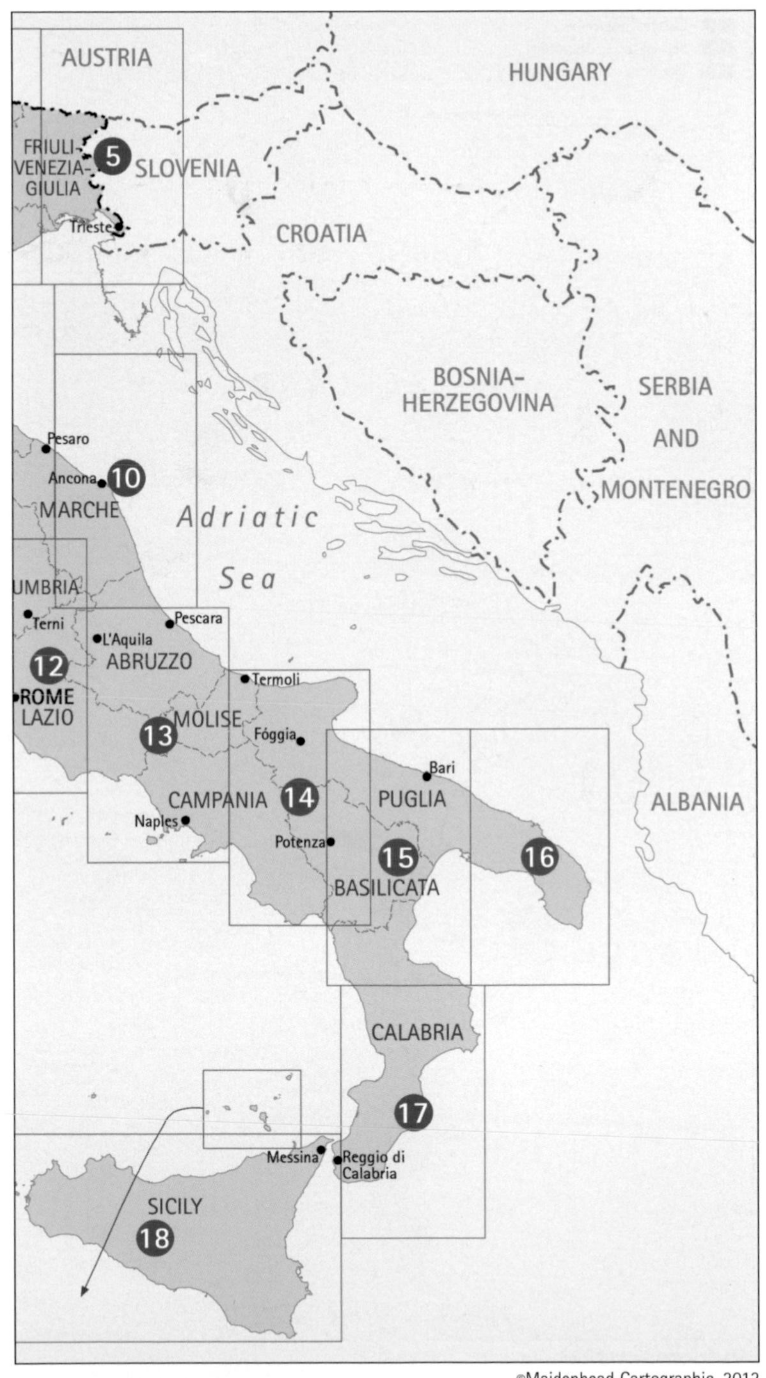
AUSTRIA
HUNGARY
FRIULI-
VENEZIA-
GIULIA
5
SLOVENIA
Trieste
CROATIA
BOSNIA-
HERZEGOVINA
SERBIA
AND
MONTENEGRO
Pesaro
Ancona
10
MARCHE
Adriatic
Sea
UMBRIA
Terni
Pescara
L'Aquila
ABRUZZO
12
ROME
LAZIO
Termoli
MOLISE
13
Fóggia
Bari
CAMPANIA
14
PUGLIA
ALBANIA
Naples
Potenza
15
16
BASILICATA
CALABRIA
17
Messina
Reggio di
Calabria
SICILY
18

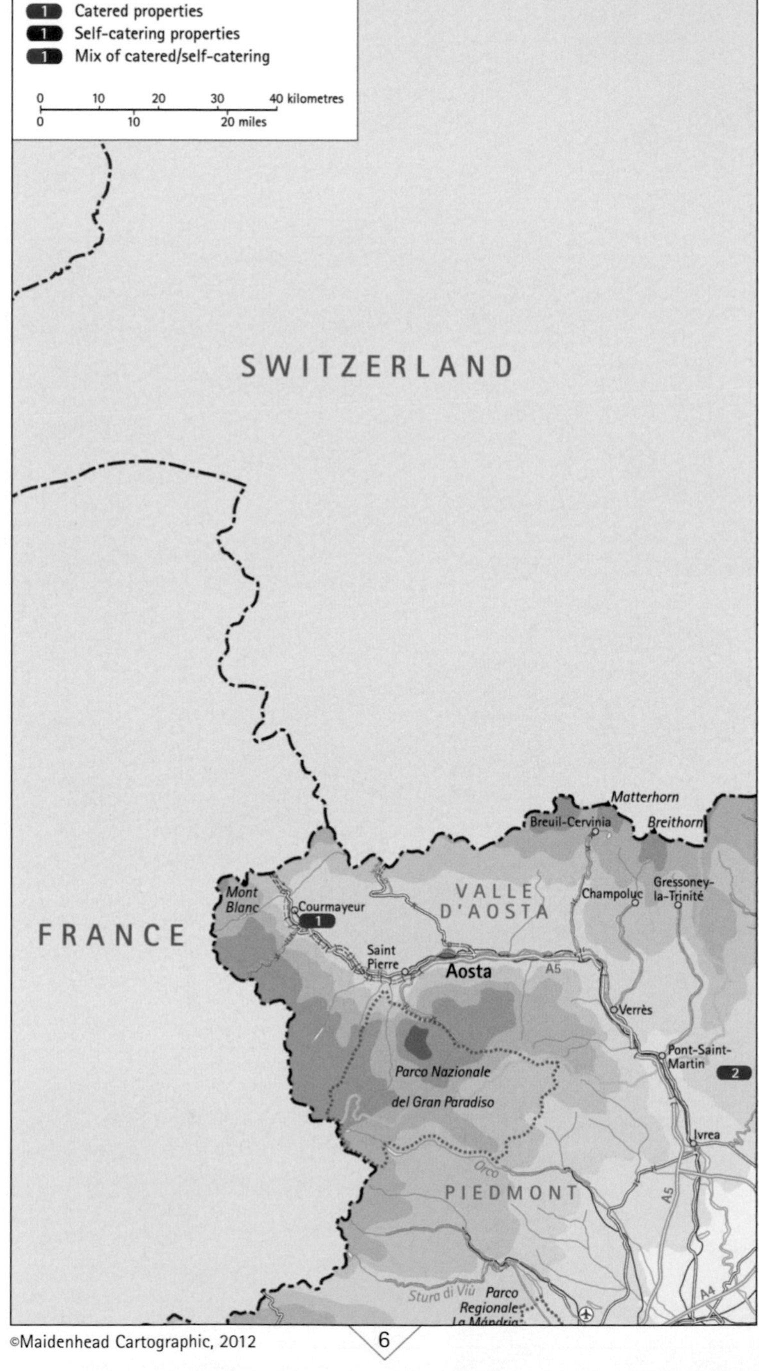
Catered properties
Self-catering properties
Mix of catered/self-catering
0 10 20 30 40 kilometres
0 10 20 miles
SWITZERLAND
FRANCE
Matterhorn
Breuil-Cervinia
Breithorn
Gressoney-la-Trinité
Champoluc
VALLE D'AOSTA
Mont Blanc
Courmayeur
Saint Pierre
Aosta
A5
Verrès
Pont-Saint-Martin
Parco Nazionale del Gran Paradiso
Ivrea
Orco
PIEDMONT
A5
A4
Stura di Viù
Parco Regionale La Mandria

6

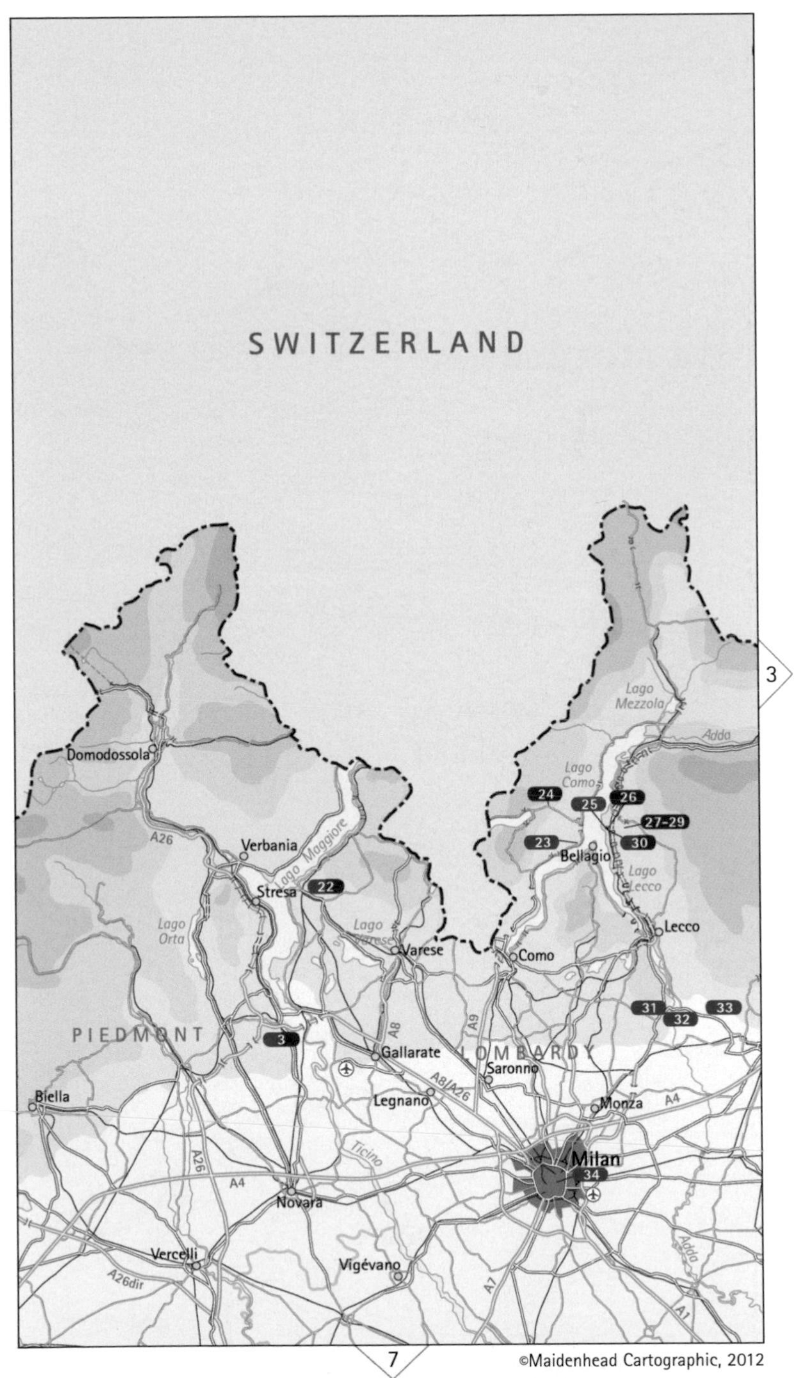
SWITZERLAND
3
Lago Mezzola
Adda
Domodossola
Lago Como
24
25
26
27-29
30
23
Bellagio
A26
Verbania
Lago Maggiore
Lago Lecco
Stresa
22
Lecco
Lago Orta
Lago Varese
Varese
Como
31
32
33
A9
A8
PIEDMONT
3
Gallarate
LOMBARDY
Saronno
A8/A26
Biella
Legnano
Monza
A4
Ticino
A26
Milan
34
A4
Novara
Vercelli
Vigévano
A26dir
A7
Adda
A1
7

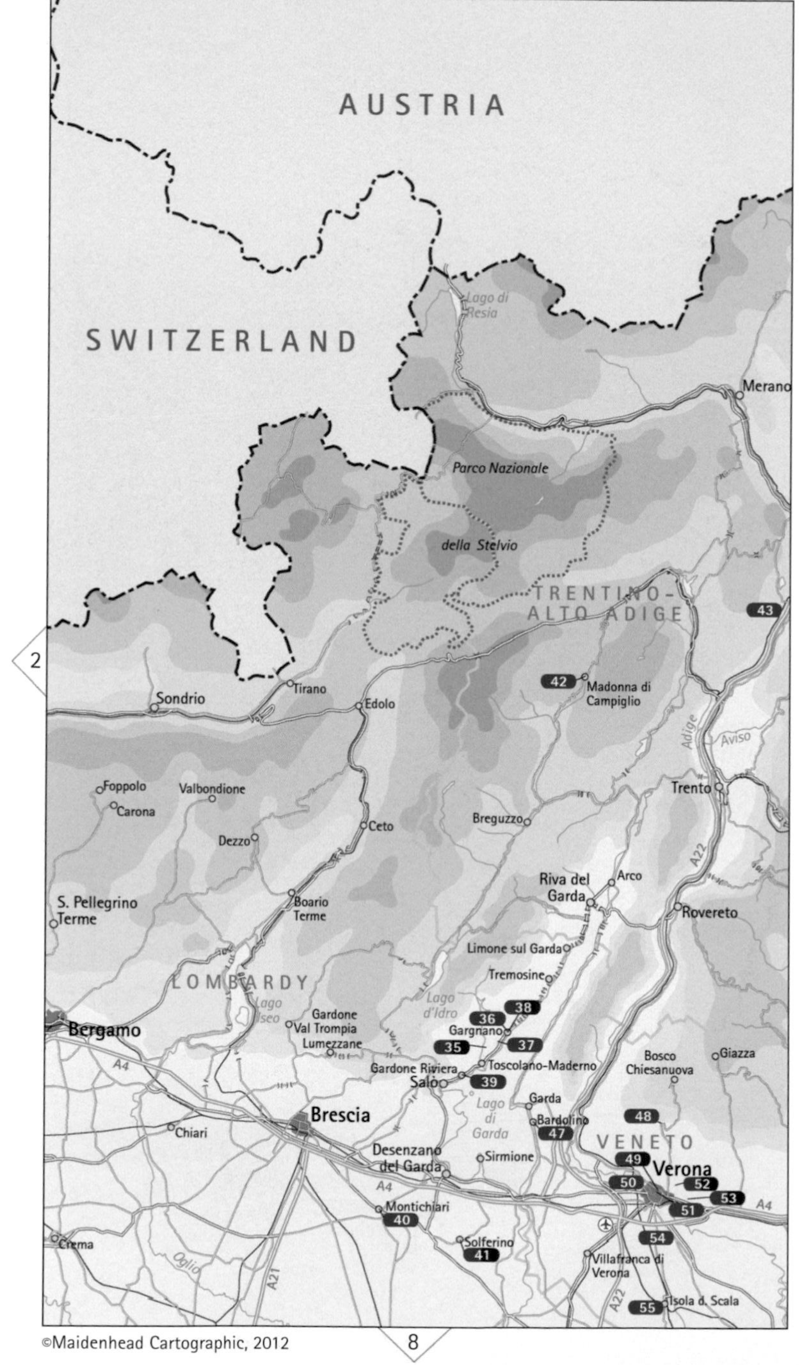
AUSTRIA
SWITZERLAND
Lago di Resia
Merano
Parco Nazionale
della Stelvio
TRENTINO-
ALTO ADIGE
43
2
Tirano
Sondrio
Edolo
42
Madonna di Campiglio
Adige
Aviso
Foppolo
Valbondione
Carona
Trento
Ceto
Breguzzo
Dezzo
A22
Riva del Garda
Arco
S. Pellegrino Terme
Boario Terme
Rovereto
Limone sul Garda
Tremosine
LOMBARDY
Lago Iseo
Lago d'Idro
38
36
Gardone Val Trompia
Gargnano
Bergamo
37
Lumezzane
35
Bosco Chiesanuova
Giazza
A4
Gardone Riviera
Toscolano-Maderno
Salò
39
Garda
Lago di Garda
48
Brescia
Bardolino
Chiari
47
VENETO
Desenzano del Garda
Sirmione
49
Verona
52
50
A4
53
A4
Montichiari
51
40
54
Crema
Solferino
Oglio
41
Villafranca di Verona
A21
A22
55
Isola d. Scala
8

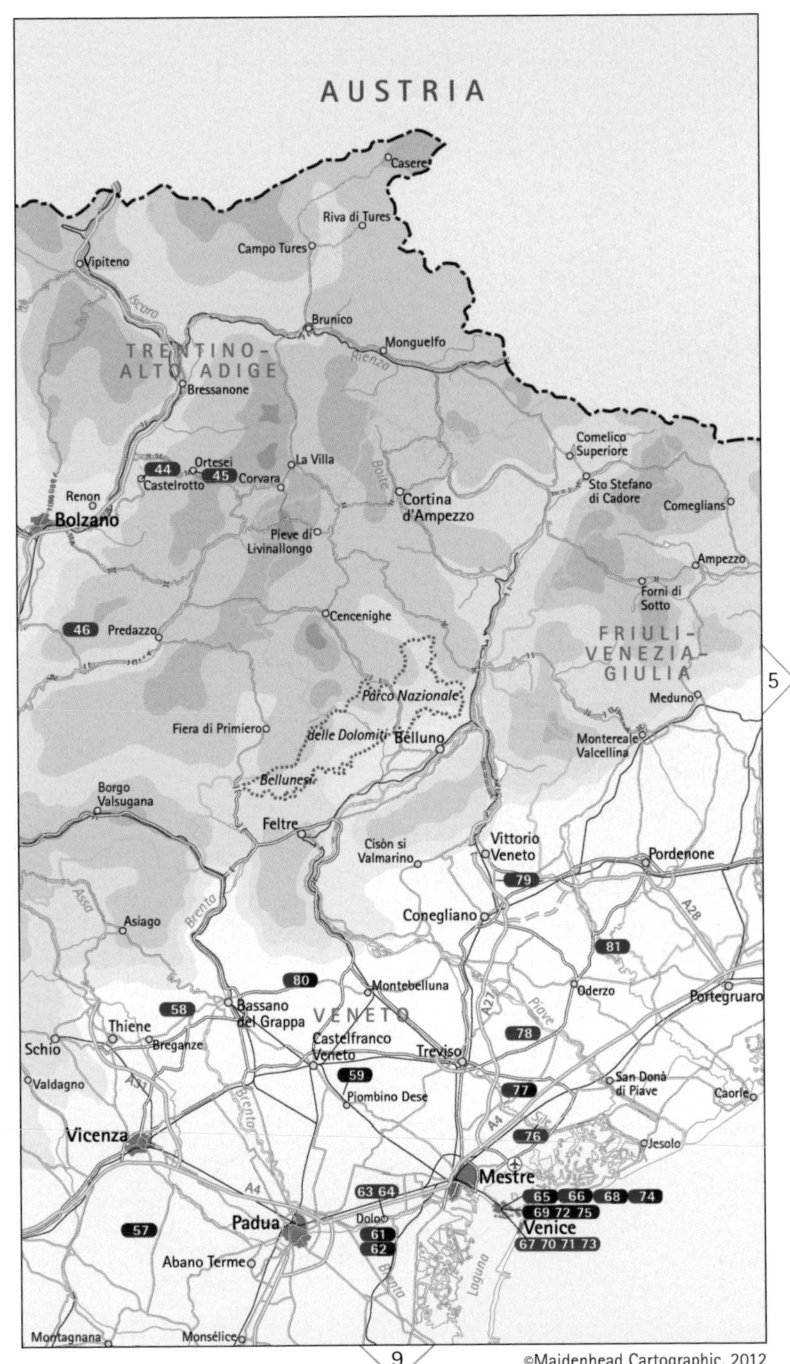
AUSTRIA
Casere
Riva di Tures
Campo Tures
Vipiteno
Iscaro
Brunico
Monguelfo
Rienza
TRENTINO-
ALTO ADIGE
Bressanone
Comelico Superiore
La Villa
Ortesei
44
45
Corvara
Castelrotto
Boite
Sto Stefano di Cadore
Renon
Cortina d'Ampezzo
Comeglians
Bolzano
Pieve di Livinallongo
Ampezzo
Forni di Sotto
Cencenighe
46
Predazzo
FRIULI-
VENEZIA-
GIULIA
Parco Nazionale
delle Dolomiti
Bellunesi
Meduno
Fiera di Primiero
Belluno
Montereale Valcellina
Borgo Valsugana
Feltre
Cisòn si Valmarino
Vittorio Veneto
Pordenone
79
Assa
Conegliano
A28
Asiago
Brenta
81
80
Montebelluna
Oderzo
Portegruaro
58
Bassano del Grappa
VENETO
A27
Piave
Thiene
Castelfranco Veneto
78
Schio
Breganze
Treviso
59
San Donà di Piave
Valdagno
A31
77
Caorle
Piombino Dese
Brenta
A4
Sile
Vicenza
76
Jesolo
Mestre
A4
63 64
65 66 68 74
69 72 75
Dolo
Padua
Venice
57
61
62
67 70 71 73
Abano Terme
Laguna
Montagnana
Monsélice
5
9

AUSTRIA
Tarvisio
A23
Tolmezzo
Gemona di Friuli
FRIULI-VENEZIA-GIULIA
Tagliamento
4
Faèdis
84
Povoletto
83
Udine
SLOVENIA
Codroipo
A23
Gorizia
85
Palmanova
A4
A4
Monfalcone
82
Lignano Sabbiadoro
Grado
Lignano Riviera
Bibione
Trieste
CROATIA

In Italy, with all the saints' days and local sagras ('sagre', in Italian), you'll find something being celebrated almost every day of the year. Think of the tortello and truffle festas, the prosciutto and chocolate fairs, and the numerous wine and olive oil sagras. These events are cultural experiences, too – you don't have to be a foodie to enjoy them. Check before you go to see if something is going on where you are staying, for every region and town has its own festivals – usually great fun, but occasionally frustrating if you unwittingly get caught in the middle!

In autumn there are a variety of harvest related gastronomic events throughout the country, grape festivals in particular. Perhaps the most famous is in Marino in the Castelli Romani (Lazio), where a huge fountain spouts white wine instead of water.

If you are lucky enough to be travelling to Italy over the Christmas period, you will find Christmas markets everywhere. Mingle with noisy Italian families around the 'presepi' (nativity scenes) in the squares, with a slice of panettone and a glass of spumante. Soak up the magical festive mix of roasting chestnuts, Christmas lights, church bells, music and gifts galore.

It is impossible to list all the food festivals here, but these are among my favourites.

Sagra dei Garagoi (April)

In Marotta, near Pesaro (Marche), this sagra is dedicated to sea snails; the locals say one should take a sip of wine for every seven snails eaten!

Sagra del Carciofo (April)

In Ladispoli, near Rome, find mountains of rotund mammola artichokes, cooked in all sorts of different ways in the town's piazza.

Sagra delle Uova Sode (Easter)

In Tredozio, near Forli (Emilia Romagna), the townsfolk celebrate Easter; a hard-boiled egg-eating contest is the highlight.

Campionato Nazionale dei Mangiatori d'Anguria (July)

The National Watermelon Eating Championship – a summer treat that takes place in Sissa, near Parma.

Festa della Cipolla (August)

In Giarratana, Sicily, huge onions, weighing up to 2kg each, are anointed with olive oil and roasted slowly, and lorry loads of vendors line the streets exhibiting their biggest onions.

Jill Greetham

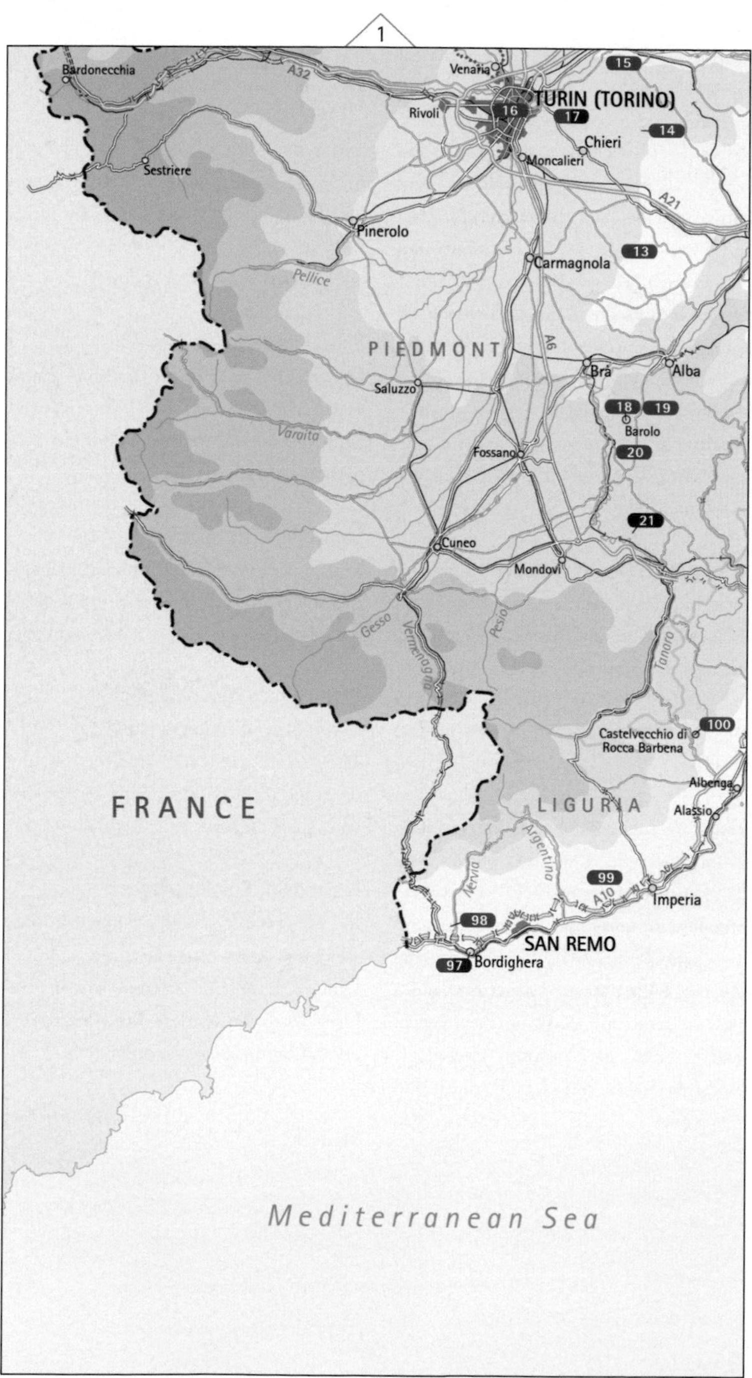
1
Bardonecchia
A32
Venaria
15
TURIN (TORINO)
16
17
Rivoli
Chieri
14
Moncalieri
Sestriere
A21
Pinerolo
13
Carmagnola
Pellice
PIEDMONT
A6
Brà
Alba
Saluzzo
18
19
Barolo
Varaita
20
Fossano
21
Cuneo
Mondovì
Gesso
Vermenagna
Pesio
Tanaro
Castelvecchio di
Rocca Barbena
100
Albenga
FRANCE
LIGURIA
Alassio
Argentina
Nervia
99
A10
Imperia
98
SAN REMO
97
Bordighera
Mediterranean Sea

2
Pavia
Casale Monferrato
Lomello
LOMBARDY
Po
A1
A21
A7
Vignale
Monferrato
Valenza
A21
Piacenza
4
Voghera
Asti
A21
Alessandria
12
11
Tortona
Nibbiano
Trebbia
Bagnaria
PIEDMONT
10
9
A26
Novi
Ligure
5
Bobbio
EMILIA-
ROMAGNA
Acqui Terme
8
7
6
Bardi
89
Casella
Rezzoaglio
Sassello
LIGURIA
A12
102
GENOA
(GENOVA)
Nervi
Rapallo
Camogli
Santa Margherita Ligure
103
Chiávari
Savona
Portofino
Sestri Levante
A10
Moneglia
104 105
101
Barcelona/Palma
Tunis/Bastia
106
107
108 109
Levanto
8
Finale Ligure
Golfo
di Genova
Mediterranean Sea

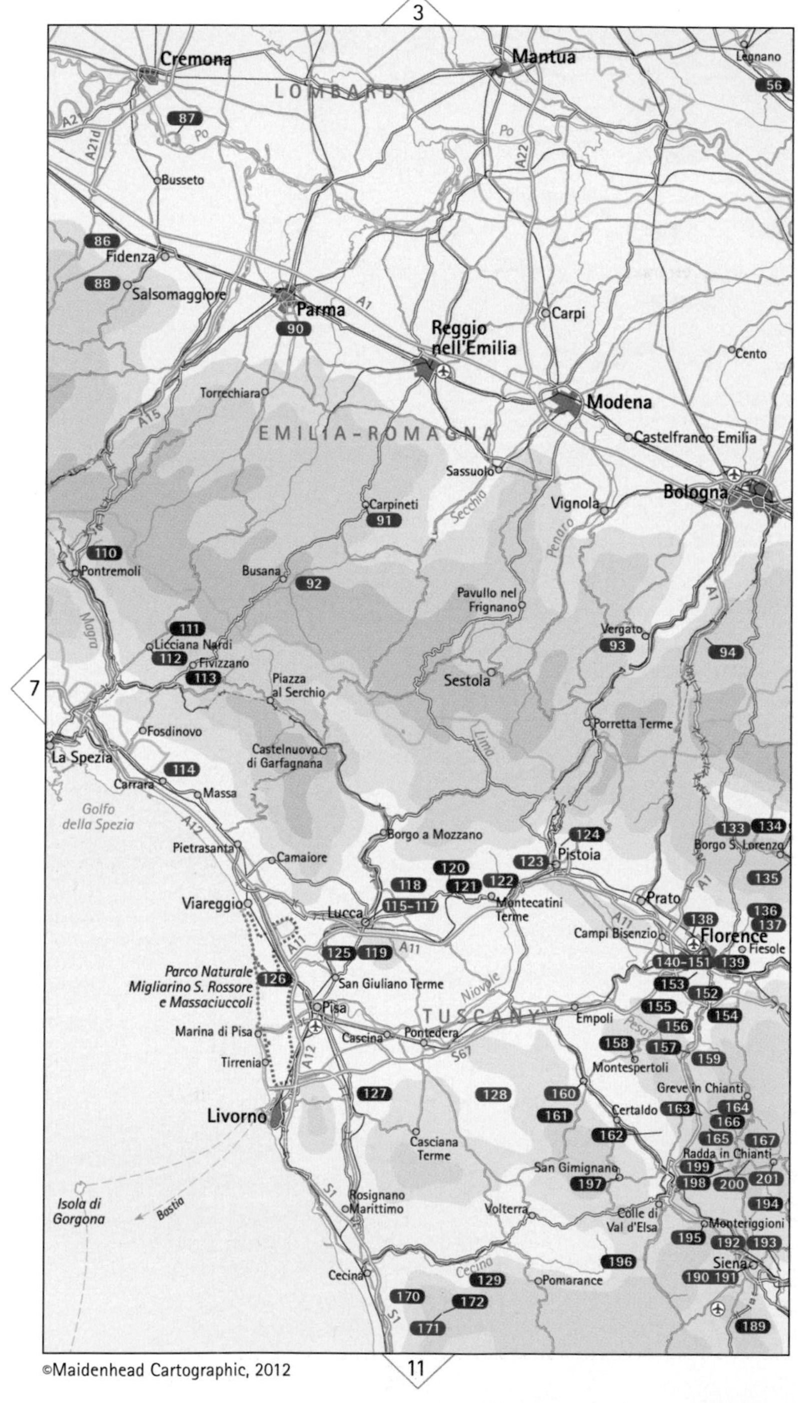
3
7
11
Cremona
Mantua
Legnano
56
LOMBARDY
87
Po
A21
A21d
A22
Busseto
86
Fidenza
88
Salsomaggiore
Parma
90
A1
Carpi
Reggio nell'Emilia
Cento
Torrechiara
Modena
A15
EMILIA-ROMAGNA
Castelfranco Emilia
Sassuolo
Bologna
Carpineti
91
Secchia
Vignola
Panaro
110
Pontremoli
Busana
92
Pavullo nel Frignano
A1
Magra
111
Licciana Nardi
112
Fivizzano
113
Vergato
93
94
Piazza al Serchio
Sestola
Porretta Terme
Fosdinovo
La Spezia
114
Castelnuovo di Garfagnana
Limo
Carrara
Massa
Golfo della Spezia
A12
133
134
124
Borgo a Mozzano
Pistoia
Borgo S. Lorenzo
Pietrasanta
Camaiore
123
120
118
121
122
135
Viareggio
115-117
Lucca
Montecatini Terme
Prato
136
137
138
Campi Bisenzio
Florence
Fiesole
A11
125
119
140-151
139
Parco Naturale Migliarino S. Rossore e Massaciuccoli
126
San Giuliano Terme
Niovole
153
152
Pisa
TUSCANY
Empoli
155
154
Marina di Pisa
Cascina
Pontedera
Pesa
156
158
157
S67
Tirrenia
A12
Montespertoli
159
127
128
160
Greve in Chianti
Certaldo
163
164
Livorno
161
166
162
165
167
Casciana Terme
Radda in Chianti
199
San Gimignano
197
198
200
201
S1
Rosignano Marittimo
194
Isola di Gorgona
Bastia
Volterra
Colle di Val d'Elsa
Monteriggioni
195
192
193
196
Siena
Cecina
129
Pomarance
190
191
170
172
171
189

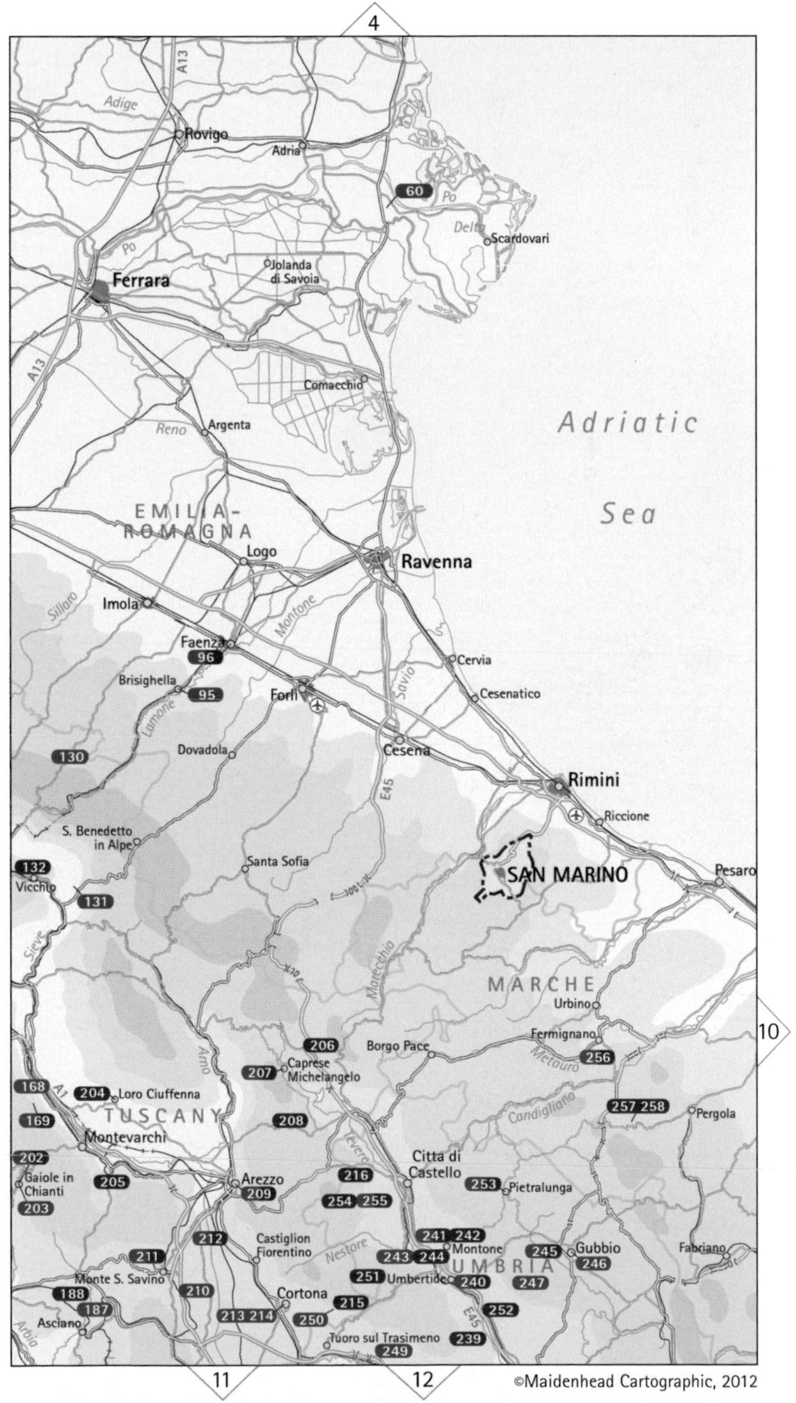
4
A13
Adige
Rovigo
Adria
60
Po
Delta
Scardovari
Po
Jolanda di Savoia
Ferrara
A13
Comacchio
Reno
Argenta
Adriatic
Sea
EMILIA-ROMAGNA
Logo
Ravenna
Sillaro
Imola
Montone
Faenza
96
Cervia
Brisighella
95
Lamone
Forlì
Savio
Cesenatico
130
Dovadola
Cesena
E45
Rimini
Riccione
S. Benedetto in Alpe
Santa Sofia
132
Vicchio
131
SAN MARINO
Pesaro
Sieve
Marecchia
MARCHE
Urbino
10
Fermignano
Metauro
256
206
Borgo Pace
Caprese Michelangelo
207
Arno
168
A1
204
Loro Ciuffenna
169
TUSCANY
208
Candigliano
257 258
Pergola
Montevarchi
Tevere
202
Citta di Castello
Gaiole in Chianti
205
Arezzo
216
253
Pietralunga
203
209
254 255
212
Castiglion Fiorentino
Nestore
241 242
Montone
245
Gubbio
Fabriano
211
243 244
UMBRIA
246
Monte S. Savino
251
Umbertide
240
247
188
210
Cortona
215
252
187
213 214
250
E45
Asciano
Arbia
Tuoro sul Trasimeno
239
249
11
12

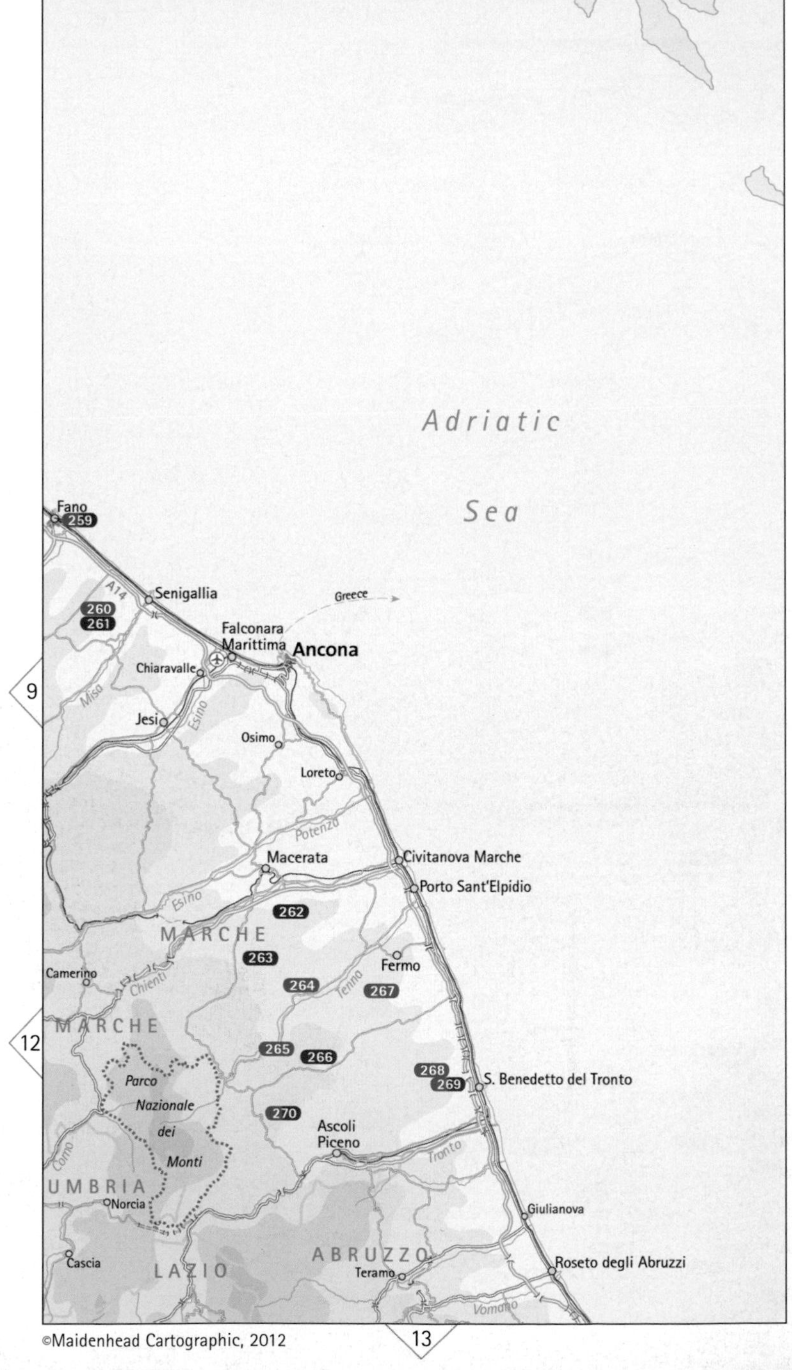
Adriatic
Sea
Fano
259
A14
Senigallia
260
261
Greece
Falconara
Marittima
Ancona
Chiaravalle
9
Misa
Jesi
Esino
Osimo
Loreto
Potenza
Macerata
Civitanova Marche
Porto Sant'Elpidio
Esino
262
MARCHE
263
Fermo
Camerino
Chienti
264
Tenna
267
MARCHE
12
265
266
268
269
S. Benedetto del Tronto
Parco
Nazionale
dei
Monti
270
Ascoli
Piceno
Tronto
Corno
UMBRIA
Norcia
Giulianova
Cascia
LAZIO
ABRUZZO
Teramo
Roseto degli Abruzzi
Vomano
13

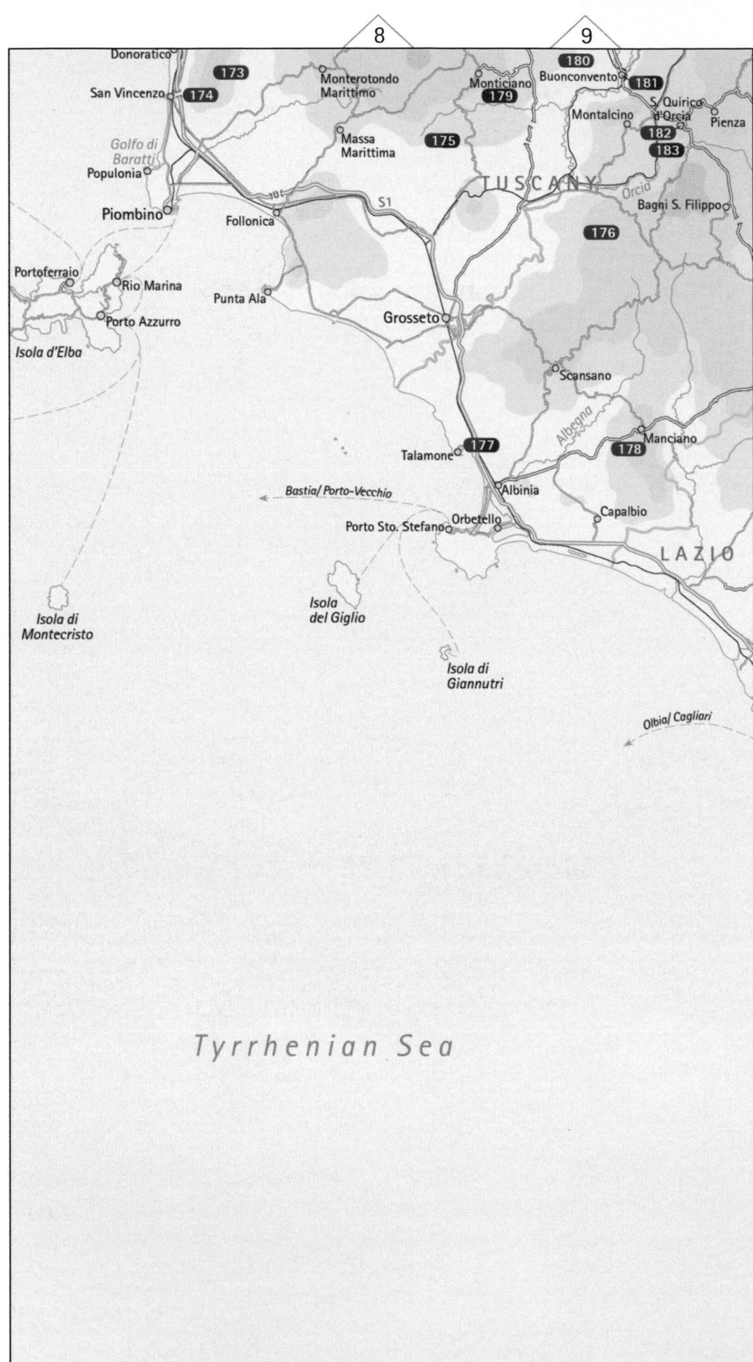
8
9
Donoratico
173
San Vincenzo
174
Monterotondo
Marittimo
Monticiano
179
180
Buonconvento
181
S. Quirico
d'Orcia
Pienza
Montalcino
182
183
Massa
Marittima
175
Golfo di
Baratti
Populonia
TUSCANY
Orcia
Bagni S. Filippo
Piombino
Follonica
S1
176
Portoferraio
Rio Marina
Punta Ala
Grosseto
Porto Azzurro
Isola d'Elba
Scansano
Albegna
Manciano
178
Talamone
177
Bastia/ Porto-Vecchio
Albinia
Capalbio
Orbetello
Porto Sto. Stefano
LAZIO
Isola di
Montecristo
Isola
del Giglio
Isola di
Giannutri
Olbia/ Cagliari
Tyrrhenian Sea

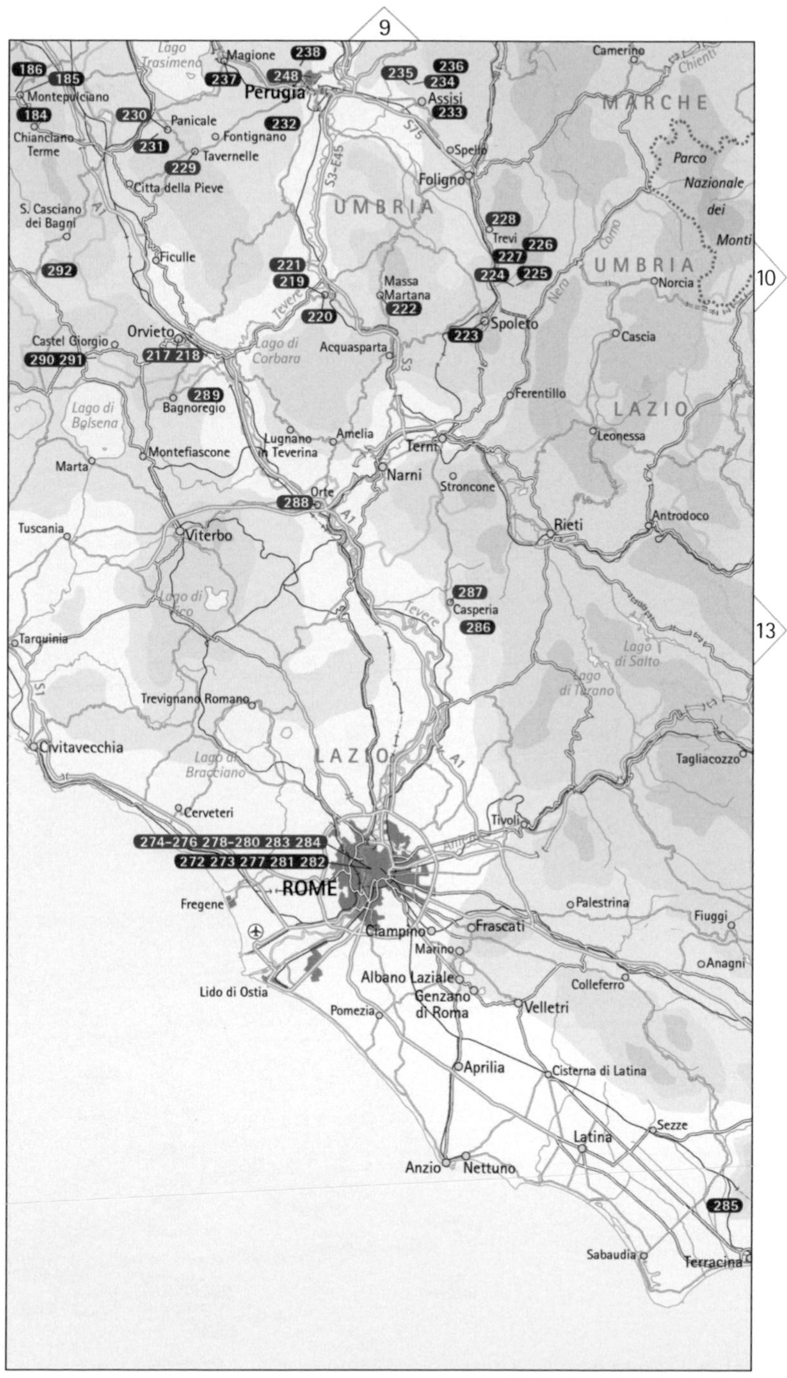
9
10
13
Lago Trasimeno
Magione
Perugia
Assisi
Camerino
Chienti
MARCHE
Montepulciano
Chianciano Terme
Panicale
Fontignano
Tavernelle
Spello
Foligno
Parco Nazionale dei Monti
Citta della Pieve
UMBRIA
S. Casciano dei Bagni
Trevi
Ficulle
Massa Martana
Norcia
Spoleto
Cascia
Castel Giorgio
Orvieto
Lago di Corbara
Acquasparta
Ferentillo
Bagnoregio
Lago di Bolsena
LAZIO
Leonessa
Lugnano in Teverina
Amelia
Terni
Montefiascone
Marta
Narni
Stroncone
Orte
Tuscania
Viterbo
Rieti
Antrodoco
Casperia
Tarquinia
Lago di Salto
Lago di Turano
Trevignano Romano
Civitavecchia
LAZIO
Lago di Bracciano
Tagliacozzo
Cerveteri
Tivoli
ROME
Fregene
Palestrina
Fiuggi
Ciampino
Frascati
Marino
Anagni
Albano Laziale
Lido di Ostia
Colleferro
Genzano di Roma
Pomezia
Velletri
Aprilia
Cisterna di Latina
Sezze
Latina
Anzio
Nettuno
Sabaudia
Terracina
186 185 184 230 231 229 237 238 248 232 235 236 234 233 228 226 227 224 225 221 219 220 222 223 292 290 291 217 218 289 288 287 286 274-276 278-280 283 284 272 273 277 281 282 285

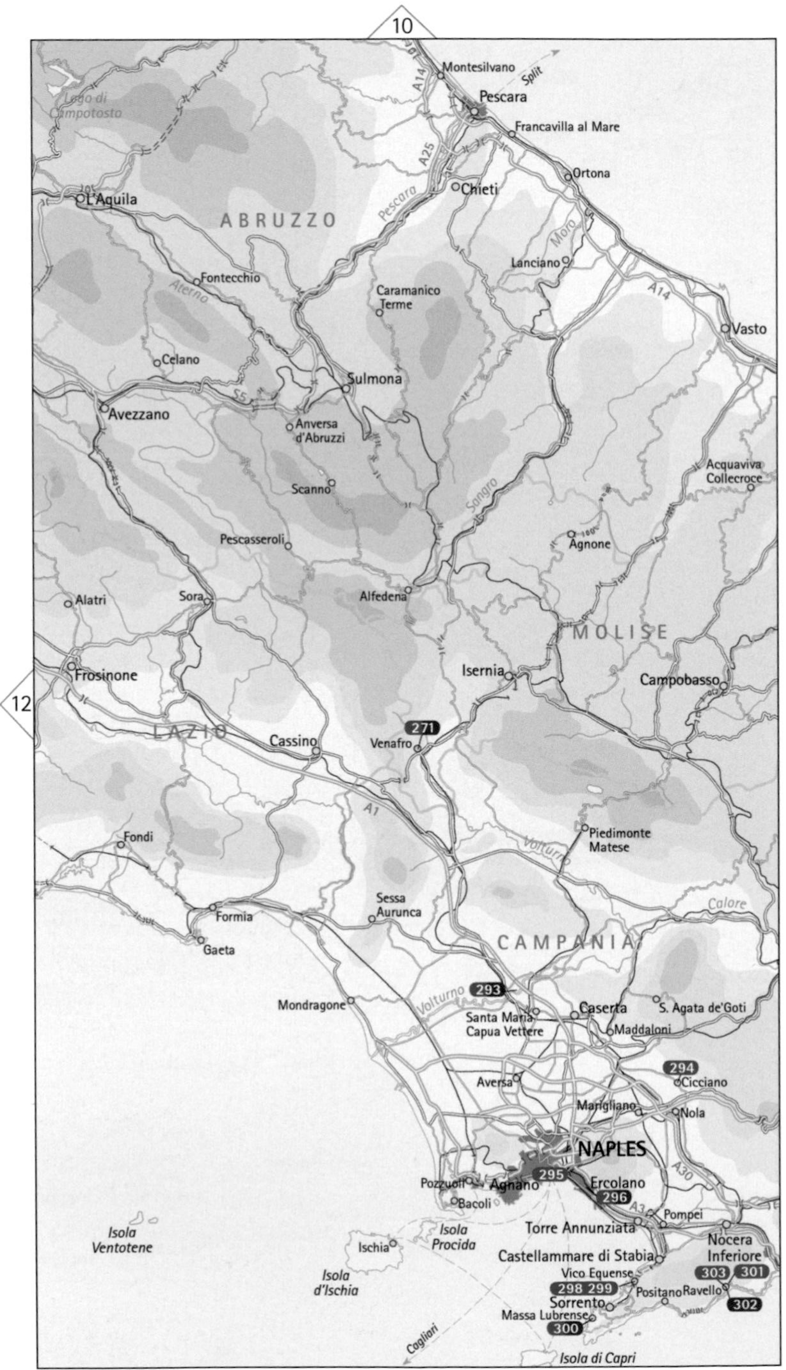
10
12
Montesilvano
Split
Pescara
Francavilla al Mare
Ortona
Chieti
L'Aquila
ABRUZZO
Lago di Campotosto
Pescara
Moro
Lanciano
A14
A25
Fontecchio
Aterno
Caramanico Terme
Vasto
Celano
Sulmona
Avezzano
Anversa d'Abruzzi
Acquaviva Collecroce
Scanno
Sangro
Agnone
Pescasseroli
Alfedena
Alatri
Sora
MOLISE
Frosinone
Isernia
Campobasso
LAZIO
Cassino
271
Venafro
A1
Fondi
Piedimonte Matese
Volturno
Sessa Aurunca
Calore
Formia
Gaeta
CAMPANIA
293
Mondragone
Volturno
Santa Maria Capua Vettere
Caserta
S. Agata de'Goti
Maddaloni
294
Aversa
Cicciano
Marigliano
Nola
NAPLES
A30
Pozzuoli
Agnano
295
Ercolano
296
Bacoli
A3
Pompei
Isola Ventotene
Ischia
Isola Procida
Torre Annunziata
Nocera Inferiore
Castellammare di Stabia
303
301
Isola d'Ischia
Vico Equense
298 299
Positano
Ravello
Sorrento
302
Massa Lubrense
300
Cagliari
Isola di Capri

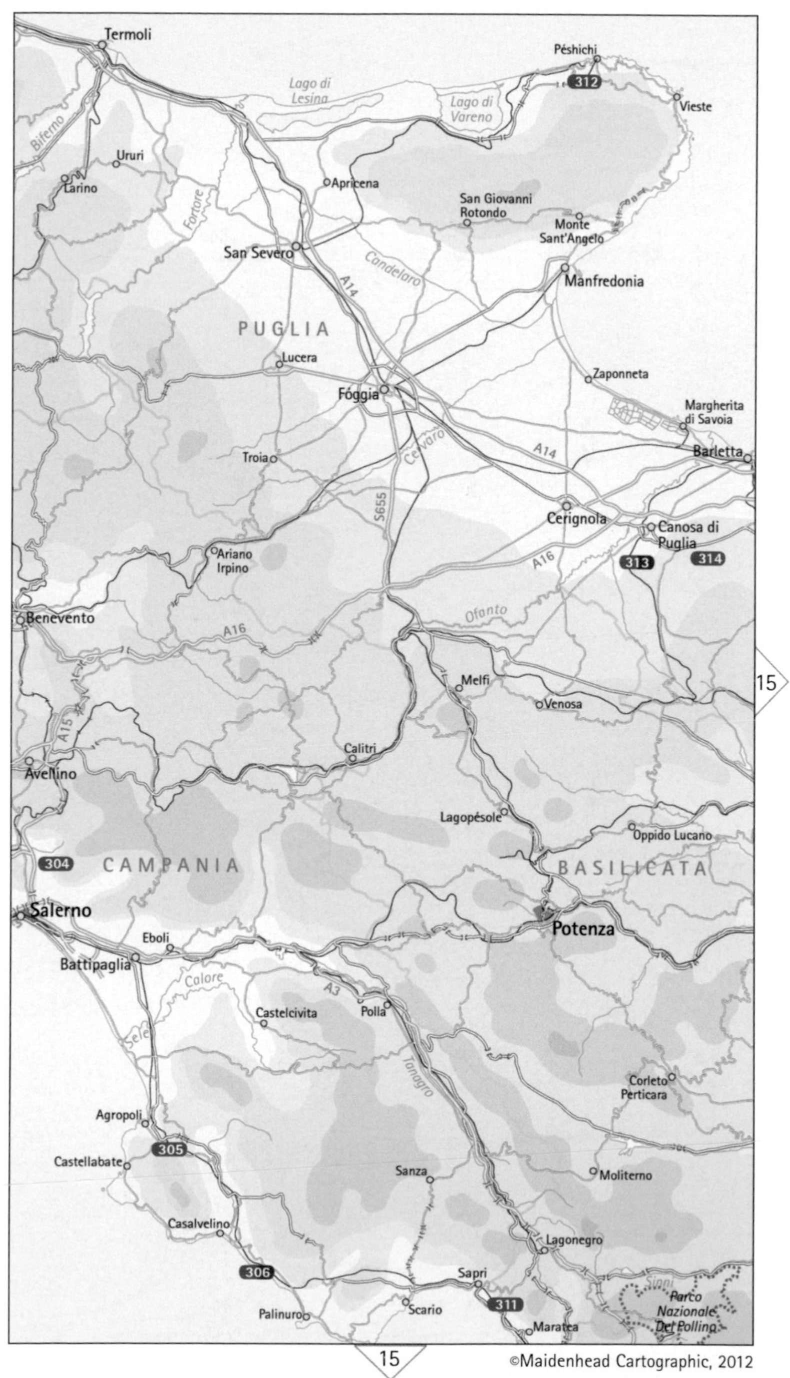
Termoli
Péshichi
312
Vieste
Lago di
Lesina
Lago di
Vareno
Biferno
Ururi
Larino
Apricena
Fortore
San Giovanni
Rotondo
Monte
Sant'Angelo
San Severo
Candelaro
A14
Manfredonia
PUGLIA
Lucera
Zaponneta
Fóggia
Margherita
di Savoia
A14
Barletta
Troia
Cervaro
S655
Cerignola
Canosa di
Puglia
Ariano
Irpino
313
314
A16
Benevento
Ofanto
A16
Melfi
Venosa
A15
Calitri
Avellino
Lagopésole
Oppido Lucano
304
CAMPANIA
BASILICATA
Salerno
Eboli
Potenza
Battipaglia
Calore
A3
Castelcivita
Polla
Sele
Tanagro
Corleto
Perticara
Agropoli
305
Castellabate
Sanza
Moliterno
Casalvelino
Lagonegro
306
Sapri
Sinni
Parco
Nazionale
Del Pollino
311
Scario
Palinuro
Maratea

15

15

Zaponneta
Margherita di Savoia
Barletta
Trani
Split
Dubrovnik
A14
Cerignola
Canosa di Puglia
Andria
Molfetta
Giovinazzo
Bari
A16
313
314
Corato
Terlizzi
A14
Ruvo di Puglia
Bitonto
Triggianno
Mola di Bari
Noicattaro
315
PUGLIA
Conversano
Monopoli
316
Venosa
Acquaviva delle Fonti
A14
Castellana
Putignano
Gravina in Puglia
Altamura
Alberobello
Gioia dei Colle
Santeramo in Colle
Oppido Lucano
Matera
Castellaneta
Massafra
Potenza
Basento
Bradano
308
Ginosa
S106
317
Tàranto
BASILICATA
Stigliano
Metaponto
309
Corleto Perticara
Agri
Policoro
Sinni
Moliterno
Golfo di Taranto
Lagonegro
Sinni
Parco Nazionale Del Pollino
Roseta Capo Spulico
Maratea
310
Monte Pollino
Pràia a Mare
Lao
Castrovillari
Scalea
CALABRIA
A3
Sibari
Firmo
Cascile
Diamante
Corigliano
Rossano
307
Cropalati
Acri
Crucoli Torretta

14

17

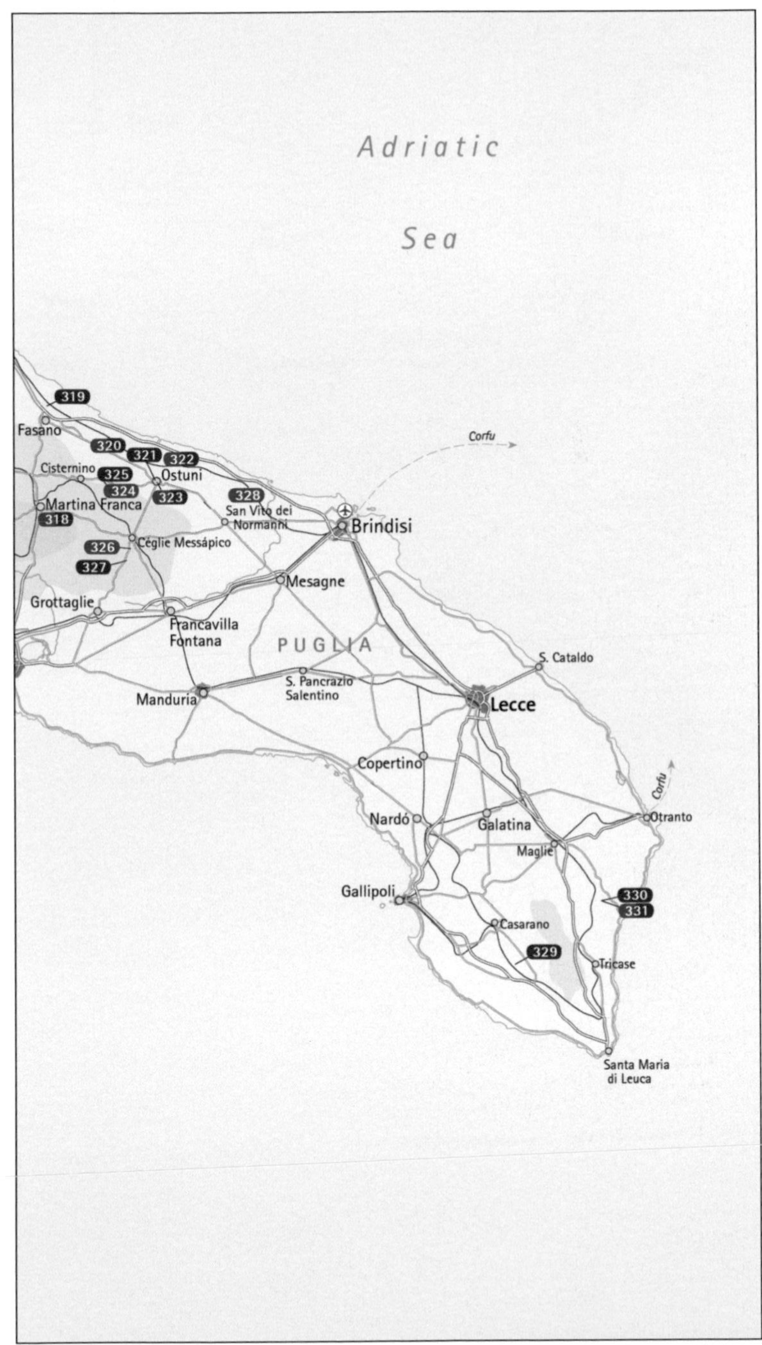
Adriatic
Sea
Corfu
319
Fasano
320
321
322
Cisternino
325
Ostuni
324
323
Martina Franca
318
328
San Vito dei Normanni
Brindisi
326
Céglie Messápico
327
Mesagne
Grottaglie
Francavilla Fontana
PUGLIA
S. Cataldo
S. Pancrazio Salentino
Manduria
Lecce
Copertino
Corfu
Nardó
Galatina
Otranto
Maglie
Gallipoli
330
331
Casarano
329
Tricase
Santa Maria di Leuca

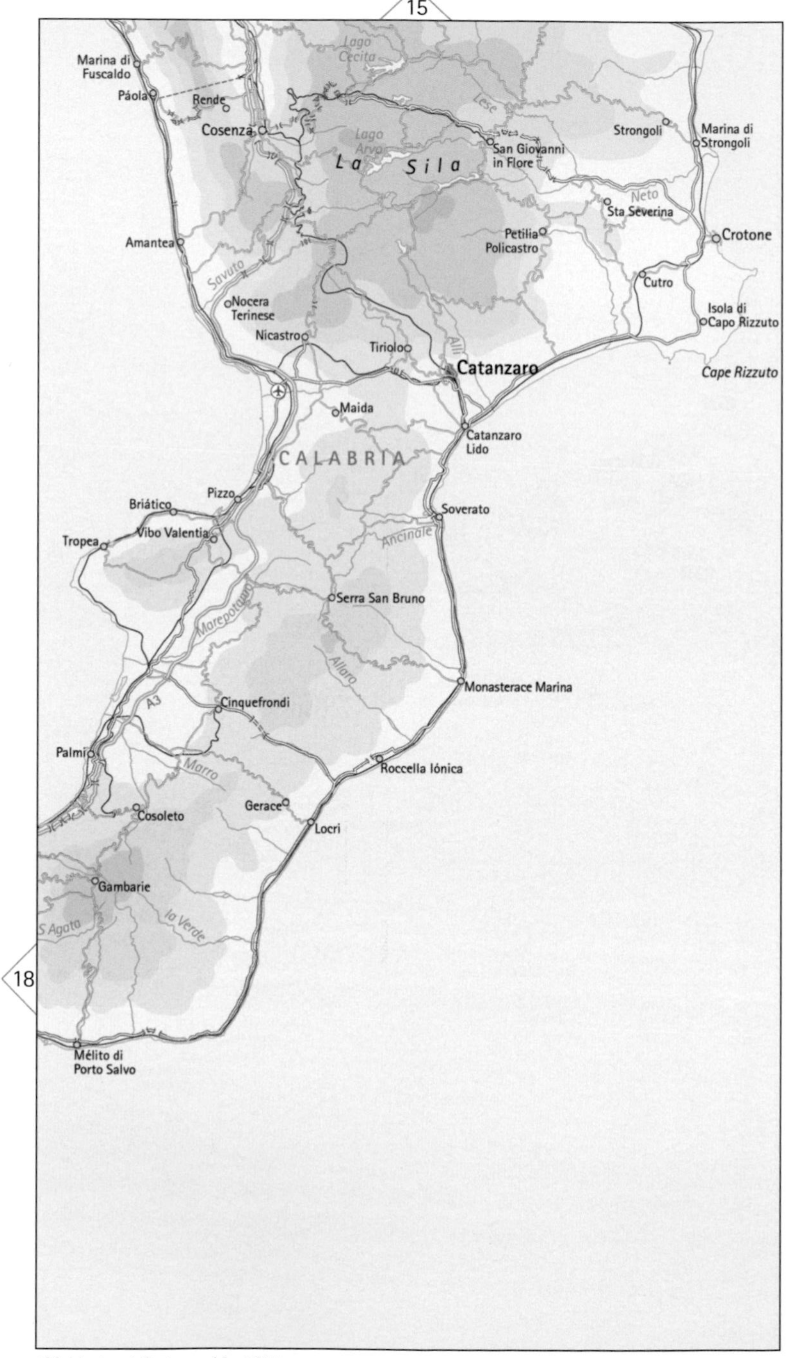
15
Lago Cecita
Marina di Fuscaldo
Páola
Rende
Cosenza
Lago Arvo
La Sila
San Giovanni in Fiore
Strongoli
Marina di Strongoli
Neto
Sta Severina
Crotone
Petilia Policastro
Amantea
Savuto
Cutro
Nocera Terinese
Isola di Capo Rizzuto
Nicastro
Tiriolo
Catanzaro
Cape Rizzuto
Maida
Catanzaro Lido
CALABRIA
Pizzo
Briático
Soverato
Vibo Valentia
Tropea
Ancinale
Serra San Bruno
Marepotamo
Allaro
Monasterace Marina
A3
Cinquefrondi
Palmi
Roccella Iónica
Marro
Gerace
Cosoleto
Locri
Gambarie
S Agata
la Verde
18
Mélito di Porto Salvo

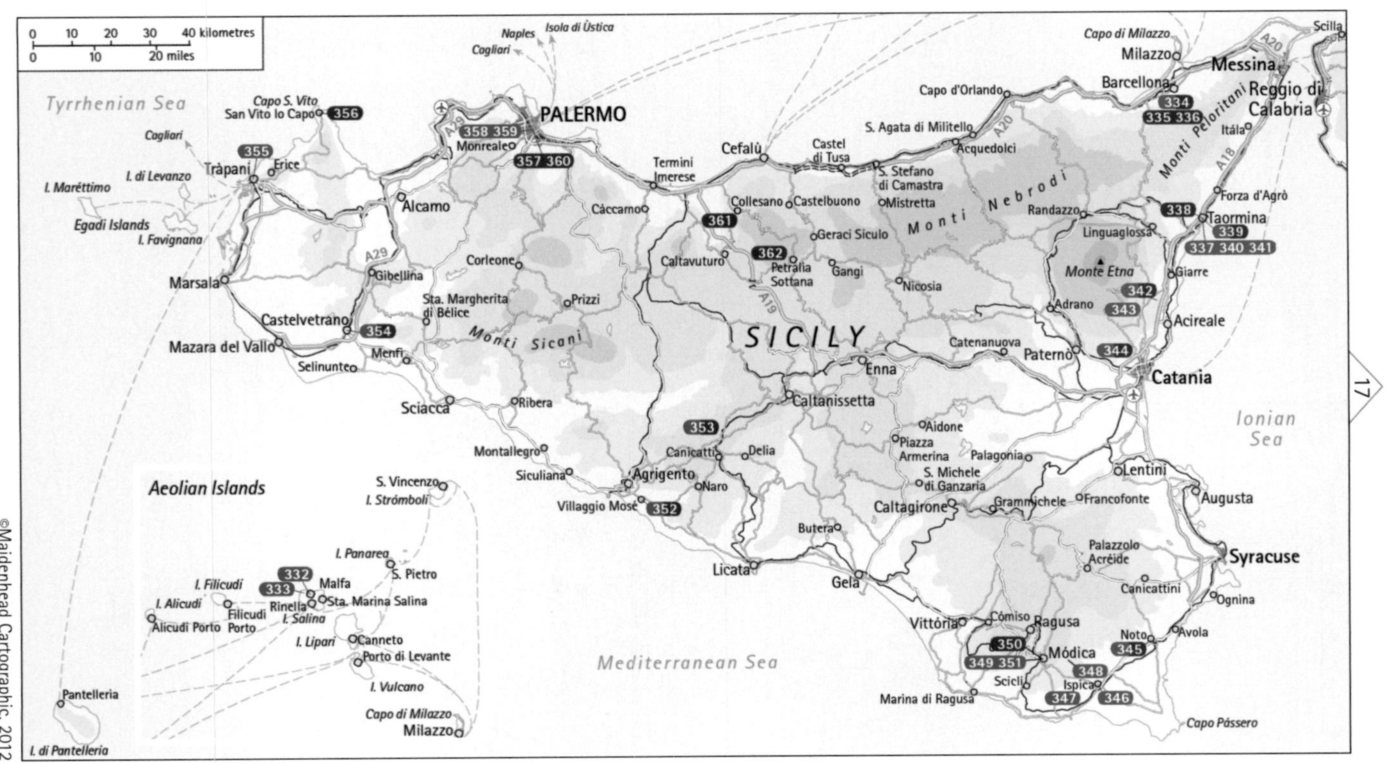
0 10 20 30 40 kilometres
0 10 20 miles
Naples
Isola di Ùstica
Cagliari
Tyrrhenian Sea
Capo S. Vito
San Vito lo Capo
356
PALERMO
358 359
Monreale
357 360
Cagliari
355
Tràpani
Erice
I. Maréttimo
I. di Levanzo
Egadi Islands
I. Favignana
Alcamo
Càccamo
Termini Imerese
Cefalù
Castel di Tusa
S. Agata di Militello
Capo d'Orlando
Capo di Milazzo
Milazzo
Messina
Barcellona
334
335 336
Reggio di Calabria
Scilla
Itála
Monti Peloritani
A20
A18
A29
A19
S. Stefano di Camastra
Acquedolci
Collesano
Castelbuono
Mistretta
Monti Nebrodi
Randazzo
Forza d'Agrò
338
Taormina
339
337 340 341
361
Geraci Siculo
Linguaglossa
362
Caltavuturo
Petralia Sottana
Gangi
Monte Etna
Giarre
Nicosia
342
Adrano
343
Acireale
Corleone
Gibellina
Marsala
Sta. Margherita di Bèlice
Prizzi
Castelvetrano
354
Mazara del Vallo
Monti Sicani
SICILY
Catenanuova
Paternò
344
Catania
Menfi
Selinunte
Enna
Sciacca
Ribera
Caltanissetta
17
Ionian Sea
353
Aidone
Piazza Armerina
Palagonia
Montallegro
Canicattì
Delia
S. Michele di Ganzaria
Lentini
Siculiana
Agrigento
Naro
Villaggio Mosè
352
Caltagirone
Grammichele
Francofonte
Augusta
Aeolian Islands
S. Vincenzo
I. Strómboli
Butera
I. Panarea
S. Pietro
Palazzolo Acrèide
Syracuse
Licata
Gela
332
333
I. Filicudi
Malfa
Canicattini
I. Alicudi
Filicudi Porto
Rinella
Sta. Marina Salina
Ognina
Alicudi Porto
I. Salina
Vittòria
Còmiso
Ragusa
I. Lipari
Canneto
Porto di Levante
350
349 351
Módica
Noto
345
Avola
Mediterranean Sea
348
I. Vulcano
Scicli
Ispica
347
346
Pantelleria
Marina di Ragusa
Capo di Milazzo
Milazzo
Capo Pàssero
I. di Pantelleria

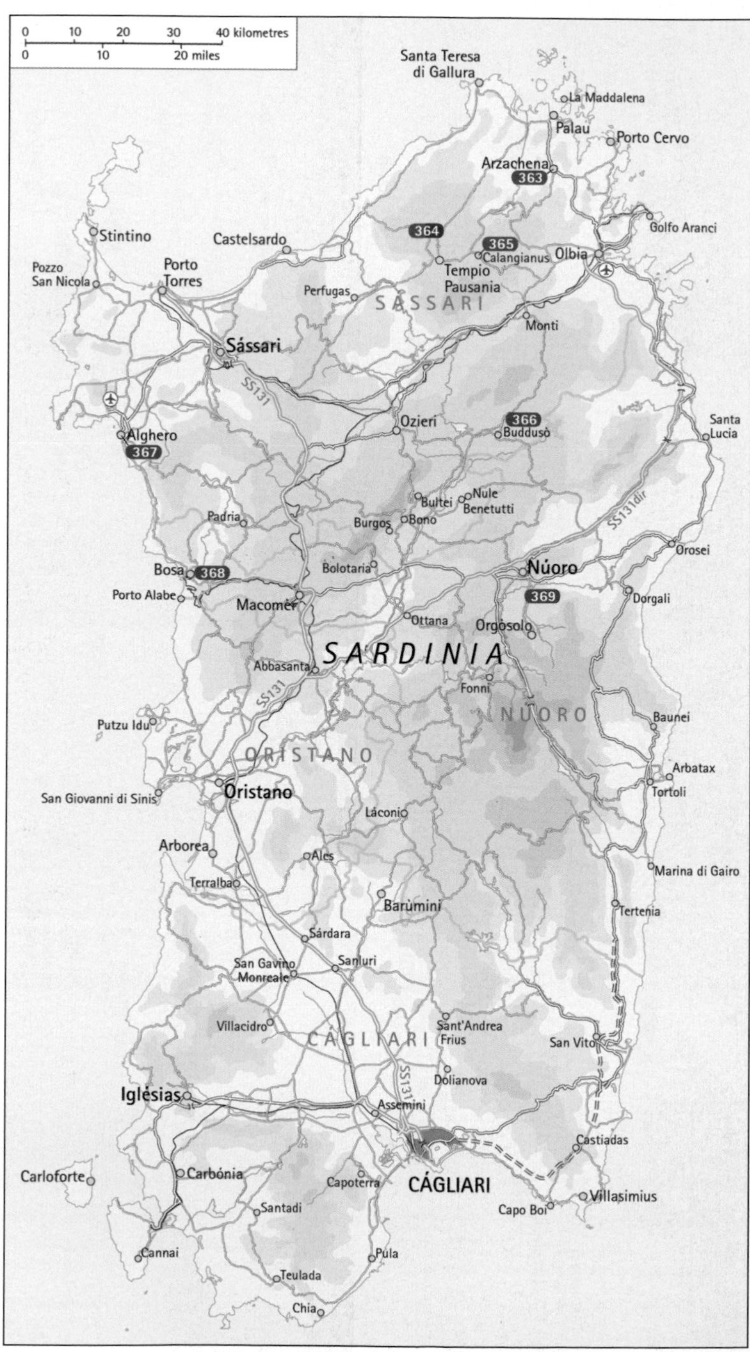
0 10 20 30 40 kilometres
0 10 20 miles
Santa Teresa di Gallura
La Maddalena
Palau
Porto Cervo
Arzachena
363
364
365
Golfo Aranci
Stintino
Castelsardo
Pozzo San Nicola
Porto Torres
Calangianus
Olbia
Tempio Pausania
Perfugas
SASSARI
Monti
Sássari
SS131
Ozieri
366
Buddusò
Santa Lucia
Alghero
367
Nule
Bultei
Benetutti
Padria
Burgos
Bono
SS131dir
Orosei
Bosa
368
Bolotaria
Núoro
Porto Alabe
Macomer
369
Dorgali
Ottana
Orgosolo
SARDINIA
Abbasanta
Fonni
SS131
NUORO
Baunei
Putzu Idu
ORISTANO
Arbatax
Tortolì
San Giovanni di Sinis
Oristano
Láconi
Arborea
Ales
Marina di Gairo
Terralba
Barùmini
Tertenia
Sárdara
San Gavino Monreale
Sanluri
Villacidro
CAGLIARI
Sant'Andrea Frius
San Vito
SS131
Dolianova
Iglésias
Assemini
Castiadas
Carloforte
Carbónia
Capoterra
CÁGLIARI
Villasimius
Capo Boi
Santadi
Cannai
Pula
Teulada
Chia

Aosta Valley and Piedmont

Auberge de la Maison

What a setting! You're in the old part of the village of Val Ferret, three kilometres from Courmayeur, in sight of Mont Blanc, surrounded by gentle terraces, gardens, meadows and majestic views. The Auberge has a quietly elegant and exclusive feel yet is not in the least intimidating, thanks to the cheerful (and efficient) staff. Bedrooms are uncluttered, stylish and comfortable with mellow colours. Many have a third bed disguised as a sofa; nearly all have balconies and the views ranging from good to superb. A Tuscan influence is detectable in the décor; the owner is passionate about the region. Her impressive collection of images of the Valle d'Aosta, from old promotional posters to oil paintings, makes a fascinating display, while a reassembled wooden mountain house is a most unusual feature of the reception and sitting area. There's a wellness centre, too, with a sauna and hydromassage. Come in any season: to fish for trout or play a round of golf, or to ski (right to the ski lift) or don crampons for a winter ascent.

Price	€140-€310. Half-board €195-€340.
Rooms	33: 14 doubles, 2 family rooms, 4 suites, 13 triples.
Meals	Dinner €38. Wine €12.
Closed	15 days in March; 15 days in November.
Directions	From south, direction Entreves; signed. From France, signed after Mont-Blanc tunnel.

Alessandra Garin
Via Passerin d'Entrèves 16/A,
Fraz. Entrèves, 11013 Courmayeur

Tel	+39 0165 869811
Email	info@aubergemaison.it
Web	www.aubergemaison.it

Villa Tavallini

Wind your way up, up the curvy drive, past broad banks of rhododendrons, splendid in late spring, to an airy 1900s villa built as a summer retreat. Step inside to find rugs on wooden floors, colourfully painted walls and fine framed photographs from trips around the world; welcome to the Versaldos' charming home. It is wonderful for kids, super hospitable and, refreshingly, does not ooze perfection. Gaetano and his elderly mother greet you with charming English and show you to your rooms: in a separate wing, with bright-tiled, near-retro bathrooms (two with box showers, one with a tub) and family furniture professionally restored by Gaetano. The sitting room is cosy with filled bookshelves and big sofas, the old-fashioned furnace is lit in winter, and the kitchen for breakfast is homely and inviting. Best of all is outdoors: manicured lawns, five acres of forest to explore, shrubs for kids to get lost in. All feels fresh and lofty. Gaetano is proud of the natural beauty of his territory and eager to take guests on hikes of the mountains and hills. And for winter? Skiing is a 30-minute drive.

Price	€70. Single €50.
Rooms	3: 2 doubles; 1 double with separate bathroom.
Meals	Restaurants in Biella, 6km.
Closed	Never.
Directions	Sent on booking.

Gaetano Versaldo
13814 Pollone

Mobile +39 393 0162580
Email info@villatavallini.it
Web www.villatavallini.it

Cascina Motto

Flowers everywhere: spilling from the balcony, filling the patio, clasping the walls of the cottage… wisteria, vines, azaleas, roses. It's an immaculate garden, with lawns, spreading trees, boules pitch and a discreet summer pool. Roberta's lovely, too, so warm and friendly; you are made at once to feel part of the family. They came here years ago – she and David, their daughters, Roberta's parents Sergio and Lilla, three dogs. They clearly love the house, which they've restored and filled with paintings and beautiful things. In a quiet street, in a quiet village, this is a happy and restful place to stay. The twin room, named after Roberta's grandmother, has windows facing two ways – over the garden and towards Monte Rosa – plus whitewashed walls, blue cotton rugs, blue-painted iron beds, books, a comfy sofa, a big bathroom. The cottage, its bedroom in the hayloft, is bright, airy, charmingly romantic, with country furniture, a well-equipped kitchenette, a balcony; it's completely independent of the main house. Breakfast is a feast, and the lakes of Orta and Maggiore are a 20-minute drive. *Minimum stay two nights.*

Ethical Collection: Environment.
See page 419 for details.

Price	€75. Cottage €85-€150.
Rooms	1 + 1: 1 twin. Cottage for 2-4.
Meals	Restaurants 800m.
Closed	December-February.
Directions	From Milan A4 (Laghi); after Gallarate, A26 for Alessandria exit Castelletto Ticino. Signs for Novara SS32, 3rd exit for Divignano (via Boschi di Sopra). At Divignano, 2nd left for Via Marzabotto.

Roberta Plevani
Via Marzabotto 7,
28010 Divignano
Mobile +39 340 7625711
Email cascinamotto@interfree.it
Web www.cascinamotto.com

Cascina Alberta Agriturismo

Cascina Alberta is an attractive hilltop farmhouse deep inside a famous wine-producing area. Marked by two stately cypress trees, the house is two kilometres from the town and has sensational panoramic views of the surrounding vineyards and hills. The business is run on agriturismo lines by smiling, capable, real-farmer Raffaella, who lives just across the courtyard with her town-planner husband, their 18 year-old son and two boisterous dogs. Tiled guest bedrooms are country-pretty: an old marble-topped table here, a rustic wardrobe there, beds painted duck-egg blue, walls in soft pastel and many pieces beautifully painted by Raffaella. Both the bedrooms and the frescoed dining room lie across the yard from your hosts' house; if you choose to eat in, you dine at your own table on well-priced local dishes with wines from the estate, some of them pretty special, having been aged in wooden barrels and are hard to find outside the area. Raffaella speaks excellent English and is happy to help guests get the most out of this enchanting area. It may be off the beaten track but it's only an hour's drive to the coast.

Price	€64-€75. Triple €80-€90.
Rooms	5: 4 twins/doubles, 1 triple.
Meals	Dinner with wine, €16-€22.
Closed	20 December-February; August.
Directions	From Vignale, follow signs to Camagna. After 2km left at roadside shrine. Cascina Alberta is 400m on right.

Raffaella de Cristofaro
Loc. Ca' Prano 14,
15049 Vignale Monferrato
Tel +39 0142 933313
Email cascinalberta@netcomp.it
Web www.cascinalberta.net

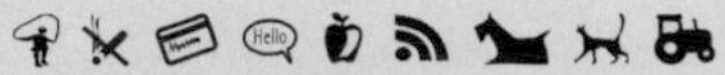

La Traversina Agriturismo

Come for the roses, the irises, the hostas! You'll find over 230 different varieties of plant here – they are Rosanna's passion. With drowsy shutters, buzzing bees and walls festooned in roses, the house and outbuildings appear to be in a permanent state of siesta. As do the seven cats, basking on warm window sills and shady terraces. There's a touch of *The Secret Garden* about the half-hidden doors, enticing steps and riotous plants, and the air is fragrant with lavender, oregano and roses, many from France. The house and farm, on a wooded hillside, have been in Rosanna's family for nearly 300 years; she gave up a career as an architect to create this paradise 40 minutes from Genoa. Homely, imaginatively decorated, bedrooms have handsome furniture, books, pictures; bathrooms come with baskets of goodies. Everyone eats together at a long table in the conservatory or outside, where lights glow in the trees at night. Rosanna, Domenico and young Vijaya are the most delightful hosts and the home-grown food is a revelation: agriturismo at its best. *Children over 12 welcome. Rose courses Feb-May. Ask about cookery classes.*

Ethical Collection: Food.
See page 419 for details.

Price	€90-€110. Half-board €70-€80 extra p.p. Apartments €115-€135. All prices per night.
Rooms	2 + 3: 1 double, 1 family room. 3 apartments for 2.
Meals	Dinner €25-€35, by arrangement. Wine €8. Restaurant 7km.
Closed	Rarely.
Directions	A7 Milan-Genova exit Vignole Borbera for Stazzano; 4km; signed.

Rosanna & Domenico Varese Puppo
Cascina La Traversina 109,
15060 Stazzano

Tel	+39 0143 61377
Email	latraversina@latraversina.com
Web	www.latraversina.com

Castello di Tagliolo

The low beams and the warm walls entice you in, demand you unwind and make this captivating place your home. The castle, part of a medieval borgo, has been in the family since 1498; from the windy cobblestone paths to the 900-year-old church the place oozes history. And it's a very peaceful, very safe place for young families to stay, with child-friendly gardens below. The apartments, neither huge nor hugely luxurious, have heaps of charm. Thick walls are painted the family's trademark ochre and terracotta, sweet flowery duvets cover down comforters, wardrobes are antique, Grandpa's sketches are lovingly framed, showers are spacious. You can use the communal oven in the garden, or rustle up a meal in your own decent-sized kitchen in the corner; expect antique marble sinks with cute curtains hiding cupboard space below, cheery oil cloths covering tables and copper pots adorning walls. A Swedish housekeeper shows you the ropes and settles you in. This is arguably Italy's best wine region so book up wine tastings at the family's cantina or head to Asti for a nice glass of bubbly. *Minimum stay two nights.*

Price	€140-€160 (€600-€1,000 per week).
Rooms	5 apartments for 2-6.
Meals	Breakfast €10. Dinner with wine, €40-€45. Restaurant in village.
Closed	November to mid-April.
Directions	A21 (from Turin) to A26 dir. Genova. Exit at Ovada & follow signs to Tagliolo Monferratto. The castle is in the old village centre.

Luca Pinelli Gentile
Via Castello 1,
15070 Tagliolo Monferrato

Tel +39 0143 89195
Mobile +39 335 261336
Email castelloditagliolo@libero.it
Web www.tagliolo.se

Castello di Rocca Grimalda

Wander off Piedmont's tourist trail up into the clouds to a grand castle fringing a charming village. It's an imposing sight with its manicured gardens and 13th-century tower, but Giulia and family give you the warmest of Italian welcomes. Highlights are a beautiful domed and stuccoed chapel swirling with frescoes and trompe l'oeil paintings, and a courtyard with a solar clock where summer concerts and exhibitions are held – among deeper, darker rooms and secrets. The sisters serve Italian coffee and breakfast pastries in a giant ballroom of soaring ceilings and chequered floor – a favourite wedding spot – and have created bright bedroom suites among the thick stone walls and beams. One has a kitchenette, but self-caterers take an apartment – sweet, ancient, up winding castle stairs. From the elegant garden and scented herb patch, views swoop over village and valleys. Seek out hiking, biking, golf, Acqui Terme's hot springs, the Castle or Wine Route, or Genova and the Ligurian coast, under an hour away. There are restaurants and shops beyond the castle gates; rich history and the family's warm generosity within.

Price €100-€120.
Rooms 2: 1 suite for 2, 1 suite for 3, with kitchenette.
Meals Restaurants within walking distance.
Closed December-February.
Directions Sent on booking.

Anna Giulia de Rege Sola
Piazza Borgatta 2,
15078 Rocca Grimalda
Mobile +39 334 3387659
Email info@castelloroccagrimalda.it
Web www.castelloroccagrimalda.it

Casa degli Orsi

You are sandwiched between vineyards, hot springs and the Ligurian coast. 'Romeo' and 'Juliet' – once simple stone cottages in a lovely Piedmontese hilltop village – exemplify excellent restoration and Peter and Carolyn's love of antiques and art. Crunch over the gravel of the shared courtyard and enter Romeo's chunky walls. This is medieval charm polished to a shine. Elegant bedrooms hold antique wardrobes, and the double has both shower and tub. The kitchen is a delicious blend of vintage limed wood with state-of-the-art appliances: chop and chat at a central island, dine at an antique table. Or eat under a shady portico in the private courtyard, with a side dish of green valley views (if the sun's hot, there's an outdoor solar shower). In the large tiled living room, cushions pile high on leather sofas and artworks dance on limewashed walls. If you're a big party, you may take on Juliet's three extra suites. Find a super four-poster, en suite massage showers and an antique tiled breakfast room with a sunny balcony. The local trattoria can deliver meals. Alba (famous for white truffles) and Genoa are close.

Price	From €1,000 per week.
Rooms	2 houses: 1 for 4, 1 for 6.
Meals	Restaurant 200m.
Closed	Never.
Directions	A26 exit Alessandria Sud and follow signs to Acqui Terme. After Cassine, follow signs to Rivalta Bormida. Owners will provide further detailed directions.

Peter & Carolyn Bear
Via XX Settembre 3,
15010 Orsara Bormida

Tel	+33 (0)4 70 67 58 34
Email	p.bear@wanadoo.fr
Web	www.orsara.biz

La Granica

When Karen, with Mark, went in search of her Italian roots, their adventure ended in an 18th-century grain barn in a secluded dell surrounded by rolling vineyards. Enter the beautifully renovated *granica* through a foyer of limestone floors, a wet bar and exposed brick walls: to the left is the library with deep leather sofas and chocolate and lime colours; to the right is the dining room, sleekly minimalist with polished marble floors and Lithuanian oak chairs. Here, fresh buffet-breakfasts and seasonal four-course dinners are served. Beneath a high cathedral ceiling, the four bedrooms are luxuriously furnished with lashings of silk, velvet chenille armchairs (or chaise longue), splashes of raspberry tones, Egyptian cotton sheets. In the more traditional rooms are mahogany sleigh beds and resplendent bohemian chandeliers. The self-catering terrace house holds a diminutive sitting room, a fully equipped kitchen and double and twin bedrooms in house style – the former with a 'Jacobean' four-poster. Trees and lawns neatly frame the discreet swimming pool. *Minimum stay two nights in cottage.*

Ethical Collection: Environment. See page 419 for details.

Price	€115-€165. Cottage €155-€210 (€644-€1,176 per week).
Rooms	4 + 1: 4 doubles. Cottage for 2-4.
Meals	Breakfast €10 for self-caterers. Dinner with wine, €30-€35. Buffet supper €10. Snacks €5-€8. Restaurant 3km.
Closed	Rarely.
Directions	From A26 exit Alessandria Sud direction Nizza Monferrato; signs for Fontanile.

Karen Langley
Cascina Mulino Vecchio 5, Regione Mulino Vecchio, 14044 Fontanile

Tel	+39 0141 739105
Email	info@lagranicahotel.com
Web	www.lagranica.com

La Villa Hotel

Welcome to the winding narrow roads and rolling vineyards of Piedmont. Built in 1600, this ochre-hued villa has breathtaking views – all the way to the snow-topped Alps. Lovely hands-on Chris and Nicola have created a small hotel where you are wrapped in luxury yet feel totally at home; their passion to do things well runs deep. The style is laid-back country chic, with floppy sofas and big worn-leather chairs, painted wood furniture and old brick walls… and the welcome breeze swishing through the French windows. Meals are taken at individual tables under a shaded arbour in summer, the menu changes daily, the food is local, simple and delicious. Start the evening with an aperitivo in the bar, then drift into the cellar to choose the perfect wine. Learn to make pasta or hunt for white truffles, spin off on a bike or hop off to the coast: it's only an hour away. Or loll by the pool-with-views. Then retire to bedrooms with lofty ceilings and tons of natural light, books, music, natural soaps, luxurious linens and amazing walk-in showers. Many of the rooms get their own terraces or balconies.

Price	€165-€260. Minimum 2 nights at weekends.
Rooms	14: 6 doubles, 6 suites, 2 singles.
Meals	Cooked breakfast €5. Dinner, 4 courses, €40. Restaurants 3km.
Closed	December-March.
Directions	Sent on booking.

Chris & Nicola Norton
Via Torino 7, Fraz. Casalotto,
Mombaruzzo, 14046 Asti

Tel +39 0141 793890
Email info@lavillahotel.net
Web www.lavillahotel.net

Casa Isabella

What a renovation! Computer programmer and whizz-at-cocktails Alessandro, and architect/designer Monica, alive with happiness and creativity, gave up lives in Turin for this dream: to renovate a village farmhouse in lovely Piedmont with glorious vineyard views. Casa Isabella is heaven. Doors and tiles have been reclaimed and walls painted in classic hues (ochre, slate blue, a dash of claret); elegant 1920s furnishings mix with unusual paintings and contemporary quirkery; lights have been inserted into stone stairs, bathrooms have exquisite hand-made mirrors, and coloured candles illuminate grandmother's cutlery. Bedrooms are huge and two have balconies. Monica's food is delicious, the breads and pastas homemade, the menus regional, the wines local; a sample of salami or a snack of crudités from the kitchen garden are yours whenever you like. Heavenly breakfasts are served, when you want them, in the dining room or in the shade of a tree; in winter, logs smoulder. Books by the score, boules in the garden, a charmingly natural pool for swimmers, and a bustling market town 15 minutes down the road.

Price	€100-€140.
Rooms	4: 2 doubles, 2 twins.
Meals	Dinner €30. Wine €9-€38.
Closed	Rarely.
Directions	A26 Alessandria-Genova; exit Alessandria Sud. Follow signs for Nizza Monferrato; signs to Vaglio Serra on SP40. After 4km in Vaglio Serra, signs for Casa Isabella.

Monica Molari & Alessandro Barattieri
Via La Pietra 5, 14049 Vaglio Serra

Tel +39 0141 732201
Email info@casa-isabella.com
Web www.casa-isabella.com

Bramaluna

Welcome to a little-known corner of Italy. Up in the forested hills on the edge of a small village outside Asti, this neat, chic conversion of an 18th-century cascina is quite a surprise. The renovation is a beautifully romantic gesture from architect Maurizio, who saw just how much his wife Mara loved her father's old home. Maurizio's artistic eye is everywhere, and much of the original charm has been preserved: exposed brick the wooden beams blend with both minimalist and whimsical touches, such as the huge oversized flowers that line the steel staircase. Bedrooms are a similar mix of bare wood and bold colours, with no compromise on the amount of natural light they receive, nor indeed on the quality of the linen. The dining room sits at the heart of this modern country retreat, the setting for a deliciously sweet and savoury breakfast – unless you prefer your pastries on the terrace overlooking a sylvan scene. After a wonderful day's walking, dinner, cooked by Mara, is the best way to sample Piedmontese produce – and to enjoy very personal style of these attentive hosts.

Price	€90. Suite €90-€120.
Rooms	3: 1 double, 2 suites for 3-4.
Meals	Dinner, with wine, €25-€35. Restaurant within walking distance.
Closed	Rarely.
Directions	Sent on booking.

Maurizio Lazzarini
14100 Asti

Mobile +39 335 7464211
Email relax@bramaluna.it
Web www.bramaluna.it

Cascina Papa Mora Agriturismo

Authentic agriturismo in northern Italy. Adriana and Maria Teresa run grandmother's old house, speak fluent English and make you truly welcome. The farm produces wine, vegetables and fruit; the pantry overflows with oil, wine, chutney and jam. (This is one of the main regions for Barbera, Dolcetto, Bracchetto, Spumante.) We can't say that the farmhouse has been lovingly restored – more razed to the ground and rebuilt, then bedecked with simple stencils of flowers. Bedrooms, some hiding in the roof area, have no-nonsense 1930s furniture and light floral spreads. There's a little sitting room for guests with a wood-burning stove and, outside, a garden with roses, lavender and herbs sloping down to the pool and stables. The sisters also run a restaurant here and are passionate about their organic credentials. Dinner is a feast of gnocchi and tagliatelle, pepperoni cream puffs, anchovies in almond sauce, all delicious, and fun. Don't leave without sampling some homemade organic ice cream. Breakfast on the veranda where the blossom is pretty, the hills surround you, the bread comes fresh from the wood oven.

Price	€70. Singles €40. Triple €85. Quadruples €95. Half-board €60 p.p.
Rooms	7: 4 twins/doubles, 1 triple, 2 quadruples.
Meals	Lunch/dinner with wine, €25-€30.
Closed	December-February.
Directions	A21 exit Villanova d'Asti & for Cellarengo. On outskirts of village left into Via Ferrere, past small chapel to farm.

Adriana & Maria Teresa Bucco
Via Ferrere 16,
14010 Cellarengo

Tel	+39 0141 935126
Email	papamora@tin.it
Web	www.cascinapapamora.it

Viavai

Alberto and Francesca inherited a big country house in hilltop Casalborgone, exploited the family's talent, taste and respect for Viavai's origins, renovated and then moved in. Now three generations live here, cheerfully spread across the big first floor. The second and third floors, reached via a small lift and a beautiful stone stair, are devoted to six uncluttered guest rooms, four with lush valley views. At ground level is a huge courtyard with a pool to one side and a courtyard garden dotted with wicker chairs. The stylishness spreads into the bedrooms, all harmonious colours, perfect wooden floors and striking textiles – linen, silk, organza, hessian. Bathrooms have plaster and brick walls, eco soaps and fluffy colour-matched towels. On this level you'll also find the dining room for (delicious) breakfasts. And then there's Francesca, full of life and ideas, keen to introduce you to the highlights (cultural, oenological, gastronomic) of this undiscovered region. There are eco walks from the village, personal shoppers (just ask!) and special prices at the little restaurant down the hill. A treat for all seasons.

Price	€70-€95.
Rooms	6: 3 doubles, 2 suites, 1 family room for 4.
Meals	Restaurant 5-minute walk.
Closed	Rarely.
Directions	From Chivasso, SS590 to San Sebastiano da Po; right onto SS458. At Casalborgone, right onto Corso Vittorio Emanuele II; signs to "centro storico".

Francesca Guerra Vai
Via Valfrè 7,
10020 Casalborgone

Mobile +39 347 1520513
Email info@viavai.to.it
Web www.viavai.to.it

Castello di San Sebastiano Po

You arrive at the top of a tiny medieval town. An ancient red-washed door buzzes you in – to a courtyard of centuries-old trees, chirruping birds and warm, gentle Luca, whose family has lived here for 25 years. Eleven bedrooms are divided between the 'noble' (early 1800s) part of the estate and the farmhouse that goes back to medieval times. Each room is steeped in character: thick stone walls, cool tiled floors, huge chunky beams. There are old wooden sleigh beds and wrought-iron day beds, pretty patches of worn paint and humble bathrooms with box showers, and a suite with a wonderful claw foot tub; it oozes charm. Views – into a courtyard with glorious trees or over the valley below – do not disappoint; breakfasts are enjoyed at cheery check-clothed tables. It's a special place for weddings but also for families, with so much outdoor space to roam… old oaks give glorious shade, there are magnolias, palms and a greenhouse that dates from the 1700s. A delightful family runs this place, and are totally hands-on. Come for nature, authenticity, a relaxed feel… and log fires ablaze in winter.

Price	€110. Singles €75.
Rooms	11: 9 doubles, 1 suite for 4, 1 suite for 6.
Meals	Dinner €25. Wine €8. Restaurants 2km.
Closed	Rarely.
Directions	Sent on booking.

Luca Garrone
Via Novarina 9,
10020 San Sebastiano da Po

Tel	+39 0119 191177
Email	info@castellosansebastiano.it
Web	www.castellosansebastiano.it

Alla Buona Stella

Turin: grandiose home to baroque architecture and art, irresistible cafés, divine chocolatiers, prestigious opera house… and capital of the aperitivo. Here, in a respectable residential street in the heart of the old town, is Roberta's B&B. Up the lift of this very elegant building to a wide landing on the fourth floor and there is Roberta to greet you, with her lovely big smile and infectious laugh. There's an elegant oval dining table for breakfast, a cluster of shiny blue matching sofa and chairs, a little computer corner and a comforting, comfortable décor. Then there are the guest quarters on the floor above, high under the eaves, reached by a wooden open-tread stair. Expect three big, friendly, generous, traditional rooms, all polished antiques, gleaming floors, patterned rugs and easy chairs. The suite has its own little terrace, looking right down to the courtyard below, and the bathrooms are excellent, with showers and baths, bottles of shampoo, coloured towels. Roberta is super-organised, loves the city, loves her B&B, knows all there is to know. You could not be in better hands.

Price	€100-€110.
Rooms	3: 1 twin/double, 1 suite for 2-3, 1 triple.
Meals	Restaurants nearby.
Closed	Rarely.
Directions	10-minute walk from centre of Turin. Train station Porta Susa (1km) and Porta Nuova (5km). Airport A. Pertini of Torino Caselle (35km).

Roberta Simonetti
Via del Carmine 10,
10122 Turin

Tel +39 0111 9710823
Email info@allabuonastella.it
Web www.allabuonastella.it

Casa Ale Bed & Breakfast

Alessandra's home in the Turin hills is as warm and inviting as she: a perfect antidote to impersonal city hotels. The old country villa sits in lush gardens in which birds and wildlife run free – your children can join them – just a few kilometres from Turin city centre. It's a lovely Italian home, pale yellow with racing green shutters, flanked by pond, palms and potted plants. You breakfast in the kitchen or garden gazebo, and sleep tight in bedrooms of pale blue or blush, with sweet curtains, tea kettles and tidy shower rooms. Families can self-cater in the apartment with its cheery orange kitchen and antique table, or dine on 'fritto misto' and 'bagna cauda' in the local trattorias – Alessandra will point out those with authentic Piedmontese cuisine. Follow the riverside boardwalk into the city for museums, shops, cafés and festivals – the Salone del Gusto (Slow Food fair) is a favourite. Or leap into the hills for some of Italy's best wines and walking country. Not luxurious but spacious, quiet and immensely welcoming... a place where the hostess's grace and generosity shine through.

Price	€85-€120. Apartment €120-€190. Minimum 2 nights.
Rooms	2 + 1: 2 twins/doubles. Apartment for 2-4.
Meals	Restaurant 1.5km.
Closed	Rarely.
Directions	Sent on booking.

Alessandra Oddone
Strada comunale di Mongreno 341,
10132 Turin

Tel	+39 0118 990808
Mobile	+39 333 4376220
Email	info@casaale.it
Web	www.casaale.it

Il Gioco dell'Oca Agriturismo

People love Raffaella: her home is full of tokens of appreciation sent by guests. She spent much of her childhood here – the farm was her grandparents'. She is happy to be back, looks after her guests beautifully, feeds them well, and has tampered with the pretty, 18th-century farmhouse as little as possible. The well-worn, welcoming kitchen, much as it must have been 50 years ago, is for you to use as and when you like – the warm hub of a sociable house. Next door is a breakfast room set with little tables, but if it's fine you'll prefer to breakfast under the portico in the garden, which is big enough for everyone to find their own secluded corner. The bedrooms are simple and cosy, with family furniture and wooden beds, one with a hob, sink and fridge – a bonus if you have little ones. Bathrooms are bright and new. The farm, up in the hills near Barolo – a wonderful area for cheeses and wines – produces wine, fruit and hazelnuts. A pity the road is so close but you'll forgive that for the pleasure of staying at such a relaxed, welcoming and thoroughly Italian agriturismo.

Price	€65-€75. Triple €75-€85.
Rooms	7: 6 twins/doubles, 1 triple.
Meals	Restaurant 500m.
Closed	January.
Directions	From Asti (east) exit autostrada TO-PC. Follow sign for Alba & Barolo. Left 2km before village, 50m on right sign for house.

Raffaella Pittatore
Via Alba 83,
12060 Barolo

Tel +39 0173 56206
Email info@gioco-delloca.it
Web www.gioco-delloca.it

Hotel Castello di Sinio

Sitting atop the tiny village of Sinio surrounded by rolling hillsides, hazelnut plantations and a multitude of vineyards, this 12th-century castello belonged to the noble Carretto family for some 600 years. On the village side, the stone façade appears impregnable, but move to the courtyard and a different mood prevails: lush green lawn, colourful flower beds, cascades of geraniums falling from windows boxes…a delicious little swimming pool has been tucked to one side of the castle. American Denise has done a tremendous job of restoration, at the same time becoming an ardent Piemontesi exponent of the region's wines, gastronomic delights and traditions. Denise is also the chef, personally creating the memorable meals which can be taken in the upstairs dining room. Good-sized bedrooms have terracotta floors, many with exposed stonework, beams and individual examples of beautiful vaulted stonework and fine Barocco furniture. Bathrooms are equipped with shower cabins and handy magnifying mirrors. Stunning. *Minimum stay two nights.*

Price	€150-€325.
Rooms	16 doubles.
Meals	Breakfast €8. Dinner, 4 courses, €45 (Wed-Sun). Wine from €15.
Closed	8 January-February.
Directions	From Alba dir. Cuneo, Barolo & Gallo. At Gallo, dir. Grinzane Cavour; immed. left for Sinio, 7km. Signed.

Denise Pardini
Vicolo del Castello 1,
12050 Sinio
Tel +39 0173 263889
Email denise@hotelcastellodisinio.com
Web www.hotelcastellodisinio.com

Relais Divino

Ah, the heavenly trio of good food, good wine and seclusion: that's the secret of Relais Divino. Thread through Piemonte's rolling landscapes, up a rural drive to a working estate and you're greeted by the all-pervasive perfume of vines. The holiday bodes well... Definitely opt for dinner: it's a four-course extravaganza here, of meat-stuffed pastas, savoury tarts and mouthwatering morsels paired with the estate's wines. Ugo and Petra's local specialities are irresistibly more-ish, and the brick arches, candlelight and crisp linen create a magical atmosphere from which to glide up to bed. Great care has been taken over the colourful king-size bedrooms and the mezzanine family rooms – the level of comfort is consistent but the individual styling means you can try a different room each visit. Breakfast at leisure under the portico or indoors, savour your espresso as you survey hazelnut groves, grazing horses, and gardens that are a child's delight. After a swim, if you fancy a jacuzzi or a Turkish bath, just ask Ugo and he'll prepare it for you, with a smile. Italy at its best.

Price	€120. Family suites €150-€180.
Rooms	6: 3 doubles, 3 family suites for 3-5.
Meals	Lunch €20. Dinner €35. Wine €10-€25.
Closed	January-February.
Directions	Sent on booking.

Petra Stechert
Loc. San Sebastiano 68,
12065 Monforte d'Alba

Tel	+39 0173 789269
Email	info@relaisdivino.it
Web	www.relaisdivino.it

Cascina Adami - Il Nido

A short drive down a country lane, the 17th-century farmhouse is set into its hill with superb views over a gentle patchwork landscape of wheat fields and vineyards – leading the eye to snowy peaks beyond. This is the best wine-producing area of Italy, and opposite the lane is a dairy where you can stock up on the sheep's cheese – soft, mild, delicious Murazzano. Discreetly distant from the main house, down a steep unpaved track – watch your wheels – is a four-square, two-storey stone structure, once a goats' shed. Il Nido (the nest) is a delicious bolthole for two. Owner Paolo is a master at putting salvaged finds to unusual use with charming results, so expect pale new stone floors and chunky old rafters, a delicate wooden fretwork door, a stylish steel table and chairs, a charming kitchen tucked under a chunky white stone stair, a bedroom with a big cream bed and small blue shutters, driftwood and pebbles prettifying quiet corners. Outside is smart wooden furniture from which to gaze on the views and a huge linen parasol. Contemporary rusticity, ancient peace. *Minimum stay two nights.*

Price	€700 per week (€350 for weekend). Heating extra.
Rooms	House for 2.
Meals	Restaurants in Murazzano, 1.5km.
Closed	October-April.
Directions	A6 from Turin exit Carrù dir. Clavesana, Murazzano.

Paolo & Flavia Adami
Fraz. Mellea 53,
12060 Murazzano

Tel	+39 0118 178135
Mobile	+39 347 9721761
Email	flavia.adami@yahoo.it
Web	www.cascinaadami.it

Lombardy and Trentino-Alto Adige

Polidora

Are you in a Fitzgerald novel, a guest at some expat's ridiculously lush estate? From the vast botanical garden on the shores of Lake Maggiore, where islands hover on the glistening water and the Alps stand protectively in the distance, you will feel at total peace with the world. The changing light mischievously catches rare species of plant, flower and tree in moods you would not think possible, in supernatural shades. What luck that GianLuca decided to convert the stables in the grounds of his elegant 1900s villa into a spacious and stylish B&B. Now the WWF-protected acres of rare plants and trees, which he still tends and adds to so passionately, are yours to explore; with lonely benches, pebble beaches and shady patches inviting you to unwind, we defy you to read a book without being distracted by the beauty – or to not swim in the cool waters of the lake the moment you see their enticing ripples. While GianLuca is away, his staff are on hand for breakfasts and conversation. Lunch in the nearby village of Cerro or picnic in the grounds, it's so big you can stay here all day and not see another soul.

Price	B&B €150. Whole house €3,000 per week.
Rooms	3: 2 doubles, 1 suite for 5.
Meals	Restaurants 1-3km.
Closed	Rarely.
Directions	From Milan A8 exit Sesto Calende; follow shores of Lake Maggiore, through Angera. Entrance before Cerro di Laveno Mombello.

GianLuca Sarto
Via Pirinoli 4,
21014 Cerro di Laveno Mombello
Mobile +39 349 7826474
Email info@polidora.com
Web www.polidora.com

Alberghetto La Marianna

On the banks of Lake Como, a very charming family-run hotel, housed in a villa simply modernised and redecorated with a nicely laid-back feel. Bedrooms are humble, functional, with cheery shower rooms and (mostly) lakeside views. Some have balconies, one has its own little terrace. A road runs between you and the busy lake, so if you're a light sleeper, it may be worth giving up those shimmering views for a room at the back – at least in summer. No need to tip-toe round the owners: Paola is a delight, very generous and treats guests as friends. Breakfasts include homemade bread, cakes, savoury offerings and jams, husband Ty prepares a different menu of wholesome food every day, while Paolo is a "mistress of desserts". You can eat inside and admire the ever-changing local art work lining the walls or outside where you can embrace the lake views on the terrace that juts onto the water. You won't be short of advice here on things to do: visits to gardens and villas, boat tours to Isola Comacina, day trips to St Moritz and the Engadine. The ferries are a step away.

Price	€85-€95. Single €60-€65.
Rooms	8: 7 doubles, 1 single.
Meals	Dinner with wine, €30.
Closed	Mid-November to mid-March (open 26 December-6 January).
Directions	From Como direction Menaggio on west lakeside road to Cadenabbia 30km; 300m after ferry port to Bellagio.

Paola Cioccarelli
Via Regina 57,
22011 Cadenabbia di Griante
Tel +39 0344 43095
Mobile +39 333 9812649
Email inn@la-marianna.com
Web www.la-marianna.com

Villetta Il Ghiro & Villetta La Vigna

The setting is wonderful, on the isthmus between two grand lakes, just by a cobbled village, surrounded by mountains, meadows and winding country lanes. Wisteria was growing through the old convent when Ann fell in love with the house. The roof had fallen in too but, undeterred, she went ahead and turned it into the lovely place it is today. She thoroughly enjoys welcoming guests to the two guest apartments that stand alongside: traditional, comfortable, homely and quiet. Find big airy rooms, well-equipped kitchens and independent outside stairs. Il Ghiro is on the first floor of a former hay barn and La Vigna is above the garages, its second bedroom and en suite bathroom opening off the first, its little balcony catching the afternoon sun. Best of all is the garden with big lawns, fenced pool and tennis court tucked away. A treat to stroll amongst the shrubs and the trees, recline on a lounger, nod off to the river, take tea on the terrace. Birdsong and water are the only sounds yet you are no distance from the excitements of Menaggio and Lake Como. *Flexible rental periods. Minimum five nights.*

Price	€450-€900 for 2-3; €900-€1,800 for 4-6. €200-300 for extra double room. Prices per week.
Rooms	2 apartments: 1 for 2-3, 1 for 4-6.
Meals	Breakfast not included. Restaurants 5-minute walk.
Closed	October-April.
Directions	From Menaggio N340 for Porlezza/Lugano, after 3km Grandola is signed. Right at 'panificio' (bakery); immediately right for Cardano. Right into Via al Forno.

Ann Dexter
Via al Forno 5, Cardano,
22010 Grandola ed Uniti

Tel +39 0344 32740
Email ann.dexter@libero.it

Albergo Olivedo

Laura runs her quayside hotel – by the ferry, a stroll from the town centre – like a tight ship. There are balconies and Art Nouveau lamps on the outside, polished parquet floors, grandmother's furniture and starched cotton inside, and, from several rooms, wonderful views over the lake. The little reception with burr maple counter and speckled floor could grace a French pensione; this is its Italian equivalent. Just a few steps away is the family's more recent acquisition, a classic, 19th-century villa, the Toretta, with large lovely bedrooms and more superb views of the harbour. Frescoes, decorative iron staircase and lofty ceilings have been carefully restored, while traditional tiles, handsome beds and fine old furniture give the rooms a distinguished air. It stands in its own pretty garden, so relax in the shade of the trees or bask on the terrace, before wandering over to the Olivedo for a traditional meal; Laura's brother is chef). Inside or out you have a view of the harbour and the charming Como ferry. The hotel has been in Laura's family for 60 years and her staff are warm and friendly.

Price	€110-€170. Half-board €160-€200 for 2.
Rooms	19: 14 doubles. Villa Torretta: 5 doubles.
Meals	Dinner €27. Wine from €8. Restaurant 100m.
Closed	2 November-20 December.
Directions	From north, SP72 from Colico to Varenna.

Laura Colombo
Piazza Martiri 4,
23829 Varenna

Tel +39 0341 830115
Email info@olivedo.it
Web www.olivedo.it

Agriturismo Castello di Vezio - Casa delle Rose

Tucked down a narrow street in tiny Vezio is a family house that makes you feel like a local – with access to the Castello di Vezio's fabulous facilities. The Vezio estate, draped around a medieval castle with panoramic views over Lake Como and the mountains, contains several other holiday homes, a tennis court, swimming pool, games room and large lawn; the Greppi family press olive oil from the estate's gnarled trees. Vezio itself is a sweet hamlet of church bells and cobblestones, with a steep rocky path to Varenna below. The house is in the village centre, and immaculately up to date: sleek modern bathrooms, large state-of-the-art kitchen with Villeroy & Boch, elegant bedrooms (one with bunks), floral fabrics, heavy curtains, crisp linens. Highlights are the stone grotto living room with its open fire and shelves of English tomes, and little grassy garden where you can eat under a rose-covered arbour and jasmine perfumes the air. Spend your days lounging in the estate, evenings cosied up at home or dining in Perledo or Varenna. For the tourist treatment, roll down the hill to Como.

Price	€1,900-€2,600 per week.
Rooms	House for 6 (1 double, 1 twin, 1 room with bunks).
Meals	Breakfast €15, by arrangement. Restaurant 800m.
Closed	Rarely.
Directions	Sent on booking.

Maria Manuela Greppi
Via del Castellano 16,
23828 Varenna

Tel +39 0258 190940
Email vezio@robilant.it
Web www.agriturismocastellodivezio.it

Agriturismo Castello di Vezio - Case Cima & Casa Selva

With views stretching over Lake Como from your dining room, a balcony hugging the exterior and sun-trapped terraces at every turn – lovely to eat out – Casa Cima is a delightful family getaway high in the historic hamlet of Vezio. Behind the entrance gates, the lake far below, Vezio is, in essence, a small friendly holiday village. Shared with four other houses are a tennis court, a huge games room (with table football) and heaps of outdoor space. The children may play football or rounders on the lawn while you nod off in the shade of one of numerous trees, or sunbathe in peace beside your very own pool; you can also look over the 12th-century castle. And, if the party is a large one, you can rent Casa Cima's ground-floor companion, Casa Selva. Throughout, pretty bedrooms have fresh painted walls and 18th-century floral furnishings, and bathrooms are spotless and functional. Stock up in the delicatessens of Perledo, walk to restaurants (one lies at the foot of the castle) or hop in the car to beautiful Varenna. Tons of space to explore and play makes Vezio a dream for families.

Price	Cima €2,600-€3,300. Selva €1,100-€1,400. (€3,500-€4,200 together.) Prices per week. Minimum 2 nights.
Rooms	2 houses: 1 for 4, 1 for 8. Can be rented together.
Meals	Breakfast €15, by arrangement. Restaurant 800m.
Closed	Never.
Directions	Sent on booking.

Maria Manuela Greppi
Via del Castellano 41,
23828 Varenna

Tel +39 0258 190940
Email vezio@robilant.it
Web www.agriturismocastellodivezio.it

Agriturismo Castello di Vezio – Casa Pupa

The *castello* of Vezio, a must-see for visitors to the area and with 360° panorama of the lake, belongs to the Greppi family; everyone staying here has free and private access. So you have it all: a slice of history, activities for the family, well-kept gardens and pools with views over what is debatably Italy's most beautiful lake. The castle goes back to the Middle Ages and stands high above the shore, with a sheer drop down to lovely Varenna. Admire the owls and hawks who reside in the battlements; imagine barbaric invaders approaching from Como, or aggressors advancing from Lecco. When you've had your fill of history, return to Casa Pupa to rest and unwind. The Greppi family themselves lived in the house in the 1970s and photos of their sailing days line walls. There's a light-hearted boating theme throughout, even a rope to help you up the spiral stair. At the top, slightly faded bedrooms flooded with light await. It's a great place to stay for a large party, and note, the two simple loft-apartments (each for four) have their own kitchens. Best of all, Casa Pupa comes with its own pool.

Price	€2,600-€5,800 per week. Minimum 2 nights.
Rooms	House for 7-15 (min. 8 people in high season).
Meals	Breakfast €15, by arrangement. Restaurant 800m.
Closed	Never.
Directions	Sent on booking.

Maria Manuela Greppi
Via del Castellano 16,
23828 Varenna

Tel	+39 0258 190940
Email	vezio@robilant.it
Web	www.agriturismocastellodivezio.it

Agriturismo Castello di Vezio - Case Milena, Giovanni & Donato

Spectacularly secluded from the other houses inside the entrance gates of Castello di Vezio (and 700 metres down a steep path) the two-up, two-down Casa Milena crouches in a cliff yards from the craggy edge and then… there's the lake, inviting deep breaths and wide eyes every time you open the front door. The cottage is one of the most romantic places we know and it would be impossible not to feel inspired here: your gaze falls on that glittering view from wherever you are. One of the bedrooms has a terrace for those who wish to share the experience. Back up the path and you can play a spot of tennis with the other guests staying in the castle grounds; there are also secret spots for those who like their privacy. Casa Giovanni is set in its own orchard below the castle – nicely private. Again, its grey granite exterior is softened inside by floral bed spreads and friendly, modern kitchens. The latest in the Vezio pack is the very lovely Casa Donato, a contemporary bolthole for two, with beautiful slate-grey shutters and a balcony for the views. *Children over eight welcome at Casa Milena.*

Price	€1,200-€1,600 per week. Minimum one week October to May.
Rooms	3 houses: 1 for 2, 2 for 4.
Meals	Breakfast €15, by arrangement. Restaurant 800m.
Closed	Rarely.
Directions	Sent on booking.

Maria Manuela Greppi
Via del Castellano 16,
23828 Varenna

Tel +39 0258 190940
Email vezio@robilant.it
Web www.agriturismocastellodivezio.it

Albergo Milano

You wander down the cobbled streets of Varenna and, suddenly, there it is: the grand lake. The life of the village bustles below, where colourwashed houses cluster round the church on a rocky promontory perched above Lake Como. The setting is enchanting. Smack on the lakeside is Albergo Milano, pretty, traditional and disarmingly small. Owners Bettina and Egidio are engaging people, delighted to be running their own small hotel. Everywhere is freshly and stylishly furnished, bedroom floors are covered in colourful old tiles, traditional furniture makes a striking contrast with sleek modern bathrooms and each has a balcony or terrace with a lake view. The dining room's big new windows open onto a wonderful wide terrace where you eat out on fine days, the lake stirring beside you. The food is divine gourmet-Italian, the wine list irresistible. A step away, in the old part of town, is a charming sister dwelling housing apartments with kitchenettes and living rooms. Bettina is a mine of information about this area and there's a regular train service into Bergamo and Milan. It's a gem. *Book garage parking in advance.*

Price	€135-€205. Apartments €130-€300.
Rooms	13 + 3: 12 doubles, 1 triple. 3 apartments for 2-5.
Meals	Dinner €35. Wine from €18. Restaurant 500m.
Closed	December-February.
Directions	From Lecco SS36 to Sondrio; 1st exit for Abbadia Lariana. After 15km, before tunnel, left for Varenna. Park in Piazza San Giorgio. 150m to hotel (map in piazza).

Bettina & Egidio Mallone
Via XX Settembre 35,
23829 Varenna

Tel	+39 0341 830298
Email	hotelmilano@varenna.net
Web	www.varenna.net

Il Torchio

Marcella's happy personality fills the house with joy. She and Franco are artists – she an animator, he a painter; if you love the bohemian life you will love it here. Franco also has an antiquarian bookshop in Milan, which explains the shelves in the sitting room. Their home began life in 1600 as the stables of the noble Calchi family; you enter through a fine stone archway into a courtyard. Franco's paintings enliven the walls and every corner is adorned with stained-glass, prints and curios that Marcella has found on her flea market forays. Bedrooms are endearingly old-fashioned – no frills but good, comfortable beds. The big private suite, entered via French windows, has green views down to Calco, a great big bed, family photos on the walls, and a cabinet filled with children's old toys. The bathrooms are basic but have lovely hand-painted tiles. The whole family is a delight – including the cats – and Marcella's cooking is superb, with many delights from the garden. Active types can canoe in summer and ski in winter (just a one-hour drive); or visit Verona, Lake Como, and the stunning shops of Milan. *Free WiFi.*

Price	€50.
Rooms	4: 2 doubles, 2 sharing bathroom.
Meals	Dinner with wine €20, by arrangement. Restaurant 2km.
Closed	Rarely.
Directions	From Milan to Calco; right at r'bout, over 2 speed bumps, right onto Via Ghislanzoni; follow signs for Vescogna; at top of hill.

Ethical Collection: Food.
See page 419 for details.

Marcella Pisacane
Via Ghislanzoni, Loc. Vescogna,
23885 Calco

Tel +39 0395 08724
Mobile +39 348 8124929
Email il_torchio@hotmail.com
Web iltorchio.wordpress.com

Villa La Vescogna

A courtyard heavy with the scent of jasmine leads to a pair of mile-high, gleaming doors: welcome to this opulent, 17th-century palazzo. It is home to the delightful Fasoli family, wonderfully easy-going and kind. Signore is a particularly passionate ambassador for this (surprisingly) unsung area, a font of knowledge on historic villas, day trips to Como and Lecco, and shopping in Milan. Use the gracious, ground-floor rooms if you wish... but you're most likely to be lured by the captivating, tiered, Italianate garden where formal hedging, urns and romantic pathways lead inexorably to a sublime pool – large enough to do a few laps (and there's a pool house with a tiny kitchen if you fancy a lazy day in). Bedrooms, on the same floor as your hosts, are of the romantic variety with a touch of whimsy – "Laura Ashley meets Alice in Wonderland" says our inspector – while the double with the en suite has a vaulted ceiling bright with frescoed cherubs. Breakfast on locally cured meats, home-baked breads and jams in the cheery blue and white kitchen, or on the atmospheric patio shaded by ancient trees.

Price	€90-€120. Minimum stay 2 nights.
Rooms	3: 1 double; 2 doubles sharing bath.
Meals	Restaurant 2km.
Closed	October-April.
Directions	Sent on booking.

Lorenza Bozzoli Fasoli
Loc. Vescogna 2,
23885 Calco

Mobile	+39 339 8927777
Email	bozzoli@tiscali.it
Web	www.lavescogna.com

Agriturismo Casa Clelia

The agriturismo has been sculpted out of the 11th-century convent, using the principles of eco-bio architecture. Cows peer from sheds as you arrive, chickens, geese and sheep bustle – this is a working farm. The main house stands proud against wooded hills and beyond are convent, outhouses, orchards and barns. Anna is a darling, so welcoming and kindly informal you feel right at home the minute you arrive. There is a talented local cook and one of the treats is the taster menu, your chance to sample – guilt-free – numerous delicacies all at once. The bedrooms, a good size, are uncluttered and original, all wood, stone and bold colours; bathrooms are modern, lighting subtle. Heat comes from a wood-burner integrated with solar panels; cork and coconut ensure the sound-proofing of walls. Children are most welcome, free to run wild in the gardens, orchards and eight hectares of woods. Hard to imagine a more wonderful place for families… or for a get-away-from-it-all weekend. There's horse riding nearby, too, and Bergamo, mid-way between Lake Como and Lake Iseo, is a cultural treat.

Price €100-€125.
Rooms 9: 6 doubles, 1 double/quadruple, 2 triples.
Meals Lunch/dinner with wine, €20-€35. Closed Mondays.
Closed Never.
Directions From A4 exit Capriate; signed.

Ferruccio Masseretti
Via Corna 1/3,
24039 Sotto il Monte Giovanni XXIII
Tel +39 0357 99133
Email info@casaclelia.com
Web www.casaclelia.com

Antica Locanda dei Mercanti

Entering the great courtyard of this 18th-century building in the heart of Milan, you wouldn't imagine the lightness and charm of the small, discreet boutique hotel on the second floor. Heavy glass doors slide open to a simple reception where chic Italians and visitors mingle; young staff whisk you off to rooms whose individuality and style promise country-house comfort rather than the spartan modernity associated with this energetic city. The place is run by real people with passion. From the smallest room with its elegant Milanese fabrics and wicker chair with cherry striped and piped cushions to the largest, airy room with its muslin-hung four-poster, terrace, olive tree and scented climbers, each space surprises. Fine linen, deep mattresses, dramatic murals, fresh posies, stacks of magazines, small, gleaming shower rooms – and air conditioning: each room bears the distinctive hallmark of the energetic owner. In the new grey-floored, aubergine-sofa'd communal space, too, for basic breakfast beneath glistening chandeliers. Cool simplicity, and La Scala a heartbeat away.

Price	€205-€325. Suites €245-€295.
Rooms	14 doubles (4 with terrace).
Meals	Breakfast €10 (€15 in bedroom). Light lunch & dinner in room on request. Restaurants nearby.
Closed	Never.
Directions	Via S. Tomaso is a small street off Via Dante, halfway between the Duomo and Piazza Castello. No sign, just a brass plate.

Alessandro Basta
Via San Tomaso 6,
20121 Milan

Tel	+39 0280 54080
Email	locanda@locanda.it
Web	www.locanda.it

Agriturismo Cervano B&B

Surrounded by wild orchids and violets at the highest point of the garden, the sun splashing colour across the sky as it sets over majestic Lake Garda, you could be fooled into believing you were a 19th-century wine merchant returning from Milan for the harvest of your country estate. What a pleasant surprise you would have on entering your house if that were true. Charming Anna and her husband Gino have mastered the restoration of Gino's once-crumbling family home, a fine example of Lombard 'fort' design, and the interior is stylish and contemporary: bathrooms are slick Italian, new beds are dressed in handmade linen, there's a marble breakfast bar in the luminous kitchen and an American-style fridge packed with breakfast goodies. Despite the modernity, Anna and Gino have constantly kept the 1800s in mind: exposed beams have been perfectly restored, floors imitate the original style and the marble is Verona's most rare: speckled pink and red. Wine is still produced on site but now it's organic, and solar panels heat water. A superb restoration in a beautiful and peaceful setting.

Price	B&B €100-€150. Whole house €500-€900. Apt for 4, €110-€130 (€15 per extra person). Apt for 10, €150-€300 p.p. Prices per night.
Rooms	3 + 2: 2 doubles (1 with sofabed), 1 triple. 2 apts: 1 for 4, 1 for 10.
Meals	Restaurant 1km.
Closed	Never.
Directions	From Gargnano, right towards golf club; signed. If you're following GPS, look for Via Golf in Toscolano Maderno, then Via Sassello 30 (car entrance).

Gino & Anna Massarani
Via Cervano 14,
25088 Toscolano Maderno

Tel +39 0365 548398
Email info@cervano.com
Web www.cervano.com

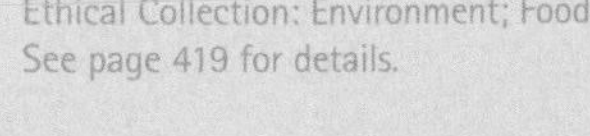

Ethical Collection: Environment; Food.
See page 419 for details.

Hotel Gardenia al Lago

Jasmine-scented gardens and green lawns reach to Lake Garda's edge: lounge here, drinking in the views, and drop down the ladder to the sparkling water, said to be the purest in Italy. There's also a small beach 100 yards away. The hotel stands, a feast of colour and design, against the steep, wooded foothills of Mount Baldo. It was bought by the Arosio family as a summer home in 1925. They were piano-makers from Lodi – note the original piano in the music room – and in the 1950s turned the house into a guesthouse. Today it is a small, restful, civilised hotel with that light 1920s charm. The entire family, parents and sons, are delightful. Some bedrooms have been renovated – frescoes were uncovered in the process – and are beautiful, with distinctive Empire antiques, exquisite floor tiles, muslin billowing at French windows and superior Edwardian-style bathrooms. Many have balconies or terraces. Others, more functional, less charming – and cheaper – await regeneration. In summer you eat under the trees, by candlelight, surrounded by lemon and olive trees – they produce wonderful olive oil.

Price	€90-€226. Singles €67-€169.
Rooms	25 doubles.
Meals	Menu à la carte, from €30. Wine from €12.50.
Closed	10 October; week before Easter. Out of season call +39 0365 71269
Directions	From Brescia-Salò dir. Riva del Garda. After Bogliaco, 400m slip road on right to Via Colletta. Parking at hotel.

Giorgio & Andrea Arosio
Via Colletta 53,
25084 Villa di Gargnano

Tel +39 0365 71195
Email info@hotel-gardenia.it
Web www.hotel-gardenia.it

Hotel du Lac

The hotel oozes old-style charm. A 1900s townhouse in a quieter, less touristy part of the lake, it's in the same street as the villa where DH Lawrence eulogised about the "milky lake" of Garda. The oxblood façade, with white relief and green shutters, is as striking as the view from the patio that overhangs the water; you can swim from here. Valerio's grandparents had a piano shop in Milan and lived here until 1959; much of their furniture remains. The family could not be more helpful. Roomy bedrooms are wonderfully old-fashioned with big beds and wardrobes, 30s' lights and polished terrazzo floors; beds are deeply comfortable and dressed in crisp cotton. Six rooms look onto the lake and have small balconies or terraces. The dining room, around a central courtyard with a palm tree that disappears into the clouds, looks directly onto the water. You can also dine upstairs on the open terrace, where metal tables and chairs are shaded by an arbour of kiwi – a magical spot at night, the water lapping below, the lights twinkling in the distance. There's even a small music room with a piano to play – guests sometimes do.

Price	€100-€144.
Rooms	12 doubles.
Meals	Menu à la carte, from €30. Wine from €13.
Closed	1st week of November; week before Easter. Out of season call +39 0365 71269.
Directions	From Brescia-Salò dir. Riva del Garda. After Bogliaco, 400m slip road on right to Via Colletta. Parking at hotel.

Valerio Arosio
Via Colletta 21,
25084 Villa di Gargnano

Tel +39 0365 71107
Email info@hotel-dulac.it
Web www.hotel-dulac.it

Villa Muslone

Muslone is a walkers' paradise. Lake Garda is bordered by olive groves, lemon trees and vines; climb higher for alpine pastures; gaze beyond to snow-capped mountains. The climate is as clement as that of the Bay of Naples. Your house, half way up a rocky hill, belongs to the young Campanardis and you couldn't wish for a kinder pair. They live in the basement, you live upstairs, sharing your space with the other guests. Emma and Mirko speak a little English, and German, and give you maps for walks and timetables for ferries for the outstandingly beautiful Italian Lakes. Breakfast's organic eggs, ricotta, olive oil and tomatoes are their own. Step into a sitting/dining room with lovely high rafters, magazines, candles and a super new kitchen to the side; each guest has a shelf in the fridge. Off here lie the bedrooms, very comfortable and pristine, one with a wonderful lake view, another opening to the garden. Bathrooms are squeaky clean, with stacks of coloured towels; upstairs are two rooms for cards, cushions and CDs. For sociable self-caterers, this is a treat.

Ethical Collection: Food.
See page 419 for details.

Price	€110-€130.
Rooms	3 doubles (sharing sitting room & kitchen).
Meals	Guest kitchen. Restaurant/pizzeria 1km.
Closed	November-Easter.
Directions	From Gargano, 6km to Muslone. Before Muslone, sign right for no. 64A, Villa signed.

Emma Campanardi
Via Muslone 64/A,
25084 Gargnano

Tel +39 0365 72648
Mobile +39 334 8165513
Email info@villamuslone.it
Web www.villamuslone.it

Dimora Bolsone

Film-like, the lake glitters between the cypress trees – an expanse of blue far below. Gaze in wonder as gentle, cultured, charming Raffaele – and spaniels Rocky and Glenda – settle you on the terrace with a jug of freshly squeezed orange juice. Economist, lecturer, sailor, antique collector, big game hunter and green aficionado, Raffaele is the lifeblood of this property, meets and greets you and gives you free run of these 46 acres, a glorious mix of of protected parkland and terraced gardens. The 15th-century house reposes gracefully among jasmine-strewn loggias and lemon trees; step in to a cool, ordered calm. Big, dark, immaculate bedrooms have light polished floors, soft washed walls, family portraits, delicious linen. All are different – gilt cornices and flirty rococo in one, sober masculinity and a 15th-century bed in another. Start the day feasting on almond cookies, local cheeses, cold meats, fresh fruits; tour Verona, or the lake; return to a salon/library with green leather armchairs and huge stone fireplace. An essay in perfection, a feast for the senses. *Children over 12 welcome. Min. stay two nights.*

Price	€200. Singles €170.
Rooms	5 doubles.
Meals	Restaurants 1km.
Closed	30 November-28 February.
Directions	A4 exit Desenzano del Garda or Brescia Est, then 45 Bis for Gardone Riviera. Left at Il Vittoriale, signed San Michaele; 2km, on left.

Raffaele Bonaspetti
Via Panoramica 23,
25083 Gardone Riviera

Tel	+39 0365 21022
Email	info@dimorabolsone.it
Web	www.dimorabolsone.it

Villa San Pietro Bed & Breakfast

A splendid 17th-century home run by Annamaria, warm, vivacious and multi-lingual, and Jacques, French and charming. This is a family affair and long-term friendships may be formed. It's a rather grand name for a house that is one of a terrace, but once inside you realise why we have included it. Annamaria's interiors are not luxurious but they are immaculate, with oak beams, ancient brick floors, family antiques and floral fabrics; not a speck of dust! Guests have their own sitting room with a frescoed ceiling, the bedrooms are delightful and original frescoes were discovered in the *sala da pranzo* during the restoration. Another exceptional thing about San Petro is its large garden and terrace. There is also a pretty ground-floor loggia for meals: Annamaria's dinners are regional and, we are told, delicious. Clearly they pour their hearts into the operation and their enthusiasm is contagious. You are in a peaceful street near the town centre, off the beaten path yet perfectly sited for forays into Garda, Brescia, Verona and Venice. Rustically special.
Ask about Italian & French language courses.

Price	€85-€110. Minimum stay 2 nights.
Rooms	5 doubles.
Meals	Dinner with wine, 4 courses, €30. Restaurants 50m.
Closed	Rarely.
Directions	From Milan motorway A4 exit Brescia east towards Montichiari, city centre & Duomo. Via S. Pietro leads off corner of central piazza.

Jacques & Annamaria Ducroz
Via San Pietro 25,
25018 Montichiari

Tel +39 0309 61232
Email villasanpietro@hotmail.com
Web www.abedandbreakfastinitaly.com

Tenuta Le Sorgive - Le Volpi Agriturismo

One cannot deny the beauty of Lake Garda, but it's a relief to escape to the unpopulated land of Lombardy. This 19th-century *cascina* has been in the Serenelli family for two generations; siblings Vittorio and Anna are justly proud of their 28-hectare working family farm. Everything is organic, solar panels provide electricity and a wood-chip burner the heating. Le Sorgive, crowned with a pierced dovecote, houses the rooms, flanked by carriage house and stables. Big guest rooms, with wooden rafters, are a mix of old and new. Some have attractive, metalwork beds, some a balcony, two have a mezzanine with beds for the children, all are crisp and clean. This is a great place for families to visit as there's so much to do: horse riding and mountain biking from the farm, go-karting and archery nearby, watersports, including scuba diving courses, at Garda. There is also a large gym and a well-maintained pool. Anna runs Le Volpi, the *cascina* only a stroll away where you can sample gnocchi, Mantovan sausages and mouthwatering fruit tarts – great value. *Min. stay three nights in high season; one week in apt.*

Price	€85-€105. Apartments €550-€900 per week.
Rooms	8 + 2: 8 doubles/triples/quadruples. 2 apartments for 4.
Meals	Breakfast €5 for self-caterers. Dinner with wine, €15-€28. Closed January & Mon/Tues evening. Restaurant nearby.
Closed	Never.
Directions	Exit A4 Milano-Venezia at Desenzano for Castiglione delle Stiviere; left at lights; left after 20m to Solferino. At x-roads, left. Signed.

Ethical Collection: Environment. See page 419 for details.

Vittorio Serenelli
Via Piridello 6,
46040 Solferino

Tel	+39 0376 854252
Email	info@lesorgive.it
Web	www.lesorgive.it

Bio-hotel Hermitage

It's not often that a bio-hotel comes with such a splash of luxury. Built a century ago, the old Hermitage has been entirely refashioned – with a modern 'eco' eye and a flourish of decorative turret. A wooden floor spans the reception area; behind is a vast and comfortable living room. A Tyrolean-tiled wood-burner dominates the centre; windows open onto a balcony with the best views in the Alps. You eat at red-clothed tables on Trentino dishes and homemade pasta in the *stübe*, with its lovely panelled ceiling of old, recycled wood. The main restaurant is larger but as beautiful. Bedrooms are serene, some are under the eaves, most have a balcony and the suites are huge. Wooden floors are softened by Persian rugs or pale carpets from Argentina, curtains and bedspreads are prettily checked. There's a superb wellness centre and an indoor pool with a ceiling that sparkles. Bars and chic boutiques are a ten-minute walk, and the hotel has its own bus that shuttles you to the slopes. Santa tips up at Christmas distributing presents for the children from a little cabin at the end of the garden.

Price	Half-board €140-€340 p.p.
Rooms	25: 18 twins/doubles, 7 suites for 3-4.
Meals	Half-board only. Wine from €15.
Closed	October-November.
Directions	Exit A22 St Mich & Mezz for Madonna di Campiglio for 75km; at Madonna di Campiglio, bypass through mountain; next exit. Signed on left.

Barbara Maffei
Via Castelletto Inferiore 63,
38084 Madonna di Campiglio

Tel +39 0465 441558
Email info@biohotelhermitage.it
Web www.biohotelhermitage.it

Schwarz Adler Turm Hotel

All around are the soaring, craggy Dolomites – and if you feel overawed, you'll be soothed on arrival. Manfred and Sonja – calm, elegant, intelligent – will be delighted to see you, and eager to do all they can to please. Though the building is young, it is a faithful reproduction of a 16th-century manor and blends in beautifully with the pretty village of Cortaccia (known as 'Kurtasch' by the locals). Light roomy bedrooms, alpine-cosy with lots of pine and warmly carpeted, have blissful views to vineyards, orchards and mountains; each has a loggia, a balcony or access to the garden. This was Austria (the area turned Italian in 1919) and the hotel's cuisine, served in the family restaurant opposite – a fascinating example of German Renaissance architecture – reflects this; it's a tour de force of Italian and South Tyrolen dishes, and comes with a well-stocked bar: the perfect place to gather after a day's hiking. Take a trip to Bolzano or Merano, go on a wine tour, rent bikes, play golf – there are three courses nearby. Return to sauna, steam room and lovely pool.

Price	€150-€195. Half-board €80-€115 p.p.
Rooms	24 doubles.
Meals	Lunch/dinner €42. Restaurant in village.
Closed	2 weeks in February; 22-27 December.
Directions	From A22 exit Egna/Ora. On for 8km dir. Termeno; left for Cortaccia; immed. after church on left.

Famiglia Pomella
Kirchgasse 2,
39040 Kurtatsch/Cortaccia

Tel +39 0471 880600
Email info@turmhotel.it
Web www.turmhotel.it

Hotel Cavallino d'Oro

In a postcard-pretty Tyrolean village, the 'Little Gold Horse' has been welcoming travellers for 600 years. The market runs every Friday in summer, the local farmers set up their stalls at the foot of the 18th-century bell tower. This was Austria not so very long ago: the local customs are still alive, and regular concerts take place at the inn over dinner. Inside, all is as charming and pretty as can be, and bedrooms mostly delightful (note a few rooms have roof windows only). Some look onto the medieval square, the best have balconies with incredible views. There's a fascinating mix of antique country beds – some hand-decorated, some four-poster, some both. Room 9 has the original ceiling. Dine in the sparkling dining room, breakfast in the rustic *stübe*, a wood-panelled room with checked tablecloths and geraniums at the window. Susanna and Stefan are as friendly as they are efficient and the service throughout is wonderful. Take the free shuttle to the cable car up to the stunning Alpe di Siusi; swim, hike or bike in summer, sleigh ride and ski in winter, steam in the spa all year round. *Secure free parking. Free laundry.*

Price	€90-€140. Singles €55. Half-board €62-€85 p.p.
Rooms	20: 7 doubles, 2 twins, 4 singles, 3 suites, 4 triples.
Meals	Lunch €18. Dinner €25. Wine from €14.
Closed	November.
Directions	A22 motorway, exit Bolzano Nord. Castelrotto signed at exit. Hotel in market square in town centre.

Susanna & Stefan Urthaler
Piazza Kraus 1,
39040 Castelrotto

Tel	+39 0471 706337
Email	cavallino@cavallino.it
Web	www.cavallino.it

Hotel Grones

Drama from the mountains, deep peace from the lush plateaux – you have the best of everything here. Valley views climb to craggy peaks from every bedroom window and stars and silence wrap you up at night. The Grones family converted their B&B into an immaculate hotel in 2008 and the combination of Austrian efficiency and Italian bubbliness is unbeatable: personalised menus pop up at dinner, your waitress can guide you through the wine list, and if you think five courses a night will beat you – it won't: every plate is light, fresh and totally irresistible. Take a digestif at the bar with other guests and you'll be swapping tips on where to find the most powdery snow or magnificent view. Bedrooms are capacious, light and quiet; new bathrooms gleam. Walk downhill for five minutes and you're in the centre of Ortisei, a sweet town famous for its wood carving, with shops for souvenirs and ski gear, and bars and cafés for excellent local wines and cream cakes. Above: a magical landscape, superb for skiing, cycling and hiking. Our inspector heard one English voice on a whole week's trip – and was enchanted.

Price	Half-board €88-€178 p.p.
Rooms	25 doubles.
Meals	Wine from €15.
Closed	May & November.
Directions	A22 exit Chiusa/Val Gardena. Follow signs to Ortisei.

Nadia Grones-Feichter
Via Stufan 110, Val Gardena,
39046 Ortisei

Tel	+39 0471 797040
Email	hotel@grones.info
Web	www.hotelgrones.com

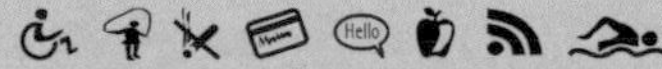

14 Suiten Hotel Villa Berghofer

At the end of the meandering track: birdsong and fir trees, cowbells and meadows, the scent of larch and pine. The tranquillity continues: there are shelves of books and magazines beside the fire, pale modern furniture, an abundance of flowers, a cuckoo clock to tick away the hours. Bedrooms, named after the peaks you can see from large windows, have glazed doors to private balconies, and breathtaking Dolomites views. Rugs are scattered, pale pine floors and light walls are offset with painted wardrobes and stencilled borders. Some rooms have an extra store room, a few can be linked – ideal for a family; all have a separate sitting area and a spacious bathroom. Dine in the charming 1450 pine-cossetted *stübe*; the wood was purchased from a local farmer and painstakingly moved, up the hill. The restaurant is warmed by a wonderful 18th-century stove; the food is regional and stylish. Hike among the alpine flowers in summer, return to a massage or hay-sauna, catch the sunset over the mountain. The small ski resort Passo Oclini/Jochgrimm has seven kilometres of piste and is recommended for families.

Ethical Collection: Food.
See page 419 for details.

Price	Half-board €270-€360 for 2.
Rooms	14: 13 suites for 2, 1 chalet for 3.
Meals	Half-board only. Wine from €20. Restaurant 500m.
Closed	5 November-26 December; 9 January-25 April.
Directions	A22 exit Neumarkt/Auer; SS48 to Kaltenbrunn; 200m after garage, left for Radein; on to Oberradein; signed.

Renate Ortner-Huber
Oberradein 54, South Tyrol,
39040 Radein

Tel +39 0471 887150
Email info@berghofer.it
Web www.berghofer.it

Veneto and Friuli-Venezia Giulia

All'Eremo Relais Agriturismo

Far from the madding crowds, you are ensconced in a solid 1970s farmhouse overlooking Lake Garda – what a setting! Adorable Elena, ex-lawyer from Verona, loves her guests, loves the country life and bakes a different cake for breakfast each day. The open-plan downstairs is the heart of the house, all chunky beams, wall paintings and agrarian artefacts on white walls, while outside is a small summer kitchen in the garden with a barbecue – a great extra addition for guests. Now that Elena's parents have moved to Verona you have three bedrooms to choose from, two with magnificent views, all with very comfortable beds and charmingly decorated in palest pinks and creams by Elena. Terraces have been furnished with loungers on every level: settle back and absorb the tranquillity and the views with a glass of Bardolino rosé. Elena is full of recommendations of where to go and what to do, and which restaurants to try – slip off to the lake, dine on fabulous fish, sample the opera in Verona, come and go as you please. Brilliant value – you'll love this place.

Price	€80-€110.
Rooms	3: 2 doubles, 1 family room for 2-4.
Meals	Guest kitchen & barbecue. Restaurants 1km.
Closed	Never.
Directions	A22 exit Affi; to Garda for 3.5km. In Albare, left at lights towards Bardolino; after 3km, 'Corteline'; 500m on right, take minor road Sem e Pigno until end; follow dirt track on left to house. Unsigned.

Elena Corsini Piffer
Strada della Rocca 2, Loc. Casetta Rossa, 37011 Bardolino

Tel	+39 0457 211391
Mobile	+39 329 0516400
Email	info@eremorelais.com
Web	www.eremorelais.com

Relais Ca' delle Giare

Enrico and Giuditta are a cultured and elegant couple who have made their B&B rooms, in the rose-clad coaching house and converted barn, as homely as their own. They welcome you with an old-fashioned, easy charm and their friendly pets like to pad around and say hello too. An old stone archway leads to the guest quarters. All have chunky ceiling beams, antique Sicilian furniture, shiny tiled floors and colourful rugs. The two upstairs rooms look over rolling wine groves; the garden room, with its own entrance and kitchenette, has French windows leading to a courtyard, and a sofa to snuggle on in front of an open fire. Bathrooms are luxurious: bright spotlighting, showers over baths, sumptuous thick towels. Enormous Sicilian urns ('giare') dot the pretty, sloping garden bordered by woods and hydrangeas. Tuck into breakfast on the well-kept lawn, then find a peaceful spot on a sunlounger with a view of Verona. Veronese Giuditta is a font of knowledge on concerts and exhibitions, and if you fancy a Valpolicella wine tour, you're in the right place: Enrico will happily take you.

Price	€120-€130.
Rooms	3: 2 doubles, 1 suite (with kitchenette).
Meals	Restaurants 3km.
Closed	Rarely.
Directions	A4/A22 exit Verona Nord; signs to Tangenziali. At end, left dir. Borgo Trento. At lights left dir. Quinzano; over r'bout, thro' Quinzano, up hill & hairpin bends. At top after 5km sign for Negrar, left; house immed. right.

Enrico & Giuditta Corpaci
Via Campi di Sopra 1,
37024 Negrar - Verona

Tel +39 0456 015059
Email info@cadellegiare.it
Web www.cadellegiare.it

Ca' del Rocolo

Such an undemanding, delightful place to be and such an enthusiastic young family to be with. Maurizio ran a restaurant in Verona, Ilaria was a journalist and has three cookbooks to her name; they gave it all up for a country life for their children. Their 1800s farmhouse is on the side of a hill overlooking forested hills and the vast Lessinia National Park. Over a decade has passed since their move; Maurizio did much of the renovation himself and the result is authentic and attractive. Simple cotton rugs cover stripped bedroom floors, rough plaster walls are whitewashed, rooms are big and airy, with solid country furniture and excellent beds and bathrooms. There's also a shared kitchen. Breakfasts are at the long farmhouse table or out on the terrace, making the most of the views: delicious food, seasonal cakes, home-grown fruits, happy conversation. Dinner, mostly vegetarian, is an occasional affair. This is a seven-hectare, all-organic farm, with olives and fruit trees, hens, horses and beehives; there are nature trails galore, and always something going on. *Ask about apiary visits & pony rides.*

Ethical Collection: Environment; Food.
See page 419 for details.

Price	€63-€75 (€410-€450 per week). Suite €90-€120 (€600-€800 per week).
Rooms	3: 2 doubles, 1 suite with kitchenette.
Meals	Light meals €16. Wine €6-€8. Restaurant 4km.
Closed	Rarely.
Directions	Sent on booking.

Ilaria & Maurizio Corazza
Via Gaspari 3, Loc. Quinto,
37142 Verona

Tel +39 0458 700879
Email info@cadelrocolo.com
Web www.cadelrocolo.com

Relais Villa Sagramoso Sacchetti

Nothing quite prepares you for the splendour of this 16th-century Venetian villa, gazing over the Valpolicella valley to the mountains of Lessinia; from bedrooms to gardens and pool it exudes atmosphere and style. The 40-year-long restoration by the Sagramoso Sacchetti family has been a labour of love and is a source of pride; sisters Chiarastella and Ludovica take huge pleasure in sharing its bounty. Enter the lofty hallway, marvel at the frescoed drawing room, climb the stone stair to luxurious suites. Who would not love the elegant wallpapers and the perfect counterpanes, the chunky chestnut beams and the sweeping terracotta, the huge flowers and the family antiques? Bathrooms are bliss. The day starts at the big oval table overseen by the ancestors; fruits are from the orchard, butter from the farmer up the road, special diets are no problem. Outside the gate is the bus to Verona, the cycle path too (five miles); there's a stunning new cable car to Monte Baldo, wine lovers can follow the Strada del Vino Valpolicella, foodies can swoon over the Veneto risottos. *Children over nine welcome.*

Price	€140-€160.
Rooms	4: 1 double, 1 twin/double, 2 suites for 2-3.
Meals	Restaurants 500m.
Closed	10 November-31 March.
Directions	A22 Brennero-Modena exit Verona Nord; 6km to Corno / A4 Torino-Venezia exit Sommacampagna; 12km to Corno.

Chiarastella & Ludovica Sagramoso Sacchetti
Via Giovanni Battista Dalla Riva 5/1, Loc. Corno, 37139 Verona

Mobile +39 345 3010330 or +39 333 7236582
Email info@villasagramososacchetti.it
Web www.villasagramososacchetti.it

B&B Domus Nova

Stroll down the Via Mazzini, nod at Gucci and Bulgari. People-watch on the Piazza delle Erbe, where the crowds throng until 2am. Soak up grand opera beneath a starry summer sky at the Roman amphitheatre. And return to the warmth and classicism of the Domus Nova, in the car-free heart of Verona; it is wonderfully quiet. This is a grand family house that has been restored to its former splendour. Giovanni grew up here, three relatives are architects and his wife's sister is an interior designer – no wonder it's perfect. The look is luxy hotel, the feel is B&B and the views are fabulous: onto the large and lovely Piazza dei Signori and its historic tower. Bedrooms, on the third and top floors, are spacious yet cosy, immaculate yet friendly... natural pigments on walls, rich fabrics, painted beams, fine antiques, and one with a balcony so you can be Juliet for a day. The salon is equally inviting, with its comfortable leather armchairs and elegant breakfast tables, classical music and antique books. You'll imagine yourself in another century staying here. *Minimum two nights. Parking available.*

Price	€200-€230. Suite €250-€280. Extra bed €60.
Rooms	4: 1 double, 2 twins/doubles, 1 suite (with kitchenette).
Meals	Restaurants nearby.
Closed	Epiphany-February.
Directions	In "centro storico", next to Piazza delle Erbe.

Anna & Giovanni Roberti
Piazza dei Signori 18,
37121 Verona

Mobile +39 380 7071931
Email info@domusnovaverona.com
Web www.domusnovaverona.com

Agriturismo Musella Relais & Winery

There's a canoe at your disposal, to ply the small river that runs through. And bikes for the roads, towels for the plunge pool and pastries for breakfast each day. Such is the generosity of the Pasqua di Bisceglie family, two of whom live within the walls of Musella; the rest live on the estate. Sweep through electric gates, park under the pergola and there's Paulo to greet you, with impeccable English and an irresistible smile. This 16th-century estate, built around a vast courtyard of grass, is a modern winery and superb B&B; and there are four apartments should you wish to do your own thing. Expect chunky rafters and country antiques, wrought-iron beds and crisp cotton sheets, harmonious colours and art on the walls. Some rooms are on the upper floors, others have their own outdoor space; others have open fires. Bathrooms are fabulous, and spacious. You may replenish your fridges from the small shop a walk away, make friends in the guest sitting room (books, open fire), savour the olive oils and the valpolicella, fish on the river – bring your rod. Special place, special people. *Wine tasting €15.*

Price	€145-€165. Single €100. Triple €175. Apts €225-€295. Minimum 2 nights.
Rooms	11 + 4: 9 doubles, 1 single, 1 triple. 4 apts for 2-4.
Meals	Breakfast for self-caterers included. Restaurant nearby.
Closed	15 December-1 February.
Directions	A4 exit Verona Est dir. Valpent; exit Via Mattarana (Borgo Venezia, white sign). Left at exit, straight on for 2km; in Ferrazze right at end; Musella courtyard on left after 250m.

Famiglia Pasqua di Bisceglie
Via Ferrazzette 2, San Martino
Buon Albergo, 37036 Verona

Tel	+39 0459 73385
Mobile	+39 335 7294627
Email	paulo@musella.it
Web	www.musella.it

La Rosa e Il Leone

Everything about La Rosa e Il Leone, from the ancient Roman columns in the flower-filled garden to the Juliet-style balcony of the marble-floored master bedroom, breathes feeling and romance. Named after Valeria's Veronese father and Milanese mother – the Rose of Lombardy, the Lion of the Veneto – the villa is an ode to their love both for each other and for the arts. The walls sing with framed musical scores and programmes from nights at La Scala (Milan) and L'Arena (Verona), while adjoining first-floor sitting rooms celebrate the juxtaposition of the masculine (hard lines, dark colours, stacks of leather-bound books) and the feminine (curves, pastel colours, a passion for music and dance). The soft hand-woven sheets on antique-framed beds were part of Valeria's mother's dowry, the furniture part of her parents' lifetime collection. Stroll under leafy pergolas; listen to the history humming in the ancient cypresses; breakfast, deliciously, outside and admire an extraordinary replica of the Louvre's Winged Victory. Like her house, Valeria is a gold-mine of high culture. A must for anyone visiting Verona.

Price	B&B €135. Whole house €1,890 per week.
Rooms	3: 1 double; 2 doubles sharing bath.
Meals	Restaurants nearby.
Closed	Mid-October to mid-April.
Directions	From Verona for Vicenza to Caldiero; left for Illasi. Right after 2km, then right again, then left at end.

Valeria Poli
Via Trieste 56, Colognola ai Colli,
37030 Verona

Tel	+39 0457 650123
Mobile	+39 342 1084622
Email	vvpoli@libero.it
Web	www.larosaeilleone.it

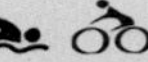

Delser Manor House Hotel

The views from your chic hilltop hotel are amazing, sailing over vineyards to the city of Verona. This ancient flat-topped Sicilian-like building, rescued from disrepair by designer-owner Alberto, is now (eight years on) a minimalist, museum-like hotel. Vaulted brick ceilings, Roman columns and stone arches have been reclaimed and revived in one man's homage to stone – daringly unusual for Italy! Alberto's church-like lobby and breakfast area are an archaeologist's dream. As for the bedrooms, they're a unique blend of modern luxury, natural materials and a handsome scattering of 16th-century furniture. Be spoiled by pure linen sheets and un-rugged oak floors, subtle behind-brick lighting and rainforest showers. Bio wines and olive oil are produced on the estate; breakfasts are feasts served on designer white china: tuck into local cheeses, hams, jams, fruits, cakes and breads. And then there's Verona, just ten minutes below, with all the romance of cobbled alleyways, Juliet's balcony and opera beneath starry skies in a Roman arena, illuminated by hand-held candles. Sensational.

Price	€110-€220.
Rooms	9: 3 doubles, 6 twins/doubles.
Meals	Dinner on request. Restaurants in Verona, 3-minute drive.
Closed	Rarely.
Directions	Sent on booking.

Alberto Delser
Via Strada dei Monti 14/B,
37129 Verona

Tel +39 0458 011098
Mobile +39 339 8153601
Email info@hoteldelser.it
Web www.manorhousehoteldelser.it

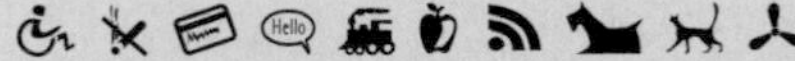

Tenuta Agrituristica Otto Ducati d'Oro

Across the road is autumn's Fiera del Riso – the biggest rice event in Italy. You're in the heart of risotto land and they grow it right here, along with maize for polenta and poplar trees for paper. The friendly, hard-working Artegiani sisters run the agriturismo while the farm is the domain of the signori; this B&B venture, substantial in size, runs on immaculate wheels. New stone floors, new beams and pastel shades have been introduced in harmonious style to outbuildings that were previously on the point of collapsing. A beaded chandelier here, a crucifix there: every room is different. Expect air conditioning and double glazing and all the latest wizardry including electronic cards not keys; a couple of bathrooms have the added excitement of colour light therapy and dual showers. The breakfast room is open all day for hot drinks, there's a TV-free sitting room and heaps of space for all, thanks to a huge courtyard/farmyard. With trains close by to whisk you into Verona and beyond this is an excellent base in a foodie area; you can birdwatch in the Tartaro valley and swim in Lake Garda. Fab for families.

Price	€90-€95. Suites €110-€150.
Rooms	10: 5 twins/doubles (2 doubles interconnect), 4 suites, 1 family room for 4.
Meals	Restaurants on doorstep.
Closed	Rarely.
Directions	Sent on booking.

Veronica Artegiani
Via Bastia 6, Isola della Scala,
37063 Verona

Mobile	+39 349 7002200
Email	info@ottoducatidoro.it
Web	www.ottoducatidoro.com

Agriturismo Tenuta La Pila

Raimonda and Alberto will soon have you chatting over a welcome drink; he speaks a clutch of languages, she's bubbly, both are committed to the green way of life. Each B&B room is named after a fruit and smartly decorated: find cream walls, exposed brick, crisp linen, fluffy towels, and antique furniture to add a homely touch. Two of the apartments are in a separate building once used for drying tobacco; they have immensely high beams and are decorated in a similar style. You get a table, chairs and sofabed in the large central living area, and a neat corner kitchen; cheerful bedrooms have flower prints and checked bedspreads; two further apartments have oak floors and country antiques. Breakfast is a spread of home produce: kiwi jam, eggs, fruit, bread, yogurt. The farm is surrounded by fertile fields, trees and kiwi vines meandering across the plains, with the beautiful towns of Rovigo and Chioggia close by. Return to a peaceful patio-garden, a dip in the pool, and skittles and boules beside the huge magnolia. A happy place. *Minimum stay two nights.*

Price	€65-€80. Singles €45-€55. Apts €678-€905 per week.
Rooms	5 + 4: 2 twins/doubles, 3 triples. 4 apts: 2 for 2-4, 2 for 4-5.
Meals	Breakfast €5 for self-caterers. Dinner €20. Wine €5-€10. Restaurants 2km.
Closed	Rarely.
Directions	From SS 434 Verona-Rovigo exit Carpi. Left at stop; after 500m left onto Strada dell'Argine Vecchio della Valle & onto Via Gorgo da Bagno. After 1km along asphalt road, left into farm.

Raimonda & Alberto Sartori
Via Pila 42, Loc. Spinimbecco,
37049 Villa Bartolomea

Tel	+39 0442 659289
Email	post@tenutalapila.it
Web	www.tenutalapila.it

Il Castello

A narrow road winds up to the *castello* at the foot of the Berici hills – a special getaway. Also known as the Villa Godi-Marinoni – it was built by Count Godi in the 15th century – its massive hewn walls enclose a compound of terraced vines, orchard, Italian garden and views that stretch all the way to Padua. You enter via an arched entrance, ancient cobbles beneath your feet. The villa itself is still lived in by the courteous owners, Signora Marinoni and her son, who run this vast estate together. Olive oil is produced, and there's a wine cellar in the bowels of the castle – ask if you can buy a bottle. The apartments (note, one with its kitchen on the far side of the courtyard), are in an outbuilding with gothic details in the plastered façade; all are simply, pleasantly furnished with family antiques and modern pieces. Hidden below the castle walls is the garden with fish pond; in spring, hundreds of lemon trees are wheeled out to stand on grand pedestals. The climate is mild and the hillside a mass of olive groves; recline on the lawns, stroll down to the village for supper.

Price	€58 for 2. Minimum 3 nights.
Rooms	4 apartments for 2-4.
Meals	Restaurant 500m.
Closed	Never.
Directions	A4 exit Vicenza Est; at r'bout follow signs to Riviera Berica for 15km. In Ponte di Barbarano, at lights right towards Barbarano. In main square, left to Villaga; villa 500m on left.

Elda Marinoni
Via Castello 6,
36021 Barbarano Vicentino

Tel	+39 0444 886055
Email	info@castellomarinoni.com
Web	www.castellomarinoni.com

Due Mori

On a pretty street plumb in the heart of medieval Marostica lies an 18th-century townhouse. Step through the glass doors and it's bright and inviting: modern design abounds, wood and stone blend with glass and steel. Choose from 12 blissfully quiet, sleek bedrooms, four on each floor and all en suite: think white walls, dark linseed-oiled floors, cherry-wood headboards, perhaps a sofa. Bathrooms have soft lighting and sleek taps. The 'Castle' rooms with beams and tile ceilings are the most luxurious – and you can glimpse the upper castle through the skylight. 'King' bedrooms are brilliant for families, 'Queen' are for those on a budget. Out on the small patio, feast on a breakfast of Asiago cheese, fruit and pastries. The lovely young family who run Due Mori live nearby; Monica is a tourist guide and knows her stuff. Explore the two castles, tranquil squares and untouristy shops – you might even witness the giant chess game enacted with human chess pieces! And taste Marostica's legendary cherries before you leave. *Ask about cookery and pottery courses.*

Price	€94-€179. Singles €64-€84.
Rooms	12: 11 twins/doubles, 1 single.
Meals	Restaurant 50m.
Closed	Rarely.
Directions	2nd right to Marostica centre (hotel signed), right again into Corso Mazzini - 200m, yellow building on right.

Monica Facchini
Corso Mazzini 73,
36063 Marostica

Tel +39 0424 471777
Email info@duemori.it
Web www.duemori.it

Ca' Marcello

Mythical statues, manicured lawns, potted lemon trees, Italian fountain: the grounds are rich in wonderful plants and the woods consist of century-old trees. Such is the setting for this Palladian-style villa with its warm, elegant, slightly faded cream facade, and your wing comes with its own private garden. Venice owes her history of great naval battles in part to the long line of captains in the Marcello family: this represents their legacy. So take a private tour of the main house and its fresco-filled ballroom; peer in awe at the ancestral portraits on the walls. Despite its history and significance Ca'Marcello is still a family home, and the atmosphere is relaxed and inviting: kind, softly spoken Jacopo grew up here and will ensure a luxurious stay. Expect beeswax-polished stairs and lovely low-ceiling'd rooms spread over two floors, in perfect condition yet virtually untouched since the 18th-century; a well-equipped kitchen (though a chef can be arranged if that's what you'd prefer; a stylish salon and your own exquisite pool. Guiding art tours are on request. *Chef, chauffeur & babysitter available, by arrangement.*

Price	€2,660-€4,000 per week. Min. one week in high season.
Rooms	Apartment for 8.
Meals	Breakfast €10. Dinner €30-€40. Wine from €10. Children's menu €15. Restaurants 2km.
Closed	Never.
Directions	From Venice-Treviso airport, left until Quinto; right & follow signs to Badoere. Signed from Badoere.

Jacopo Marcello
Via del Marcello 13,
35017 Levada di Piombino Dese

Tel +39 0499 350340
Email info@camarcello.it
Web www.camarcello.it

Agriturismo La Presa

The agriturismo is Lucia's baby, she looks after both 400-acre farm, growing crops and cattle, and guests wonderfully, having done B&B for five years now. So bowl along the flatlands of the Po delta, pass the chicken factory, sweep up the poplar-lined drive – Lucia has planted hundreds – into a peaceful, jasmine-scented farmstead, resuscitated after carpet insect-bombing and now humming with frogs, bees and birds. Bats and swallows are back, too, and Lucia's nature trail is brilliant. Brick paths link the main house (two bedrooms) to the rest in a converted farm building. Inside, all feels clean, simple, spacious and cool. Shower rooms are new, floors are warm with rugs, walls are light green and the 'single' beds in the annexe are more like small doubles. The beamed dining room is most inviting, meat roasts (and pizzas) are done in Lucia's new wood-fired pizza oven. Breakfasts promise homemade tarts and the chestnut table seats 16. Friend Alberto knows the delta deeply – let him take you up the river for oysters. Or bicycle out into the flat reclaimed countryside. *Minimum stay two nights.*

Price	€85. €145 for 4.
Rooms	8: 1 double, 1 suite for 2 + cot; 2 doubles sharing bath. Annexe: 4 mezzanine suites for 4-6.
Meals	Dinner with wine, €30. Restaurant 6km.
Closed	6-31 January.
Directions	From Taglio di Po follow right bank of river Po for 5km until poplar lined driveway.

Lucia La Presa
Via Cornera 12, Taglio di Po,
45019 Rovigo

Tel	+39 0426 661594
Mobile	+39 338 8683431
Email	info@lapresa.it
Web	www.lapresa.it

Villa Colloredo

Handsomely ranged around a courtyard, these 18th-century Venetian buildings – all peachy stone and olive shutters – hold a cool surprise. Bold paintings, modern sculptures and colourful collages dot their interiors: part of the collection of the Meneghelli family. Architecturally, these former stables and grain stores, next to the family villa, fuse modern styling with original features. Beamed ceilings and wooden or tiled floors contrast with streamlined kitchens, simple rustic furniture and artwork on white walls. Spaces have been imaginatively used – a shower, perhaps, in a glass-topped cube – to maximise the open feel. Upper floors have lovely low windows, with views to fields, orchards or courtyard. Two of the larger apartments can be joined together – great for families. The outdoor cloisters are a tranquil place to sit and read, or set out lunch; behind the villa are wonderful natural gardens to explore. Drop in on Padua, look forward to the restaurants of Dolo, cool off in the Dolomites, or catch the water bus (from Fusina) to Venice. Family-run with a welcoming feel – plus two friendly dogs and a cat.

Price	€60-€80. Apartments €80-€110. Minimum 2 nights.
Rooms	1 + 4: 1 double. 4 apartments for 4.
Meals	Restaurant 500m.
Closed	7 January-4 February; 17 February-26 March; 3 November-20 December.
Directions	From A4, exit Dolo dir. Sambruson; right opp. church.

Sara Frison
Brusaura 24,
30030 Sambruson di Dolo

Mobile +39 348 2102337
Email info@villacolloredo.com
Web www.villacolloredo.com

Villa Tron Carrara Mioni

You're in a wonderfully central spot – perfect for exploring the delightful towns of the Veneto. Gabriella and Sandro are a considerate, charming couple who love to share their home with guests. Standing on the site of a palace destroyed by Napoleonic troops, it's typical of the grand villas built by Venetian patrician families in the early 19th century. They travelled by water; now a busy road sweeps between the house and the river. But the house is set well back and is surrounded by five hectares of elegant gardens and woodland, including an ice house and a lake. Inside, the rooms are big and beautifully proportioned, filled with fresh flowers, antiques and gracious sofas. Old family photos record generations of the Carrara and Mioni families (ask for the full story!). The super airy double room on the first floor has its own small terrace and two views onto the garden; there's a faint hum of traffic but nothing serious. On the second floor is the family suite. Gabriella serves you a lovely breakfast of homemade cakes, jams and fruit, out under the trees in summer, elegantly presented.

Price	€120-€170. Apts €770-€1,260 per week. Minimum 2 nights B&B, 4 nights self-catering.
Rooms	2 + 3: 1 double, 1 suite for 3 (1 twin, 1 single). 3 apts: 2 for 2-4, 1 for 4-6.
Meals	Restaurants 200m.
Closed	Rarely.
Directions	A4 exit Dolo-Mirano. Left at lights in front of church dir. Venice; on for 1km, house on left after bend in road, 4th gate.

Alessandro & Gabriella Mioni
Via Ca' Tron 23,
30031 Dolo

Tel	+39 0414 10177
Email	villatron@libero.it
Web	www.villatron.it

Hotel Villa Alberti

Pluck fruit from the orchard, wash it in the fountain, pick a quiet spot in the walled garden. This 17th-century villa, once the summer residence of Venetian nobility, has been restored by the delightful Malerbas to combine grand features with a warm and unstuffy mood. Beautiful shutters and floors, Murano lights and chandeliers, decorative ironwork lamps and balconies… all has been reclaimed and revived. And it is no wonder Gianni is proud of his garden, its box-lined paths, statues and century-old trees, its exceptional roses, its carpets of wild flowers; it develops as it matures. The reception hall – a sweep of dark polished wood, rich rugs and deep sofas – leads to three floors of bedrooms furnished in a simple but refined style: wooden or stone floors, silky bedspreads, a few antiques; ask for one overlooking the garden rather than the road. The rooms in the *barchessa* are more rustic and somewhat blander. Feast on delicious risottos on the terrace in the summer; you could get used to the aristocratic life! A direct bus runs to Venice from Dolo; here you are peacefully out of town.

Price	€90-€130.
Rooms	20 doubles.
Meals	Dinner €25. Wine €15. Restaurant 300m.
Closed	Rarely.
Directions	A4 exit Dolo-Mirano. At lights in Dolo, left, direction Venice. 2km along river, over bridge & cont. in same direction along opp. bank for 1.5km. Hotel on right.

Famiglia Malerba
Via E. Tito 90,
30031 Dolo

Tel	+39 0414 266512
Email	info@villalberti.it
Web	www.villalberti.it

Hotel Villa Gasparini

Follow the scenic route from Padua to Venice along the Riviera del Brenta waterway, to drive past pretty towns and palatial villas that evoke the Italy of old. On the edge of sleepy Dolo, you arrive at a tall, green-shuttered 18th-century house restored by the current owners, descendants of the family who built it. Big beamed bedrooms – those at the front double-glazed against the road – come with family heirlooms, long curtains, and antique beds with fine silk covers; mod cons include well-disguised mini-bars and jacuzzi baths in some rooms. Take your morning coffee and pastries out to the leafy garden patio, or linger in a chandeliered dining room of high beamed ceilings, ornate mirrors and plush crimson velvet. Burchielli river boats once carried noblemen from Padua to Venice along this route; tourist cruises stop at the most impressive villas on the way. Hire a bike to explore the Riviera del Brenta's lively towns – Stra, Fiesso d'Artico, Mira, Oriago, Malcontenta – with their weekly markets, boutiques and historic architecture. Or hop on one of the frequent buses to Venice, 15 kilometres away.

Price	€65-€165. Family rooms €100-€195.
Rooms	15: 13 doubles, 2 family rooms for 3-4.
Meals	Breakfast included. Restaurants within walking distance.
Closed	Rarely.
Directions	Sent on booking.

Michela Pegorer
Riviera Martiri della Libertà 37,
30031 Venice

Tel	+39 0415 608156
Email	info@villagasparini.it
Web	www.villagasparini.it

Dune Agriturismo Relais

Why stay in Venice, when half an hour away (by boat or train) lies this estate, deeply rural and a sandal stroll to a private beach space at Eraclea Mare? The family farm (mostly beef) is going strong but it's daughter Francesca who runs the show. And what a splendid show it is: an airy reception bright with art by cousin Lorenzo; a huge garden with barbecue and big swimming pool; an inexpensive restaurant whose young chef cooks with passion (ask about the half-board option); and a little shop selling home-grown produce you can cook yourself. The apartments are fabulously well-equipped: simple stylish bedrooms dressed in earthy tones, luxurious bathrooms, dreamy kitchens. You can tell the family care about the environment and love seasonal, organically grown food – some of the produce comes from the fields outside. Local staff give a great performance, smile spontaneously and do their utmost to make you feel part of the family, even when they're packed out in summer. A poster in reception sums it all up: "Good company, good wine, good welcome: good people." *Flexible out of season booking.*

Price	€90-€190. Apts €70-€160 for 2; €100-€200 for 4. Minimum 3 nights in apts.
Rooms	15 + 11: 5 doubles, 2 singles, 2 suites, 2 family rooms for 4, 4 triples. 11 apts: 3 for 2, 4 for 4, 4 for 4-6.
Meals	Breakfast €8 for self-caterers. Dinner €20-€30. Closed mid-October to mid-April. Restaurant 100m.
Closed	Rarely.
Directions	A4 Trieste-Venezia exit San Donà di Piave/Noventa. Follow directions for Eraclea Mare, then Dune Verde, until Via dei Fiori.

Francesca Pasti
Via S. Croce 6, Eraclea Mare,
30020 Venice

Tel	+39 0421 66171
Email	info@adriabella.com
Web	www.adriabella.com/dune

B&B Corte 1321

Go down a narrow alleyway, through a large and lovely courtyard, high walls towering above, and enter a 15th-century palazzo. The apartment is on the ground floor, the B&B on the first. Inside, catch your breath at the calm, eclectic décor of oriental rugs, silk curtains, fresh flowers and influences from Bali and Morocco. Amelia is a Californian artist and her paintings hang on every wall. She, her baby and her mother Deborah live nearby; it's her likeable assistants Maria and Suhbash, both with good English, who minister impeccably to your needs. Most guests are English speaking and bedrooms have been designed to meet American expectations: the best linen, mattresses and showers; hand-crafted beds; the internet. One room looks onto the canal, the other two onto the courtyard. In the apartment downstairs the style is uncluttered, the whitewashed walls making the most of the light. Breakfast is a pretty basket of brioche and bread in the courtyard. The little vaporetto is five minutes away – no bridges! – the local shop is across the square and the Rialto, markets and Accademia are nearby. *Minimum stay two nights.*

Price	€125-€180 for 2; €140-€190 for 3; €150-€220 for 4. Apt €125-€220.
Rooms	3 + 1: 3 family rooms: 1 for 2-3, 2 for 2-4. Apartment for 4.
Meals	Restaurants nearby.
Closed	Rarely.
Directions	From Piazzale Roma, water bus towards Lido; exit San Silvestro; walk towards Campo San' Aponal; 3rd left; 3rd right.

Amelia Bonvini
San Polo 1321,
30125 Venice

Tel +39 0415 224923
Email info@corte1321.com
Web www.corte1321.com

Oltre Il Giardino

A corner of paradise in off-beat San Polo – take a water taxi to the door! What a joy to find, behind the iron gates, a dreamy courtyard garden scented with jasmine and lavender... to breakfast under the pergola – April to October – is a serious treat. This enchanting cream stone villa once belonged to Alma Mahler, the composer's widow; now it is the home of Signora Zambelli Arduini and her son Lorenzo, and is run by the sweetest staff. Gaze from your bedroom window onto a magnolia, an olive and a pomegranate tree – wonderfully restorative after a day discovering Venice. Each room is elegant, spacious and filled with light, each has its own charm; three have sitting rooms and the ground-floor suite its own lovely piece of garden terrace. Colours range from vibrant turquoise to dark chocolate to pale ivory, there are family antiques and art on the walls and lovely mosaic'd bathrooms with Bulgari products. Deep green sofas in the lounge, the international papers on the table: all feels calm, inviting, intimate. The Rialto is a 15-minute walk; artisan shops and eateries wait outside the door.

Price	€150-€250. Suites €200-€500.
Rooms	6: 2 doubles, 4 suites.
Meals	Restaurant 200m.
Closed	Mid-January to mid-February
Directions	Vaporetto to San Tomà; cross Campo San Tomà. Exit left into Calle del Mandoler; right, then left to end. Right into Campo dei Frari; over bridge, left. Over 2nd bridge, right; hotel at end.

Lorenzo Muner
San Polo 2542,
30125 Venice

Tel	+39 0412 750015
Email	info@oltreilgiardino-venezia.com
Web	www.oltreilgiardino-venezia.com

Palazzo Tiepolo

Old-fashioned grandeur at its best, and the approach down the narrow alley gives nothing away. This 16th-century beauty has been in the Tiepolo family forever and friendly Lelia oversees the ongoing restoration. Tiepolo, the ground-floor studio, has been cleverly thought out. A beautifully equipped and stocked kitchen tucks behind cupboard doors, the shower room is in a corner and the gem of a dining area overlooks the life of the Grand Canal, and you fall asleep to the lapping waters: such a privileged position. Valier, the more spacious apartment across the garden, is beautifully peaceful; enjoy a glass of wine in your own courtyard and listen to the chirruping birds. Cream and pale terracotta walls bedecked with prints and gilt mirrors set off rich rugs and Venetian furniture in the living room, the walk-in shower and kitchen are in opposite corners and wide wooden stairs lead to the mezzanine's bed, encased in embroidered linen. For grand old style, go B&B and take the antique-filled suite in the house. Breakfast is formally served on bone china and the history of the Tiepolos surrounds you.

Price	Suite €1,750-€1,850. Apartments €850-€1,050. Prices per week. Min. 3 nights in apts.
Rooms	1 + 2: 1 suite. 2 apartments for 2.
Meals	Restaurants nearby.
Closed	Never.
Directions	Vaporetto 1 to San Tomà; straight on, right at end. Cross Campo San Tomà, right into Campiello San Tomà. Over canal into Calle dei Nombolithen, right Calle Centani; house at end on left. Bell marked M. Passi.

Lelia Passi
Calle Centani, San Polo 2774,
30125 Venice

Tel	+39 0415 227989
Email	leliapassi@gmail.com
Web	www.cortetiepolo.com

Casa San Boldo – Grimani, Loredan & Manin

Your own tennis court – in Venice! Borrow a racket, or watch others from the jasmine-covered bandstand in the garden. Francesca's parents live on the ground floor and share both court and garden. These well-restored apartments are elegant yet cosy, with family antiques, fresh flowers, smart sofas and Persian rugs on parquet floors. There are intriguing quirks too: an original window and its glass preserved as a piece of art, a 1756 dowry chest from Alto Adige. And you're never far from a window with bustling canal views. The smaller apartment on the first floor has a sweet twin/double tucked away beneath the rafters, and a larger double room downstairs with modern paintings by a local artist. The little kitchen is beautifully equipped, the dining room has high ceilings and a Venetian marble floor. Grimani has a bedroom on the ground floor with garden views and another up; the super new Manin is also on the ground floor. Multi-lingual Francesca who lives nearby is kind, friendly and runs cookery courses that include buying the produce from the Rialto market, just around the corner. *Minimum stay three nights.*

Price	Grimani €1,550-€1,950. Loredan €1,150-€1,550. Manin €900-€1,200. Prices per week.
Rooms	3 apartments: 1 for 4, 2 for 4-6.
Meals	Breakfast €8. Restaurants 50m.
Closed	Never.
Directions	Park at Piazzale Roma nearby. Details on booking.

Francesca Pasti
San Polo 2281,
30125 Venice

Tel +39 0421 66171
Email info@adriabella.com
Web www.adriabella.com

Pensione La Calcina

Catch the sea breezes of early evening from the terrace butting out over the water as you watch the beautiful people stroll the Zattere. Or gaze across the lagoon to the Rendentore. Ruskin stayed here in 1876, and for many people this corner of town, facing the Guidecca and with old Venice just behind you, is the best. The hotel has been discretely modernised by its charming owners; comfortable bedrooms have air con, antiques and parquet floors. Those at the front, with views, are dearer; the best are the corner rooms, with windows on two sides. A small top terrace can be booked for romantic evenings and you can breakfast, lunch or dinner at the delightful floating restaurant, open to all – delicious dishes are available all day and the fruit juices and milkshakes are scrummy. Pause for a moment and remember Ruskin's words on the city he loved: "a ghost upon the sands of the sea, so weak, so quiet, so bereft of all but her loveliness, that we might well doubt, as we watched her faint reflection on the mirage of the lagoon, which was the City and which the shadow." The vaporetto is a step away.

Price	€110-€310. Singles €90-€150.
Rooms	27: 20 doubles, 7 singles.
Meals	Lunch/dinner, with glass of wine, €26-€35. Restaurant closed Mondays.
Closed	Never.
Directions	Water bus line 51 or 61 from Piazzale Roma or train station; line 2 from Tronchetto.

Alessandro Szemere
Fondamenta Zattere ai Gesuati,
Dorsoduro 780, 30123 Venice

Tel +39 0415 206466
Email info@lacalcina.com
Web www.lacalcina.com

Fujiyama Bed & Breakfast

Jasmine, wisteria, shady trees – hard to believe this pool of tranquillity is minutes from the hurly-burly of Venice's streets and the grandeur of the Rialto and St Mark's Square. Even more unusual – for this city – is to step through an oriental tearoom to reach your bedroom. The four bedrooms are on the upper two floors of this tall, narrow 18th-century townhouse and continue the gentle Japanese theme. Carlo worked in Japan for eight years – also Algeria, Egypt, Holland – and his love of the Far East is evident throughout. With views over the garden or the lovely Venetian rooftops, the rooms exude a light, airy and ordered calm with their polished dark wood floors, white walls, Japanese prints and simple oriental furnishings. Shower rooms are small but neat and spotless. Breakfast on the terrace in summer or in the tea room in winter. A charming and warm host, full of stories and happy to chat, Carlo will recommend good local restaurants – especially those specialising in fish. Retreat here after a busy day exploring this magical city and sip a cup of jasmine tea on the shady terrace.

Price	€70-€150.
Rooms	3 doubles.
Meals	Restaurants next door.
Closed	Never.
Directions	From station, water bus line 1. Get off at stop Cà Rezzonico & walk to end of Calle Lunga San Barnaba.

Carlo Errani
Calle Lunga San Barnaba 2727A,
Dorsoduro, 30123 Venice

Tel +39 0417 241042
Email info@bedandbreakfast-fujiyama.it
Web www.bedandbreakfast-fujiyama.it

Terrazza Veronese

You're in a creative corner of 'La Serenissima' – the City otherwise known as Venice. In fact, you would be forgiven for missing the little red door altogether, hemmed in as it is between one art gallery (parading a mouthwatering collection of Venetian treasures) and another. Inside, at the top of the staircase, awaits a delightful top-floor flat. In the little red sitting room are glistening crystal chandeliers, their reflections bouncing off pretty mirrors; in the bedroom, ornate French armoires and matching side tables; in the bathroom, pretty blue and white tiling from top to toe. Striking orange walls express the colours of the Mediterranean in the kitchen, and then it's out onto a narrow terrace where window boxes perch on sills, spilling red geraniums in summer – a sunny spot for a morning coffee. It's very central here, yet quiet; the street leads to a vaporetto stop so there's no through traffic, and the Rialto is five minutes away. Sara has compiled a bumper pack of information: essential reading for the first time visitor and Venice buff alike. *Minimum stay three nights. Cot available.*

Price	€150.
Rooms	1 apartment for 2-4.
Meals	Restaurants within walking distance.
Closed	Never.
Directions	Vaporetto 82 to S. Samuele; up Calle delle Carozze (Palazzo Grassi on left) into Salizzada San Samuele; house between Profumo Santa Maria Novella & Venice Design Art Gallery, on right.

Sara Tidy
3147 Salizzada San Samuele,
San Marco, 30124 Venice
Mobile +44 (0)7973 560142
Email sara.tidy@btinternet.com
Web www.terrazzaveronese.com

Bloom & Settimo Cielo Guest House

In the heart of Venice, yet not overwhelmed by tourists, is a perfectly restored house and *residenza*. You check in round the corner, then delightful reception escorts you to your room. No lift, so be prepared to carry bags to the second (Settimo Cielo) and third (Bloom) floors; on the fourth is the sitting room – books, guide books, your own prosecco in the fridge. From here, step out to the roof top terrace, a privileged spot with a panoramic view, magically lit at night. Back down to the six bedrooms – what fun the owners had in their creation! Spacious and filled with light, named after colours not numbers, they are a beguiling mix of funky and grand. Bows in navy, lilac, cerise attach themselves to doors behind which a heady mix of Venetian baroque and modern minimalism lies; romantic too, though Cream takes the biscuit. Expect raw silk and floating organza, button-back leather and pale painted beams, gilt mirrors and glass-fronted fridges, fine antiques and bathrooms small but exquisite. Buffet breakfasts are elegant and the Chiesa San Vidal is three minutes away – a peerless setting for Vivaldi.

Price	€90-€250. Minimum stay 3 nights (high season), 2 nights rest of year.
Rooms	6: 4 doubles, 2 triples.
Meals	Restaurants nearby.
Closed	Never.
Directions	Vaporetto 1 to Sant'Angelo. Walk until tall redbrick building, then 1st turning on left of building (Ramo Narisi); on until small bridge then left. Along Calle del Pestrin until courtyard on right (Campiello Nuovo); hotel just in front.

Alessandra Vazzoler & Paolo Battistetti
Campiello Santo Stefano,
San Marco 3470, 30124 Venice

Mobile	+39 340 1498872
Email	info@bloom-venice.com
Web	www.bloom-venice.com

Locanda al Leon

Such friendly people and such a perfect spot: three minutes walk from everything that matters (like the Basilica end of St Mark's Square, the airport bus and the vaporetto stops). This small, unpretentious, family-run hotel, its characterful old entrance down a tiny alley, is an excellent choice if you're visiting Venice on a tightish budget but want to be at the centre of it all. It's been modestly modernised. Clean, carpeted bedrooms (the biggest on the corner of the building, looking onto the Campo San Filippo e Giacomo and the Calle degli Albanesi) have Venetian-style bedheads with scrolled edges and floral motifs; there are matching striped counterpanes and curtains, modern Murano chandeliers and neat shower rooms. The new flat, a five minute walk from the hotel, is ideal for families. Breakfast is taken at a handful of tables on the big, first-floor landing (no lift) buffet-style: breads and croissants, yogurts and fruit juice – what you'd expect for the price. And there's no shortage of advice – one or two members of the delightful dall'Agnola family are always around. *Minimum stay two nights at weekends.*

Price	€80-€210. Singles €60-€130. Triple €100-€250. Apt €100-€300. All prices per night.
Rooms	11 + 1: 8 doubles, 2 singles, 1 triple. Apartment for 4.
Meals	Restaurants nearby.
Closed	Rarely.
Directions	Water bus line 1 or 82 to San Zaccaria. Follow Calle degli Albanesi until last door on left; signed.

Marcella & Giuliano dall'Agnola
Campo Santi Filippo e Giacamo 4270,
Castello, 30122 Venice

Tel	+39 0412 770393
Email	leon@hotelalleon.com
Web	www.hotelalleon.com

Giudecca Mare Riva

On the site of an old gondola boathouse, on the southern side of Giudecca, is a luxurious waterfront development with spectacular views. Life's quieter on this side of the lagoon but there are still plenty of trattorias, shops and bars, the vista of islands is a dream, and in eight minutes you can be stepping from the vaporetto onto the Piazza San Marco. Or bring your own boat to the private jetty. Inside, huge sheets of glass pull in the water and sky, polished marble sweeps from living room to bathroom past Italian furniture and pictures in gold frames. The kitchen is white and duck-egg blue, contemporary and cool. The bedroom floor is of pale ash, the wardrobe is fitted glass, the bed is vast. Almost every modern gadget you can think of is here: air conditioning, underfloor heating, huge fridge-freezer, electric sun blind, DVD and CD players, flat-screen TV, WiFi. Outside is a courtyard with a metal staircase spiralling its way up to a roof terrace tangled in jasmine with two perfect loungers... the sunsets are fabulous. *Two vaporetto stops from San Marco. Ask about boat rentals.*

Price	£215 (£1,493 per week). Minimum stay 3 nights.
Rooms	Apartment for 2-3.
Meals	Restaurants within walking distance.
Closed	Rarely.
Directions	Private water taxi from Marco Polo airport or vaporetto from Piazzale Roma to Zitelle; walk length of Calle Michelangelo to lagoon end.

Nick & Wendy Parker
D3 Giudecca Mara Riva,
Calle Michelangelo, 30133 Venice

Tel	+44 (0)2380 456710
Mobile	+44 (0)7785 350376
Email	nickyp43@hotmail.com
Web	www.venicefortwo.com

Relais Ca' Maffio

The delightful young Levi Morenos welcome you to their huge villa in the Sile nature reserve; they live at one end, their parents at the other and the guests in between. They're a family with a history: in 1939 they bought Jesurum, legendary producers of Venetian lace; some historic examples are on display here. The guest bedrooms are on the first floor, classically elegant, harmoniously colour-themed, immaculately furnished. Imagine the best of new (gleaming wooden floors, luxurious fabrics) and a touch of the old (an antique bibelot, a gilt-framed botanical print) and bathrooms that are top of the range. The villa's round-arched façade is striking, its vast open 'veranda' furnished with sofas, tables and an open stone fireplace; breakfast out here in summer and let Nicolò help you plan your day. The house is perfectly placed for birdwatching rambles and bike rides along the river Sile, as well as for cultural forays into Treviso and Venice (drive to Quarto d'Altino, then take the train). Or ask Nicolò to ferry you on his little boat down the river – it flows by at the end of the garden.

Price	€135-€165. Suite €190-€230.
Rooms	4: 3 doubles, 1 suite for 2-4.
Meals	Restaurant 1km; choice 8km.
Closed	Occasionally.
Directions	A4 Milano-Trieste, exit Quarto d'Altino. Follow signs for centre, left at r'bout for Roncade, right after bridge onto Via Principe; after 2km, right.

Nicolò Levi Morenos
Via Principe 70,
31056 Roncade

Tel +39 0422 780774
Email info@camaffio.com
Web www.camaffio.com

Castello di Roncade Agriturismo

An imposing entrance, a garden full of statues and roses and a 16th-century villa do not mean impossible prices. A stately double room furnished with antiques is available in the house itself and there are five simply furnished apartments in the corner towers, some ideal for families. All have big wardrobes and dark wooden floors, heating for winter, air con for summer, and thick walls to keep you cool. The newly refurbished garden apartment is bright and airy, a perfect little place for two with its own terrace. Surrounding the castle and village are the estate vineyards which produce some excellent wines; try the Villa Giustinian Rosso della Casa or the Pinot Grigio and you'll be tempted to take a case home; at the very least make sure you join a tasting session. The owners and their son Claudio are helpful hosts and proud of their wines. No dinner but you're welcome to throw a rug on the lawn for a picnic for an evening meal. Don't take the car to Venice but catch instead the bus to Treviso – an ancient place of cloisters and canals, frescoes and churches – then the train.

Price	€85-€110. Apartments €70-€100.
Rooms	1 + 5: 1 double. 5 apts: 2 for 2, 3 for 4.
Meals	Occasional dinner, €50. Restaurants 500m.
Closed	Rarely.
Directions	Exit A27 Venice-Belluno at Treviso sud, follow Roncade. You can't miss the castle's imposing entrance and magnificent gardens.

Vincenzo Ciani Bassetti
Via Roma 141,
30156 Roncade

Tel +39 0422 708736
Email info@castellodironcade.com
Web www.castellodironcade.com

Locanda RosaRosae

Nothing prepares you for the charm and creaky charisma of this rose-smothered flour mill, lost down narrow lanes by the Meolo river. Rescued from ruin and imaginatively restored, reclaimed wooden floors, beams and brickwork abound with an undressed exuberance: gentle hosts Silvio and Elisabetta have flair! High ceilinged common rooms are decked out simply with antique finds from France and Morocco and quirky touches: exposed mill machinery, a festoon of crystal baubles, antique wall sconces with candles, suspended books,an old woolly mattress-cum-sofa. The restaurant's four dining alcoves are enchanting. Rooms have pretty wooden or metal bedsteads with antique bed linen, linen curtains, ceramic lamp holders with matching switches. Wooden columns make for bedside tables and each has a pièce de résistance: a large Vuitton trunk, an antique metal bath tub or a clad mannequin. Stencilling flounces polished cement bathrooms. Try their own wine, relax in the lovely long riverside garden, drift off to the creak of the mill wheel. Or borrow bikes for the day. A boost for the soul.

Price	€120.
Rooms	4 doubles.
Meals	Dinner €50 (Friday-Sunday; closed August). Restaurant 5-minute walk.
Closed	Rarely.
Directions	Sent on booking.

Elisabetta Pagnossin
Via Molino 1,
31030 S. Bartolomeo di Breda di Piave

Tel +39 0422 686626
Mobile +39 335 8136706
Email info@locandarosarosae.it
Web www.locandarosarosae.it

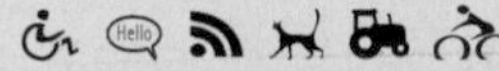

Giardino di Mezzavilla

In a town with a history – it was the site of the Italian victory over the Austro-Hungarian forces: the end of the First World War – is a house of bohemian beauty owned by the nicest people. The pretty 17th-century courtyard is still intact, as are the haylofts, the wine cellar and the greenhouse, all enveloped by acres of garden, theirs and their neighbours'. And a big old tree that fell in last year's storm has been kept, roots and all. The character continues inside, up to two big guest rooms with sober planked floors, colourwashed walls, old-fashioned radiators and the odd antique; no safes or gadgets, just good books, natural soaps, extremely comfortable beds. Janine (who speaks five languages) will lend you maps for free council bicycles – yes, really; her breakfasts, organic feasts of homemade everything, set you up beautifully. Or you could jump in the car and visit the Dolomites or the sea. Return to Aga-cooked dinners that are pure pleasure – fruit and veg from the garden, local meats, Angelo's well-chosen wines. All this and fresh mountain air at night... you'll sleep like a baby.

Price	€70-€110.
Rooms	3: 1 single, 1 family room for 3, 1 family suite for 4.
Meals	Dinner with wine, €20. Vegans catered for. Restaurant 300m.
Closed	Rarely.
Directions	S. Giacomo di Veglia by church after Albergo da Carlo, 1st left at bread shop onto Via Mezzavilla; house on right.

Janine Raedts & Angelo Vettorello
Via Mezzavilla 26, 31029
Vittorio Veneto

Tel	+39 0438 912585
Mobile	+39 320 0525289
Email	info@giardinomezzavilla.com
Web	www.giardinomezzavilla.com

Asolo House

Asolo is a medieval gem, home to Freya Stark, Robert Browning and the Queen of Cyprus – to name a few. Asolo House is a charming 19th-century farmhouse, rural but not isolated, high on a country lane not far from town, with blissful views of woodland, fields, vineyards and mountains and a babbling stream at the foot of the slope. In winter you have books, music and wood-burning stoves, in summer, three waggy dogs, the neighbour's goats, and terraces for views. And Lara, Sicilian-born Italian with a Slovakian mother, educated in Toronto, working as a translator, open, friendly and delightful. Living room and bedrooms (the suite up, the others down) are quirky, eclectic, rustic and homely: chunky rafters, lots of steps, striped throws, prints, mirrors, objets and a bed suspended from the ceiling; another bed sits on a mezzanine reached by a ladder. The downstairs bathroom is spacious and stylish, with a mosaic'd steam room to the side. Paints are eco, veg home-grown and milk comes from a nearby farm. Brilliant for walkers, foodies, culture vultures, couch potatoes – and the young at heart! *Minimum stay two nights.*

Price	€45-€120. Whole house €750-€900 per week.
Rooms	3: 1 double with kitchenette, 1 family suite for 6; 1 double with sofabed sharing top-floor shower. Whole house available.
Meals	Restaurant 500m.
Closed	Rarely.
Directions	Asolo-Pagnano to Via Vallorgana. After Trattoria Ponte Peron, right into Via del Barbo; road veers to left, 1st right to Via Val Sesilla (country lane). 500m, house on right.

Lara Fabiano
Via Carreggiate 18/A,
31011 Pagnano d'Asolo

Mobile	+39 349 6003672
Email	larysafabiano@gmail.com
Web	www.asolohouse.com

Hotel Villa Luppis

Stefania is brimful of ideas and energy, poised to breathe new life into her husband's ancestral home. It's a grand country mansion on the border of Veneto and Friuli, surrounded by acres of flat farmland and 40 minutes from Venice. All creamy peeling stucco and terracotta roof tiles, the hotel stands in 12 acres of lawns and venerable trees, with a fountain and a fabulous terrace. Inside, formal reception and dining areas are graced with antiques and presided over by a friendly and helpful staff. Bedrooms, in need of refurbishment, have comfortable beds, small fridges and fluffy bathrobes. You can go for walks along the river bank but this place is made for excursions; there's a daily shuttle into Venice, Palladian villas populate the river Brenta and you're a 20-minute drive away from one of the biggest McArthur Glen outlets in Italy. Return to a Turkish bath or a blast in the sauna, and wine tastings in the old monks' ice cellar: a must. The two restaurants, elegant and romantic, the smartest with white upholstered chairs and massive fireplace, are a further lure. *Ask about cookery courses.*

Price	€220-€265. Singles €115-€125. Suites €280-€320.
Rooms	39: 27 doubles, 2 singles, 10 suites.
Meals	Buffet breakfast included. Dinner from €28. Wine from €14.
Closed	Never.
Directions	From Oderzo towards Pordenone. Right at Mansue, signed. From A4, exit Cessalto (12km) for Motta di Livenza & Meduna di Livenza. Hotel before village of Rivarotta.

Stefania Ricci Luppis
Via San Martino 34,
33087 Pasiano di Pordenone

Tel	+39 0434 626969
Email	hotel@villaluppis.it
Web	www.villaluppis.it

Tenuta Regina Agriturismo

Views stretch to Croatia on a clear day. Great for a sociable family holiday: an hour to Treviso, Trieste (beloved of James Joyce) and Udine, a 12m x 6m pool with snazzy loungers and a big garden with volleyball. Table tennis, bikes and a children's playground too; the owners, who have children themselves, are proud of their restoration. Now grandfather's farmhouse and grain store are manicured outside and in, and there's a distinct small-resort feel, but the lovely old ceiling rafters remain. The most homely apartment is the largest, on the western end of the farmhouse: two storeys of wooden floors and gleaming doors, pristine white kitchen, four immaculately dressed beds, a sprinkling of family pieces. Perhaps even a bunch of fresh roses – Giorgio's passion. The other apartments, some in front of the pool, some just over the road, feel more functional. Comfortable and open-plan, two on the ground floor, they come with spotless showers, dishwashers and safes, and top-quality linen. A relaxed and untouristy spot for families who love to make new friends. *Flexible rental periods.*

Price	€80-€120. Apts €400-€1,360 per week.
Rooms	3 + 4: 3 suites. 4 apts: 3 for 2-4, 1 for 4-5.
Meals	Breakfast €7 for self-caterers. Restaurants 1.5km.
Closed	Rarely.
Directions	A4 Venezia-Trieste, exit Latisana; signs for Trieste. At Palazzolo, right at 1st lights for Piancada; continue for 7km.

Alessandra Pasti
Casali Tenuta Regina 8,
33056 Palazzolo dello Stella

Tel +39 0421 66171
Email info@adriabella.com
Web www.adriabella.com/tenutaregina

Agriturismo La Faula

An exuberant miscellany of dogs, donkeys and peacocks on a modern, working farm where rural laissez-faire and modern commerce happily mingle. La Faula has been in Luca's family for years; he and Paul, young and dynamic, abandoned the city to find themselves working harder than ever. Yet they put as much thought and energy into their guests as into the wine business and farm. The house stands in gentle countryside at the base of the Julian Alps – a big, comfortable home, and each bedroom delightful. Furniture is old, bathrooms new. There is a bistro-style restaurant where wonderful home-reared produce is served (free-range veal, beef, chicken, lamb, just-picked vegetables and fruits); on summer nights there may be a barbecue. An enormous old pergola provides dappled shade during the day; sit and dream awhile with a glass of estate wine or aqua vita. Or wander round the vineyard and *cantina*, watch the wine-making in progress, practice your skills with a golf club on the residents' driving range, cool off in the river, visit the beaches of the Adriatic. Perfect for families. *Minimum stay two nights.*

Ethical Collection: Environment; Community; Food. See page 419 for details.

Price	€80. Apartments €455 per week.
Rooms	9 + 4: 9 twins/doubles. 4 studio apartments for 2-4.
Meals	Lunch/dinner €19. Wine €10. Restaurant 500m.
Closed	16 September-14 March.
Directions	A23 exit Udine Nord dir. Tarvisio/ Tricesimo. From SS13 Pontebbana dir. Povoletto-Cividale. At r'bout, right dir. Povoletto. At Ravosa, pass Trattoria Al Sole on left; right after 20m. Signed.

Paul Mackay & Luca Colautti
Via Faula 5, Ravosa di Povoletto,
33040 Udine

Mobile +39 334 3996734
Web www.faula.com

Casa del Grivò Agriturismo

This is the house that Toni built – or, rather, lovingly revived from ruin. The smallholding sits in a hamlet on the edge of a plain; behind, wonderful, high-wooded hills extend to the Slovenian border, sometimes crossed to gather wild berries. Your lovely hosts have three young children. Simplicity, rusticity and a 'green' approach are the keynotes here; so you'll sample traditional wool-and-vegetable-fibre-filled mattresses. Beds are comfy and blanketed, some with wonderful quilts. Your children will adore all the open spaces, the animals and the little pool that's been created by diverting a stream. Adults can relax with a book on a bedroom balcony, or in a distant corner of the garden. Maps are laid out at breakfast, and there are heaps of books on the region; the walking is wonderful, there's a castle to visit and a river to picnic by. Paola cooks fine dinners using old recipes and their own organic produce. There's a lovely open fire for cooking, and you dine by candlelight, sometimes to the gentle accompaniment of country songs: Paola was once a singer. *Minimum stay two nights; five in high season.*

Price	€70. Half-board €60 p.p.
Rooms	4: 1 double, 2 family rooms sharing 1 bathroom; 1 family room with separate bathroom.
Meals	Picnic by arrangement. Dinner from €25. Wine from £10.
Closed	Mid-November to Easter.
Directions	From Faédis, Via dei Castelli for Canébola. After 1.5km right, over bridge; 2nd house on left.

Toni & Paola Costalunga
Borgo Canal del Ferro 19,
33040 Faédis

Tel	+39 0432 728638
Email	info@casadelgrivo.com
Web	www.casadelgrivo.com

Palazzo Lantieri

In Gorizia, through an archway off a beautiful piazza, you pull up into a courtyard of luscious lawns and elegant palms. This 14th-century palazzo may have grand proportions, but the immediate feel is of an affectionately tended home. The amiable Contessa guides you past chandeliers and fresh flowers, broad stone staircases and miles of herringbone parquet to two light-filled bedrooms, each intended to delight. Wooden floors creak charmingly, sunlight floods in through soft white curtains, and bathrooms ooze thick fluffy towels and indulgent luxury: just bliss. 'La dolce vita' surrounds you here, with vineyards and good restaurants to visit, country walks to build up your appetite and operas and Roman history to quench cultural thirst. Do explore the palazzo's Persian-style garden and ask the Contessa for a guided tour of the hand-drawn frescoes, the modern art and the memorabilia. Elegant, atmospheric Lantieri: Napoleon, Schiller and Casanova stayed here – and wrote about it; but as you rest in the garden listening to birdsong, you will think yourself the only one to have discovered this Italian jewel.

Price	€140. Suite €150. Apt for 2, €160. Apt for 4, €220.
Rooms	2 + 2: 1 double, 1 suite. 2 apts: 1 for 2, 1 for 4.
Meals	Restaurant walking distance.
Closed	Rarely.
Directions	Sent on booking.

Carolina di Levetzow Lantieri
Piazza Sant'Antonio 6,
34170 Gorizia

Tel	+39 0481 533284
Email	contatto@palazzo-lantieri.com
Web	www.palazzo-lantieri.com

Emilia-Romagna

Villa Bellaria

Off the track, but not isolated, tucked under a softly green hillside, this cream-painted *casa di collina*, with its wide hammock'd veranda and well-established garden, has been a retreat from summer heat since 1900. Having moved here with her husband 20 years ago, Marina, warm and kind, herself a keen traveller, decided to throw open her doors – and share her enthusiasm for this under-sung area, all medieval villages, castles and thermal cures. A much-loved, ornately carved mirror, made by her cabinet maker father at his renowned atelier in Milan, graces one wall. Immaculate bedrooms in old-fashioned style are a friendly mix of wrought-iron bedsteads, delicately embroidered blinds, tile floors and contemporary art. After breakfast al fresco – perhaps a delectable homemade tart – head off through leafy lanes to the walled hill town Castel Arquato, or Piacenza and Parma. After a hard day exploring or being sporty, consider the area's gastronomic treats: nothing sums up Emilia-Romagna so well as its food. A comfortable, cute, civilised home to return to – and great value, too.

Price	€60-€70. Singles €40-€50.
Rooms	4 doubles.
Meals	Restaurant 300m.
Closed	Rarely.
Directions	At lights after Alseno on to Vernasca. On for 5km, right into small street for Cortina; house 2km with green gate on left.

Marina Cazzaniga Calderoni
Via dei Gasperini Loc. Fellegara 380,
29010 Cortina di Alseno

Tel	+39 0523 947537
Email	info@villabellariabb.it
Web	www.villabellariabb.it

Antica Corte Pallavicina Relais

As you turn down the estate's driveway, ancient breeds of cattle and horse pause their grazing, and geese and hens shuffle out of your way. You have arrived at the home of one of Italy's most cherished salami producers, the Spigarolis, who opened their relais with the intention of winning tourists over to the gastronomy of the region. Elegant guest rooms nod to the past in their traditional guise, but have an exquisitely modern edge thanks to their round zinc basins, medusa-like lamps whose bulbs cascade to the floor, and delicious poplar-wood decked showers. Days can be spent in the kitchen with inspiring Massimo learning how to chop and stir, or out exploring the area on one of the estate's bikes. But you cannot leave without visiting the castle's famed cellars, where thousands of culatelli di Zibello and Parmigiano Reggiano cheeses are left to age. Savour both delights at either of the family's two restaurants here. Then finish your day with an aromatic bath in your suite's tub, next to the glowing fire. Look forward to fresh brioches at breakfast beneath frescoed ceilings.

Price	€140-€250.
Rooms	6: 4 doubles, 2 suites.
Meals	Dinner €50-€75. Restaurant nearby.
Closed	Rarely.
Directions	From A1, exit Fidenza. Follow signs to Busseta, then Polesine Parmense.

Massimo Spigaroli
Strada del Palazzo Due Torri 3,
43010 Polesine Parmense

Tel	+39 0524 936539
Email	relais@acpallavicina.com
Web	www.acpallavicina.com/relais

Antica Torre Agriturismo

The farm dogs ambling across the pristine gravel paths in the lee of the 14th-century tower and enormous colonnaded barn, covered in vines, exude a peaceful contentment – which belies the energy that the family pour into this enterprise. From sweeping flagstones at dawn to the final flourish of a delicious bottle at dinner, this family is devoted to agriturismo. Don't expect to stumble across farm machinery or be set upon by winsome lambs: Antica Torre, with its many buildings, has the air of a model farm. The big rooms in the *casa rustica*, with their ancient polished brick and tile floors, have strange and wondrous rustic furniture, and curly metal bedheads inject a light-hearted air. Otherwise, expect simple bathrooms, immaculate housekeeping and an honest rurality. With its huge fireplace and long tables covered in red gingham, the barn, where generous breakfasts are served, has a distinctly alpine air. In the evening, deep in the ancient Cistercian cellar, to the strains of plain chant and Verdi, feast with guests on Vanda's astonishingly good cooking. *Ask about wine tasting.*

Price	€110. Half-board €75 p.p.
Rooms	8 twins/doubles.
Meals	Dinner €20. Wine €5-€12.
Closed	December-February.
Directions	From Salsomaggiore centre, SP27 for Cangelasio & Piacenza. Fork left (signed Cangelasio); 1.5km; left for Antica Torre. Driveway left after 1.5km.

Francesco Pavesi
Case Bussandri 197, Loc. Cangelasio,
43039 Salsomaggiore Terme

Tel	+39 0524 575425
Email	info@anticatorre.it
Web	www.anticatorre.it

Tiglio

Extremely gorgeous and utterly remote! You're way off the beaten track here, at the top of a curvy, slow road with mountain views and gentle rocky river streams. Claudio and Donna, clever restorers of this three-storey 1800s farmhouse – in the family for over a hundred years – are usually there to meet and greet and can stock up with food for you before you arrive. Inside is lovely. The open-plan kitchen/living room is spacious yet cosy, with the original deep butler sink, a long antique wooden table and pretty vintage china. The views over the mountains are stunning and there's a rustic open fireplace with plenty of logs to keep you cosy on chilly days. Bedrooms (stairs are tricky) have a charming, fresh feel: exposed stone work, oriental rugs and family made, antique hand-carved furniture. More woodwork in the bathroom – paired with a stylish modern sink and a walk-in glass shower. A little patio by the front door is the perfect spot for a glass of wine, or laze in a hammock under an arbour of vines. Discover tiny villages, hillsides and creeks, pick berries and mushrooms... country lovers will swoon.

Price	£300-£475 per week.
Rooms	House for 4.
Meals	Restaurant 15km.
Closed	Never.
Directions	Sent on booking.

Donna Lucas
Loc. Tiglio,
43032 Pione

Mobile +39 346 0830047
Email donnalucas2@hotmail.com
Web www.tiglio112.com

Villino di Porporano

It may be surrounded by smart houses, but this impressive B&B stands out in the village of Porporano. A converted stone stable, it oozes Italianness, sitting behind wrought-iron gates in an enclosed (but overlooked) park of trees, roses and lawn – great for picnics. The neat villa attached is where welcoming owner Elena lives with four children and two dogs. She keeps everything in apple-pie order, and can also (as befits Emilia-Romagna) arrange cooking courses. The five compact double rooms are a delight. Expensive linens and embroidered drapes, all whites and creams, soften exposed stone and wooden floors; inviting bathrooms have cotta tiles and goodies (fluffy towels, slippers, nice smellies); Le Rose comes with flowery touches and an antique bath in the bedroom. Lots of high windows (note the building's hayloft heritage) flood the place with light, including the spacious living room where buffet breakfast is served: homemade cakes, local hams and cheeses. Dinner s available on request, there s an excellent restaurant 500m away, and the gastronomy of Parma is a ten-minute drive.

Price	€110. Suite €150. Min. 2 nights: March-October & December.
Rooms	5: 4 twins/doubles, 1 suite for 4.
Meals	Dinner on request. Restaurants nearby.
Closed	Rarely.
Directions	Sent on booking.

Elena Maria Ciotti
Strada Bodrio 26,
43123 Parma

Tel	+39 0521 642268
Mobile	+39 349 4126037
Email	info@villinodiporporano.com
Web	www.villinodiporporano.com

B&B Valferrara

On an ancient road between Canossa and Carpineti, this 17th-century travellers' lodge sits in the silent hamlet of Valferrara. Weary merchants would rest their heads in peace – and absorb the calm and protection of the surrounding forested hills and distant castle of Carpineti. Ruined when Giuliano and Cosetta discovered it in 1994, the *casa di scale* ('tiered house'), complete with flat-roofed Emilian tower – where a clutch of apartments are almost ready – has been completely and masterfully restored with local materials, and parquet flooring fashioned from recycled beams of oak. Cosetta restores local antique furniture and the house is full of it; crisp cotton envelops large, beautifully framed beds and an eye-catching walnut writing desk stands elegantly near one of her several finely polished wardrobes. Expect a warm welcome and a delicious breakfast – under the cool portico, in the walled garden or in the dining room: a fabulous conversion of the old stables. Fresh parmesan can be sampled locally and smiling Cosetta, also a great cook, provides dinner on request.

Price	€76-€90.
Rooms	3: 1 double; 2 doubles sharing bath.
Meals	Restaurants 1km.
Closed	November-March.
Directions	A1 Bologna-Milano exit Modena Nord. SS via Emilia to Reggio Emilia, exit Scandiano to Viano; to Carpineti, dir. Casina, thro' Cigarello. After 1.5km, right at small Valferrara sign; 100m on left.

Cosetta Mordacci & Giuliano Beghi
Via Valferrara 3, Pantano,
42033 Carpineti

Mobile	+39 340 1561417
Email	info@bb-valferrara.it
Web	www.bb-valferrara.it

La Stella

The long, twisting road to La Stella dances from Modena into the Apennines and this secluded farmhouse set in deepest nature. The reward: magnificent views of Monte Cusna, an enthusiastic welcome, a nighttime carpet of stars. No wonder Belgian Peter and Christine fell for this rural spot by the Tuscan-Emilian National Park, with hiking, biking, a river beach on the Secchia, skiing in winter, stunning mountains year-round. You will fall for it too – if you value tranquillity – and for the house with its chunky stone walls, fire-warmed sitting room, antique piano and breakfast room with chandelier. The bedroom, just as charming, has dainty pillows, a reading corner, a sofabed for a child – and views. Outside, a delicious bite-sized plot of birds, trees, flowers: a taste of what lies beyond. In summer, breakfast out here on cured meats and Christine's scrumptious pastries. La Stella may be off the beaten path but it is well-positioned between several wonderful cities. For those who love nature: an adventure to arrive, a pleasure to stay... and there's a restaurant a ten-minute drive. *Ask about cupcake decoration & astronomy.*

Price	€95.
Rooms	1 twin/double.
Meals	Restaurant 10-minute drive.
Closed	Rarely.
Directions	Sent on booking.

Christine Tiebout
Via San Venerio 7/2,
42030 Carù di Villa Minozzo

Mobile	+39 348 6354836
Email	info@bb-lastella.it
Web	www.bb-lastella.it

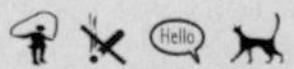

La Piana dei Castagni Agriturismo

Write, paint, read or potter: here, deep in the woods, there's nothing to distract you. This is a secret little Hansel and Gretel house with a vegetable patch, demure shutters and lace-trimmed curtains. It stands isolated among chestnut and cherry trees, reached via a long, wriggling track; below are bucolic meadows, falling to a farm or two, and a further distant descent along the yawning valley. An old stone farmhouse converted and adapted for B&B, La Piana is a modest place to stay. The bedrooms, named after local berries, are a good size and painted in clear pastel colours; tiny pictures hang above beds and little windows set in thick walls look out over the glorious valley. The shower rooms – one of them a restyled chicken shed! – are simply tiled. Valeria lives ten minutes away at La Civetta. She is gentle, kind, spoiling; even the breakfast *torte di noci* are homemade. She will also help organise everything, from trekking to truffle hunting. An ideal spot for those who love the simple pleasures of life: good walks by day, good food by night. *Ask about gastronomic tours.*

Price	€70-€95. Singles €40. Triples €80-€100. Minimum 2 nights.
Rooms	5: 2 doubles, 1 single, 2 triples.
Meals	Dinner €19-€21. Wine €8-€20. Restaurant 3km.
Closed	November-March.
Directions	From Tolè, follow signs for S. Lucia & Castel d'Aiano; signed.

Ethical Collection: Food.
See page 419 for details.

Valeria Vitali
Via Lusignano 11,
40040 Rocca di Roffeno

Tel +39 0519 12985
Email info@pianadeicastagni.it
Web www.pianadeicastagni.it

Lodole Country House

An exceedingly well-renovated 17th-century stone cottage with views over breathtaking Apennine countryside; it's a treat to arrive. Flowers brighten windows, wooden shutters are hung and varnished, terracotta planters march up to the front door, and a paved path curves up to a swimming pool from which you can exclaim at the view. Bedrooms – Sun, Sky, Stars – reflect their names, and are wonderfully romantic; Moon has semicircular end tables and in its bathroom a skylight; Dawn, pale pink, faces east; Sunset, pale orange, faces west. All have low lighting, wooden boards, exposed beams, soothing hues. Well-chosen pieces add interest: polished armoires, antique vanities, free-standing antique washbasins and fine wrought-iron beds, some canopied in soft cotton. The living room has a fireplace, big white sofas, a window to the hills, and a raised area beyond for delicious, lovingly sourced breakfasts served at separate tables by Alice. Numerous local trattoria provide discounted meals to guests and the Molino del Pero golf course lies handily next door.

Price	€90.
Rooms	6: 5 doubles, 1 triple.
Meals	Restaurants nearby.
Closed	Rarely.
Directions	A1 exit Rioveggio; left dir. Monzuno/ Loiano. To Monzuno; continue to Loiano. After 2km, Borgo Lodole on left. Left; on for 100m to 'Lodole B&B.'

Alice Frontini
Loc. Lodole 325,
40036 Monzuno

Tel +39 0516 771189
Email info@lodole.com
Web www.lodole.com

Relais Varnello

In young gardens just above the pretty town of Brisighella – you'll need the car, it's quite a hike – the brick buildings stand sparkling and tickety-boo. Nicely-furnished rooms have views across the valley or the garden; the suites are in a separate building with a sauna. The setting among the calanchi (chalk hills) is stunning and the farm produces Sangiovese DOC wine and olive oil, which you can buy along with Faenza pottery showing the family crest. Giovanni has been producing oil and wine all his life and you won't leave here without a bottle or two – it's delicious. If you speak a little Italian, pick his brains, he has a vast knowledge of Italian grapes (over 1,000 varieties) and will happily tell tales of some of the best wines going. Spend your days lounging by the pool (he's also very proud of his fully plumbed poolhouse): there are wide views over the Padana and to the Adriatic, and just a stroll away there's a private wild park, Giovanni's pride and joy: a lovely place for a picnic and a book. Higher up the hill is the Pacro Carné, with Club Alpino Italiano (CAI) walking trails. *Minimum stay two nights.*

Price	€130. Suites €180.
Rooms	6: 4 twins/doubles, 2 suites.
Meals	Restaurant 300m.
Closed	January-15 March.
Directions	From Brisighella on SP23 Montecino & Limisano road, signed to Riolo Terme. After 3km, left after Ristorante Manicômi, signed to Rontana. 1st building on left.

Giovanni Liverzani
Via Rontana 34,
48013 Brisighella

Tel +39 0546 85493
Email info@varnello.it
Web www.varnello.it

Azienda Vitivinicola e Agrituristica Trerè

Braided vines, with their companion grasses, stretch as far as the eye can see... in the middle of this flat green patchwork stands a compact group of rosy buildings and a clump of tall trees to one side. The entertainingly angular farmhouse is surrounded by barns and stables, modernised as apartments and a conference room. This is very much a wine-growing estate – around the house are certificates and awards, a shop and a little rose-and-gold wine museum – but there's a family feel with the owners' children, a tribe of peacocks and an easy atmosphere. The bedrooms in the house have the light and pretty elegance of beamed ceilings, pastel walls, lovely old family furniture and books, and memorable touches such as the deep lace trim of a white sheet folded over a jade bedcover. The apartments (with kitchenettes) are attractive but more functional in feel. Each has French windows opening onto a private patio and a mezzanine with an extra bed tucked under a skylight – always fun for kids. Eat in a stall in the unspoilt former cowshed, now the restaurant, open for four days a week (there are other restaurants nearby).

Ethical Collection: Food.
See page 419 for details.

Price	€68-€78. Singles €52. Suite €135-€150. Apts €80-€92 for 2; €108-€190 for 4-6.
Rooms	7 + 4: 4 doubles, 1 twin, 1 suite for 4-6, 1 triple. 4 apts for 2-6.
Meals	Breakfast €6.50. Dinner €30 (except Jan/Feb & Mon-Wed). Wine €7-€22. Restaurants 5km.
Closed	Rarely.
Directions	From Faenza via Emilia SS9 for Imola/ Bologna; 3km left after Subaru garage on Via Casale; signed.

Morena Trerè & Massimiliano Fabbri
Via Casale 19,
48018 Faenza

Tel	+39 0546 47034
Email	trere@trere.com
Web	www.trere.com

Liguria

© iStockphoto.com/
Rechitan Sorin

Villa Elisa

The climate is kind: visit at any time of the year. The hotel was created in the 1920s when Bordighera, a pretty town with sloping tree-lined roads and pastel houses, became a winter retreat. The owner's father-in-law ran it for years, was a painter and had artists to stay – bedroom walls are still hung with the works they left. Some still come, following in the steps of Monet. This is a friendly place for walkers and families: Rita and husband Maurizio take groups off into the Maritime Alps in their minibus, then guide them back on three-hour treks. They also have a playroom for children, and organise special activities for summer. The restaurant is traditional and charming, the bedrooms are old-fashioned and double-glazed. Bathrooms are white-tiled with floral friezes and heated towel rails; the larger rooms have terraces with views to the hills. Best are the gardens: the courtyard bright with bougainvillea and oranges, the pool area lushly planted. Set off for the pebbled beach, a ten-minute dash down the hill; return to fresh fish on the menu served by attentive and delightful staff.

Price	€120-€180. Singles €80-€110. Suite €200-€250. Apt €220-€300.
Rooms	34 + 1: 30 doubles, 3 singles, 1 suite. Apartment for 4-6.
Meals	Lunch/dinner from €40. Wine €16-€50. Half or full-board option for week-long stays.
Closed	5 November-22 December.
Directions	Via Romana parallel to main road through town (Via Aurelia), reachable by any x-road that links the two. Villa at western end of Via Romana.

Rita Oggero
Via Romana 70,
18012 Bordighera

Tel	+39 0184 261313
Email	info@villaelisa.com
Web	www.villaelisa.com

Casa Villatalla Guest House

Revel in the peace – and the views: they sweep across the wooded valley to the blue-grey mountains beyond. Roger (British) and Marina (Italian-Swiss) moved not long ago to Liguria and had the delightful Casa Villatalla built in traditional style, ochre-stuccoed and green-shuttered. They are wonderfully welcoming hosts – and the cheerful, eclectic décor of the house reflects their warm personalities and love of travel. Through the brick archway, a Swiss armoire presides over a dining room furnished with rustic wooden tables on which seasonal breakfasts and dinners (do book) are served. Upstairs, charming modern bedrooms, some lead to balconies and those views. All are different – in Quercia, a bedstead woven from banana tree fronds, in Corbezzolo, rose tones and a flowery patchwork quilt. Marina, a keen horticulturist, nurtures her garden full of roses, and there's a swimming pool terrace which is crowned by a fine oak tree, beautifully illuminated at night. Together they organise occasional painting and yoga courses: another reason to stay. *Minimum two nights July/August.*

Price	€80-€90.
Rooms	5: 1 double, 4 twins/doubles.
Meals	Dinner with wine, from €25. Restaurant 5km.
Closed	Never.
Directions	Follow Val Nervia road from coast. 1km after Dolceacqua, left to Rocchetta Nervina. After 3km, left to La Colla. Villatalla on right, after 2km.

Roger & Marina Hollinshead
Loc. Villatalla,
18035 Dolceacqua

Tel +39 0184 206379
Email info@villatalla.com
Web www.villatalla.com

Relais San Damian

Wind your way up through endless olive groves to this organic working estate. Through the gate... to find child-free seclusion and spa-like calm. Manicured lawns give way to a fine terrace, and breathtaking bougainvillea-framed views over village-studded hills to the glinting sea (even better appreciated from the stunning infinity pool!). Rooms, all with their own private outdoor space, are savvy and sophisticated yet simple: open brickwork, marble basins, cream iron beds and sofas, bare wooden floors, beautiful country antiques. Relaxation is what San Damian is about. Bring a book or browse the library, slip into the pool, feel time go slow-mo to the serenade of the cicadas. Local osteria dining tips are readily provided by serene hosts Pamela and Roberto; breakfast – an abundant buffet of homemade breads and cakes, fresh fruit, cheeses and cured meats served under portico'd arches – should under no circumstances be slept through. Should you stray from the garden and grounds, the surrounding hills promise superb hiking – and the lavish Ligurian coast is the shortest drive.

Price	€140-€170.
Rooms	10 doubles.
Meals	Restaurant 4km.
Closed	December-February.
Directions	Sent on booking.

Pamela Kranz Gardini
Azienda Agricola Strada Vasia 47,
18100 Imperia

Tel +39 0183 280309
Email info@san-damian.com
Web www.san-damian.com

Casa Cambi

You can hardly believe that such a magical hilltop village, with its tangle of winding cobbled streets and medieval stone houses, has survived unspoilt into the 21st century. A square, brooding old castle dominates the hill. All around are dramatic mountains and stupendous views; in the streets is perfect peace. Walk the cobbles down to Anna's entrancing house (the splendid apartment for families is further up the hill); a tiny front door (the house is 700 years old, after all) takes you straight into a fine vaulted room done in a soothing mix of creams and whites, ochres and umbers. Pale walls contrast with a gleaming wooden floor and old polished furniture; its subtle, restrained country charm sets the tone for the rest. All the rooms are a delight, all full of unexpected touches – jugs of fresh wild flowers, a rack of old kitchen implements stark against a white wall... Vivacious Anna adores her house and has lavished huge care on it. She's bubbly and friendly and loves cooking in her lovely kitchen. Breakfast out in the pretty terraced garden among olive and fig trees and revel in those mountain views.

Price	€90-€110.
Rooms	4: 2 doubles, 1 twin, 1 family room.
Meals	Dinner €25-€30. Wine from €10.
Closed	30 September-1 May. Out of season fax +39 010 812613.
Directions	A10 exit Albenga. S582 Garessio for Castelvecchio di Rocca Barbena, 12km. Free car park outside pedestrianised Borgo, 5-minute walk.

Anna Bozano
Via Roma 42,
17034 Castelvecchio di Rocca Barbena

Tel +39 0182 78009
Mobile +39 329 1667507
Email casacambi@casacambi.it
Web www.casacambi.it

Ca' de Tobia

In the little fishing village of Noli – a big surprise! Behind the potted box trees is a friendly B&B with a boutique feel. Enter a communal space, sharp, chic, white, a reflection of the dazzling seaside beyond. Traditional furniture (a wooden hutch full of antique plates) is juxtaposed with funky modern (a ceramic collage) and whimsical touches ('plastic' dishes that turn out to be glass). A big restoration has taken place to lick this former warehouse into shape and Andrea does it all – reception, breakfast, laundry. He loves both house and guests so lap up the luxury. There are currently three bedrooms but more will follow; ceilings are high and windows generous (though views are unmemorable), thick curtains flow, down pillows are heaped high, bursts of colour come from pleasing art and bathrooms are hugely spoiling. Best of all are the breakfasts, served on the terrace in summer: prosciutto and melon, buffalo mozzarella, fresh smoothies, homemade cakes; some of it finds its way into picnic baskets if you set off on the bikes. There's hiking in the hills and delicious villages to be discovered. *Ask about parking.*

Price	€170-€250. Min. 2 nights in high season.
Rooms	3 doubles.
Meals	Restaurants nearby.
Closed	September.
Directions	Sent on booking.

Andrea Tobia
17026 Noli Savona

Tel	+39 0197 485845
Mobile	+39 346 9923318
Email	info@cadetobia.it
Web	www.cadetobia.it

Sognando Villa Edera

At the top of the ever-winding road from Rapallo you are rewarded with a sweet surprise: a family agriturismo with spectacular views. These 1.5 hectares of olive groves and orchards, planted by Sara's grandfather, are home to well-behaved dogs, cats, a donkey and a pony, and Rosanna's delightful tiered gardens. Below the gardens are five simple, spotless apartments not so long ago created from the farmworkers' houses: two on the the ground floor, three above, each with its own piece of garden or terrace. Set off for the beaches of Portofino, three kilometres away... or the peaceful palmed promenade, harbours and little castle of Rapallo. You could happily spend all day here too, high up among the birds and the roses, the views swooping from your deckchair to the coast. In among the trees and verdant terraces is a swimming pool that families love. No breakfasts here but plenty of cafés in historic Rapallo, down the hill. The Cinque Terre is 40 minutes by car and the buses run three times a day. *Min. stay three nights; five July-August. Air con extra charge.*

Price — €100-€200 per night.
Rooms — 5 apartments: 4 for 2-4, 1 for 4-5.
Meals — Restaurants 2km.
Closed — Rarely.
Directions — A12 Genova-Livorno exit Rapallo. Round central reservation, right onto Via Savagna for 1.5km; into Via Sotto la Croce. Right into Salita S. Giovanni, gate on left.

Sara Piaggio
Salita San Giovanni 3,
16035 Rapallo
Mobile +39 338 5211381
Email info@sognandovillaedera.com
Web www.sognandovillaedera.com

Villa Gnocchi Agriturismo

Once you've negotiated the steep and windy access drive, you are rewarded with sensational views over Santa Margherita. Roberto, a Ligurian farmer, trained at Pisa University and inherited the house from his grandfather in a dilapidated state; he's made a few changes! He is a wonderful host and loves this place, deep in the country but within sight of the sea... enjoy breakfast or a glass of wine from the terrace and gaze down the coast: a treat. Each bedroom is colourful, spotless, different: white, ochre or saffron; all are simply furnished and decorated with dried flowers. Bright bedcovers dress grandfather's beds, muslin curtains flutter at windows, old framed prints hang on the walls and many shower rooms are tiny. Apart from the hoot of the train and the faint hum of the traffic below, the only sound to break the peace is birdsong. Forget the hire car: Santa Margherita – a 15-minute walk downhill, a bumpy bus or taxi up – is a charming little town, with beach, fishing boats, shops, bars and restaurants. Paths lead to most of the villages and buses from the gate. *Access for cars from via San Lorenzo.*

Price	€90-€110. Strict check-in/out times (before 13.30 or between 16.30-19.45).
Rooms	9: 5 doubles, 2 twins, 2 family rooms.
Meals	Restaurant 500m.
Closed	Mid-October to mid-April.
Directions	From Santa Margherita for S. Lorenzo, 4km. Past big sign 'Genova & S. Lorenzo' on left, Rapallo & A12 on right, 50m ahead, left down narrow road. At red & white barrier ring bell.

Roberto Gnocchi
Via San Lorenzo 29, San Lorenzo della Costa, 16038 Santa Margherita Ligure

Tel	+39 0185 283431
Email	roberto.gnocchi@tin.it
Web	www.villagnocchi.it

Hotel Villa Edera

The villa is perched above the beautiful town of Moneglia and is a beautifully run, family owned hotel. The hosts make any stay a joy; Orietta and Francesca pour themselves into their business. Orietta is a mine of information about Ligurian art and history, sings in the local choir and loves meeting people who share her interest in music. Rooms are light and airy if a little retro, but there are plans to update the décor. Chef Adriano will prepare Ligurian dishes, some vegetarian, with the freshest organic produce, and does fabulous breakfasts; sister Edy is a cake-making genius. Orietta is a keen walker who may take guests out for real hikes – though you can always catch a boat to Portofino and explore the Cinque Terre by sea. You are fairly close to the railway here (a significant part of the landscape, threading the Cinque Terre villages together) but you'd never know, and now there's a lift up to the hotel from the street – handy! Lots of treats to come back to: a fitness room, sauna, a lovely pool. The beach is a ten-minute walk. *Gluten-free meals available. Ask about wine tasting.*

Price	€130-€280. Singles €85-€135. Half-board €75-€125 p.p. Minimum 3 nights.
Rooms	26: 21 doubles, 2 singles, 2 suites, 1 family room.
Meals	Lunch/dinner €28-€35. Wine €12.
Closed	November-March.
Directions	Exit A12 at Sestri Levante; signs for Moneglia tunnel. Immed. after 5th tunnel right (at sports field); signed. Free parking.

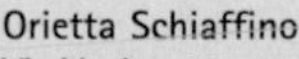

Orietta Schiaffino
Via Venino 12,
16030 Moneglia

Tel +39 0185 491119
Email info@abbadiasangiorgio.com
Web www.villaedera.com

Abbadia San Giorgio

Sublimely romantic and peaceful, this 15th-century monastery recalls the life of St Francis in frescoes and sculptures beneath vaulted ceilings. You can almost hear the sandalled Franciscans padding round the cloister garden. Dipping into a delicious spread for breakfast, served by candlelight in the refectory, you will breathe more monastic air. Nothing monkish about the bedrooms: Orietta and Francesca, a mother and daughter team, have searched Italy for antique furniture and sensual fabrics to make them both sumptuous and individual. Many of the beds are wrought-iron; one's a four-poster. Floors are of original octagonal terracotta or terrazzo tiles. The large and ethereal honeymoon suite is swathed and festooned with gauze and ivory furnishings. Elsewhere, tones range from lavish red to green, apricot and gold, all opulently matched. Neat marble bathrooms sport spa shower cabins with pretty olive-oil-based toiletries. An amorous evening might begin with wine tasting in the cellar, then stepping out for dinner. A haven of peace in the centre of beautiful Moneglia. *Pool at hotel next door.*

Price	€190-€250. Suites €210-€310. Minimum stay 3 nights.
Rooms	6: 3 doubles, 1 twin/double, 2 suites for 4.
Meals	Restaurants 100m.
Closed	November.
Directions	A12 exit Sestri Levante dir. Moneglia; under bridge towards town centre, immed. left down palm tree-lined street, right at end after pharmacy; entrance to Abbadia next to church. Or 5-minute walk from station.

Orietta Schiaffino
Piazzale San Giorgio,
16030 Moneglia

Tel	+39 0185 491119
Email	info@abbadiasangiorgio.com
Web	www.abbadiasangiorgio.com

Villa Margherita by the Sea B&B

Federico is the understated owner of this family hotel, and his bubbly sister Paola. A five-minute walk above Levanto – count the steps! – is the Villa Margherita, built in 1906. It once mingled with the smart set and played its part in the summer seasons between the wars, when Levanto was seriously fashionable. The town is still full of character, still worth exploring; fishermen fish, children build sandcastles, but the glitterati have moved on. Sensitively renovated in classic Liguria ochre and decorative fresco, the house sits in leafy, terraced gardens sprinkled with pots of flowers, tables, loungers and tall palms; lap up the lushness over an aperitivo. White walls, muslin-clad windows and deep armchairs welcome you and charm abounds, in each marble stair, graceful iron banister and decorative floor tiles. Simply furnished flowery bedrooms, family bathrooms and unfussy style imbue the house with the spirit of a well-loved, long-established *pensione*, and the updated garden rooms, one reached through the (breakfast-noisy) kitchen, are delightful, each with its own little terrace.

Price	€85-€160.
Rooms	11: 9 doubles, 2 triples.
Meals	Restaurants 5-minute walk.
Closed	Never.
Directions	From A12 exit Carrodano & Levanto; right after station; left onto main street; right onto Corsa Italia up hill; hotel on left; parking, signed.

Federico Campodonico
Via Trento e Trieste 31,
19015 Levanto

Tel +39 0187 807212
Email info@villamargherita.net
Web www.villamargherita.net

Agriturismo Villanova

Villanova is where Barone Giancarlo Massola's ancestors spent their summers in the 18th century, and has barely changed. It's a mile from Levanto yet modern life feels far behind as you wind your way up the hills through olive groves, then down an unremarkable street... to an unexpected gem. Behind its gates the red and cream villa – with private chapel – stands in a small sunny clearing. Giancarlo, quiet, charming, much-travelled, loves meeting new folk; his golden retriever will welcome you too. Guest bedrooms are in the main house and in two small stone farmhouses behind; all have an elegant, country-house feel and rooms are large, airy, terracotta tiled. Furniture is of wood and wrought iron, beautiful fabrics are yellow and blue. As for the apartments, they have private entrances and terraces with pretty views. Two apartments are separate, a third is in the farmhouse. Giancarlo grows organic apricots, figs and vegetables and makes his own wine and olive oil; breakfasts are delicious. This is a great place to bring children: swings and table tennis in the garden, space to run around in, the coast nearby.

Price	€95-€130. Suites €120-€170. Apartments €600-€1,300 per week.
Rooms	9 + 4: 3 doubles, 6 suites for 2-3. 4 apartments for 2-6.
Meals	Breakfast €12 for self-caterers. Restaurants 1.5km.
Closed	January.
Directions	Exit A12 at Carrodano Levanto dir. Levanto. Signs from junction before town (direction Monterosso & Cinque Terre).

Giancarlo Massola
Loc. Villanova, 19015 Levanto

Tel	+39 0187 802517
Email	info@agriturismovillanova.it
Web	www.agriturismovillanova.it

La Sosta di Ottone III

Legend has it that Otto III stayed here on his way to his coronation in Rome in 996, creating La Sosta, a 'stopover' of some magnificence. Now a listed building, the house's unadorned stone façade stands proudly over the hamlet of Chiesanuova, scanning a vista from all rooms of olive groves, village and vineyard-clad hills, before dropping down to Levanto and the sea. The terrace is a superb breakfast and dinner setting, perfect too at sunset with a glass of chilled vermentino. At night, the glow from a host of illuminated bell towers is enchanting. Angela has taken great care to gather the best local slate, marble and wood in the renovation of dining and sitting rooms. Bedrooms, named after Otto and his family members, come in an elegant range of neutrals and corals. There are parquet floors, antique pieces, indoor shutters and iron beds graced by fine bedspreads... take time to pamper yourself in stylish marble and slate bathrooms. Aficionados of all things Ligurian, Angela and Fabio can be depended on for local information, the freshest ingredients and one of the best wine cellars around. Superb.

Price	€200. Extra bed €20-€40. 10% discount for stays of 7 nights; minimum stay 2.
Rooms	4: 1 double, 1 suite for 4, 2 family rooms for 2-4.
Meals	Breakfast €15; €7.50 for children under 12. Dinner €40. Restaurant 5km.
Closed	Beginning October-end April.
Directions	From Levanto dir. Cinque Terre. Ignore signs on right for Chiesanuova. After 400m park on left near cement watertank. Follow path for 150m.

Angela Fenwick
Loc. Chiesanuova 39,
19015 Levanto

Tel	+39 0187 814502
Email	lasostadiottone@hotmail.com
Web	www.lasosta.com

L'Antico Borgo

Oozing tranquillity, it could be a setting for a film, so private is it with its gorgeous views over green hills and down to the sea. Once you reach tiny Dosso, leave the car and walk intrepidly down the short steep path to the B&B. Surrounded by olive groves and pocket vineyards, it's hard to believe Levanto is only four kilometres. A pretty pebbled square and a stone arch form the entrance to this 1700s *casa padronale*, fully restored with the soft-ochre façade and dark green shutters so typical of Liguria. The panoramic terrace is a fine place for breakfast or an aperitif and Cecilia is happy for guests to have their own picnics here. Relax in the sitting room with a book from the small library, breakfast at round tables in the rustic taverna. Bright and generous bedrooms, two with sea views, have timber beams; all are comfortably furnished with wrought-iron beds and warmed by gentle shades of yellow. Modern bathrooms use solar-heated water. Siblings Cecilia and Carlo, a local surfing hero, are shy but natural hoteliers and are both supporters of the Slow Food movement so they know the best places for dinner.

Price	€80-€110. Family rooms €130-€160. Triples €110-€135.
Rooms	7: 1 double, 1 twin/double, 2 family rooms for 4, 3 triples.
Meals	Restaurant 1km.
Closed	Rarely.
Directions	A12 Genova-Livorno exit Carrodano-Levanto; on for Levanto. Left after gallery, signs for Dosso; free parking at entrance.

Cecilia Pilotti
Loc. Dosso,
19015 Levanto

Tel	+39 0187 802681
Email	antico_borgo@hotmail.com
Web	www.anticoborgo.net

Tuscany

Podere Conti

Set in an organically certified, 200-acre olive estate beneath the magnificent Appennini mountains, this 17th-century hamlet, procured by Corrado and English Cornelia, recently renovated whilst raising a family, is agriturismo perfection. Follow a winding five-kilometre drive through chestnut, hazelnut and oak forest (ensuring utter seclusion), be greeted by charming Cornelia, decant into rooms beautifully designed with Arabian (not Tuscan) flair; both spent time in Abu Dhabi. Find exquisite rugs on cotto floors, raw beams, antique screen bedheads, richly textured cushions, delicious cotton bedding, little chandeliers, creaky trunks, glass bedside lights, and breezy bathrooms with free-standing tubs and monogrammed towels... all feels uncluttered and balanced. La Tavolata, their restaurant, serves delicious estate-produced meals (game in season) against sensational valley sunsets. There's loads to do both on the estate and off – this is heaven for free-range kids. And, with secluded nooks, poolside daybeds and hammocks in secluded crannies, it's pretty nice for adults too. Oh, and a haunted ruin!

Ethical Collection: Environment.
See page 419 for details.

Price	€95-€180 (min. stay 3 nights). Apartments €160-€290.
Rooms	9 + 3: 6 doubles, 3 suites for 4. 3 apartments: 2 for 4, 1 for 5.
Meals	Breakfast €10. Lunch/dinner with wine €25. Book in advance.
Closed	Mid-January to mid-February.
Directions	From A15/E31 Parma/La Spezia m'way, exit Pontremoli. Right onto SP31, 1st right Via di Caritá e Lautro; T-junc. left SS62, 1st right Via Dobbiana. Follow signs to Podere Conti (approx. 6km).

Cornelia Conti
Via Dobbina Macerie 3,
51023 Filattiera

Email	info@podereconti.com
Web	www.podereconti.com

Casa Gisella

In the chestnut-mantled Lunigiana mountains, Bastia village is quaint, cobbled, labyrinth'd with lanes and dominated by an ancient, surely unassailable fort. Sitting on the breakfast terrace at Casa Gisella, distracted by gaspworthy views, you feel on top of the world. In the dream holiday home of Irish owners Ronnie and Alison the bedrooms are cosy, comfortable and classy all at the same time and show exceptional attention to detail; nothing too flash, just carefully considered and harmonious: a clean use of space and the odd contemporary painting; big wrought-iron beds covered with beautiful cream fabrics, textured throws and lots of cushions; power showers, snazzy lighting and WiFi. Thick, exposed medieval walls and beams make rooms snug and the big sitting room has a fire for winter. The very modern kitchen is charming and there are guest discounts to be had at local restaurants. The place is a walkers' paradise – you could veer off in any direction for hours – and, being close to both sea and snow, is family-fabulous all year round. *Minimum stay three nights. Flexible rental periods.*

Price	£550-£890 per week.
Rooms	House for 6.
Meals	Welcome pack. Dinner with wine, €32, by arrangement. Restaurants 3km.
Closed	Never.
Directions	A1 to A15, exit A15 Aulla. Follow signs for Licciana Nardi on SS665. From Licciana, signs for Bastia.

Ronnie & Alison Johnston
Via Bastia 20, Bastia,
54016 Licciana Nardi

Mobile +44 (0)7967 188017
Email info@casagisella.com
Web www.casagisella.com

Dimora Olimpia

When they arrived it was a ruin; a decade on, Olimpia and Gaetano's 16th-century farmhouse is an exquisitely restored home for them and their little girl. For the full force of its charm, approach by the cobbled back street where chickens potter. There are long views of fields, woods and rumpled hills from elegant terrace and pool. Passionate lovers of old things, your hosts are also fluent guides to the region. Gorgeousness abounds: bare beams and exposed brickwork have been lovingly preserved, there are old wall hangings, fine, early country furniture and, in the snug bedrooms, original shutters at tiny windows. The small apartment is simple and charming, peaceful and cool, the beds aligned with the Earth's magnetic field to ensure perfect sleep. The shower room is first-class, the kitchen tiny, the pillow cases lined with lace. You will dine well in nearby restaurants and self-caterers are most welcome to join B&B guests round the antique Indian table. Outside, you have a verdant, unspoilt and unsung part of Tuscany to explore – country roads, tiny villages, good walks, fine wines. *Minimum stay two nights.*

Price	€80. Apt €380-€450 per week.
Rooms	2 + 1: 1 double, 1 suite for 4. 1 apt for 2-3.
Meals	Breakfast €5. Restaurants 4km.
Closed	Never.
Directions	From Aulla SS62 to SS665, then Monti & Amola. Right for Dimora Olimpia in middle of village; on right.

Olimpia De Caro & Gaetano Azzolina
Via Molesana,
54017 Licciana Nardi

Tel +39 0187 471580
Email info@dimoraolimpia.it
Web www.dimoraolimpia.it

The Watermill at Posara

Enjoy secluded millstream gardens in little Posara, with the wonderful Rosario cascading below. This was a working mill until the 80s and downstairs nothing has changed: the flagged floors, the beams, the ancient passageways to different sections. Bill, Lois, their daughters and their dogs have moved from a castle in Scotland; and if they're not here to greet you, charming Kerstin will. Apartments have lovely views and an eclectic combination of furniture old and new, from a faux leopard skin-clad chaise longue to flowery shower curtains. Beds are new, fabrics are in natural colours, shower rooms are spotless and there are some marvellous old floor tiles. In summer, cool off in the plunge pool and cross the bridge to the "bamboozery" – a vast thicket of giant bamboo, a joy for hide and seekers. The little town of Fivizzano is a 20-minute walk and treks and horse tracks abound, but most people come for the spring and autumn courses, a vibrant programme of workshops in painting and writing. There's a kiwi garden near the courtyard, picnics at millstone tables, and a lovely sociable barbecue.

Price	£315-£715 per week. Minimum stay one week.
Rooms	3 apartments: 1 for 2, 2 for 4.
Meals	Restaurant 2km.
Closed	Rarely.
Directions	Autostrada A15 to Aulla. From Aulla, SS63 towards Fivizzano. 5km from Fivizzano, left for Posara. In village pass church, right at pink house down to mill.

Bill Breckon
Via del Mulino 12-20, Loc. Posara,
54013 Fivizzano

Tel	+44 (0)20 7193 6246
Mobile	+39 366 4882587
Email	info@watermill.net
Web	www.watermill.net

Castello di Fosdinovo

Dante stayed here – crossing the Lunigiana on a pilgrimage. Built in the 12th-century, Fosdinovo is one of the most important castellos in Tuscany, and one of the most fascinating. Pietro, eloquent, hospitable son of the Marquis Malaspina, knows the history. If the journey up the winding road is an adventure, then the arrival is thrilling; the views swoop to the Tyrrhenian coast and you sail into a fairy tale. Spiralling staircases run up and down, to Throne Room, Arms Room, Watchtower, terraces. The drawing room is faded but inviting, the dining hall is remarkable (note the ceiling fresco of a goat's behind!). Bedrooms are spacious and have breathtaking views, particularly those in the South Wing. Two come with vast marble baths, one with a wood-burning stove you have to stoke... all have high ceilings, old polished floors, fine white towels – great sober spaces in which nothing jars, just right for a castle. Stroll the small streets of the castle hamlet, hop in the car to Sarzana, catch the train to the sea. Return to a delicious (menu-free) dinner as you gaze on the setting sun. *Resident artists/writers in summer.*

Price	€80-€150.
Rooms	7: 5 twins/doubles; 2 twins/doubles each with separate bath.
Meals	Restaurant 50m.
Closed	November-April.
Directions	Sent on booking.

Pietro Torrigiani Malaspina
Via Papiriana 2,
54035 Massa-Carrara

Tel	+39 0187 680013
Mobile	+39 339 8894423
Email	info@castellodifosdinovo.it
Web	www.castellodifosdinovo.it

 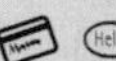   

Albergo Villa Marta

The travel book-strewn table in reception, crafted from an Indonesian bed, sets the mood: very elegant, not stuffy. The villa-hotel is the creation of the young Martinellis who personally welcome you and attend to your every whim… a Tuscan Christmas? A wine and chocolate tour? All can be arranged. With two flights of steps leading to an entrance on either side, the elegant, loftily positioned 19th-century villa stands in sweeping lawns enfolded by the Monti Pisani, from whose verdant hills you can spot Pisa's leaning tower. The whole feel is intimate yet there's masses of space, and a terrace for spring and summer wafted by magnolias, jasmine and pines. Bedrooms ooze subtlety and comfort: fabrics with flowers and stripes, peach and grey walls, modern art. Bed linen is delicious, walk-in showers luxurious, views bucolic. Return after a day in Lucca (catch the bus) to cocktails in the garden and a dip in the pool. The chef gives an international twist to her delicious Tuscan dishes, and in winter you breakfast by an open fire, on breads and brioche straight from the oven. Gorgeous.

Price	€99-€330. Singles €79-€330.
Rooms	15: 8 twins/doubles. Annexe: 7 twins/doubles.
Meals	Menu à la carte, €28-€40. Wine €20-€80.
Closed	January.
Directions	A11 Firenze-Mare exit Lucca Est; signs for Pisa onto SS12; signs to Albergo Villa Marta; after 250m, left into Via del Ponte Guasperini; entrance 500m on left. Can be tricky; ask for detailed directions on booking.

Andrea Martinelli
Via del Ponte Guasperini 873,
San Lorenzo a Vaccoli, 55100 Lucca

Tel	+39 0583 370101
Email	info@albergovillamarta.it
Web	www.albergovillamarta.it

Albergo San Martino

What a position: in a secluded corner of Lucca, a minute from bars, restaurants and ramparts. There's a fresh-faced enthusiasm about the little San Martino now that the young Morottis have taken over; smiling faces behind reception and breakfasts that shine. Expect cheese and salami platters, baskets of different breads, homemade cakes, yogurts and fresh fruits every day – enjoyed in the courtyard in summer. No architectural flourishes, no rushes to the head – just a simple, comfortable, family-run hotel in one of Italy's loveliest towns. Gone are the fitted carpets, new are the wooden floors. The traditionally furnished, uncluttered bedrooms have creamy silk-like curtains and soft coloured walls, cute shuttered windows and interesting paintings, refurbished bathrooms, the odd fresco. Two new suites in the adjoining building have hydromassage baths and showers and Room 108 gets its own terrace, but all of them will please you. The Duomo is a stroll, there's a concert in San Giovanni every night, and bike rental – for Lucca's cycle-friendly walls – is nearby. *Private car park €15.*

Price	€80-€110. Suites €130-€170.
Rooms	11: 9 doubles, 2 suites. Some rooms interconnect.
Meals	Breakfast €10. Special price for guests at osteria, 500m.
Closed	Rarely.
Directions	In the Old Town next to cathedral. Ask for directions. Parking 100m; €15 per day.

Andrea Morotti
Via della Dogana 9,
55100 Lucca

Tel	+39 0583 469181
Email	info@albergosanmartino.it
Web	www.albergosanmartino.it

Da Elisa alle Sette Arti

Some cities are to be escaped – for cooler breezes, respite from the crowds. Lucca isn't like that. More serene than its Tuscan cousins, it is one of the most beguiling medieval cities in Europe, and it is the locals, not the tourists, who set the pace. The elegant shop fronts – dark wood, gold lettering, sparkling glass – are piled high with cheeses, bread, wines; and the entire city is encircled by a wide city wall along which you may cycle or walk! Da Elisa sits within the embrace of the walls, like a little youth hostel for grown ups (good beds, some flourishes in the décor); a rare place. The big wooden door off the street opens to an unprepossessing staircase; then through a little hall are six rooms and a shared kitchen – a blessing for those on a budget. A note says 'help yourself to supplies and leave something for others, too'. Breakfast is DIY: nip up to the bakery while the coffee brews. It's frill-free, functional and could do with a spruce-up, but good prices and delightful staff make up for these shortcomings. Note their second building is a 600m walk from reception; you may need a cab. *Free WiFi.*

Price	€45-€70.
Rooms	10: 4 doubles; 6 doubles sharing 3 bathrooms.
Meals	Breakfast €6. Restaurants within walking distance.
Closed	Never.
Directions	Follow signs to train station, around walls; after 1st bend, through Porta Elisa gate; on for 50m.

Andrea Mencaroni
Via Elisa 25,
55100 Lucca

Tel +39 0583 494539
Email info@daelisa.com
Web www.daelisa.com

Fattoria Mansi Bernardini

Extra virgin olive oil is pressed from the groves that clothe this ancient estate in rural Lucca, and a cluster of vines produce DOC wine. It doesn't get much more Mediterranean than this: a hamlet of farmhouses immersed in gardens, all stone walls and steps, climbing vines and nodding roses. It's a bucolic scene that could come straight from an easel – indeed, you may meet an artist or two, sketching in the shade of the big magnolia, finding inspiration in the hills around. Generations of the Bernardini family have lived and loved this place; we were equally enamoured. There's B&B in the cottages of Il Borghetto – you skip across to the greenhouse for breakfast – and self-catering in the big 'villas' (one the old farm manager's house, another the hayloft). All have been beautifully renovated in a palette of Tuscan colours. Original stonework, cotto floors and beams are softly illuminated, kitchens are fitted, each house has its pool and garden and there's maid service most days. The owner lives in the main villa; Monica runs the office. A taste of Italy you thought no longer existed: elegance, comfort and peace.

Price	€110-€150. Villas €1,000-€6,000 per week.
Rooms	15 + 5: 8 doubles, 3 twins, 4 suites. 5 villas for 8-14.
Meals	Dinner €30, on request. Wine €6-€10. Restaurant 5km.
Closed	Rarely.
Directions	A11 exit Capannori for Capannori/Porcari, then Porcari/Bagni di Lucca; 500m with Esselunga on right, r'bout dir. Pescia/ Bagni di Lucca; 2.4km signed Lunata; 200m, Via Pesciatina. Right for Pescia; 600m to lights; yellow sign for Villa Mansi.

Marcello Salom
55018 Lucca

Tel +39 0583 921721
Email info@fattoriamansibernardini.it
Web www.fattoriamansibernardini.com

Villa Michaela

A lifetime's treat. Writers, celebrities and a First Lady have all stayed here, in the opulent Tuscan villa with its *House & Garden* interiors. You can even make it your own: indulge family and friends and get married in its chapel. It's beautiful throughout the seasons here. Come for a few days, join a Slow Food house party, sample local wines, listen to opera. An interior designer has worked his magic on every room, mingling fine English furniture with classic Italian style, while Puccini, Verdi and Dante lend their names to the grander bedrooms, awash with frescoed ceilings, lavish fabrics, king-size beds and double sinks. Also: a family kitchen, a formal dining room, a library and a multimedia room, tennis and an outdoor pool. Dine al fresco, on divine Tuscan cuisine, and let your gaze drift over the floodlit gardens, heady with gardenias, to the 50 acres of pine forests and olive groves beyond. You are bathed in tranquillity yet it's a five-minute walk to the delightful village of Vorno, and unspoilt Lucca is a ten-minute drive. *Coach house for six occasionally available. Minimum two nights. Personal driver and/or cook available by arrangement.*

Price	€200-€300. Whole villa & wedding chapel on request.
Rooms	15 suites.
Meals	Lunch/dinner by arrangement. Restaurant within walking distance. Other restaurants few minutes' drive.
Closed	Never.
Directions	SS12 from Lucca to Guamo. Follow signs for Vorno; villa behind church.

Vanessa Swarbreck
Via di Valle 8, 55060 Vorno

Tel	+39 0583 971112
Mobile	+44 (0)7768 645500
Email	vanessaswarbreck@yahoo.co.uk
Web	www.villamichaela.com

Fattoria di Pietrabuona

Drink in gulpfuls of mountain fresh air in the foothills of the Svizzera Pesciatina – Tuscany's 'Little Switzerland'. Home to a beguiling brood of ancient breed Cinta Senese pigs, this huge estate immersed in greenery is presided over by elegant, bubbly Signora – an unlikely pig farmer. The farm buildings have been cleverly divided into apartments that fit together like a puzzle; we like the three oldest best, near the main villa, each very private. The rest – near the pool – are quite a drive up winding roads, precipitous in parts: not for the faint-hearted nor heavily-laden hire cars! All have gardens, barbecues and outside seating. The exteriors are full of character, the interiors are simple, and some of the newer have steep stairs. Help with the harvests, bring a Tuscan cookbook: the kitchens, with old sinks but with new everything else, beg to be used, and there's a lovely shop next to the office selling their delicious vin santo and Cinta Senese sauce. The views are stunning – particularly from the pool – and the villages are worth a good wander. *Ask about the Italian frisbee/golf phenomenon, Disc Golf.*

Price	€400-€1,400 per week. Minimum 2 nights.
Rooms	13 apartments: 4 for 2, 4 for 4, 4 for 6, 1 for 8.
Meals	Breakfast €7. Restaurants 1km.
Closed	Never.
Directions	Exit A11 at Chiesina Uzzanese towards Pescia, then Abetone & Pietrabuona. After P. left for Medicina; left again. After 500m road becomes an avenue of cypresses. Villa & Fattoria at end.

Maristella Galeotti Flori
Via per Medicina 2, Pietrabuona,
51017 Pescia

Tel	+39 0572 408115
Email	info@pietrabuona.com
Web	www.pietrabuona.com

Villa Sermolli

Country lanes from Borgo Buggiano ferry you up to the castle and borgo of Buggiano – still inhabited by locals – and the entrance to this 16th-century palace. It's the loveliest place, aglow with light and space, a villa with 18th-century frescoed ceilings, and Martin and Francesca are renovating in style. There are five terraces, four kitchens, two living rooms, 12 bedrooms, a library with a bar, winding little staircases, wrought-iron railings, chunky beams and arches in brick and stone. The interiors are labyrinthine and getting lost the only downside we can see! The main kitchen is huge, with a Tuscan fireplace and a pizza oven down below, bathrooms are marble vintage or luxy new, bedrooms are lavish. Enchanting too are the gardens, all wisteria and vines, oranges and lemons, wrought-iron railings and antique urns, fountains, palm trees, terraces, pool and long lovely views to Monticatini. Take it all on for a big occasion – the 'limonaia' would be heaven for weddings... or rent an apartment or two. Seriously special all year round, and gourmet wine tasting tours, too. *Shuttle service to Pisa & Florence airports.*

Price	House €4,000-€6,500. Apts €750-€1,200. Prices per week.
Rooms	House for 15 (6 doubles, 1 twin, 1 single). 3 apartments for up to 13.
Meals	Breakfast, lunch & dinner on request, €10-€30. Restaurant 5-minute walk.
Closed	Rarely.
Directions	A11 (Pisa-Firenze) exit Chiesina Uzzanese. Follow signs to Borgo a Buggiano. Thro' town, follow signs to Buggiano Castello.

Martin Pleiner
Via Umberto I, 2-8,
51010 Buggiano Castello

Mobile +39 348 3220293
Email martin.pleiner@gmx.net

Antica Casa "Le Rondini"

Imagine a room above an archway in an ancient hilltop village, within ancient castle walls. You lean from the window and watch the swallows dart to and fro; there are *rondini* inside too, captured in a 200-year-old fresco. The way through the arch – the via del Vento ('where the wind blows') – and the front door to this captivating house await just the other side. Step into a lovely room, a study in white – fresh lilies and snowy walls and sofas – dotted with family antiques and paintings. Fulvia and Carlo are warm, interesting hosts who have lovingly restored the house to its original splendour. The delightfully different bedrooms have wrought-iron bedheads, big mirrors and some original stencilling. Several, like the Swallow Room, have pale frescoes. All have good views. The little apartment, too, is simple, charming, peaceful. Just across the cobbled street is a walled garden with lemon trees – an idyllic place for breakfast on sunny mornings. A short walk brings you to the square where village ladies sit playing cards, children scamper and the church bell rings every hour, on the hour.

Price	€75-€130. Apartment €65 for 2. Breakfast not included.
Rooms	5 + 1: 5 doubles. Apartment for 2-4.
Meals	Restaurant 200m.
Closed	Rarely.
Directions	A11 Firenze-Pisa Nord. Exit Montecatini Terme. Follow signs to Pescia. Left after 2nd lights, right after petrol station. Follow sign "Colle-Buggiano". Up hill to parking area.

Fulvia Musso
Via M. Pierucci 21,
51011 Colle di Buggiano

Tel	+39 0572 33313
Email	info@anticacasa.it
Web	www.anticacasa.it

Tenuta di Pieve a Celle

Fiorenza welcomes you with coffee and homemade cake, Julie – the retriever – escorts you round the garden, and there are freshly-laid eggs for breakfast. This is pure, genuine hospitality. Off a country road and down a cypress-lined drive, the shuttered, ochre-coloured *colonica* sits amid the family farm's olive groves and vineyards. The Saccentis (three generations) live next door but this house feels very much like home. Bedrooms (one downstairs) are furnished with well-loved antiques, rugs on tiled floors and handsome wrought-iron or upholstered beds. Cesare, Fiorenza's husband, designed the fabrics – pretty country motifs – and his collection of African art is dotted around the rooms. Books, flowers, soft lighting give a warm and restful feel. There's an elegant but cosy sitting room, with fireplace, where you eat breakfast if it's too chilly on the patio, and dinner – delicious – is by request. Sometimes the Saccentis join you: a real family affair. Laze by the pool with views to distant hills, walk in the woods, borrow bikes or visit nearby Lucca.

Price	€140-€160.
Rooms	5 twins/doubles.
Meals	Dinner €30, by arrangement. Wine €10-€25. Restaurant 200m.
Closed	Rarely.
Directions	A11 for Pisa Nord. Exit Pistoia; signs for Pistoia Ovest to Montagnana; 2km, Tenuta on right. Ring bell at gates.

Ethical Collection: Food.
See page 419 for details.

Cesare & Fiorenza Saccenti
Via di Pieve a Celle 158,
51030 Pistoia

Tel +39 0573 913087
Email info@tenutadipieveacelle.it
Web www.tenutadipieveacelle.it

Villa de' Fiori

With its formal rose gardens, immaculate lawns and neat box-hedged gravel paths, Villa de' Fiori lives up to its name. Pass through impressive gates and follow the cypress-lined drive to the main house, a renovated, 17th-century confection of peach and white with smart green shutters, a loggia for candlelit dining with live music in the evenings, terraces and, hidden beyond a high hedge, a pool with sophisticated white sun umbrellas, fringed with orange trees. Modernistic awnings provide cover for al fresco dining on the lawns. Inside, simple, uncluttered décor justifies the agriturismo status: vaulted sitting rooms, a music room, original geometric tiles, paintings, good solid furniture, high windows and massive fireplaces. There are six bedrooms in the main house, two of which are large, child-proof family suites. The excellent restaurant is host to a dining club; yoga, ayurvedic treatments and Polynesian massage complete your relaxation; and the olive groves, woodland and vineyards are perfect for exploring – for child and adult alike. Gabriele merrily oversees this lovely, lively place.

Ethical Collection: Food.
See page 419 for details.

Price	€102-€152. Apartments €90-€165. Half-board extra €22 p.p.
Rooms	7 + 1: 5 doubles, 2 family rooms. 1 apt for 3-5.
Meals	Dinner €20-€60. Wine €12-€150. Restaurant open to public.
Closed	January-March closed during the week.
Directions	A11 exit Pistoia, 2nd exit at r'bout; through two sets of lights. 2nd exit at next r'bout; past industrial estate. Right at end of road; signed.

Gabriele Prosperi
Via Bigiano e Castel Bovani 39,
51100 Pistoia

Tel +39 0573 450351
Email info@villadefiori.it
Web www.villadefiori.it

Villa Anna Maria

The wrought-iron gates swing open to reveal a strange and atmospheric haven. You feel protected here from the outside world, miles from the heat and bustle of Pisa. It is an intriguing place. Secret rooms lurk behind locked doors; some bedrooms seem untouched since the 17th century. They are all different, themed and with high ceilings, the most curious being the Persian and the Egyptian. The entrance hall is decked in marble, graced with columns and chandeliers; the library – a touch over the top for some – is nevertheless in tune with the rest, and in tune, it must be said, with its eccentric owner. Claudio and his wife collect anything and everything and rooms are crammed with curios and collectibles. Yes, it's shambolic – but your host cares more about people than about money and there are no rules, so treat it as your home. There's a game room with billiards and videos (3,000 of them), table tennis, a garden with tall palms and woodland paths, a pool with piped music issuing from clumps of bamboo, a barbecue area for those who choose to self-cater, and a romping dog. *Minimum stay two nights.*

Price	€120-€150. Singles €90. Apartments €800-€2,000 per week. Cottage €1,000 per week.
Rooms	6 + 1: 6 doubles/triples (or 2 apartments for 2-8). Cottage for 2-3.
Meals	Dinner with wine, €40.
Closed	Rarely.
Directions	From Pisa SS12 for Lucca. At S. Giuliano Terme, SS12 left down hill; after Rigoli to Molina di Quosa. On right opposite pharmacy.

Claudio Zeppi
SS dell'Abetone 146,
56010 Molina di Quosa

Mobile	+39 328 2334450
Email	zeppi@villaannamaria.com
Web	www.villaannamaria.com

Agriturismo Fattoria di Migliarino

On 3,000 farmed hectares between the Alps and the sea is a gated agriturismo run on well-oiled wheels. This is due to the indefatigable energy of Martino and Giovanna, a couple who understand families – they have four children themselves. The B&B rooms are in the main house, all great sizes, all different: Tuscan beds, soft wall lights and prints, mosquito-proofed windows, big arched sitting areas. There's a lovely communal sitting room with plenty of sofas, and a raftered dining room with two sociable tables. In the buildings beyond are 13 two-storey apartments of every shape and size, with terraces divided by hedges of jasmine so you may be as private or as sociable as you like. There's a pool open from June to September, fringed by neatly gravelled pathways and lawned spaces with sunloungers. On the Pisa road are restaurants, their farm shop – turkey, game, wine, vegetables, olive oil – and a well-being centre brimming with treatments. Football, tennis and ping-pong are on tap, riding and sailing can be arranged, and the sandy beaches are a bike ride away. *Call ahead for access code to entrance gates.*

Price	€100-€130. Apartments €380-€1,900 per week.
Rooms	10 + 13: 10 doubles. 13 apartments for 2-10.
Meals	Breakfast €5 for self-caterers. Agriturismo's taverna 200m. Dinner (min. 15 people) on request.
Closed	Never.
Directions	Exit A11-A12 Pisa Nord, left for Pisa; 1st lights right under r'way bridge to Viale dei Pini. Left after 800m; in Via del Mare.

Martino & Giovanna Salviati
Viale del Mare 2,
56010 Migliarino

Tel	+39 335 6608411
Mobile	+39 348 4435100
Email	info@fattoriadimigliarino.it
Web	www.fattoriadimigliarino.it

Tenuta Poggio al Casone

You won't forget your first sight of this Tuscan villa, standing alone on top of the world. Alone but for the vast vineyards it oversees; this is wine country and the Castellani family have been in the business since Dante's time. The current generation cultivate organic Chianti and now they've transformed the villa and two cottages into supremely elegant apartments. These would not look out of place in an Italian design show, so sophisticated is their décor, so generous their space. Some apartments have mezzanine levels, others attics or terraces; yet others have jacuzzis and four-posters. The rooms are dressed in gorgeous fabrics and shades of soft ivory and latte, enlivened by splashes of aqua and Tuscan red. If the interiors are finely tuned, the views are utterly untouched. From organising wine tours and tastings to lake fishing and mountain biking, Michela and her team take care of you with consummate professionalism. Swim in the pool, fire up the barbecue, visit Pisa and the Etruscan coast. Fresh, stylish, memorable – a huge treat. *Minimum stay one week in high season.*

Price	€700-€2,900 per week.
Rooms	9 apartments: 3 for 2, 2 for 3, 2 for 4, 1 for 5, 1 for 6-8.
Meals	Breakfast €15. Restaurant 400m.
Closed	Rarely.
Directions	A1 exit Scandicci then m'way FI-PI-LI dir. Livorno exit Lavoria. Follows signs for Cenaia centre; thro' village for 2km until Quattro Strade, right at lights dir. Crespina. House after 500m on left, big gates.

Famiglia Castellani
Via Volpaia 16,
56042 Crespina

Tel	+39 0506 42259
Email	resort@poggioalcasone.com
Web	www.poggioalcasone.com

Antica Dimora Leones

A labyrinth of vaulted ceilings, stone fireplaces and original frescoes in the heart of the medieval *borgo* of Palaia. The palazzo was restored in the 1800s but goes way back to AD1000, when it formed part of the castle. Now it is an antique collector's paradise – which is no surprise: the owner's grandparents were antique dealers. It almost feels as though they are still here, wandering the historic corridors and rooms. Specialness is everywhere, from the high frescoed ceilings of the 'noble floor' to the bare beams and rooftop views of the characterful servants' quarters. Every floor (the lift is for luggage only) has a wonderful sitting room or library, with books, comfy chairs and something precious in each corner. A tray of drinks awaits your arrival; the buffet breakfast (salami, cheeses, homemade cakes) is served in the beamed dining room or under wisteria in the pretty garden. So much history, yet there are some winning modern touches – notably the seven-person hydropool. Restorative, soothing, special – head out to discover Tuscany and don't miss the lovely Etruscan town of Volterra. *Ask about parking.*

Price	€95-€120.
Rooms	10: 9 doubles, 1 single.
Meals	Lunch or dinner with wine, €35, on request (small groups only). Restaurant 100m.
Closed	Rarely.
Directions	Superstrada Firenze-Pisa-Livorno, exit Pontedera, follow signs for Palaia centre. Just beyond clock tower on the corner.

Andrea Soldani
Via della Rocca 2,
56036 Palaia

Tel +39 0587 622024
Email info@leones-palaia.it
Web www.leones-palaia.it

Castello Ginori di Querceto

Here's something for families who want the Tuscan sun but don't want to spend the earth. Querceto is a hamlet, a rambling medieval *borgo* on many levels, whose nucleus is a castle around which workers' cottages have evolved (and in the family since 1543!). Leave the car outside the walls and enter a timewarp; the Liscis may own 15 hectares of vineyards and produce a number of important red wines but no-one is in a hurry here. The apartments too will charm you: a clean plain décor in a rustic style, comfort without the frills. There are bright tartan cotton bedspreads, dark shutters to keep out the light, resuscitated floor tiles and nice old doors, simple kitchens with copper pans; the farmhouse sleeping eight (set apart with a small private pool) is brilliant value. The restaurant in the village sells fresh pasta and milk, fruit and vegetables, a bread van calls three times a week and the wine is on the spot. The grounds (not the gardens) are yours to roam, picnic spots are close and the big swimming pool is down the steep track, surrounded by olive trees. *Not all bathrooms are en suite.*

Price	Apartments €400-€750. House €740-1,220. Farmhouse €1,050-€1,900. Prices per week. Min. 2-7 nights.
Rooms	5 apartments for 2-4. 2 houses for 6. Farmhouse for 8.
Meals	Restaurants within walking distance.
Closed	January-February.
Directions	Exit A12 Rosignano; SS1 (via Aurelia) exit Cecina. Signs for Volterra & Ponteginori. In Ponteginori, right, over railway & River Cecina bridge. At end of road, signed.

Cristina Sannazzaro
Loc. Querceto,
56040 Montecatini Val di Cecina

Tel	+39 0588 37472
Mobile	+39 335 5405006
Email	info@castelloginoridiquerceto.it
Web	www.castelloginoridiquerceto.it

Locanda Senio

Food is king here, slow food: genuine home cooking with home-grown fruit and veg from Roberta and, in the restaurant, much gastronomic lore from Ercole. Echoing the movement to revive lost medieval traditions, they are passionate about wild herbs and 'forgotten' fruits. Take a cookery course (included if you stay three nights). The prosciutto from rare-breed *maiale medievale* is delicious; breakfast is a feast of homemade delights; dinner a leisurely treat served in the cosy little log-fired restaurant. The inn (*albergo diffuso*) occupies a stunning spot in a quiet town in the Mugello valley, surrounded by rolling hills... there are guided walks through the woods, gastronomic meanders through the valley. Bedrooms are comfortable and pretty with country antiques – but lash out on a suite if you can; they're in the 17th-century building with original fireplaces. Roberta and Ercole are very proud of their wellbeing centre, too – the jacuzzi, sauna and Turkish bath have a delicious, calming aroma. Steps lead up to a pool with an amazing view; body and soul are nurtured; walkers are in heaven. Special indeed.

Price	€115-€200. Suites €190-€230. Half-board €100-€145 p.p.
Rooms	8: 6 twins/doubles, 2 suites for 2-3.
Meals	Dinner from €35. Wine from €10.
Closed	6 January-13 February.
Directions	From Bologna A14, exit Imola for Rimini; 50m; for Palazzuolo (40 mins). House in village, right of fountain & Oratorio dei Santi Carlo e Antonio.

Ercole & Roberta Lega
Via Borgo dell'Ore 1,
50035 Palazzuolo sul Senio

Tel	+39 0558 046019
Email	info@locandasenio.com
Web	www.locandasenio.com

Le Due Volpi

Twenty miles from Florence, yet utterly unspoilt: the gentle hills of the Mugello valley have escaped development and the drive from Borgo is truly lovely. At the end of a long white track is a big house strewn with ivy; outside two snazzy little foxes – 'le due volpi', – splash water into a trough. Step into spaciousness and light and a charming Tuscan interior. Heidi is Italian, well-travelled and speaks perfect English; Lorenzo has a passion for old radios and antiques. They are naturals at looking after guests, love cooking on their Aga, dispatch meals to the loggia in summer and are embarking on a greener lifestyle, introducing solar panels and wood-fired central heating. The bedrooms, with their wooden floors and chunky rafters, couldn't be nicer. Beds are large and lighting soft, wood-burners keep you cosy in winter, Chini-tiled shower rooms have a stylish rusticity. Note that the two top-floor rooms are reached via several stairs. Vicchio, full of history, is a ten-minute drive and there's a riding stables down the road. Bliss. *Minimum stay two nights.*

Price	€80-€95. Extra bed €20-€30.
Rooms	4: 3 doubles (one with kitchenette), 1 twin.
Meals	Picnic with wine, €15. Dinner, from €25. Restaurant 3km.
Closed	Rarely.
Directions	A1 exit Barberino; SS551 to Vicchio. From town square, Molezzano/Caselle road. 2km after Caselle, over bridge; at x-roads, right up track signed Villa Poggio Bartoli for 900m; cypress trees on right.

Heidi Flores & Lorenzo Balloni
Via di Molezzano 88,
50039 Vicchio

Tel	+39 0558 407874
Mobile	+39 338 6220160
Email	info@leduevolpi.it
Web	www.leduevolpi.it

Agriturismo Fattoria I Ricci

Down winding Tuscan lanes with perfect Tuscan views, through wrought-iron gates that glide open to greet you, you enter a courtyard 'twixt an old mill and a 16th-century villa. Discover majestic cedars in the garden, a spacious pool surrounded by lawns, smartly furnished patios scattered here and there and the Cecchinis' olive groves beyond: the first impression is wonderful. And then there's Caterina, who looks after you all with her big open smile. Welcome to self-catering with a difference: breakfast, served at large tables beneath chunky beams, is included in the price, and lunches and dinners are on request (gluten-free if you wish). All feels genuine, friendly and family-run, with two generations living in the main villa and the old mill beautifully renovated: guest apartments above, dining areas below. The apartments are Italian traditional, each individual and pleasing, with pretty curtains and peaceful colours, each as neat as a new pin. La Cascina, a Hansel & Gretel cottage in the garden, is the choice of romantics – and free bikes for guests are a boon.

Price	€400-€1,260. Whole house €3,200-€3,700. Prices per week.
Rooms	3 apartments: 1 for 2, 1 for 4-5, 1 for 4-6. Cottage for 2. Whole house available (sleeps 12-15).
Meals	Breakfast included. Lunch & dinner €35, on request. Restaurants 4km.
Closed	Rarely.
Directions	A1 exit Barberino di Mugello; dir. Borgo San Lorenzo, then Vicchio. After 1.5km, left to Rostolena. House 4km on right.

Caterina Cecchini
Via Rostolena 14,
50039 Vicchio

Tel	+39 0558 44784
Mobile	+39 347 7920638
Email	info@fattoriairicci.it
Web	www.fattoriairicci.com

Il Fienile di Scarperia

Scarperia is famous for its Mugello race track and colourful festivals, but Il Fienile (the Haybarn) is tucked over the hill in a quiet pocket of Tuscan countryside. Here is Italian family life at its most genuine and welcoming. Francesca brims with enthusiasm for the corn-yellow stone house and neat gardens which she, Paris, their two young children (and fluffy little dog) share happily with guests. There are just two cosy chunky-beamed guest rooms here; one tinged in dusky pink with shuttered windows and fancy new shower; the other smaller but just as homely, with a claw-foot bath. Like many in this foodie region, Francesca loves to cook. Tuck into dinner by a roaring fire in a vaulted country kitchen hung with Tuscan crockery; on summer mornings, taste grandma's jams out on the garden terrace. Beyond the rustic wooden fence lie rolling hills, bike trails, a sailing lake, championship golf course and horse riding ranch; Francesca will help with maps and bookings. A short stroll takes you to town and a bus whisks you south: you can be in Florence in 40 minutes. A genuine, family-run B&B.

Price	€75-€95.
Rooms	2: 1 twin/double; 1 twin/double with separate bath.
Meals	Dinner with wine, €25.
Closed	Never.
Directions	A1 exit Barberino di Mugello dir. Scarperia. After 1st r'bout, signs for Autodromo/Sant'Agata. At 2nd r'bout cont. to Autodromo/Firenzuola. 2nd white road on left, Via della Resistenza; 300m, last house on left.

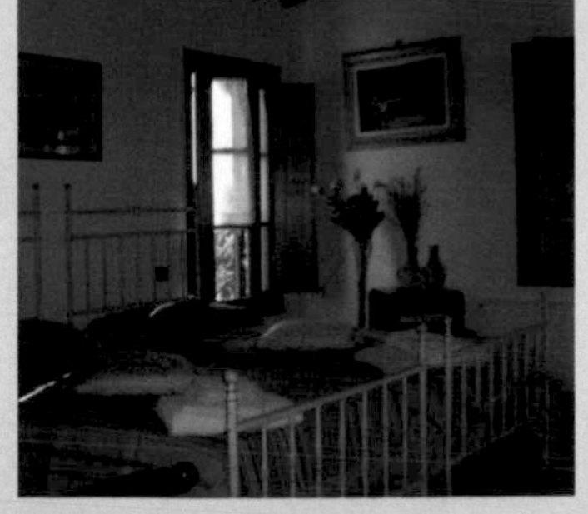

Francesca Parigi
Via della Resistenza, 15/F,
50038 Scarperia

Tel	+39 0558 430578
Email	info@ilfienilediscarperia.it
Web	www.ilfienilediscarperia.it

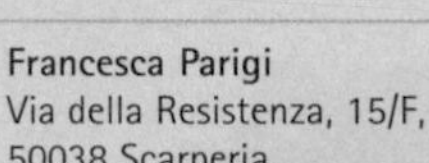

Podere Capitignano

Welcome to the Mugello Valley! Up a country lane, at the end of a cypress-lined drive, is a peaceful Tuscan farmstead with far-reaching views over the Apennines. A farmhouse and outbuildings make up this neat and tidy complex – much-loved and sympathetically restored. Let the caretakers settle you in – or the owners, generous, energetic and in residence part-time. With its 400 olive trees and small vineyard, Capitignano feels like a farm, with the added luxuries of tennis court and pool. Fienele, a converted old hay barn, makes a roomy holiday home, with its big friendly living room and French windows to two terraces; there's an art studio above. If you're a big party the Fattoria is for you, all exposed beams and vaulted ceiling, smart kitchen, large terrace and private courtyard. La Stalla, an old stable, is bright and spacious and sleeps up to five; la Casetta is a neat stone cottage on a hill, with terraces front and back, a charming bolthole for two. There's a library with WiFi, DVDs and open fires for all. So much to see and do – and a train nearby that whisks you to Florence in half an hour.

Price €420-€1,520.
Rooms 5 houses: 1 for 2-3, 3 for 2-5, 1 for 6-9.
Meals Restaurant 4km.
Closed Never.
Directions Sent on booking.

Lynn Fleming Aeschliman
Via San Cresci 48,
50032 Borgo San Lorenzo
Tel +39 0558 495600
Mobile +41 (0)792 004222
Email lfa@tasis-schools.org
Web www.capitignano.org

La Campanella

The big gates are a welcoming sight after the steep crawl up the unmade road, and the views across the valley and the breezes are a joy. The delightful Jill will soon have you seated in her farmhouse kitchen (or under the parasol on the patio): a glass of homemade lemonade, a slice of something sweet; you can't help but feel there's nowhere else you'd rather be. The airy sitting room has high ceiling arches interrupted by the odd beam, and deep sills; white walls are busy with paintings, puffed-up white sofas sit under mounds of cushions, fresh flowers rest on polished tables; there's more than just a touch of Englishness about the place. Pretty bedrooms have terracotta floor tiles, patchwork quilts and more views. Children will entertain themselves for hours in the charming garden, on the swing under the mulberry tree or in the pool. Adults may flop into the hammock with a chilled glass of the neighbour's organic wine; the peace is broken only by the faint shuffles of next door's hens. Walk straight into the woods carpeted in spring with orchids, or pop into Borgo, a five-minute drive.

Price	€75-€95.
Rooms	2: 1 twin/double, 1 family suite for 2-4. Cot available.
Meals	Lunch €12. Dinner with wine, €30. Restaurant 500m.
Closed	Rarely.
Directions	A1 exit Barberino di Mugello; signs for Borgo San Lorenzo; SP41 to Sagginale; 1st right into Via di Zeti. Follow track up & fork right; 1st yellow house on right at top.

Ethical Collection: Food.
See page 419 for details.

Jill Greetham
Via Romignano 9, Loc. San Cresci,
50032 Borgo San Lorenzo

Tel	+39 0558 490373
Mobile	+39 333 1923031
Email	info@atuscanplace.com
Web	www.atuscanplace.com

Casa Palmira

A medieval farm expertly restored by charming Assunta and Stefano who, being Italian, have a flair for this sort of thing. You are immersed in greenery yet half an hour from Florentine bustle. The views on the road to Fiesole are stunning; Stefano will ferry you around neighbouring villages in his mini-van, or you could hire mountain bikes and take one of Assunta's wonderful picnic baskets with you. For lazier days, the wonderful pool beckons. The log-fired sitting room sets the tone: the *casa* has a warm, Tuscan feel, and bedrooms open off a landing with a brick-walled 'garden' in the centre – all Stefano's work. Two have four-poster beds dressed in Florentine fabric, all have polished wooden floors and pretty views, either onto the gardens where Assunta grows her herbs and vegetables or onto vines and olive trees. You are 500 metres above sea level so... no need for air conditioning, no mosquitoes! Breakfast on apricots and home-produced yogurt; dine on delicious Tuscan food. There is also an excellent restaurant up the road. *Minimum stay two nights. Ask about cookery classes.*

Price	€85-€115. Single €65-€75. Triple €115-€130. Apt €125-€135 (€700-€850 p.w.).
Rooms	6 + 1: 4 twins/doubles, 1 single, 1 triple. Apt for 3.
Meals	Dinner with wine, €30. Restaurant 700m.
Closed	10 December-10 March.
Directions	Sent on booking.

Assunta & Stefano Fiorini-Mattioli
Via Faentina 4/1,
Loc. Feriolo, Polcanto,
50030 Borgo San Lorenzo

Tel +39 0558 409749
Email info@casapalmira.it
Web www.casapalmira.it

Il Fornaccio

Half way up the hill, high above the Mugnone valley, is this blissful and bucolic spot; you could be miles from anywhere. But no: there's a pizzaria you can walk to and Florence can be glimpsed through the trees. Surrounded by olive orchards and fields, Il Fornaccio (the 'bread oven') is a 16th-century farmhouse whose oak and chestnut beams and terracotta floors have been beautifully restored. Loredana lives here with young daughter Eleonora, loves company (and dogs: meet the elderly German shepherd), gives you private sunbeds and tranquil seating corners and prepares breakfasts of homemade cakes, yogurts, fruits and jams before she leaves for work. Bedrooms feel lived in and loved, one reached via the living room, the other below, with a private kitchenette and a charming courtyard under the spreading linden tree: perfect for families. Both rooms have spectacular views. On cooler days you can share Loredana's books, fire and CDs; in summer you be sitting at the rustic stone table in the refreshing shade of the ancient oak, or plucking cherries and figs from the trees. Lovely.

Price	€80-€120.
Rooms	2: 1 double (+ sofabed for 1), 1 twin (+ sofabed for 2) with kitchenette, both with separate baths.
Meals	Dinner with wine, on request. Restaurant 1km.
Closed	Rarely.
Directions	Sent on booking.

Loredana Pecorella
Via di Campolungo 297/B,
50036 Vaglia

Mobile +39 348 7723629
Email info@ilfornacciofirenze.com
Web www.ilfornacciofirenze.com

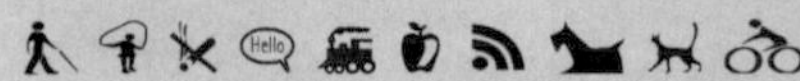

Casa Valiversi

Perched on a hill, painted in pretty pink, this distinctive, distinguished B&B was once, incredibly, a laboratory. Just four rooms – one with a balcony, one with an open fire – and Mirella, warm, friendly and living next door. Tired of commuting to Florence every day, she opened her Casa to guests, popping in to serve generous breakfasts. Inside are 20th-century antiques from her years of dealing, sprinkled over three floors with originality and taste. Armchairs range from cream Thirties Art Deco to Sixties bubblegum pink, bold art beautifies pale walls, a white Fifties lamp dominates the glass dining table, the six dining chairs are immaculately upholstered. Bedrooms are serene spaces that breathe comfort and class and monogrammed linen while big arched windows overlook groves of olives. For self-caterers, the kitchen is fitted in contemporary style (plus one perfect antique cupboard from France), opening to the lovely garden, rose-climbed pergola and large terrace. Here in the hillsides of Sesto Fiorentino, five miles from Florence's centre, is a relaxing, refreshing and peaceful place to stay. *Airport 3km.*

Price	B&B €100-€120. Whole house €3,000-€5,000 per week.
Rooms	4 twins/doubles.
Meals	Use of kitchen €10. Restaurants 1km.
Closed	Never.
Directions	A1 exit Sesto Fiorentino for Centro & Colonnata; signed. Ring for further directions.

Mirella Mazzierli
Via Valiversi 61,
50019 Sesto Fiorentino

Tel +39 0553 850285
Email mirella@casavaliversi.it
Web www.casavaliversi.it

Casa Howard Guest Houses – Florence & Rome

A five-minute walk from the bus and railway station is this handsome palazzo, the talk of the town. No reception staff, no communal space, just a big fur throw on a welcoming divan and smiling housekeepers who bring breakfast to your room. On each floor an honesty fridge carries soft drinks, wine and champagne. Best of all are the bedrooms. Eclectic, original and humorous, they have great elegance. If you can splash out on a larger, more lavish room, do, though all are delightful. One, with a sunken bath and Japanese prints on the walls, is a deep sensual red; another is 18th-century elegant with a black velvet sofa and gold taffeta curtains. The apartment, its queen-size bed at the top of a spiral stair, is ultra-modern. There's a room specially for those who arrive with their pooches (dogs' beds, baskets, large terrace), and another, the Play Room, for families (Disney videos, a climbing wall!). Bathrooms are memorable; nights are air-conditioned and peaceful, providing you keep windows shut. A breath of fresh air, and decent value for the heart of old Florence. *Minimum two nights at weekends in high season.*

Price	€120-€250. Apartment €1,500-€2,200 per week.
Rooms	12 + 1: 10 doubles, 2 suites. Apartment for 2-3.
Meals	Breakfast €12. Restaurants nearby.
Closed	Never.
Directions	50m from Santa Maria Novella train station.

Via della Scala 18, 50123 Florence

Tel	+39 0669 924555
Email	info@casahoward.it
Web	www.casahoward.com

Palazzo Niccolini al Duomo

One minute you're battling with tourists in the Piazza del Duomo, the next you're stepping into a piece of history, this extraordinarily lovely palazzo. Take the lift to the *residenza*; two small trees, a brace of antique chairs and a brass plate announce the friendly reception. Built by the Naldini family in the 16th century on the site of the sculptor Donatello's workshop, the building has steadily grown in grandeur; the recent restoration hasn't detracted from its beauty, merely added some superb facilities. It's all you hope such a place will be – fabulously elegant and luxurious, with 18th-century frescoes, trompe l'œil effects, fine antiques and magnificent beds… but in no way daunting, thanks to many personal touches; your host is a delight. The top suite looks the Duomo in the eye – staggering. Relax in the gracious drawing room with family portraits and books. Two signed photographs were sent in 1895 by the King of Italy to Contessa Cristina Niccolini, the last of the Naldini. She married into the current owner's family, bringing the palazzo as part of her dowry. An exceptional place. *Parking available.*

Price	€150-€380. Singles €150-€220. Suites €300-€500.
Rooms	10: 5 doubles, 5 suites.
Meals	Dinner, by arrangement. Restaurants nearby.
Closed	Never.
Directions	In Florence "centro storico". A1 exit Firenze south; head for town centre & Duomo; Via dei Servi off Piazza del Duomo. Park, unload & car will be taken to garage: €25-€30.

Filippo Niccolini
Via dei Servi 2,
50122 Florence

Tel	+39 0552 82412
Email	info@niccolinidomepalace.com
Web	www.niccolinidomepalace.com

Mr My Resort

Here's something different: a small B&B with a luxurious décor and a theatrical flourish. One room is called Actor, another Diva, all exude glitter and glam. Step off the street into a wonderful courtyard – a sun-dappled surprise with seats, plants, flowers and objets – off which the swish bedrooms lie. There are antique majolicas and evocative lighting, mirrors in abundance, velvet and stucco, big beds and sumptuous cushions, and black lava stone in shower rooms to create a fantastic effect. And history to match – lunatics were once housed in the medieval cloisters below. (Anything less like an asylum is hard to imagine today...). Instead: a fresh, cool and charming little spa with jacuzzi, sauna and hammam. Friendly, cosmopolitan owners Christina and Giuseppe have thought of everything: a sitting area with guidebooks, teas, coffees, WiFi and a fridge at your disposal; breakfast coupons to a stylish café nearby. Outside are fascinating streets to wander while the famous sites are a ten-minute stroll. A refreshing escape from the enticements of Florence. *Minimum stay two nights.*

Price	€95-€170.
Rooms	5: 4 doubles, 1 single.
Meals	Breakfast included (served at Nabucco café). Restaurants within walking distance.
Closed	Rarely.
Directions	10-minute walk from Santa Maria Novella train station. Exit station, Via Nazionale; 7th street on right (Via delle Ruote).

Cristina Gucciarelli
Via delle Ruote 14A,
50100 Florence

Tel +39 0552 83955
Email info@abacusreservations.com
Web www.mrflorence.it

Relais Grand Tour & Grand Tour Suites

Step straight off the street into the 18th-century elegance of Giuseppe and Cristina's home. Your hosts are jolly, enthusiastic (as is Albert, the dog), a mine of information on all things Florentine. The bedrooms – three very large ones on the ground floor overlooking the patio, four doubles on the second floor, all with showers – have traces of the original frescos and are furnished with family paintings and antiques. You're given a breakfast voucher for the Nabucco café-bar down the road (to be used at any time of day), but if you're staying upstairs, you have the option of breakfast, at extra charge, in your room. A charming bonus is an 18th-century theatre attached to the house, a fabulous room with original seats and Neapolitan tiles that Giuseppe and Cristina open to guests for recitals, readings and wine tastings. This is a terrific position in super-central Florence, with the Accademia Museum next door, and the Duomo and the Market of San Lorenzo a five-minute stroll. If you come by car, you'll pay to park, but the station is within walking distance – come by train! *Minimum stay two nights.*

Price	€95-€110. Suites €110-€170.
Rooms	7: 3 doubles, 4 suites.
Meals	Breakfast included (served at Nabucco café). Restaurants within walking distance.
Closed	Never.
Directions	From Santa Maria Novella station onto Via Nazionale, straight on; then turn 4th right, Via Guelfa; 2nd left Via Reparata.Bus No. 1, 11, 16, 22, & 25.

Cristina Gucciarelli
Via Santa Reparata 21,
50129 Florence

Tel	+39 0552 83955
Email	info@abacusreservations.com
Web	www.florencegrandtour.com

Le Stanze di Santa Croce

A great find, this very old 'terratetto', nestled between its neighbours on a small street off the Piazza Santa Croce – perfect for those who want to stay in the historic centre. There's attention to detail at every turn; everything has been thought through beautifully. The four elegant rooms, one with a four-poster, aren't large but are beautifully presented, each named after famous Florentine bells, each with its own refined identity; they provide sanctuary from the heat of the city, while the jasmine-garlanded breakfast terrace is the perfect place from which to enjoy Mariangela's exceptional baking. Your charming host runs her own highly acclaimed Tuscan cookery courses so make sure you book a lesson during your stay. Freshly baked cakes, homemade jams and a variety of teas are in constant supply. There's a cool lobby with comfortable seating and plenty of books, the internet and useful local info on where to go and what to see, and cheery Mariangela is always on hand to tell you more: the best markets, the artisan workshops, the hidden corners. Fresh and inviting.

Price	€145–€160. Ask about prices for singles.
Rooms	4 doubles.
Meals	Restaurant 50m.
Closed	Rarely.
Directions	In historic centre. Detailed directions upon booking.

Ethical Collection: Food.
See page 419 for details.

Mariangela Catalani
Via delle Pinzochere 6,
50122 Florence
Mobile +39 347 2593010
Email info@lestanzedisantacroce.com
Web www.lestanzedisantacroce.com

Residenza Casanuova

Live like a Florentine in the heart of the city, high above the madding crowds. The top floor of this handsome palazzo belonged to Beatrice and Massimiliano's grandmother and is filled with her elegant taste. There are panelled doors and parquet floors, creamy walls and tall windows. Light-filled rooms are furnished with antiques, grand mirrors and pretty chandeliers, polished surfaces are dotted with china vases, walls hung with engravings, portraits and a collection of oils by great-grandfather. Calm, uncluttered bedrooms are soft and spacious, each with an amusing theme: a collection of umbrellas, hats or tin boxes. One has a magnificent Murano mirror. Breakfast on beautiful china in the handsome dining room or on the terrace before plunging into the hubbub of the city's museums, galleries and churches. The owners, with an apartment on the same floor, will help with tours, museums and shopping trips. Friendly and easy-going, they're on hand when you need them or happy to leave you alone. Return to a private terrace for a glass of wine and rooftop views. *Ask about Gelato Lovers tours & tiramisu-making sessions.*

Price	€120-€170.
Rooms	5: 4 doubles, 1 single.
Meals	Restaurants within walking distance.
Closed	Rarely.
Directions	Exit Firenze Sud. Follow directions to city centre & S. Ambrogio market. Bus No. 6, 23, 14 or C2.

Beatrice & Massimiliano Gori
Via della Mattonaia 21,
50121 Florence

Tel	+39 0552 343413
Mobile	+39 338 5450758
Email	info@residenzacasanuova.it
Web	www.residenzacasanuova.it

Antica Dimora Firenze - Antiche Dimore Fiorentine

You'll reach the relaxed *residenza* via the small lift or the wide stone stairs, then come and go as you please – a friendly receptionist is here to welcome you. It's a treat to come back to a decanter of vin santo and a book of love stories by your bed. If it's not a four-poster you'll have a jasmine-scented balcony... Italian love of detail is evidenced by rose-pink and pistachio-green walls, luscious fabrics woven by local artisans, striped sofas, silk curtains and little vases of dried lavender. Black and white 19th-century prints and antique tiled floors combine beautifully with waffle towels and walk-in showers, modems and satellite TV: the best of old and new. Settle down in the sitting room, dip into almond biscuits and a cup of tea and plan where to have dinner; all the info's there. Browse a glossy book or a magazine, choose a DVD, be as private or as sociable as you like. There are homemade cakes and jams at breakfast, you are on a quietish street near the university and it's great value for the centre of Florence. *Ask about special packages.You cannot park in central Florence; ask about garage on booking.*

Price	€90-€150.
Rooms	6: 3 doubles, 3 twins.
Meals	Restaurant 30m.
Closed	Never.
Directions	In Florence "centro storico"; San Marco square, then Via San Gallo. 10-minute walk from train station.

Lea Gulmanelli
Via San Gallo 72,
50129 Florence

Tel +39 0554 627296
Email info@anticadimorafirenze.it
Web www.anticadimorafirenze.it

Residenza Johlea - Antiche Dimore Fiorentine

Discover life in a real Florentine *residenza*... a particularly charming home. The restored, late 19th-century building is in an area well-endowed with musuems (the Museum of San Marco and Michelangelo's David are just around the corner). It has good access to train and bus stations, and Laura, Giovanna or Anna will be there to welcome you. The big bedrooms have long, shuttered windows, subtle colours and lovely fabrics. All are different and all are comfortable, with sofas, polished floors topped with rugs, and super bathrooms; the feel is friendly and cosy. There are antiques and air conditioning, books, a shared fridge – and now a new small breakfast room, or you can enjoy buffet-style breakfast in the seclusion of your own room. There's a well-stocked honesty bar, too, available all day long. Like the rest of Lea's *residenze* (there are four altogether in this book, Antica Dimora Johlea being right next door – see overleaf), this is excellent value considering how close it is to the city centre. *Ask about special packages. You cannot park in central Florence; ask about garage on booking.*

Price	€70-€140. Single €50-€90.
Rooms	8: 2 doubles, 4 twins, 1 single, 1 triple.
Meals	Restaurant 30m.
Closed	Never.
Directions	In Florence "centro storico"; San Marco square, then Via San Gallo. 10-minute walk from train station.

Lea Gulmanelli
Via San Gallo 76,
50129 Florence

Tel	+39 0554 633292
Email	johlea@johanna.it
Web	www.johanna.it

Antica Dimora Johlea - Antiche Dimore Fiorentine

A cross between B&B and hotel – no room service but a friendly face on reception all day – the *residenza* idea is perfect for the independent traveller. Lea Gulmanelli has got her *residenze* down to a fine art and what's special about this one is the roof terrace. Weave your way past antiques tucked under sloping ceilings and up to a wide, sun-flooded, pergola'd space for breakfast and sundowners with a classic panorama of Florence – thrilling at night! The entire top floor of this restored 19th-century palazzo feels bright, light and inviting. Furnishings are colourful and fresh, bedrooms – some lofty, some more intimate – have beautiful silk-canopied four-poster beds, delicate prints on walls and mozzie-protected windows. Luxurious extras include radios, WiFi and satellite TV, there's an honesty bar for drinks and polished tables for breakfast. Romantics could ask for a room with a balcony. Michelangelo's David is at the Accademia round the corner, the Duomo is a ten-minute walk. *Ask about special packages. You cannot park in central Florence; ask about garage on booking.*

Price	€100-€170. Single €75-€120.
Rooms	6: 2 doubles, 2 twins, 1 single, 1 triple.
Meals	Restaurant 30m.
Closed	Never.
Directions	In Florence "centro storico"; San Marco square, then Via San Gallo. 10-minute walk from train station.

Lea Gulmanelli
Via San Gallo 80,
50129 Florence

Tel +39 0554 633292
Email anticajohlea@johanna.it
Web www.johanna.it

Residenza Johanna I - Antiche Dimore Fiorentine

Astonishingly good value in the historic centre of Florence – and what an attractive, friendly place to be. You really feel as though you have your own pad in town, away from tourist bustle. Owner Lea has several other *residenze* (see previous entries). They were such a success that she and Johanna opened this one in a lovely 19th-century palazzo, shared with notaries and an embassy. Take the lift or marble stairs to a big welcome on the second floor from charming people, keen to make your stay a happy one. Graceful arches, parquet floors and soft colours give a feeling of light and space to the two corridors, classical music wafts past and there are plenty of books and guides to browse through. The bedrooms are airy and cool, silk beautifies beds (some four-posters) and give the rooms a feeling of charm and elegance. All have good, stylish bathrooms. There's a new breakfast room, too. Slip out to a bar for a cappuccino before wandering happily off to the Duomo, the San Lorenzo market and the Piazza della Signora. *Ask about special packages. You cannot park in central Florence; ask about garage on booking.*

Price	€71-€140. Single €50-€90.
Rooms	10: 5 doubles, 4 twins, 1 single.
Meals	Restaurants nearby.
Closed	Never.
Directions	In Florence "centro storico"; San Marco square, then Via San Gallo. 10-minute walk from train station.

Signora Ilanit
Via Bonifacio Lupi 14,
50129 Florence

Tel	+39 0554 81896
Email	lupi@johanna.it
Web	www.johanna.it

Relais Villa Antea

A peaceful 1900s villa a 15-minute walk from Piazza San Marco – with parking! Off a leafy residential square, close to restaurants, antique shops, botanic gardens and Russian Orthodox church, is a friendly Italian-family concern, a lovely little find. The Antea is overseen from early morning until 8.30 at night by owner Delitta, her sister Serena and mascot Marta (the Jack Russell); when they go home, Florina takes over. Enjoy continental breakfast with fruits in season – and perhaps homemade 'bombolone' (mini doughnuts) – served at tiny round tables in the elegant dining room. Up the white stone stair are big airy bedrooms with tall windows and timeworn parquet, lavish silken drapes in yellows and greens, net curtains, pristine covers, walk-in wardrobes, posies of plastic flowers. Extras include air con, mini bar, WiFi and a restaurant guide put together by Delitta. Beds are extra-king in size and bathrooms are vast, with hydromassage showers. Through the side gate is a courtyard shaded by horse chestnut trees; a further pebbled courtyard makes a tranquil spot for an aperitivo before a night on the town.

Price	€100-€180.
Rooms	6 doubles.
Meals	Restaurant 2-minute walk.
Closed	Rarely.
Directions	15-minute walk from S. Lorenzo, Accademia or Piazza San Marco. Bus No. 12 from Piazza della Stazione to Via Ruffini.

Dileita Lenzi
Via Puccinotti 46,
50129 Florence

Tel +39 0554 84106
Email info@villaantea.com
Web www.villaantea.com

Villa La Sosta

It's a five-minute bus ride to the Duomo, yet the 1892 villa on the Montughi hill stands in large landscaped gardens where songbirds lull you to sleep. The mansard-tower sitting room with sofas, books and views is a lofty place in which to relax, and there's billiards. Bedrooms, with large windows and wooden shutters, are equally stylish with striking toile de Jouy or checks and dark Tuscan pieces. Interesting, too, are the artefacts – wooden statues and innumerable ivory carvings – gathered from the Fantonis' days in Africa; the family ran a banana plantation there. Simple breakfast is served outside under an ivy-covered pergola in summer or in the dining room, just off the family's bright sitting room; over coffee the young, affable Antonio and Giusi – a brother-and-sister team – help you plan your stay. If the city's treasures start to pall they will organise a day in the vineyards or local pottery villages. There's parking off the main road and the number 25 bus, which stops outside the gates, will ferry you into the city or up into the hills. *Gluten-free breakfasts available.*

Price	€75-€130. Singles €70-€105. Triple €99-€160. Quadruple €120-€100.
Rooms	5: 3 doubles, 1 triple, 1 quadruple.
Meals	Restaurants 800m.
Closed	Rarely.
Directions	Signs for Centro & Piazza della Libertà, then Via Bolognese; villa on left. Bus No. 25 from r'way station; get off 800m after Via Bolognese begins, just before Total petrol station.

Antonio & Giuseppina Fantoni
Via Bolognese 83,
50139 Florence

Tel	+39 0554 95073
Email	info@villalasosta.com
Web	www.villalasosta.com

Torre di Bellosguardo

Imposing, mellow buildings, exquisite gardens fashioned by a friend of Dante, and magical views of Florence: it is breathtaking in its beauty and ancient dignity. The entrance hall is cavernous, glorious, with a painted ceiling and an ocean of floor; the view reaches through a vast plaster-crumbling sun room to streams with stepping stones, lily ponds and hothouses of exotics. A water feature meanders along a stone terrace, a twisted wisteria shades the walkway to the potager, donkeys, goats, ponies graze, and cats doze. A pool, gym and cane chairs occupy the old orangery while another pool settles into a perfect lawn. Most of the bedrooms can be reached by lift but the tower suite, with windows on all sides (very special) demands a climb. Bedrooms defy modern convention and are magnificent in their simplicity, the furniture richly authentic, the views sublime. (Ask for a room with one of the newer beds.) With luck you'll meet Signor Franchetti whose manners and English are impeccable, and Coco Bello, his charismatic pink parrot. All this, and Florence a ten-minute cab ride down the hill.

Price	€290. Single €160. Suites €340-€390.
Rooms	16: 8 doubles, 1 single, 7 suites.
Meals	Breakfast (included in winter only), €20. Restaurant 2km.
Closed	Never.
Directions	A1 exit Firenze-Certosa for Porta Romana/Centro; left at Porta Romana on Via Ugo Foscolo; keep right & take Via Piana to end; right into Via Roti Michelozzi.

Amerigo Franchetti
Via Roti Michelozzi 2,
50124 Florence

Tel +39 0552 298145
Email info@torrebellosguardo.com
Web www.torrebellosguardo.com

Villa Le Piazzole

Have the best of both worlds: live like a Florentine but eschew city heat and hassle. You'll adore this handsome, symmetrical, 17th-century villa that lies just outside Florence. Beaming Benedetta welcomes you through the imposing entrance, at once diffusing any impression of formality you may have deduced from the immaculate gardens, the dignified statues and the imperial entrance stair – which leads you from a cypress tree-lined pathway into the marbled hallway. The bedrooms are beautiful, elegant and utterly original: wooden ceilings and terracotta floors, the occasional lavish four-poster, oil paintings, smartly upholstered armchairs, window arches and fresh flowers. The self-catering apartments have their own private little gardens, and there's a stunning pool surrounded by lounging wicker chairs and cream parasols. The owners produce their own wine so ask to visit the *cantina* and stock up before you leave. This is a real Tuscan retreat with wonderfully down-to-earth hosts; the guest book bursts with praise from returning guests. *Ask about wine tasting & cookery classes.*

Price	Doubles €250. Singles €200. Apartments €1,700 per week.
Rooms	4 + 10: 3 doubles, 1 single. 10 apartments for 2-4.
Meals	Breakfast €12 for self-caterers. Dinner from €10, by arrangement. Restaurants 1km.
Closed	20 December-11 January.
Directions	Sent on booking.

Rodolfo & Benedetta
Via Suor Maria Celeste 28,
Via Gherardo Silvani 149/A,
50125 Florence

Tel +39 0552 23520
Email lepiazzole@gmail.com
Web www.lepiazzole.com

Azienda Agricola La Capannaccia

Originating in 1753, revived phoenix-like from an 18th-century fire, commandeered by the Americans in WW2, and renovated over 30 years by the current family, this country pile of an agriturismo (Chianti grapes, organic olive oil) is steeped in history and character. No pool but a large lawned garden with a hot tub to share, heaps of olive groves and vineyards to stroll, farm machinery all around and a stunning view from the top of the hill. As for the apartments, two occupy an extended wing, the other is in the main house. They exude an elegant simplicity with their solid wrought-iron beds, new fireplaces, mottled, clotted cream paint schemes, cotta floors, and classic, cosy kitchens. The flat in the main house is decoratively busier, with its many antiques and Murano glass chandeliers. Your hosts, the charming Luca and his parents, are warm, fun, love horses (the stables house six, plus two shaky-kneed foals) and happy to advise on everything; they'll even drive you to the restaurant down the road. Beautifully positioned for day trips to Florence, and a riding school nearby. *Minimum stay two nights.*

Price	€80-€250.
Rooms	3 apartments: 1 for 2, 2 for 2-4.
Meals	Basic breakfast included. Dinner arranged on request. Restaurants 500m.
Closed	Rarely.
Directions	A1 exit FI-Certosa dir. Florence. Left at 2nd lights; dir. San Casciano. After 4km, over x-roads to Scandicci. 2nd left, right into Via di Vingone; after approx. 4km right into Via Francesca, on for 1km, then right Via delle Selve; 1st house.

Luca Bini
Via delle Selve 5,
50018 Scandicci

Tel +39 0552 41839
Email info@lacapannaccia.com
Web www.lacapannaccia.com

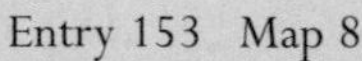

Relais Villa L'Olmo

With a bit of luck you will be greeted by Claudia, a German lady of considerable charm, married to a Florentine whose family have owned the property since 1700. The Relais is a clutch of immaculately converted apartments looking down over the valley, all shamelessly *di lusso*. Imagine soft-lit yellow walls beneath chunky Tuscan beamed ceilings and nicely designed kitchenettes, perfect for self-caterers. Find white china on yellow cloths, smartly checked sofas, glass-topped tables, fresh flowers – even a private pool with plastic loungers for the two smaller villas if you can't face splashing with others in the main one. And there's a communal barbecue, so you can mingle if you wish. Claudia runs a warmly efficient reception and rents out mountain bikes and mobile phones; she organises babysitting, cookery classes and wine tastings, too. There's a cheerful restaurant and a pizzeria, farm products for sale, and a little gym to work it all off. Florence is 20 minutes away by car or bus… this is heaven for families. *Special rates for local golf, tennis & riding clubs.*

Price	Villas €170-€400. Apts €80-€280. Farmhouse €210-€470.
Rooms	Farmhouse for 6-8. 2 villas for 2-4. 8 apartments for 2-5.
Meals	Breakfast €12. Restaurants nearby.
Closed	Never.
Directions	A1 exit Firenze-Certosa; at r'bout, signs for Tavarnuzze; there, left to Impruneta. Track on right, signed to villa; 200m past sign for Impruneta.

Claudia & Alberto Giannotti
Via Imprunetana per Tavarnuzze 19, 50023 Impruneta

Tel	+39 0552 311311
Email	florence.chianti@dada.it
Web	www.relaisfarmholiday.it

La Canigiana Agriturismo

With Florence's Duomo glistening in the distance across a carpet of olive groves, this Tuscan farmhouse has the best of both worlds. Set amongst the sparkling air of the Chianti hills, it is 15 minutes from that glorious city. Producing organic olive oil, the farm has been in Alessandra's family for over 100 years. Her family and father still live on the estate – let yourself to be swept into their warm embrace. The apartments (with private entrances) share those glorious views. A cut above those of the average agriturismo, the bedrooms here are country comfortable with colourful bedspreads, wrought-iron beds, posies of fresh flowers and prints on white walls. Traditionally tiled floors, beams and shuttered windows add charm. Kitchen areas incorporated into the living room are fine for holiday cooking and there are pretty tablecloths for dinner; choose the ground-floor apartment for its lovely terrace, or take the two together. Those Tuscan jewels – Pisa, Lucca, Siena, Florence – are under an hour away, and there's an orchard-enclosed pool for your return. Bliss. *Minimum stay three nights.*

Price	€595-€840. Whole house €1,225-€1,540. Prices per week.
Rooms	2 apartments for 3. Whole house available.
Meals	Restaurant 1.5km.
Closed	December-February.
Directions	From A1 exit Firenze-Certosa dir. Firenze. At lights left dir. Montespertoli. Junc. after 6km, right to La Romola. House after 1km on left; signed.

Alessandra Calligaris
Via Treggiaia 146,
50020 La Romola

Tel +39 0558 242425
Mobile +39 339 4463483
Email info@lacanigiana.it
Web www.lacanigiana.it

Ethical Collection: Environment. See page 419 for details.

Dimora Storica Villa Il Poggiale

Where to start? This historic 16th-century Tuscan villa is so serenely lovely. Breathe in the scent of old-fashioned roses from a seat on the Renaissance loggia. Wander through olive trees to the pool. Retreat to the house for some 1800s elegance. Much loved, full of memories, this is the childhood home of brothers Johanan and Nathanel Vitta, who devoted two years to its restoration. Rooms are big, beautiful, full of light, and everything has been kept as it was. An oil painting of their grandmother welcomes you as you enter; a portrait of Machiavelli by Gilardi hangs in the salon. Bedrooms are all different, all striking. Some have frescoes and silk curtains, others have fabrics commissioned from a small Tuscan workshop. The attention to detail is superb but in no way overpowering. The independent apartment is a restored farmhouse with original fireplace and stunning views over the rose garden. The staff clearly love being here and want you to love it too. Breakfast is a generous buffet, dinner is in the restored olive store and Florence is a 20-minute drive. *Honesty bar. Well-being, spa & fitness area.*

Price	€130-€240. Suites €195-€240. Apartment €310.
Rooms	23 + 1: 21 doubles, 2 suites. Apartment for 5.
Meals	Dinner €30. Wine from €8. Restaurants 300m.
Closed	9 January-9 February.
Directions	Rome A1 exit Firenze-Certosa; superstrada Firenze-Siena, exit San Casciano; signs for Cerbaia-Empoli. After 3km, signs on left.

Monica Cozzi
Via Empolese 69,
50026 San Casciano in Val di Pesa

Tel	+39 0558 28311
Email	villailpoggiale@villailpoggiale.it
Web	www.villailpoggiale.it

Fattoria Le Corti - Principi Corsini

The 17th-century Villa Le Corti is one of the noblest in Tuscany; the land, in the Corsini family since 1427, has been producing 'chianti classico' and rich olive oil since the beginning of time. There are cellars to visit, wines to taste, horses to ride, and fascinating tours of the 'orciaia', the most beautiful oil store in Tuscany; find, too, cookery classes in historic kitchens, a cosy restaurant above the shop, and holiday houses scattered about. It's a working estate with a wonderful buzz. A great big party would have a whale of a time in La Gugliaie, a big rambling farmhouse with two sitting rooms and bedrooms dressed in lovely fabrics and colours; discover steps, nooks, crannies, beams and polished wooden floors made from old wine barrels. The garden begins at the swimming pool and ends in the olive grove, with wondrous far-reaching views. Bake bread in an old wood-oven, take a soak in a hidden bath, sip a glass of chianti on your bedroom balcony. All this and a situation to dream of: posh but friendly San Casciano is the nearest village, Florence is a bus ride away. *Chef available, by arrangement.*

Price	B&B €100-€140. Whole house (sleeps 12-14) €4,000-€5,800 per week.
Rooms	8: 7 doubles, 1 single. Whole house available.
Meals	Breakfast from €9 for self-caterers. Restaurant on site.
Closed	Rarely.
Directions	Exit A1 Certosa; Florence-Siena m'way to Siena, exit San Casciano. Villa le Corti is signed after left turn at roundabout towards Mercatale Val di Pesa.

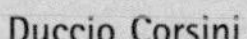

Duccio Corsini
Via San Piero di Sotto 1,
50026 San Casciano in Val di Pesa

Tel +39 0558 29301
Mobile +39 348 7215125
Email info@principecorsini.com
Web www.principecorsini.com

Il Poggetto

A deliciously green and sunny Tuscan hilltop, surrounded by vineyards and olive groves. Once through the electronic gates, you'll be captivated by the views. The gardens are delightful, too: three hectares of rose-ridden lawns, fruit trees, azaleas and heather (always something in flower), with pines and cypresses for shade and a terrace dotted with lemon and mandarin trees. Ivana and her family moved to the 400-year-old *casa colonica* in 1974 and have renovated beautifully, using original and traditional materials. The apartments are attractive, uncluttered and full of light. All have big comfortable beds, antique furniture and private patios. La Loggia was once a hay barn; the huge, raftered living/dining area is superb and the old triangular air bricks are still in place. La Cipressaia, characteristically Tuscan in style and very private, is a conversion of the stable block, and sleeps five. Il Gelsomino, named after the jasmine outside the door, and La Pergola join each other. Everyone has use of the pool, which is set apart in a stunning position: you can watch the sun rise and set from your lounger. *Minimum stay three nights.*

Price	€77-€100 (€448-€1,295 per week).
Rooms	4 apartments for 2-5.
Meals	Restaurants 1km.
Closed	Rarely.
Directions	Milan-Rome A1 exit Scandicci; take Pisa-Livorno exit Ginestra; right for Montespertoli. In Baccaiano left uphill to Montagnana; signed after 1km. 1st left into Via Montegufoni, left at the church into Via del Poggetto.

Andrea Boretti & Ivana Pieri
Via del Poggetto 14,
50025 Montespertoli

Mobile	+39 339 3784383
Email	info@poggetto.it
Web	www.poggetto.it

Villa di Riboia

Step over the threshold and into the arms of the older Mrs Renzoni; Elisabetta, her children (and computer!) now live down the road. Three generations have lived in this 16th-century villa; you'll be welcomed as friends and your children will be adored. Make yourself at home among old-school sofas and antiques in the sitting room (where doors open to the garden), or beneath the frescoes (the work of Elisabetta's uncle) in the rather lovely dining room. For reading there's a guest sitting room at the top of the grand stone staircase. Beamed and tiled bedrooms offer traditional comfort with their dark chests and iron bedsteads, patterned rugs and woodland murals; old-fashioned bathrooms are unpristine but spacious. Look forward to walks and cycle routes from the house, and the treasures of medieval Impruneta up the road. Return to a fairytale garden on multi levels, winding down to a small, beautiful pool surrounded by flowers; and heavenly views to Florence. Dine on produce from their small organic farm under the gazebo in the summer. Embrace relaxed rustic Italian family life. *Minimum stay two nights.*

Price	€80-€90. Triple €110-€120.
Rooms	2: 1 double, 1 triple.
Meals	Dinner with wine, €20. Welcome dinner with family for 4-night stays. Restaurant 2km.
Closed	Never.
Directions	A1 exit Certosa dir. Firenze; right at lights in Galluzzo main square onto Viale Gherardo Silvani dir. Impruneta; pass Pozzolatico, then Mezzomonte; after Monteoriolo 1st sharp right onto Via di Riboia; on right.

Elisabetta Renzoni
Via di Riboia 2a,
50023 Monteoriolo

Tel	+39 0552 374038
Mobile	+39 333 3154788
Email	info@villadiriboia.it
Web	www.villadiriboia.it

Locanda le Boscarecce

A sparkling star in Tuscany's firmament. Susanna is full of life and laughter, her daughter Swan is equally warm – and an accomplished sommelier. Susanna, or Swan's husband Chef Bartolo from Sicily, concocts dishes that people travel miles to discover. Fruit, vegetables, herbs and olive oil are all home grown, there are 450 wines in the cellar and, outside, the biggest pizza oven ever. The 200-year-old *locanda* is on a ridge, embracing fields and farms and heavenly sunsets. Bedrooms in the farmhouse are part rustic, part refined, with bold colours and pretty lace at the windows, each space unique. Beds are modern and comfortable, furniture 18th and 19th-century, bathrooms have bath tubs **and** showers, and some rooms have kitchenettes. Tennis, cycling, swimming in the saltwater pool with its panoramic view – all are possible; or simply relax under the dreamy gazebo and dip into an art book from the library. Even the geography is enticing, in the charmed triangle formed by Florence, Siena and Pisa. Heart-warming, creative and definitely special. *Ask about cookery courses, and wine, cheese & olive oil tasting.*

Ethical Collection: Community; Food.
See page 419 for details.

Price	€100-€145.
Rooms	12: 8 doubles, 3 triples, 1 quadruple.
Meals	Dinner €25. Restaurant 3km.
Closed	20 November-26 December.
Directions	From Castelfiorento, Via A. Vivaldi for Renai; right after dirt road, signed. Over bridge, road curves left, stay on paved road for 'di Pizzacalada'; T-junc. left; signed.

Susanna Ballerini
Via Renai 19,
50051 Castelfiorentino

Tel	+39 0571 61280
Email	info@leboscarecce.com
Web	www.leboscarecce.com

Fattoria Barbialla Nuova

An organic farm specialising in Chianina cattle, olive oil and white truffles; utter tranquillity 30 minutes from Florence. Delightful Guido and others have created somewhere bio-sensitive, Slow and stylish – special places to stay on a 500-hectare nature reserve/farm. Each of the three farmhouses, each with sweeping views, sits on top of its hill. Le Trosce – one floor but several levels – is for one big party. Doderi is divided into three apartments, simple and minimalist (Gianluca's bedcovers and 60s retro furniture adding originality and colour). The apartments in Brentina, deeper in the woods, are a touch more rustic but designers will love their whitewashed simplicity. All have books, music, delicious bathrooms, chic patios and pools. Back down at the farm: a vegetable and herb garden, a farm shop and organic produce, orchards, pigs, hens. Nature trails entice you to explore: forage in the shade of the woods in the truffle zone or stumble upon a ruined 'casa colonica'. Lovely old Montaione, San Miniato and Certaldo Alto have festivals throughout the year. *Internet in reception only. Minimum three to seven nights.*

Price	Apts €500-€720 for 2; €785-€1,120 for 4; €1,020-€1,470 for 6. Farmhouse €1,780-€2,530. Prices per week.
Rooms	7 apartments: 2 for 2, 3 for 4, 2 for 6. Farmhouse for 8.
Meals	Restaurant 3km.
Closed	January to mid-March.
Directions	From S.G.C. FI-PI-LI exit San Miniato; up hill to Montaione; 4km after Corazzano, on right opp. white 6km sign.

Ethical Collection: Environment; Food.
See page 419 for details.

Guido Manfredi
Via Casastrada 49,
50050 Montaione

Tel +39 0571 677259
Mobile +39 335 1406575
Email info@barbiallanuova.it
Web www.barbiallanuova.it

Castello di Pastine

Enthroned atop an olive-terraced hill on a Chianti vineyard sea, this 14th-century castello encloses a number of comfortable self-catering apartments in two big ancient buildings and a house tucked away in the woods. Acres of landscaped grounds, wonderfully magical, perfectly maintained, have long and spectacular views past statues and cypresses, secret hideaways and jogging trails. There's a huge pool with snazzy parasols and pergolas, multiple terraces with barbecues, slides, swings, ping pong, volleyball and floodlit tennis, and a hot tub for the lazy. All feels nicely countrified and cared for, with terracotta floors, exposed brickwork, plentiful beams, big sofas piled with cushions, eclectic prints – testament to family travels – and well-stocked kitchens. Casa Colonica can be rented as a single unit but our favourite is the house that hides in the woods; one wall was once part of a cave. Young Guido knows all the secrets and stories: the Castello is his pride and joy. Cycle tours of vineyards beckon, San Gimignano is close, Florence is half an hour. A paradise for families. *Minimum stay three to five nights.*

Price	Apts €392-€1,400. Cottage €1,176-€1,806. Prices per week.
Rooms	7 apts for 2-5. Cottage for 6.
Meals	Occasional dinner. Restaurant 3km.
Closed	Rarely.
Directions	A1 exit Firenze-Certosa; SS Firenze-Siena, exit Tavarnelle Val di Pesa. Thro' town dir. Barberino Val d'Elsa; provincial rd No. 50 right; signs for Vico d'Elsa-Sant'Appiano. Left; signs for Pastine. 1st fork, right; right.

Guido Materi
2-4 Strada di Vico - Pastine,
50021 Barberino Val d'Elsa

Tel	+39 0558 075176
Email	castellodipastine@gmail.com
Web	www.pastine.it

Sovigliano

A stone's throw from Tavarnelle, down a country lane, this ancient farmhouse stands among vineyards, olives, cypresses and pines. Though the setting is secluded you are in the middle of some of the most popular touring country in Italy; on a clear day, you can see the towers of San Gimignano. Every view is breathtaking. Sovigliano has been renovated by the family with deep respect for the architecture and traditional materials. The self-catering apartments – one palatial, with a glorious stone fireplace – are most attractive, all white walls, ancient rafters, good beds and country antiques. If you choose to go B&B, the double rooms are equally charming. The big rustic kitchen, with a private fridge for each guest, makes it easy to meet others should you wish to do so, or a delicious dinner can be arranged. Breakfast under the pines in the garden, take a lazy dip in the pool, work out in the exercise area (here children must be supervised), enjoy a pre-dinner drink. Vin Santo, olive oil and grappa are for sale. Signora is most helpful and will insist you return!

Price	€120-€175. Apartments €770-€1,780.
Rooms	4 + 4: 2 doubles, 2 twins. 4 apartments for 2-4 (some connect to make apt for 8).
Meals	Dinner with wine, €35.
Closed	Rarely.
Directions	SS2 Firenze-Siena exit Tavarnelle; on entering town, right & follow Marcialla. Sovigliano just out of town: left at 4th r'bout down lane signed Magliano; follow signs.

Patrizia Bicego
Strada Magliano 9,
50028 Tavarnelle Val di Pesa

Tel	+39 0558 076217
Email	info@sovigliano.com
Web	www.sovigliano.com

B&B Del Giglio

You'll fall under del Giglio's spell. What with the beauty, the history and your hosts' warmth and zest, you won't have a chance of resisting. Roberto and Laura bought the 12th-century house, part of delightful San Donato's fortified walls, years ago and have been working on it devotedly ever since. In the apartment, where polished antiques and Roberto's works of art blend beautifully with white walls and chunky rafters, you get a small dark wood kitchen (note, delicious continental breakfast is provided, brought to you on the terrace or the living room) and two simple, comfortable double bedrooms, each with their own shower room. No washing machine – but there is a tiny gym! Downstairs – through a courtyard with a fascinating little wine cellar – is a perfect garden, with resident tortoises and breathtaking views to San Gimignano. If you don't want to eat out, have a barbecue under the ancient olives. Once through the gate, there's walking for miles, among the olive groves and the rolling hills. Exceptional place, and people.

Price	€75-€95. €170 for 4.
Rooms	2 doubles.
Meals	Restaurants 50m.
Closed	Rarely.
Directions	Firenze-Siena road (4 corsi) to San Donato; dir. centre; park in any of free car parks then 3-minute walk.

Roberto Cresti
Via del Giglio 78,
50028 San Donato in Poggio

Tel +39 0558 072894
Email info@delgiglio.it
Web www.delgiglio.it

Palazzo Malaspina B&B

A special find. The medieval walls of San Donato are tucked away behind an arch, while the Renaissance façade belies a modern and spacious interior. Enter the big hall with its fine wooden doors and stylish staircase, sense the history. The palazzo is a listed building and Maria is enthusiastic about all she has to offer. She was born here (in Room 3), and now lives in the apartment downstairs with her pet dog. Breakfast – in your bedroom, or at a huge table on white runners and china – includes fruits, cheeses, croissants, jams. You can even request a full English; the guest book says it is sensational. Each of the bedrooms has a classic Tuscan charm with family antiques and fabrics from the House of Busatti, Anghiari. Luxurious bathrooms have mosaic tiles and huge white towels bearing the palazzo's emblem; three have a jacuzzi. From some of the rooms you can just glimpse the towers of San Gimignano, from others, little gardens that guide the eye to the countryside beyond and its treasures. There's a huge cherry tree in the small back garden. Drop your baggage off outside; car parks are a five-minute walk.

Price	€70-€110.
Rooms	5: 3 doubles, 2 twins/doubles.
Meals	Restaurant next door.
Closed	Occasionally.
Directions	A1 exit Firenze-Certosa; SS Firenze-Siena for Siena; exit San Donato; signs for San Donato; thro' arch into "centro storico"; Via del Giglio, on left.

Maria Pellizzari
Via del Giglio 35,
50028 San Donato in Poggio

Tel +39 0558 072946
Mobile +39 339 4114711
Email info@palazzomalaspina.it
Web www.palazzomalaspina.it

Fattoria Viticcio Agriturismo

You're on a hill above Greve, in Chianti Classico country. Alessandro's father, Lucio, bought the farm in the 1960s and set about producing fine wines for export. It was a brave move at a time when people were moving away from the countryside. Now the vineyard has an international reputation. Visit the vaults and taste for yourself. Nicoletta (also a sommelier) runs the agriturismo, helped by their daughters. The apartments are named after them – Beatrice, Arianna, Camilla – and lie at the heart of the estate. Much thought has gone into them. Plain-coloured walls, brick arches, beams and terracotta floor tiles give an attractively simple air, furniture is a charming blend of contemporary and antique pieces; kitchens are superb. One pool rests in a walled garden, with a small play area for children; a second lies within the olive groves. You may hear the occasional tractor – this is a working estate – but the farmyard is tidy and well-kept, with tubs of flowers everywhere. There's a family atmosphere, too, and wonderful views. *Minimum stay two nights; one week in apartments.*

Price	€115. Apartments €790-€1,200 per week.
Rooms	3 + 5: 2 doubles, 1 twin. 5 apartments: 3 for 2-4, 2 for 4-6.
Meals	Breakfast €5. Restaurants 1km.
Closed	Rarely.
Directions	A1 exit Firenze Sud; via Chiantigiana SS222. In Greve, signs for pool ("piscina"): over small bridge past pool on right; take track for Viticcio, signed.

Alessandro Landini &
Nicoletta Florio Deleuze
Via San Cresci 12a,
50022 Greve in Chianti

Tel +39 0558 54210
Email info@fattoriaviticcio.com
Web www.fattoriaviticcio.com

Villa Le Barone

The late Marchesa wrote a delightful book about her passion for this lovely old manor with its maze of stairs and crannies, in the family for 400 historic years. A gorgeous, genuinely unspoilt place, it has old-fashioned comforts. Staff bustle with easy-going friendliness under the guidance of the owners, an elegantly charming couple who spend part of the year here. Bedrooms vary, some in the villa, others in outbuildings; some small, others on a grand scale; most with fantastic fabrics, prints, oil paintings and pretty antiques; all have warm Tuscan style. In the drawing room you'll find the irresistible comfort of a log fire on chilly nights and vast coffee-table books to whet your appetite for Italy. The airy dining room, once the wine store, is a proper setting for superb, leisurely Tuscan dinners and wines. The gardens are no less appealing, full of roses, olive trees and lavender; there's tennis and a training track for the active, a parasoled terrace for the idle and a pool that is far too seductive for anyone intent upon a cultural holiday. That said, do visit the exquisite church of San Leolino, a step away.

Price	€180-€345. Half-board €110-€190 p.p.
Rooms	30: 28 twins/doubles, 2 suites.
Meals	Light lunch €20. Dinner €45. Wine from €20. Restaurants 1km.
Closed	Only three rooms available for self-catering November-March.
Directions	Panzano (not marked on all maps), 7km from Greve in Chianti; hotel signed from Greve.

Aloisi de Larderel
Via San Leolino 19,
50020 Panzano in Chianti
Tel +39 0558 52621
Email info@villalebarone.com
Web www.villalebarone.com

Podere La Casellina Agriturismo

Come here for life's slow rhythm – and for this warm, honest and lovely family. The grandparents arrived in 1936, when the little church put the *podere* into their hands; they and young Michelangelo have worked the land ever since. Anyone wishing to experience 'real' Italian peasant life (*vita del contadino*) should come here; so little has changed at La Casellina, inside or out. Simple spotless bedrooms, in the old hayloft and stables, have very comfortable beds and views of the San Pietro al Terreno's church. All the food, oil and produce is deliciously Slow, while the landscape, between Chianti and Valdarno, is exquisite; you have the chestnut woods of the Chianti mountains to one side, oaks, cypresses and olives to the other. Learn to prune vines and pick olives on the farm; gather chestnuts and wild mushrooms in the woods. Go riding or biking, then return to Grandma's recipes – the grape flan is scrumptious and there's passion fruit for breakfast. Michelangelo is a dear, talks to the animals as though they were family and speaks brilliant English. *Ask about cookery classes.*

Price	From €70. Minimum stay 2 nights.
Rooms	3 doubles.
Meals	Lunch with wine, €18. Dinner with wine, €21. Restaurant 2km.
Closed	Rarely.
Directions	A1 exit Incisa; Figline road. Just before Figline, right to Brollo & Poggio alla Croce; 5km, on right.

Ethical Collection: Environment; Food.
See page 419 for details.

Michelangelo & Silvia Bensi
Via Poggio alla Croce 60,
50063 Figline Valdarno

Tel +39 0559 500070
Email poderelacasellina@tin.it
Web www.poderelacasellina.it

Locanda Casanuova

"The beauty of simplicity" is their motto. Casanuova was once a monastery, then an orphanage, then a farmhouse... Ursula and Thierry took it on years ago, rescuing the house and returning the land to organic use. They're a generous couple and the whole place exudes an air of serene simplicity. Fresh menus are chalked up on the board each day; meals, served at large tables under the vines, are happy events. Off the refectory is a library where you can pore over trekking maps at a big round table. By the old mulberry tree 800m from the house are two apartments for self-caterers, one up, one down. But we recommend the B&B rooms, spotless and charming, furnished with natural fabrics (no TVs) and with a serenely monastic air; bathrooms are equally delightful. As well as a talented cook, Ursula is an imaginative gardener: green secret corners, inviting terraces and unusual plants abound. Best of all, in a clearing in the woods, is an enchanting swimming 'pond', a natural, self-cleansing pool with lily pads, surrounded by decking, with a paddling pool for tinies alongside. *Hall for meetings & weddings. Ask about yoga.*

Price	€90-€100. Half-board €80 p.p. Apartments €80-€120.
Rooms	18 + 2: 12 doubles, 4 singles, 2 suites. 2 apts: 1 for 2, 1 for 4.
Meals	Breakfast €10 for apartments. Dinner €30-€35. Wine €12-€50. Restaurant 3km.
Closed	7 November-15 March.
Directions	A1 from Rome exit Incisa Valdarno; dir. Figline, right for Poggio alla Croce; left before Poggio alla Croce for San Martino; on for 2km.

Ethical Collection: Food.
See page 419 for details.

Ursula & Thierry Besançon
San Martino Altoreggi 52,
50063 Figline Valdarno

Tel +39 0559 500027
Email locanda@casanuova-toscana.it
Web www.casanuova.info

Podere Le Mezzelune

A treat to find this house in the north Maremma. After a long, winding track, two big wooden gates; ring the bell and they swing open to reveal a tree-lined drive. This is a typical Tuscan, late 1800s farmhouse turned into a delightful B&B where you feel as though you are visiting friends. Downstairs, a huge dining table for breakfasts of fresh, home-baked pastries and seasonal fruits, and an open fire for winter. Upstairs are the bedrooms, two looking out to sea, all with their own terrace and a view. Painted white and cream, they have linen curtains, wooden floors, furniture made to the owners' design, candles, fresh fruit and vintage wooden pegs hung with an antique shawl. Bathrooms, too, are perfect. For longer stays there are two little private cottages in the garden, comfortable with open fires, dishwashers and beams. You are surrounded by cypresses, vines, flowers, herbs, 2,000 olive trees and seven hectares of woodland. This is a magical place, five minutes from the historic centre, 15 minutes from the sea and blissfully free of newspapers and TV. *Minimum stay two nights.*

Price	€160-€180. Cottages €180-€195.
Rooms	4 + 2: 4 twins/doubles. 2 cottages for 2-4.
Meals	Breakfast €15 for self-caterers, by arrangement. Restaurants 3km.
Closed	15 December-January.
Directions	SS1 exit La California towards Bibbona. Just before village, signs for Le Mezzelune on left. Follow for approx. 2km to farm gate.

Azienda Agricola Le Mezzelune
Loc. Mezzelune 126,
57020 Bibbona

Tel	+39 0586 670266
Email	relais@lemezzelune.it
Web	www.mezzelune.com

Relais Sant'Elena

Leaving the Etruscan coast and following the wine trail towards Bibbona, you'll meet an 'oasis' in the middle of the Tenuta Gardini Estate. Olive trees, terracotta, restored stone, glimpses of white Chianina cows: as far as you can see, the land belongs to the family, and you'll wish you had booked for longer. Even the roses creeping up the walls seem reluctant to abandon their blooms and it's easy to find yourself drawn, wine or book in hand, to one of the many covered terraces such as La Carraia where the old carriages were housed. For cooler nights there's the magnificent sitting room, with chandeliers hanging from vaulted ceilings, intimate armchair seating, and wafts from candelabra mixing with the dusky-red of handmade tiles. Each bedroom, in the main house or across the courtyard, comes with its own romantic features: canopy beds, verandas, balconies. One has a lovely view out to the ruined mill. A Tuscan breakfast is served in the old 'limonaia', and delightful manager Daniella will arrange a light lunch or a picnic basket if you plan to explore the botanical treasures of Magona Park.

Price	€160-€340. Minimum 2 nights.
Rooms	15: 11 doubles, 2 twins, 2 suites.
Meals	Bar meals available. Light poolside lunches. Tuscan buffet on request. Restaurant 1km.
Closed	November-April.
Directions	Sent on booking.

Moira Ciampolini
Tenuta Gardini, Via Campo di Sasso,
57020 Bibbona

Tel +39 0586 671071
Mobile +39 335 5395564
Email tenutagardini@gmail.com
Web www.tenutagardini.it

Ginestriccio

Fresh from the coast with a crate of Bolgheri in the boot, romantic couples will be happy to land at this peaceful old hunting lodge in the middle of the woods. it's an amazing place, part of the 280-hectare Tenuta Giardini Estate, almost hidden by greenery… it stands at the end of a white road flanked by tight coils of olive trees and the grazing pastures of the famous white Chianina cows. These five apartments really do feel cut off from the rest of the world, and nicely private too, divided by bushes and shrubs along the pathways. 'Solengo', off to one side, is the grandest with its large living room and fireplace, but all have good-sized kitchens, built-in wardrobes, store rooms and shower bathrooms. Elegant and tastefully lit interiors have been lovingly restored with style, their high-ceiling'd, wooden-floored double bedrooms decked in smart fabrics and soft natural colours. Each has its own garden space – but what you'll probably want to do is head for the sea. You can also walk to the nearby Relais Sant'Elena for use of their pool, or take a stroll in the woods – just mind the wild boar!

Price	€400-€860 per week. Minimum one week (Sat-Sat).
Rooms	5 apartments: 4 for 2, 1 for 2-3.
Meals	Restaurant 1km.
Closed	November-April.
Directions	Sent on booking.

Moira Rossi Ciampolini
Tenuta Gardini, Via Campo di Sasso,
57020 Bibbona

Tel	+39 0586 671071
Mobile	+39 335 5395564
Email	tenutagardini@gmail.com
Web	www.ginestriccio.com

La Casetta

Up a little road dotted with houses is a handsome 'colonica' with a view of the sea. Entertaining, sprightly Adriana welcomes you in perfect English to a delightful terrace with a big table, wicker chairs and dreamy wisteria. This is where you breakfast in summer, on local breads and homemade cakes, delicious coffee and fruity teas. Inside are vaulted ceilings, chunky beams and rooms awash with light and artistic colour: beiges, whites, creams; chartreuse cushions; lavender-painted doors. In the hall: a big table for leaflets and books; up the stairs: a guest sitting room with bedrooms off it. Be charmed by comfy sofas, family antiques, books on low shelves, rugs on painted wooden floors, and the occasional fine watercolour or oil. Bathrooms are past the first flush of youth; fresh bedrooms have blue and white spreads and lovely views (two have a view of the sea). There are several resorts within an easy drive, fish restaurants in little Bolgheri and history in medieval Castagneto Carducci. Return to super grounds with huge ancient olives, delectable peaches and a tucked-away pool.

Price	€90-€130.
Rooms	3: 1 double, 1 single; 1 twin/double with separate bath.
Meals	Dinner €24. Wine €10. Restaurant 4km.
Closed	Rarely.
Directions	Sent on booking.

Adriana Milla
Loc. Vallone Segalari 175,
57022 Castagneto Carducci
Tel +39 0565 763525
Mobile +39 339 1286330
Email milla.adri@alice.it

Poggio ai Santi

International sports presenter Dominique knows what people yearn for when they're away. At Poggio ai Santi, he and his wife are channelling all their imagination and flair into providing it. Here are three buildings – the main house 19th-century, the other two modern – set among roses and with spellbinding sea views. Uneven paths wind through fabulously relaxing gardens planted with a hundred exotic trees; there's even a painting hut – help yourself to art supplies and have a go at capturing the views. As for the restaurant, it is presided over by Danny, an exciting and passionate Michelin-starred chef. To eat here is a cosmic experience: the seafood and lobster bisque will linger long in the memory. Bedrooms are cool, Asian-chic and luxurious, bathrooms are astonishingly lush and the big, open-plan, parquet-floored suites have magnificent terraces and ingenious wardrobes opening to mini-kitchens. Enter the Royal Mare suite and you find a vast free-standing bath on the corner of your terrace... drink a toast to your good fortune as you soak, gazing across the sea to the isle of Elba.

Price	€142-€399. May-September: minimum 2 nights.
Rooms	11: 2 doubles, 9 suites (some with kitchenettes).
Meals	Dinner €35-€40. Wine €10-€100.
Closed	9 January-10 February.
Directions	A12 exit for SS to Vincenzo, right, then 4th right. Climb hill to top; go slow & look for hidden turning on right, big iron gates.

Francesca Vierucci
Via San Bartolo 100,
57027 San Vincenzo

Tel	+39 0565 798032
Email	poggioaisanti@toscana.com
Web	www.poggioaisanti.com

Pieve di Caminino Historic Resort

A fallen column lying deep in the grass, woods, a quiet lake... so peaceful it's hard to believe what a history this settlement has had since it was first recorded in 1075. It is set in a huge natural amphitheatre, ringed by hills and medieval fortresses, and has its own magic spring. Once you've driven through the big rusty gates and down the tree-lined drive, you'll be greeted by your hosts in an 11th-century church – part of their private quarters. It's the most lovely, airy space, with battered columns, soaring arches and elegant furniture – a subtle study in cream, gold and brown. The suites (one a romantic cottage) and the apartments are beautiful too. Each has its own terrace or balcony and is simply furnished with family antiques and fine old paintings. Enchanting windows look over the grounds, the massive walls are rough stone or plaster, the ceilings beamed or vaulted. The 500-hectare estate has been in Piero's family since 1650 and produces its own olive oil and wine. The beautiful panoramic pool has distant views to the isle of Elba. *Min. stay three nights in high season. Complimentary wine in room.*

Price	€110-€170 (€600-€900 per week). Apts €180-€250 (€900-€1,300 per week).
Rooms	5 + 2: 5 suites for 2-3. 2 apartments for 4-5.
Meals	Breakfast €10. Restaurant 5km.
Closed	Never.
Directions	From Milan m'way Bologna-Firenze exit Firenze-Certosa, for Siena-Grosseto, exit Civitella Marittima for Follonica. 5km before Montemassi right for Sassofortino. On right, 1km.

Piero Marrucchi & Daniela Locatelli
S.P 89 snc,
58036 Caminino

Tel +39 0564 569736
Email caminino@caminino.com
Web www.caminino.com

Ethical Collection: Environment; Food. See page 419 for details.

Poderi Firenze

Throw open your shutters to a rich panorama – up here, on top of the world. Ascend 20 hectares of vineyards... until you reach the farmhouse dominating its hill, the valley sweeping below. Flavia, a designer, welcomes you in, then it's up the sober 18th-century staircase to bedrooms on the second floor, and an elegant, minimalist, rustic-Tuscan perfection. Walls are exposed stone, rafters are high, floors are beautiful worn terracotta, shower stalls are ultra modern, and the suite has its extra beds on the mezzanine. Gianluigi looks after the vineyards – taste the wines – while the agriturismo is Flavia's new venture; both live just down the hill. Buffet breakfasts are laid out in a serene room with darkwood tables, a stone resin floor and a wonderful view-filled window. Tuck into fresh orange juice, eggs with bacon and homemade cakes before you set off for the wild hilly landscapes of the Maremma Grossetana or the Saturnia hot springs. Two very old olive trees guard the entrance to the west, a large flagged terrace overlooks the pool to the east and the views are enchanting from wherever you stand.

Price	€80-€90. Suites €130-€170. Min. stay 2 nights.
Rooms	5: 2 doubles, 1 twin, 2 suites for 3.
Meals	Lunch/dinner occasionally available, €15. Restaurants 8km.
Closed	October-March.
Directions	Sent on booking.

Flavia Tagliabue
Loc. l'Abbandonato,
58031 Stribugliano Arcidosso

Tel	+39 0564 967271
Mobile	+39 335 6888609
Email	info@poderifirenze.it
Web	www.poderifirenze.it

Villa Bengodi

A family house where you feel you've stepped back in time to a gentle age of old-fashioned charm and peace. Great-aunt Zia Ernesta lived in the room with the angel frescoes for most of her life. Catarina now oversees the running of the villa. Bedrooms are generous, light and spotless and house a hotchpotch of furniture from past decades; some have ceilings painted in 1940, another a terrace; all have original floor tiles in varying patterns. Modern bathrooms are excellent, views are to the garden or the sea. The villa and its gardens are the owners' pride and joy. While away the days in the enchanting palm-fringed garden or on the terrace where you might see Corsica on a clear day. Beaches and mile upon mile of surf are a hop away – or you could walk the full mile to Talamone, where a family friend takes you out on his boat to fish and swim; then eat what you've caught. The apartments, separate from the villa, have their own gardens. Dine al fresco in summer; in winter under a chandelier made of antlers and pine cones. An unusual and warmly personal house in a magical setting. *Minimum stay three nights.*

Price	€110-€170. Apartments €800-€1,500 per week.
Rooms	6 + 3: 6 doubles. 3 apartments for 2-4.
Meals	Dinner with wine, €30, by arrangement. Restaurant 1km.
Closed	Rarely.
Directions	From Grosseto-Roma at Fonteblanda, right for Talamone. 1st left & follow signs for Villa Bengodi.

Ethical Collection: Community; Food.
See page 419 for details.

Famiglia Orlandi
Via Bengodi 2, Loc. Bengodi,
58010 Fonteblanda

Mobile +39 335 420334
Email info@villabengodi.it
Web www.villabengodi.it

Quercia Rossa

The farmhouse sits on an estate of oak and cypress-scudded fields of wheat; olive groves and vineyards sweep down to the Tyrrhenian Sea. Loll on poolside loungers, soak up the peace. It's wonderfully laid-back, yet classy and romantic at the same time. As for the interiors, they are quirky and design-mag cool. A huge communal Maremma table beneath antique oil-lamps in a stunningly elegant dining room forms the focus of meals enriched by stylish young Alessandro; the chef bakes fresh cakes for breakfast each day. Fabulous furniture from Victorian voyager Augusta Belloc (daughter of Hilaire) – bought blind as a 'job lot' – catch the eye throughout: big gold mirrors and pretty gilded sconces; cherrywood pieces, intricate swans carved into their legs; a huge mahogany four-poster; an ornate bathroom mirror above an ancient marble basin; and, in the red and white-tiled sitting room, beautiful antique armchairs in deep rich blue and gold. Try to peel yourself away: medieval towns, beaches and the thermal baths at Saturnia are close. A special, unusual and remote place – made magical by Alessandro.

Ethical Collection: Food.
See page 419 for details.

Price	€81-€143.
Rooms	6 doubles.
Meals	Dinner with wine, €25-€35. Restaurant 5km.
Closed	Rarely.
Directions	A1 exit Orvieto; SS74 dir. Pitigliano/ Manciano. Thro' Manciano dir. Albinia on SS74 for 23.8km La Sgrilla; signed from here. Right at entrance to Tenuta Cavallini; follow white road for approx. 5km (avoid satnav).

Alessandro Bonanni
Montemerano, Santarello 89,
58014 Manciano

Tel +39 0564 629529
Email info@querciarossa.net
Web www.querciarossa.net

Villa Podernovo

In the Val di Merse wildlife reserve, a winding road away from San Galgano Abbey – mythical site of the King Arthur legend – is a 1700s farmhouse whose simple rooms, once for farmworkers, have become chic charming apartments for urban escapees. To ancient rusticity (mellow tiled floors, solid wood doors, chestnut beams) modern comforts have been added: big beds, white bathrooms, stainless steel kitchenettes, silent ceiling fans. A white sofa here, a country antique there, a judiciously placed black and white photo. We loved Focolare, the apartment for eight, with its big country fireplace in the kitchen/dining room and logs piled high. (Cosy in autumn – mushroom foraging time.) For summer there's a swish saltwater pool down the garden, a stylish gazebo for shade, and a communal barbecue so you can hobnob with the guests as you rustle up lunch. The set-up is managed by a brother and sister team and every last detail has been thought through, from the shop selling artisanal products and the dining room with trestle tables to the bikes on the house and the excellent photography courses. *Ask about bringing pets.*

Price	€500-€2,600 per week.
Rooms	5 apartments: 1 for 8-9, 3 for 2, 1 for 1.
Meals	Breakfast €10. Dinner from €25. All on request. Guest kitchen. Restaurant 200m.
Closed	Never.
Directions	Siena-Grosseto, exit Monticiano. From the SP32A, 15km dir. Monticiano. At x-roads, left for 50m then sharp right into Via Primo Maggio. Follow white unmade road for 200m to villa.

Diana Grandi
Loc. Podernovo 35,
53015 Monticiano

Tel	+39 0577 756611
Mobile	+39 348 8045131
Email	info@villapodernovo.it
Web	www.villapodernovo.it

Bosco della Spina

The road sign for 'pizzeria' is misleading: nothing so mundane here. Tables overlook a magical garden of pergolas, waterfalls, vines and wisteria; Castle Murlo hangs in the distance. Imaginatively restored and landscaped, these former farmhouse cellars in medieval Lupompesi have strikingly modern interiors and old Tuscan beams and terracotta; architecturally it is an interesting restoration. The restaurant, a cool space of open arches, raftered ceiling and sleek furniture, serves classic regional dishes (pizza in the summer only) accompanied by 180 wines. Reached down a series of impersonal corridors, the super comfy suites, each with fridge, sink and dual hob, have terraces, big divans and furniture made by local craftsmen. Blankets are neatly rolled, colours white and conker brown, beds hi-tech four-poster, bedcovers faux suede, shower rooms designery. All this and a wine bar, library, small gym, slimline pool (suitable for lengths only) and garden spots filled with tinkling water and views. A smoothly run and relaxed operation, popular with wedding parties, too.

Ethical Collection: Food.
See page 419 for details.

Price	€100-€170.
Rooms	14 suites for 2-4, 4-6, or 4-8.
Meals	Dinner €30. Wine from €7.
Closed	6 November-28 March.
Directions	A1 for Siena; exit Siena south; SS2 for Rome-Buonconvento; 15km; Monteroni d'Arbia; right to Vescovado di Murlo just after r'bout; 8km; right for Casciano di Murlo; 1km; in Lupompesi, on left, signed 'Residence'.

Brigida Meoni
Lupompesi,
53016 Murlo

Tel	+39 0577 814605
Email	bsturist@boscodellaspina.com
Web	www.boscodellaspina.com

Podere Salicotto

Watch sunsets fire the Tuscan hills; catch the sunrise as it brings the valleys alive. Views from this hilltop farmhouse roll off in every direction. It is peaceful here, and beautiful. Breakfast is a delicious feast that merges into lunch, with produce from the organic farm, and Silvia and Paolo, a well-travelled, warm and adventurous couple, are happy for you to be as active or as idle as you like. Eat in the big farmhouse kitchen or under the pergola, as deer wander across the field below. Paolo is full of ideas and will take you sailing in his six-berth boat that has crossed the Atlantic – or organise wine-tasting and cycling trips. The beamed and terracotta tiled bedrooms are airy and welcoming, full of soft, Tuscan colours and furnished with simplicity but care: antiques, monogrammed sheets, great showers. B&B guests are in the main house (private entrance) while the studio is in the converted barn. Visit Siena, medieval Buonconvento, Tuscan hill towns. Come back, rest in a hammock, laze around the pool with a glass of wine and a fabulous view.

Price	€150-€170 (€920-€1,080 per week). Studio €1,200 per week.
Rooms	6 + 1: 6 doubles. Studio for 2-4.
Meals	Breakfast €15 for self-caterers, on request. Guest kitchen & barbecue. Wine from €7. Restaurants 300m.
Closed	December to February.
Directions	From Siena via Cassia to Buonconvento. After Agip petrol station, 2nd left. After 2nd hill, house 2nd on right.

Ethical Collection: Environment; Food. See page 419 for details.

Silvia Forni
Podere Salicotto 73,
53022 Buonconvento

Tel +39 0577 809087
Email info@poderesalicotto.com
Web www.poderesalicotto.com

Il Rigo

The fame of Lorenza's cooking has spread so far that she's been invited to demonstrate her skills in the US (she runs courses here, too.) So meals in the big, beamed dining room at pretty check-clothed tables are a treat. Irresistible home-grown organic produce, 60 local wines to choose from and a gorgeous Tuscan setting. There are two houses on the family farm, named after the stream running through it. Casabianca, reached via a cypress-flanked drive, is ancient and stone built. A vine-covered pergola shades the entrance; beyond the reception area is a courtyard full of climbing roses. The second house, Poggio Bacoca, is about 600 metres away. Once home to the farmworkers, it's red-brick built and has two sitting rooms and panoramic views. You walk (600m) to 'Casabianca' for those wonderful meals. Bedrooms are homely, pretty and inviting; all have embroidered sheets, appealing colour schemes and matching bathrooms. No televisions: it's not that sort of place. Lorenza and Vittorio hope and believe that their guests will prefer a relaxed chat over a glass of wine.

Price	€100-€124. Half-board €144-€170 for 2.
Rooms	15 doubles.
Meals	Lunch/dinner €22-€25, by arrangement. Wine from €12. Restaurant 4km.
Closed	Never.
Directions	Exit A1 Certosa; follow SS, exit Siena South. SS.2 (Via Cassia) 2km south of S. Quirico d'Orcia; on left on 2km track, signed.

Vittorio Cipolla & Lorenza Santo
Podere Casabianca,
53027 San Quirico d'Orcia

Tel	+39 0577 897 291
Mobile	+39 342 3735370
Email	info@agriturismoilrigo.com
Web	www.agriturismoilrigo.com

Castello di Ripa d'Orcia

As you drive up the long, long white road, the castle comes into view: a thrilling sight. Ripa d'Orcia is 800 years old and one of Siena's most important strongholds. The battlemented fortress (closed to the public) dominates the *borgo* encircled by small medieval dwellings. The delightful family are descendants of the Piccolomini who acquired the estate in 1484 and are naturally proud of their heritage. Grand banquets and knights in shining armour come to mind… it's all gloriously, romantically atmospheric. Rooms and apartments have huge raftered ceilings and are furnished simply and well; most have breathtaking views. There's also a dayroom, filled with wonderful furniture and heaps of books to browse. You breakfast in a small annexe off the main restaurant, there's a cellar for wine tastings and a shop for you to stock up on your favourites. A pool too, and a beautiful chapel in the grounds. The area is a paradise for walkers and there is enough on the spot to keep lovers of history and architecture happy for hours – before the 'official' sightseeing begins. *Minimum stay two nights; three in apt.*

Price	€110-€150. Apts €110-€155 for 2; €175-€190 for 4.
Rooms	6 + 8: 6 twins/doubles. 8 apartments: 5 for 2, 3 for 4.
Meals	Breakfast €12 for self-caterers. Dinner from €12. Wine from €10. Closed Mondays.
Closed	November-March.
Directions	From SS2 for San Quirico d'Orcia; right over bridge. Follow road around town walls for 700m. Right again, signed; 5.3km to Castello.

Famiglia Aluffi Pentini Rossi
Loc. Ripa d'Orcia,
53027 Castiglione d'Orcia

Tel +39 0577 897376
Email info@castelloripadorcia.com
Web www.ripadorcia.it

Montorio

As you pootle up the drive, you will be inspired by the Temple of San Biagio. A Renaissance masterpiece designed by Antonio Sangallo the Elder, it is an unforgettable backdrop to Montorio. The house stands on top of its own little hill, 600m above sea level, overlooking a vast green swathe of Tuscany. Made of warm stone walls and roofs on different levels, it was once a *casa colonica*. It is now divided into five attractive apartments, each named after a celebrated Italian artist or poet, each with a well-equipped kitchen and an open fire. White walls, beams and terracotta floors set a tone of rural simplicity; antiques, paintings and wrought-iron lights crafted by Florentines add a touch of style; leather chesterfields and big beds guarantee comfort. The terraced gardens – full of ancient cypress trees, pots of flowers and alluring places to sit – drop gently down to olive groves and vineyards. Stefania's other villa, Poggiano, is five minutes away and historic Montepulciano, full of shops and eating places, is close enough to walk. *Minimum stay three nights.*

Price	€100-€170 for 2 (€600-€1,200 per week). €200-€250 for 4 (€1,400-€1,650 per week).
Rooms	5 apartments: 3 for 2, 2 for 4.
Meals	Restaurants 500m.
Closed	December-January.
Directions	A1 exit Valdichiana for Montepulciano. In Torrita di Siena, left at lights to Montepulciano. There, follow signs to Chianciano. Right at x-roads Bilvio di S. Biagio.

Stefania Savini
Strada per Pienza 2,
53045 Montepulciano

Tel +39 0578 717442
Email info@montorio.com
Web www.montorio.com

Fattoria San Martino

The track to San Martino is surrounded by wild roses, lavender and birds. Dutch Karin, warm and full of life, lives with her family in harmony with nature and gives you fine vegetarian dinners at a long table beneath an antique chandelier; or under the pergola in summer. This soft ochre-hued fattoria, restored with earth-tone pigments and immersed in garden, feels as though it is part of the landscape. Inside is as special. Expect limewash, wood, beeswax and stone; feast on the simplicity, indulge the senses. The feel is rustic, creative, eclectic, inventive. Bedrooms – with views that sweep in every direction – have electric current disjoiners that come into play as soon as the last light is turned off and beds positioned according to electromagnetic fields: your sleep will be deep. Wake to scrumptious spreads of yogurt, honey, cake, muesli, marmalade and bread – home-grown, homemade and biodynamic. Look forward to a day of Tuscan treats, from visits to hilltop towns, churches and monasteries to wine tastings of Vino Nobile di Montepulciano. It's as close to heaven as heaven gets.

Price	€150. Suites €180. Half-board by arrangement. Reduced rates for weekly stays.
Rooms	6: 1 double, 2 twins/doubles, 1 suite. Outbuilding: 1 double, 1 suite. Whole house available.
Meals	Dinner €35. Lunch by arrangement. Restaurant 1.5km.
Closed	Rarely.
Directions	A1 exit Chiusi for Montepulciano. At junc., right (pine tree-lined road); 30m after Bar Stella, right. Right at next junc.; after tennis court, left for San Martino (signed).

Antonio Giorgini
Via Martiena 3,
53045 Montepulciano

Tel +39 0578 717463
Email sanmartino@montepulciano.com
Web www.fattoriasanmartino.it

San Gallo Agriturismo

On Fridays they invite you to lunch with their friends – a gesture typical of this generous family. The setting is bucolic: vineyards, olive groves and views sweeping up to San Biagio and lovely Montepulciano – two kilometres away. This is a simple Tuscan farmhouse whose ground floor housed the animals and whose living quarters – dominated by big country fireplaces – were upstairs. Today the house sits in spacious gardens with mature trees for shade and benches for views. As for the apartments, these are all in the house, those on the upper floor air conditioned for hot nights; thick walls keep lower floors cool in summer. Kitchenettes, all bar one, have hobs not ovens; fabrics are plain and traditional; tiled floors and cream walls are pristine; bathrooms are in perfect order. The 20-hectare estate includes a small lake populated by ornamental ducks (not for the pot!) and a big pool surrounded by rosemary, roses and pergolas for sunloungers: comfort reigns supreme. Architecture and archaeology abound as does the lush and unsung Vino Nobile. Make the most of San Gallo's tastings!

Price	€840-€1,610 per week. Minimum 2 nights.
Rooms	6 apartments for 2-3 (each with sofabed).
Meals	Restaurants 1.5km.
Closed	Never.
Directions	A1 exit Montepulciano. Dir. San Biagio to church below town. Follow road around church to left, downhill for 700m. San Gallo signed on left down track.

Olimpia Roberti
Via delle Colombelle 7,
53045 Montepulciano

Tel	+39 0578 758330
Mobile	+39 339 7769444
Email	info@agriturismosangallo.com
Web	www.agriturismosangallo.com

Laticastelli Country Relais

In the fresh, clean air of a forested hilltop, this medieval hamlet once guarded Siena from marauding invaders. Now it's a charming hotel, with space to relax and a restaurant in the wine cellar. Rolling green views – pure Tuscany – are best enjoyed from the infinity pool, set amid flowers, lush grass and big old trees; bliss. Meals are best taken on the terrace at sunset, or cosily under rustic brick arches; food is fresh, local, and again, pure Tuscany. If you feel the belt tightening, use the communal kitchen to prepare your own snack, then settle on the sofa by an enormous stone fireplace. Two sitting rooms are dotted with eye-catching paintings and books – great conversation-starters in this sociable place. With the motorway close by, you can zip everywhere; or ask Giancarlo about wine tours, horse riding, polo lessons, hot springs. Wake to a slow buffet breakfast and take your turn guarding Siena, from the comfort of that heavenly pool. And when night and peace fall, trot across to big, bold bedrooms with chunky wood beams, terracotta floors, deep chic baths and huge walk-in showers.

Price	€127-€280.
Rooms	27: 21 doubles, 2 singles, 4 family rooms.
Meals	Lunch/Dinner €30. Wine €15-€400. Guest kitchen. Restaurant 3km.
Closed	Rarely.
Directions	Sent on booking.

Giancarlo Lorizzo
53040 Rapolano Terme

Tel	+39 0577 724419
Email	contact@laticastelli.com
Web	www.laticastelli.com

17 Via dei Goti

The whole of Tuscany is within reach of this medieval hill town that buzzes with its weekly market and year-round inhabitants. Catch brilliant views of surrounding hills through arches in ancient walls; Porta dei Tintori is a fine place to sit with a glass of wine in the evening. Your perfect townhouse is tall and narrow, on four floors, cool in the summer, cosy in winter; rusts, blues and whites bathe its walls, the interior is a welcoming mix of rustic and antique. You enter the open-plan dining area from the street; through an arched wall is a fully stocked kitchen. (Take what you need, wine included, then simply replace.) On the first floor are a double bedroom and an elegant living room with a beamed ceiling, an open fireplace, a cream sofa and chairs, some lovely art and books galore. A second salon and another bedroom are on the third floor, then right at the top (not for the un-nimble) is the master bedroom, splendid with its French antiques and embroidered linen curtains and sheets. The bathroom has a claw-foot bath from which you may gaze over rooftops, and candles are waiting to be lit. Fabulous.

Price	€450-€850 per week.
Rooms	House for 6 (3 doubles).
Meals	Restaurant 50m.
Closed	Rarely.
Directions	Sent on booking.

Sheri Eggleton & Charles Grant
53040 Rapolano Terme

Tel +44 (0)117 9081949
Mobile +44 (0)7932 186096
Email sherieggleton711@googlemail.com
Web www.17viadeigoti.co.uk

Villa Giuncheto

In a commanding position with far-reaching views – spot Siena on the horizon – is a former monastery encircled by olive groves, roses and a wrought-iron fence. Inside, find 800 square metres of tiles, beams and cotto ceilings renovated by craftsmen with no expense spared. The sitting room stretches the length of the house, its arched windows surveying the inner courtyard, its French windows overlooking the garden. Live life like a king – or a film star: they have dropped by! – in amongst grand armchairs and sofas, oils in gilt frames and swish stripey fabrics. The bedrooms sport ornate polished bedheads, harmonious colours, eclectic pictures; the bathrooms are marble, some with gold taps, one with a jacuzzi; the kitchen is awash with every device known to man. Housekeeper Rosa lives on the ground floor, shops and cooks for you if that's what you wish, and keeps the linen fresh. Slip into a big pool beneath the Tuscan sun, slide a pizza into the outdoor oven, knock a few tennis balls around the court, saunter to the gym – it lies below the as-handsome smaller house. From every window is a breathtaking view.

Price	€6,700-€12,000 per week. €160-€320 for 2 per night. Includes daily housekeeper.
Rooms	House for 14. House for 4.
Meals	Summer kitchen. Restaurant 1.5km.
Closed	Never.
Directions	Sent on booking.

Sig. Polito
Via delle Stine 1636, Ville di Corsano,
53018 Siena

Tel	+39 340 1404801
Mobile	+39 335 6277010
Email	sienapartments@libero.it

Frances' Lodge Relais

You stay in a converted hilltop lemon house, a ten-minute bus ride into the city. Catch your breath at views that soar across olive, lemon and quince groves to the Torre del Mangia of Siena. The old farmhouse was built by Franca's family as a summer retreat. Now she and Franco – warm, charming, intelligent – have filled the lofty, light-filled *limonaia* with beautiful things: an oriental carpet, a butter-yellow leather sofa, vibrant art by Franca. Guests may take breakfast in this lovely room, divided by a glass partition etched with a lemon tree from the kitchen, Franca's domain. And the first meal of the day – in the historic garden in summer – is to be lingered over: Tuscan salami and pecorino, fresh figs, delicious coffee. Bedrooms burst with personality and colour – one, funky and Moroccan, another huge, white and cream, with an outside area with a view. Chic coloured bed linen, huge walk-in showers, a fridge stocked with juice and water, towels for the pool. And what a pool – curved, it lies on the edge of the house, filled with views. A special place with a big heart.

Ethical Collection: Environment; Food. See page 419 for details.

Price	€180-€220. Suite €240-€380. Minimum 2 nights. Over 18s only.
Rooms	6: 5 doubles, 1 suite for 2-4.
Meals	Restaurant 800m.
Closed	10 January-10 March.
Directions	Past Siena on Tangenziale ring road for Arezzo-Roma; exit Siena Est to big r'bout 'Due Ponti'; road to S. Regina; 1st right Strada di Valdipugna; signed on right.

Franca Mugnai
Strada di Valdipugna 2,
53100 Siena

Mobile	+39 337 671608
Web	www.franceslodge.it

Campo Regio Relais

In bustling, beautiful Siena, step straight in from a quiet cobbled street to marble floors, frescoed walls, fine antiques and wonderful paintings. A first-floor sitting room gleams with leather sofas and vases of fresh flowers, there are striped cloths on the tables where copious breakfasts are had, the terrace looks over rooftops to the Duomo: an incomparable, dazzling, picture-postcard cityscape. This building, which dates from the 16th century, has its own peculiar architecture. One bedroom has a private terrace and that view, another a window onto the view from its bed; all are generously sumptuous with monogrammed sheets, taffeta curtains, soft creams and pale lilacs, buckets of smellies and big-mirrored bathrooms; totally pampering. The charming owners live upstairs and are unintrusively present. It's a stroll to restaurants, shops, street life and the great sights. Then back for a nightcap from the honesty bar in the candlelit salone as you watch the twinkling lights of the city below. Honeymooners will find it irresistible, architecture buffs will swoon, children may prefer somewhere a touch more robust.

Price	€150-€650.
Rooms	6 twins/doubles.
Meals	Restaurants nearby.
Closed	Beginning January to mid-March.
Directions	From m'way exit Siena west; follow signs for stadium until x-roads with Basilica di San Domenico.

Livia Palagi
Residenza d'Epoca, Via della Sapienza 25,
53100 Siena

Tel	+39 0577 222073
Email	relais@camporegio.com
Web	www.camporegio.com

Podere La Strega

Breakfast with Siena's rosy skyline before you: the Duomo and Torre del Mangia, the meandering streets studded with piazze and medieval palazzi. Talk about a dining room with a view! The corn-yellow farmhouse stands high on a Tuscan hill, flanked by olive trees and a tidy courtyard, a 20-minute country walk from Siena's ancient gates. Letizia was a designer – the house lives and breathes her French-inspired creativity. Bedrooms are doll's-house pretty: soft violets, greens, lavenders; soaring whitewashed beams; floaty drapes and canopies; antique headboards and ancient doors; picture frames fashioned from wooden vats. Two look to Siena, the others to neat gardens where roses scamper and a large covered terrace begs you to sit out with a glass of wine – or float in a sky-blue infinity pool. Letizia loves cooking, too: dine under the stars, or chat around an open fire. Tuscany explodes all around you: Florence, Pisa, San Gimignano are close; theatre, wine-tasting, cookery courses, even shopping trips can (and should) be arranged. The main villa, next door, can be rented for large groups and weddings.

Price	€130-€150.
Rooms	6: 5 doubles, 1 twin.
Meals	Restaurant 1km.
Closed	Rarely.
Directions	See owner website.

Letizia Nuti
Strada dell'Ascarello 6,
53100 Siena

Tel	+39 0577 43646
Mobile	+39 338 6649721
Email	letizia@poderelastrega.com
Web	www.poderelastrega.com

Santa 10

A couple of years ago Elisa and Gianni, with their two kids in tow, made the move here, to this breezy hill outside Siena; the city's medieval towers dominate the horizon – and there's a 1,000-year-old tower right here (where Gianni's mother lives). It was only after the renovation of this old farm had begun that they discovered the *cantina* underground. Now they are in the wine business too, and vines stretch out along the valley in both directions. There's just the one bedroom here, round the back, with views to Siena. It's simple, countrified and extremely comfortable, with flashes of blue and gold on the walls, waxed floorboards underfoot, and some lovely family pieces dotted around. The colourful bathroom has a huge shower and a handsome gilt mirror and a little porthole through which you can espy the pool and gardens. Gianni and Elisa are a kind, interesting, loveable couple who want you to enjoy their life as much as they do; their enthusiasm is infectious. Breakfast in their kitchen or in your room – and don't leave without a bottle of Santa 10 in your suitcase!

Price	€100.
Rooms	1 double.
Meals	Restaurants within 1km.
Closed	Rarely.
Directions	Sent on booking.

Gianni & Elisa
Strada di Santa Regina 10/A,
53100 Siena

Tel +39 0577 43566
Email elisa@stradadisantareginadieci.it
Web www.stradadisantareginadieci.it

Rocca di Castagnoli

Max truly wants this place to shine, and shine it does. Ancient Rocca di Castagnoli, one of Chianti's most prestigious wine-producing estates, is a one thousand-year old hilltop castle with an attached hamlet and – off a courtyard with time-polished cobbles – some swooningly beautiful self-catering apartments and rooms. Immaculately designed interiors with beamy ceilings and ancient cotta floors offset the sharply defined opulence of sleek modern fixtures, royalty-sized draped beds, gold embroidered curtains, mountains of cushions and perfectly placed antiques. Bathrooms have huge whirlpool showers and snazzy products. Kitchens and sitting rooms follow flawless suit. A communal billiards room opens onto a terrace with stop-and-stare views that are shared from the pool in the garden below. Breakfasts are predictably perfect; and there's an exquisite inn, Osteria al Ponte, a stroll away. Tour the vineyards and cellars, dig into your pool-side sunspot, let dashing manager Max advise you – in perfect English – on wine trails in Chianti, and postpone the return home. The place is a dream!

Price	€125-€210. Apartments €515-€955 per week.
Rooms	6 + 7: 6 doubles. 7 apts for 2-6.
Meals	Breakfast €8-€13. Restaurant 5-minute walk.
Closed	Rarely.
Directions	FI-SI road exit Radda in Chianti; follow signs for Giaole in Chianti until signs for Rocca di Castagnoli; signed.

Max Adorno
Loc. Castagnoli,
53013 Siena

Tel	+39 0577 731909
Email	info@roccadicastagnoli.com
Web	www.roccadicastagnoli.com

Antico Borgo Poggiarello

Totally unspoilt, with gorgeous views over the hillsides down to the sea, this tucked-away 17th-century *borgo* has been transformed into an utterly charming 'holiday village' linked by a circuit of paths. Poggiarello is a family set-up: Signora Giove does the cooking, son Roberto does front of house, and Nino, Paolo and Ciro – the perfectly behaved English setters – are there when you need them. You can self-cater or do B&B here: the arrangements are flexible. Most apartments are for two; some interconnect and are ideal for eight. Rooms are big and comfortable with wrought-iron beds, cream curtains and covers, tiled floors; all have patios and great views and one is excellent for wheelchair-users. Days are spent lolling by the pool, evenings sunset-gazing on the terrace. Though the beaches – and the treasures of Siena, Monteriggioni and Volterra – lie a short drive away, you'll find it hard to leave. Note the beautifully lit bath housed in a cave that's heated all year to 38 degrees (extra charge) and the terraced restaurant in the stables where you can sample the best of Tuscan home cooking.

Price	€100-€140 for 2 per night.
Rooms	10 apartments: 9 for 2, 1 for 4.
Meals	Breakfast €9. Dinner, 5 courses, €20; by arrangement. Wine from €12. Half board extra €37 p.p.
Closed	November-February.
Directions	From Firenze-Siena m'way exit Monteriggioni. Right after stop sign, 1.4km, left for Abbadia a Isola & Strove. After 6km, left for Scorgiano. On for 4km, left at 'Fattoria di Scorgiano'. Signed for 2km.

Roberto Giove
Strada di San Monti 12,
53035 Monteriggioni

Tel +39 0577 301003
Email info@poggiarello.com
Web www.poggiarello.com

Bichi Borghesi Scorgiano

A clutch of 17th-century buildings – some beautifully restored, others ageing gracefully – make up this glorious wine estate half an hour from Siena. The hamlet is full of life: tractors trundle around the country lanes, estate workers throw you a cheery 'Buongiorno!' as they pass, dogs scamper around your feet on arrival. Despite the activity, this is a refined, relaxed place to stay. Archways, formal gardens and courtyards beg exploration, and there's a delightful pool to laze away the afternoon by... masses of space at every turn. There's always stuff going on here too: cookery courses in the kitchens, wine and olive oil tasting in the old stables, trips to neighbouring towns and vineyards. The comfortable apartments are set back away from all the hubbub. Traditionally furnished and wonderfully spacious, they have antique pieces, exposed brickwork and strong colours on the walls – ochres, terracottas, lemon yellows. Petite, sparkly-eyed Paola throws masses of energy into everything she does; she and Vittorio are a great team and will look after you perfectly. You won't want to leave! Special. *Minimum stay two nights.*

Price	Rufini €570-€760. Cocchieri €765-€900. Fattoria €860-€1,020. Prices per week.
Rooms	3 apartments: 1 for 4, 1 for 6, 1 for 7.
Meals	Restaurants 200m.
Closed	Casa Rufini: January to mid-April. Cocchieri & Fattoria: January to mid-March.
Directions	Sent on booking.

Paola & Vittorio Mereu
53031 Casole d'Elsa

Tel	+39 0577 301020
Email	info@bichiborghesi.it
Web	www.bichiborghesi.it

Fattoria Guicciardini

San Gimignano is a must and this makes a charming base: eight self-catering apartments right within the old city walls. Once the headquarters of the family's winemaking business, they have been immaculately converted from an ancient complex of buildings. Two were granaries in a former life (their bedrooms on a mezzanine floor), another was the farm cook's house. Lovely cool rooms have huge raftered ceilings, others arched windows or original fireplaces and tiles; all have been furnished in a contemporary style with new sofas, kilim-style rugs, Tuscan colours, the occasional antique. There are entrances from both outside the city walls and from the Piazza S. Agostino (take a look at the church's stunning altar frescoes). Get up early and watch the mists fall away to reveal the vineyards in the valley, then drink in the astonishing treasures of San Gimignano before the army of tourists descends. Evening in the city is magical, too, when the city's fairytale towers are floodlit: the time of day at which San Gimignano – honey pot of Tuscan tourism, and deservedly so – is at its most lovely. *Ask about parking.*

Price	€90 for 2. €120-€140 for 4. €150 for 6 (€600-€1,000 per week).
Rooms	9 apartments: 6 for 2-4, 3 for 4-6.
Meals	Restaurant 100m.
Closed	Never.
Directions	Leave Florence-Siena m'way at S. Gimignano & Poggibonsi Nord exit. Fattoria in centre of S. Gimignano.

Tuccio Guicciardini
Viale Garibaldi 2/A, Piazza S. Agostino 2,
53037 San Gimignano

Tel +39 0577 907185
Mobile +39 329 2273120
Email info@guicciardini.com
Web www.guicciardini.com

Fattoria Tregole

A vineyard and a private family chapel. What could be more Italian? The delightful Kirchlechners – he an architect, she a restorer – make Chianti Classico, grappa and olive oil from their Tuscan manor farm. They spent seven years restoring the buildings, keeping original features – raftered ceilings, terracotta floors, large fireplaces – and furnishing with a light, country-house touch. The airy apartments and the bedrooms, including a ground-floor suite with a terrace, feel like the family's rooms; all are lovely. Walls are eye-catching with Edith's hand-painted stencils, painted brass bedsteads are cleverly restored; there are traditional lampshades, dried flowers, patchwork quilts and crochet cushions. It is light, warm and inviting. Breakfast in the sunny dining room or on the patio; twice a week Edith cooks a Tuscan dinner, accompanied by the wine from the Tregole cellars. A beautiful pool, quiet views over olive groves and vine-clad hills, a garden with shady nooks, a tiny Renaissance chapel – it is intimate and homely. *Minimum stay three nights in apartments. Ask about cookery courses.*

Price	€130-€150. Suite €180. Apts €220-€320.
Rooms	5 + 2: 4 doubles, 1 suite for 2. 2 apts: 1 for 4, 1 for 5.
Meals	Dinner €35, book ahead. Wine from €10. Restaurants 4km.
Closed	Mid-November to mid-March.
Directions	From Florence SS222 for Greve-Panzano-Castellina; 5km after Castellina in Chianti; sign for Tregole; 1km.

Edith Kirchlechner
Loc. Tregole 86,
53011 Castellina in Chianti

Tel +39 0577 740991
Email fattoria-tregole@castellina.com
Web www.fattoria-tregole.com

Podere Cogno

The deeper you follow the bumpy unlit road into the woods, the quieter it gets – until all you can hear are birds and crickets. When you alight, you find yourself in a secret place: a green clearing overlooking olive groves and hills. The land has been worked since Etruscan times and the mellow dignified house suits its setting: the tower is 13th century, the house a century younger. Marco and Giovanna love it dearly and their enthusiasm and generosity bubble over. From the billiard room and library at the top to the gym and the wonderful oak-floored sitting room below, there's masses of space. Bedrooms are restrained and stylish, with exposed beams and 18th-century furniture; bathrooms are sparkling, and supplied with a superabundance of towels. You'll have breakfast on the veranda and Giovanna, an excellent cook, will make you an evening meal if you book early in the day; all is homemade, much is home-grown. The garden is wonderful, with a pond full of frogs and goldfish, a deliciously scented rose garden (with a hot tub) and an elusive family of coypus. *Min. stay three nights in B&B; one week in apt & cottage.*

Price	€120-€230. Apt €1015-€1400 per week. Cottage €1365-€1750 per week.
Rooms	4 + 2: 1 double, 3 suites for 2. 1 apt for 2, 1 cottage for 2.
Meals	Dinner €27. Restaurant 2km.
Closed	6 January-1st weekend in March.
Directions	A1 exit Firenze-Certosa dir. Siena; exit S. Donato in Poggio, dir. Siena. After Castellina in Ch., S.R. 222 (ex SS) Chiantigiana for 4km. At km 47.450 right dir. Caggiolo & Caggio. At x-roads sign for Cogno; on for 1.5km.

Marco Matteini
Loc. Cogno,
53011 Castellina in Chianti

Tel +39 0577 740978
Email giovannamatteini@gmail.com
Web www.poderecogno.com

La Locanda

Admire the view from the pool – both are stunning. This is a magical place; a soft green lawn edged with Mediterranean shrubs slopes down to the pool, a covered terrace overlooks medieval Volpaia. (Some of the best chianti is produced here; the village itself is a 20-minute walk.) The house vibrates with bold colour and lively fabric. The beautiful raftered living room, with open fireplace, big, stylish sofas and pale terracotta floor, reveals photos of Guido and Martina, he from the South, she from the North. They scoured Tuscany before they found their perfect inn, renovated these two houses and filled them with fine antiques, delightful prints, candles and fun touches. There's a library/bar where you can choose books from many languages and where Guido is generous with the grappa. The bedrooms, some with their own terraces, are in a separate building and have big beds, great bathrooms and whitewashed rafters, as was the custom here. Martina cooks and gardens while Guido acts as host – they are a charming pair. Once settled in you'll find it hard to stir. *Minimum stay two nights.*

Price	€220-€290. Singles €190-€250. Suite €310.
Rooms	7: 3 doubles, 3 twins, 1 suite.
Meals	Dinner €35 (Mon, Wed & Fri). Wine €18-€70. Restaurants 4km.
Closed	November to mid-April.
Directions	From Volpaia village square take narrow road to right which becomes track. On for 2km past small sign for La Locanda to left; 1km further to group of houses.

Guido & Martina Bevilacqua
Loc. Montanino,
53017 Radda in Chianti

Tel	+39 0577 738832/3
Email	info@lalocanda.it
Web	www.lalocanda.it

Palazzo Leopoldo

In a corner of the hall is a stone carving of a swaddled baby – 14th-century evidence of the hospital this once was. For the last few centuries Palazzo Leopoldo has been a manor house. It's surprisingly peaceful here, in the middle of beautiful, hilltop Radda, strolling distance to several *enoteche* – taste the fine chiantis. The whole house, on several levels and teeming with nooks and crannies, has a delightful feel: the hall is light, with white-painted arches and old tiled floor, there are bright rugs and fresh flowers. Stroll onto the terrace for sensational Tuscan views. Bedrooms range from suites to doubles up under the roof, all generously equipped and with a rustic-rich Tuscan feel. Some have the old bell-pulls for service, others the original stoves and frescoes; there's a beautiful elegance. A remarkable breakfast is served in a remarkable kitchen, replete with 18th-century range: the best-ever setting for a cookery class. Add to that an indoor pool and spa, a restaurant serving delicious food and delightful staff. More than worth the steep and winding road to get here! *Private parking.*

Price	€113-€225. Suites €315-€394.
Rooms	19: 14 doubles, 5 suites.
Meals	Breakfast €9.90. Lunch €25. Dinner €35.
Closed	January-February.
Directions	Signed in centre of Radda in Chianti.

Martina Rustichini
Via Roma 33,
53017 Radda in Chianti

Tel +39 0577 735605
Email info@palazzoleopoldo.it
Web www.palazzoleopoldo.it

Castello di Tornano

How about sleeping in a listed monument? The first thing you see is the ancient stone tower, peering above the wooded hills and vineyards. Inside, a beautiful restoration has enriched the glorious stonework, the space and the sense of history. Rooms are positively regal with ornate furniture, deep rugs on tiled floors, sparkling chandeliers and richly coloured drapes and linen (plum, raspberry, royal blue, vermilion). The terrace has stunning views and bathrooms are a treat: neutral-toned mosaics blend in with the original stone, there are big mirrors and fluffy white towels and robes. Relax downstairs in the living room with its old font, soft-lighting and plush red drapes; request dinner and you are served fine Tuscan food. The hotel is also an agriturismo so chianti, olive oil, grappa and sweet vin santo are all produced here. Uncluttered self-catering apartments, some with vaulted ceilings, have exposed beams and stone walls. Come for the friendly atmosphere, the lovely pool and garden, the wine tastings (they grow their own), the riding on the estate, the luxuriousness of it all, and the peace.

Price	€130-€325. Suites €280-€510. Triples €220-€325. Apartments €120-€220 (€670-€1250 per week).
Rooms	11 + 8: 7 doubles, 2 suites, 2 triples. 8 apartments for 2-4.
Meals	Breakfast €12 for self-caterers. Dinner €40, on request. Wine from €12. Restaurant 4km.
Closed	8 January-28 February; 15 November-23 December.
Directions	A1 exit Valdarno for Cavriglia-Gaiole on road 408. Pass Gaiole, cont. for Siena for 5km; signed on left.

Maura Marasca
Loc. Tornano,
53013 Gaiole in Chianti

Tel +39 0577 746067
Email info@castelloditornano.it
Web www.castelloditornano.it

L'Ultimo Mulino

The sense of space is stunning – the vast, medieval hall, the lofty ceilings, the stone walls, the flights of stairs… a fairy tale. Original arches give glimpses of passageways beyond and many of the rooms are connected by little 'bridges' with the millstream far below. Outside the restored watermill there's a large terrace for delicious breakfasts, a lovely long pool, and a small amphitheatre where the odd concerts is held. You're in the middle of nowhere, surrounded by trees and it's immensely quiet – just the sound of water and birds. All feels fresh and clean, the atmosphere is welcoming and informal, and nothing is too much trouble for the staff. Sparsely, elegantly and comfortably furnished, the great hall makes a cool, beautiful centrepiece to the building – and there's a snug with a fireplace where you can roast chestnuts in season. Excellently equipped, smallish bedrooms have terracotta tiled floors and good, generously sized beds. You dine in the conservatory overlooking the stream, on mainly Tuscan dishes – be tempted by truffles and local delicacies. Historic Radda is a ten-minute drive.

Price	€112-€203. Suite €324-€370.
Rooms	13: 12 doubles, 1 suite.
Meals	Dinner €35-€45. Wine €15-€80.
Closed	Mid-November to mid-March.
Directions	From Gaiole in Chianti 1st right on road to Radda. Mill on right after bend; signed.

Massimo Rossinelli
Loc. La Ripresa di Vistarenni,
53013 Gaiole in Chianti

Tel +39 0577 738520
Email info@ultimomulino.it
Web www.ultimomulino.it

Odina Agriturismo

You are 650 metres above sea level and feel on top of the world – the Arno valley reaches out before you and the air is pure. Paolo is a talented gardener and each bush, tree and herb has been chosen with care, posing magnificently next to the solid, blue-shuttered house. The interiors of the house and apartments are delightfully rustic and contemporary. Each is different: kitchen surfaces are of granite, or local *pietra serena*, bathroom walls are softly ragged in varying shades. All have French windows to a patio with wooden outdoor furniture. Oil, vinegar, sugar, coffee, salt and washing-up liquid are provided; ask in advance and they'll provide more (for which you pay). The reception is in a beautifully restored, de-consecrated chapel, with an old bread-making chest and a 'shop' selling Odina olive oil, honey, lavender and beans. Take a dip in the pool, go for long, lazy walks in the olive groves and chestnut woods, prepare a barbecue. Garden courses and visits – highly recommended – are held here in May. *Min. stay one week in high season; three nights in low season. Private chef available.*

Ethical Collection: Environment; Food.
See page 419 for details.

Price	€550-€950 for 2; €800-€1,400 for 5; €950-€1,750 for 6-7. Farmhouse €2,100-€3,900. Prices per week.
Rooms	4 apartments: 1 for 2, 1 for 5, 1 for 6, 1 for 7. Farmhouse for 8-10.
Meals	Restaurants 5km.
Closed	Mid-January to end February.
Directions	Firenze-Rome A1, exit Valdarno. In Terranuova, follow Loro Ciuffenna.

Paolo Trenti
Loc. Odina,
52024 Loro Ciuffenna

Tel	+39 0559 69304
Mobile	+39 333 9556699
Email	info@odina.it
Web	www.odina.it

Borgo Iesolana Agriturismo

At the centre of a patchwork of fields, vineyards and woods stands this irresistible group of old buildings. Mellow stone and warm brick blend, flowers tumble from terracotta pots, arches invite you in from the sun, two pools beckon... and to each apartment its pool-view terrace. The Toscano brothers inherited the estate from their grandfather and live here with their young families. They have made eleven apartments in the farm buildings – a solid, sensitive conversion with room for lots of people. The décor is a classy, uncluttered mix of traditional and new: good beds and fabrics, super kitchens, thoughtful lighting. If you prefer not to cook, you can breakfast in the 'wine bar' across the way, another impeccable restoration with modern Italian furniture and big windows while lunch and dinner are available on request: local produce and traditional Tuscan fare. The farm is beautifully run (the very vines are edged with roses) and produces wine, olive oil and honey. It lies beside an old Roman road that linked Siena and Florence, with views of Chiantishire on all sides. *Minimum stay two to seven nights.*

Price	€860-€2,670 per week (€130-€180, 2 nights low season).
Rooms	11 apartments: 3 for 2, 3 for 4, 3 for 6, 2 for 8.
Meals	Breakfast €8. Lunch/dinner €25-€30, by arrangement. Wine €9-€12. Restaurant 3km.
Closed	December-February
Directions	A1 Firenze-Roma exit Valdarno; at toll, right for Montevarchi & Levane/Bucine; thro' Bucine, left to Pogi. Left for Iesolana, 150m left; over narrow bridge & cont. to Borgo.

Giovanni & Francesco Toscano
Loc. Iesolana,
52021 Bucine

Tel +39 0559 92988
Email info@iesolana.it
Web www.iesolana.it

Le Caviere

What's lovely about this tranquil place – apart from the luxuries within – are the long dreamy views and the pool that's your own. You have utter privacy from the main house, in a creamy limestone hay barn with lots of garden. It's a superb renovation in a lovely untouched corner of Tuscany, awash with space and light, true to the building's age yet the finest of contemporary. Enter an open-plan living area with rustic terracotta floors and soothing biscuit shades, deep white sofas, art, books, antiques and flowers. Off which: an immaculate kitchen, a wisteria draped terrace, and a bathroom, surely the most delicious in Italy… impeccable white fittings, vast rain heads suspended from an ancient brick arch, an olive ladder on which to sling a luxurious towel. Then it's up the open stone stair to Busatti linens and a sumptuous bed. Sansepolcro, six miles off, is a draw for art lovers but has chic shops and restaurants too – or fire up the barbecue or the old pizza oven. The owners will also cook on request – the home-grown vegetables, raspberries and olive oil are the biggest treat.

Price	€1,300-€1,500 per week. Minimum 3 nights.
Rooms	Barn for 2-4 (1 double; sofabed).
Meals	Breakfast €10. Restaurant 5km.
Closed	Rarely.
Directions	Sent on booking.

Kate Middleton
Azienda Agricola Le Caviere,
52036 Pieve Santo Stefano

Mobile +39 347 8990137
Email kate@oliveoilandraspberries.it
Web www.oliveoilandraspberries.it

Casa Simonicchi

A magical spot from which to absorb the stillness that these hills evoke. After a blissful drive through the Casentino National Park you arrive at this stone farmhouse with a barn attached, made comfortable to the point of luxury by sculptress Jenny. In the top barn (six entrance steps only) is a family apartment, simple and charming: Italian and English pieces, natural colours, paintings and sculpture. The bedrooms, each with a shower, are placed at either end; the spacious sitting room and well-equipped kitchen lie between. Best of all is your roof terrace with its breathtaking panorama of sweet-chestnut forests. Bask in the sun or the shade, take a cool shower, dine al fresco, stargaze from the jacuzzi – or the telescope. Steeply below are wonderful terraces, lavender, irises, olives, pergola and small sculptures. Jenny also does B&B in the farmhouse and gives you a suite, with one bedroom romantically over the arch: beams, antiques, a huge fireplace. Warm generous Jenny can tell you about the historic towns, the countryside of Michelangelo and St Francis of Assisi – and the welcoming taverna down the road.

Price	€175; €350 for 4. Apt €675-€975 per week. Minimum 2 nights.
Rooms	1 + 1: 1 suite for 2, with kitchen. Apt for 4.
Meals	Dinner with wine, from €30, by arrangement. Restaurant nearby.
Closed	Christmas-April.
Directions	Exit A1 Arezzo; north for Sansepolcro; signs for Caprese Michelangelo; left for Lama; right for Chiusi della Verna; after cypress-filled cemetery, house on 3rd right-hand bend; sharp descent.

Jennifer Frears-Barnard
Via Simonicchi 184, Caprese Michelangelo, 52033 Arezzo

Tel +39 0575 793762
Email jenniferbarnard@libero.it
Web www.simonicchi.com

The Tuscan Mill

The bucolic valley is edged with woods – so peaceful you could hear a pin drop. Such is the setting for this ancient water mill. Owner Lulu lives in part of the house, is kind and charming and has done a terrific job of restoring, carefully preserving the mill's inner workings through the creative use of thick glass and clever lighting. Much of the furniture has been brought from England and the slight English country-house feel is enhanced by some horsey paintings (a reminder of Lulu's past as a point-to-pointer) alongside the traditional arches, beams and cotto floors so typical of rural Italy. The treehouse in the lawned garden is heaven for children and not bad for adults either, as you watch your energetic little ones clambering about and enjoy an apertitivo on the terrace. Dine out here, too; as night falls and the stream is lit up, you'll be hard pressed to think of anywhere you'd rather be. But go out you must, particularly as Sansepolcro, birthplace of Renaissance genius Piero della Francesco, is a ten-minute drive. Arezzo with its lively, monthly antiques market is not much further.

Price	€100-€150 (€700-€900 per week). Minimum 3 nights.
Rooms	Apartment for 2-4. B&B option available.
Meals	Restaurants 1km.
Closed	Rarely.
Directions	Sent on booking.

Lulu Primavera
Il Mulino, Tavernelle 21, Anghiari, 52031 Arezzo

Mobile +39 334 2119170
Email thetuscanmill@gmail.com
Web www.thetuscanmill.co.uk

Villa I Bossi

Fifty people once lived on the ground floor of the old house and everything is as it was – the great box that held the bread, the carpenter's room crammed with tools, the robes hanging in the sacristy, the oven for making charcoal... Francesca loves showing people round the house that has been in her husband's family since 1240; it is brimful of treasures. There's even a fireplace sculpted by Benedetto da Maiano in the 1300s – his 'thank you for having me' to the family. Sleep in faded splendour in the main villa or opt for the modern comforts of the orangery: simple and beautiful. This is a magical place, full of character and memories, overseen by the most delightful people. As for the park-like gardens... set among gentle green hills, they have been enriched over the centuries: to one side of the swimming pool, a hill covered in rare fruit trees, to the west, Italian box hedges and camellias, peonies and old-fashioned roses, avenues, pond, grassy banks and shady trees, enticing seats under arching shrubs, olives and vines... And they make their own chianti and oil. *Ask about cookery courses.*

Price	€125-€165. Extra person €10. Apartment €125-€165.
Rooms	10 + 1: 2 doubles, 2 twins. Orangery: 2 doubles, 2 triples, 2 quadruples. Apartment for 2.
Meals	Dinner, 4 courses with wine, €35; by arrangement. Restaurant 100m.
Closed	January-February.
Directions	In Arezzo follow signs to stadium. Pass Esso petrol station & on to Bagnoro. Then to Gragnone; 2km to villa.

Francesca Vignali Albergotti
Gragnone 44/46,
52100 Arezzo
Tel +39 0575 365642
Email franvig@ats.it
Web www.villaibossi.com

Villa La Lodola

One of the warmest, most generous and inviting places we know. The moment you pass through the wrought-iron gates you leave the outskirts of town and the main road behind: welcome to La Lodola. Hard to believe the livestock once lived downstairs: now low velvet sofas sprawl on polished terracotta floors and interesting pictures dot rose colour-washed walls. You'll like the huge fireplace you can actually sit in, the multi-drawed sideboards, the honey-bricked arches, the rustic 18th-century beams. Bedrooms – four upstairs – are a feast for the eyes, with heavy swagged curtains and some playful trompe l'oeil; those at the back have views. Gentle Mario is head of the family, his son cooks in the Osteria, his wife and daughter sell antiques. Mario's delicious cakes are served with fruits, cheeses and hams under your chosen pergola in summer – chase the morning sun – and the cookery courses are a treat: find the best produce in the market, then bring it home. Olives, pomegranates, lemons, vines, all flourish here so linger in their shade, then wander down to the pool for a long valley view.

Price	€116-€170. Minimum 3 nights.
Rooms	5: 2 doubles, 2 twins/doubles, 1 suite.
Meals	Lunch on request. Dinner with wine, €30.
Closed	Never.
Directions	Sent on booking.

Mario Porcu
Via Piana 19, Foiano della Chiana,
52045 Arezzo

Tel +39 0575 649660
Email info@lalodola.com
Web www.lalodola.com

Castello di Gargonza

Intriguing, delightful: a fortified Romanesque village in the beauty of the Tuscan hills, whose 800-year-old steps, stones, rafters and tiles remain virtually intact. Today it is a private, uniquely Italian marriage of exquisitely ancient and exemplary modern. Seen from the air it is perfect, as if shaped by the gods to inspire Man to greater works: a magical maze of paths, nooks and crannies, castellated tower, great octagonal well, a heavy gate that lets the road slip out and tumble down, and breathtaking views. You're given a map on arrival to help you navigate your way round. No cars, no shops, but a chapel, gardens, pool and old olive press for meetings, concerts and breakfasts by the fire. The old storeroom is now a spacious and airy restaurant with wooded hillside views. As for the Count and Countess, they and their staff look after you beautifully. Bedrooms and apartments are 'rustic deluxe' with smart modern furnishings, white-rendered walls, superb rafters, open fireplaces, tiny old doors reached up steep stone staircases. There's an ancient ambience, as if time has stood still.

Price	€140-€200. Suites €175-€195. Apartments €875-€2,275 per week.
Rooms	20 + 12: 20 doubles. 12 apartments for 2-10.
Meals	Breakfast €9 for self-caterers. Lunch/dinner with wine, €25-€35.
Closed	10 January-1 March.
Directions	Exit A1 at Monte S. Savino; SS73 for Siena. Approx. 7km after Monte S. Savino right for Gargonza; signed.

Elisa & Neri Guicciardini
Loc. Gargonza,
52048 Monte San Savino

Tel	+39 0575 847021
Email	info@gargonza.it
Web	www.gargonza.it

Il Pero

A labrador called Molly, a pony called Topsy, cats, chickens and a pool with long views – this is a brilliant place for families, lived and worked in by delightful William and Miranda. With their two daughters, they have poured their hearts into a new life in Italy. Il Pero is a work in progress, a lovely old Tuscan farmhouse (1782) set in a flat plain and surrounded by barley and sunflowers, plus a haybarn, an olive press (they produce their own oil) and a kitchen garden you can help yourself to. There are four super apartments with good kitchens, cheery bright bedrooms, big wet rooms and little pergolas for private outdoor spaces – and a romantic bedroom in the square tower with an ancient wine barrel for the shower! All is new or cleverly recycled, from the adjustable mattresses to the lovely old floorboards from a nearby convent. Don't miss the minstrels' gallery, lit by a 120-candle chandelier (a wow for big celebrations) or the pizza evenings – great fun. As for cobbled hilltop Arezzo, it is stuffed with fine churches and frescoes, pretty shops and irresistible *gelati*. *Ask about photography courses.*

Price	€150. Apts €800-€1,500 per week.
Rooms	1 + 4: 1 double. 4 apts: 2 for 2, 1 for 5, 1 for 6.
Meals	Breakfast €15 for self-caterers. Welcome pack. Occasional dinner with wine, €30. Restaurants 5km.
Closed	Rarely.
Directions	A1 exit Monte S. Savino. At Montagnano dir. Rigutino/Frassineto. Leaving Frass. left off main road; past cemetery, gravel track, stone house with towers; left after farm. Right into drive, signed.

Miranda Taxis
Loc. Manziana 15,
52100 Policiano

Tel +39 0575 979593
Email info@ilpero.com
Web www.ilpero.com

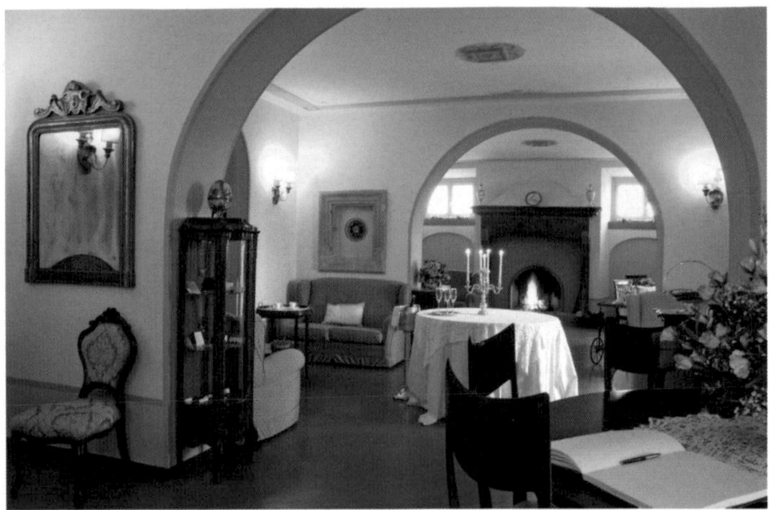

Villa Marsili

It's always refreshing to come to Cortona, set so magnificently on its hill. And the site of this smart and beautifully run palazzo-hotel is steeped in history: in the 14th century the church of the Madonna degli Alemanni stood here, built to house the miraculous image of the Madonna della Manna. Beneath, an Oratory was linked by a flight of stairs – which still connects to the breakfast room and its excellent breakfast buffet; in 1786 the church was demolished and an elegant mansion built on the site. The owners have preserved many of the original architectural features hidden over the centuries, while the hall and the light-filled bedrooms are immaculately and individually decorated with trompe l'œil and hand-painted borders. Colours are gentle yellows, bathrooms are gorgeous, most rooms are large, some are tiny, all windows have views. The front of the house looks onto a garden – with a pergola for admiring the stunning panorama of the Valdichiana and Lake Trasimeno. On the northern side is a winter garden, with the Borgo San Domenico as a mesmerising backdrop. *Ask about cookery classes & vineyard tours.*

Price	€130-€230. Singles €80-€130. Suites €250-€350.
Rooms	26: 18 doubles, 5 singles, 3 suites.
Meals	Restaurants 5-minute walk uphill.
Closed	9 January-February.
Directions	A1 exit Val di Chiana, then Siena/ Perugia m'way; 2nd exit for Cortona. Follow signs for "Cortona Centro". Parking nearby.

Caterina Caloni
Viale Cesare Battisti 13,
52044 Cortona

Tel	+39 0575 605252
Email	info@villamarsili.net
Web	www.villamarsili.net

Casa Bellavista

A glass of wine at a table in the orchard. Birdsong for background music – or occasionally foreground, if the family rooster is feeling conversational. And a panorama of Tuscan landscape. Bellavista is well-named: its stunning all-round views take in Monte Amiata, Foiano della Chiana and the old Abbey of Farneta. There was a farm here for 200 years but the house was extensively restored about 30 years ago. It still has the original brick exterior, now softened by creepers, and a welcoming, family atmosphere: lovely Simonetta and Guido have two teenage children. There's an assured, uncluttered country elegance to the rooms, while pretty, airy bedrooms are furnished with family antiques and interesting textiles; two have their own balcony with views onto the garden. Simonetta's kitchen has a huge marble table top for kneading bread and she cooks farmhouse food for her guests: delicious; breakfasts are lavish, cookery lessons are a treat. Roam the Arezzo province in true Italian style: vespas and bikes are free and there's a beautiful 65km route to test them on. Italian family B&B at its finest.

Price	€100-€145.
Rooms	4: 2 doubles, 2 twins/doubles.
Meals	Dinner €35, by arrangement. Wine from €19.
Closed	Rarely.
Directions	Autostrada Valdichiana exit Perugia; exit Foiano. After 400m, right for Fratta-S. Caterina. On for 2.8km, right next to ruined building. After 1km, right at junc.; keep to left-hand road. After 600m, right onto dirt road.

Simonetta Demarchi
Loc. Creti C.S. 40,
52044 Cortona

Tel	+39 0575 610311
Mobile	+39 335 6383377
Email	info@casabellavista.it
Web	www.casabellavista.it

La Palazzina

There is an English inflection to La Palazzina, with its quirky 14th-century watchtower planted inexplicably beside the main house. With its intimate rooms and luscious views across the wooded valley it makes a magical retreat. There's a well-equipped kitchen, a wood-burner for cosy nights, a winding stair to a half-moon double and, at the top, a twin with a stunning brick-beehive ceiling. The bathroom is shared, so this is one for close friends; and, note, no children under 16, on account of several severe drops from tower windows! The honeysuckle-strewn terrace is just as you would wish, with cypress trees marching sedately up the hill alongside, and birdsong to disturb the peace, and the beautifully maintained, terraced grounds, which include a saltwater swimming pool with views, are for you to explore; they lead to some of the loveliest walks in the valley. Hannibal defeated the Roman army at nearby Lake Trasimeno and there is little that David doesn't know about the historical importance of this area; the friendly owners live at the end of the neighbouring farmhouse. *Minimum stay one week.*

Price	£795-£1,095 per week.
Rooms	Tower for 4 (1 double, 1 twin).
Meals	Restaurants 3km.
Closed	Rarely.
Directions	Sent on booking.

David & Salina Lloyd-Edwards
Sant'Andrea di Sorbello,
52040 Mercatale di Cortona

Tel +39 0575 638111
Email davidle47@btinternet.com
Web www.palazzina.co.uk

Il Palazzetto

An unassuming barn conversion up a steep drive, this self-catering treat combines traditional architecture with fresh homely furnishings and underfloor heating. A 2.5-acre garden of fruit orchards and olives with long vistas to ancient hill-topped Tuscan towns ensures birdsong and herb-tinted peace and tranquillity. Bedrooms are understated, simple and comfortable with plenty of wood and natural colours. The spacious sitting room is made snug by an open fire in winter, while French windows keep it breezy in summer. Behind the house is a rose-rambled terraced dining area and a covered pergola; down some steps through the olive trees to the field below lies a lovely large saltwater infinity pool, a secluded sun trap for relaxing with far-reaching views; bliss too for a night-time, underwater-lit dip. There's loads to do in the area, from truffle snuffling, fishing and riding to meandering through the alley'd mazes and markets of nearby medieval towns Città di Castello, San Sepolcro and Anghiari. A well-converted, well-furnished space whose gardens, given time, will mellow. *Minimum stay one week.*

Price	€900-€2,200 per week.
Rooms	House for 8.
Meals	Restaurants 1.5km.
Closed	Never.
Directions	In Monterchi centre at large sq., over bridge on right. Follow road round old town (don't go into old town). Exit Monterchi, 1st right to Ripoli & Pianezze. On for 1.5km until small bridge on left. Over bridge, onto gravel road. At x-roads, left track for 0.2km. New drive on right; very steep.

Diane Noel
Loc. Borgacciano,
52031 Monterchi

Mobile +44 (0)7956 841895
Email diane@noelfamily.co.uk
Web www.il-palazzetto.com

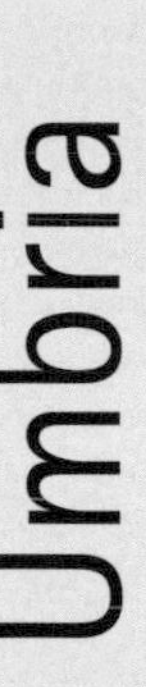
Umbria

Locanda Rosati Agriturismo

From the moment you turn off the road – whose proximity is quickly forgotten – the atmosphere is easy. The house has been gently modernised but remains firmly a farmhouse; the summer-cool rooms on the ground floor – with open fires in winter – have been furnished with an eye for comfort rather than a desire to impress, and wild flowers, books and magazines are scattered. Dinner is the thing here; it's rustic, delectable and Giampiero and Paolo are natural hosts, full of stories and enthusiastic advice on what to do and where to go. Tables are laid with simple cloths, glass tumblers and butter-coloured pottery, the recipes have been handed down the Rosati generations, the ingredients are home-grown and the wines come from a wonderful cellar carved out of the tufa seven metres below ground. Bedrooms are simple, with new wooden beds, pristine bed linen, spotless showers. Much of the furniture comes from the famous Bottega Michelangeli in Orvieto, whose jigsaw-like carved animal shapes characterise this region. From the gardens you can see the spiky skyline of Orvieto: delightful. *Ask about cookery courses.*

Price	€110-€150. Singles €90-€110. Half-board option available.
Rooms	10: 4 doubles, 1 single, 5 family rooms.
Meals	Dinner with wine, €37.50.
Closed	7 January-February.
Directions	Exit A1 at Orvieto; on for Viterbo, Bolsena & Montefiascone; 10km; on right.

Giampiero Rosati
Loc. Buonviaggio 22,
05018 Orvieto

Tel	+39 0763 217314
Email	info@locandarosati.it
Web	www.locandarosati.it

Locanda Palazzone

An imposing palazzo in the Umbrian countryside, Locanda Palazzone is full of contrasts. Built by a cardinal as a resting place for pilgrims to Rome, it was designed with urban sophistication: buttressed walls, mullioned windows, vaulted hall. Later, it fell from grace and became a country farmhouse – until Ludovico's family rescued it, planting vineyards and restoring the buildings. Despite the rustic setting, the interiors are cool, elegant, chic. The light and airy sitting room, once the Grand Hall, has huge windows overlooking the garden. Bedrooms – split-level suites, mostly – are understatedly luxurious, their modern and antique furnishings set against pale oak floors, cream walls, exposed stone. Red, claret and purple cushions add warmth; white linen sheets, Bulgari bath foams and specialist herb soaps soothe. Meals, both regional and seasonal, are served on rainbow china on the terrace, accompanied by the estate's wines. Your generous hosts are eager to please, the pool is surrounded by delphiniums and roses, and views sweep to vineyards and forests. A remarkable place. *Minimum stay two nights June-September.*

Price	€185-€320.
Rooms	7 suites: 5 for 2, 2 for 4.
Meals	Breakfast €8. Dinner, 4 courses, €43; by arrangement.
Closed	10 January-20 March.
Directions	A1 Firenze-Roma, exit Orvieto; 1.8km dir. Orvieto; at bridge for funicular, right for Allerona; cont. to Sferracavallo junc.; on for Allerona; 200m, left toward Castel Giorgio, keeping petrol station on right; 2.5km, signed.

Lodovico Dubini
Loc. Rocca Ripesena,
05010 Orvieto

Tel	+39 0763 393614
Email	info@locandapalazzone.com
Web	www.locandapalazzone.com

Tenuta di Canonica

The position is wonderful, on a green ridge with stunning views. The house was a ruin (17th century, with medieval remnants and Roman foundations) when Daniele and Maria bought it in 1998. Much creativity has gone into its resurrection. There's not a corridor in sight – instead, odd steps up and down, hidden doors, vaulted ceilings, enchanting corners. Cool, beautiful reception rooms are decorated in vibrant colours, then given a personal, individual and exotic touch: family portraits, photos, books... there's even a parrot. The bedrooms are vast, intriguingly shaped and opulent, with rugs on pale brick or wooden floors and gorgeous beds and fabrics. Ask for air conditioning if you go in summer. The dining room opens onto a covered terrace surrounded by roses and shrubs, a path sweeps down to the pool – oh, the views! And there's walking on the 24-hectare estate. This is a house that reflects its owners' personalities. Daniele and Maria are vivid, interesting and well-travelled. While they are away, Benedetta or Francesca are on hand, to welcome guests to a rich tapestry of rooms.

Price	€160-€250. Apts €1,100-€1,350 per week.
Rooms	11 + 2: 11 doubles. 2 apartments for 3-4.
Meals	Dinner €40. Wine €10-€40. Restaurants 6km.
Closed	December-February.
Directions	Firenze-Rome A1 exit Valdichiana; E45 Perugia-Terni exit Todi-Orvieto; SS448 for Prodo-Titignano; 3km, Bivio per Cordigliano; 1km, signed. Do not turn to Canonica, continue until Cordigliano sign, then on left.

Daniele Fano
Loc. Canonica m.75/76,
06059 Todi

Tel +39 0758 947545
Email tenutadicanonica@tin.it
Web www.tenutadicanonica.com

Torre Sangiovanni

This 13th-century watchtower saw many a battle from within the castle walls, but is now a peaceful spot of cooing pigeons and roses scampering up pale walls. You enter by a garden of pink petunias and shady iron tables where Umbrian and Venetian fare – wild boar, funghi, fish – is served in summer. The cosy reception (low beams, comfy sofas, Persian rugs, tasselled lamps) is replete with Catholic paraphernalia, for this is a pilgrim's stop – Il Santuario dell'Amore Misericordioso stands on top of the hill. The dining room is similarly bijou, all floral plates, pictures, clocks and copper pans polished to a shine. (Amazing that Rosary magicked this from semi-ruin.) Bedrooms – and separate self-catering suite – continue the traditional, religious theme: tasselled velvet, stencilled ribbons, doilies over dainty tables, an antique sewing machine... stone walls are two arm-lengths thick, one pierced with an arrow slit. All is spotless: Rosary likes things just so. The village has restaurants, a spa, tennis, horse riding; close by are hilltop Todi, arty Perugia, ceramics at Deruta, and Montefalco for Sagrantino wine.

Price	€85-€140. 2 apartments €100-€160.
Rooms	9 + 2: 4 doubles, 3 twin/doubles, 2 family rooms for 2-4. 2 apartments for 2-4.
Meals	Dinner €25. Wine €3-€35. Restaurants in village.
Closed	Rarely.
Directions	Sent on booking.

Rosary Pecoraro
Voc. Castello 26/G,
06059 Todi

Tel	+39 0758 87364
Mobile	+39 349 4466442
Email	info@torre-sangiovanni.it
Web	www.torre-sangiovanni.it

La Palazzetta del Vescovo Relais

Only the bells from a nearby convent or the hum of the tractor will disturb you. Paola and Stefano love to pamper their guests and there's a 'wellness' room in the cellar. Widely travelled and from the corporate world, they decided in 2000 to hang up their business suits and do something different. They bought this 18th-century hilltop palazzetta – once a summer residence for bishops, utterly abandoned in the 1960s – and restored it to its former glory. An informal elegance prevails. The four sitting rooms are cool, elegant and inviting; the bedrooms, each individual, each lovely, are composed in subtle, muted colours: pale walls, fine rugs, muslin'd four-posters, antique Neapolitan beds. What they have in common is a matchless view over steeply falling vineyards and the Tiber valley. On a clear day you can see as far as Perugia. The newly planted gardens and the pool make the most of the outlook, too – as does the terrace, where you can enjoy an aperitif before Paola's Umbrian cuisine. She, like her house, is a delight – serene, smiling and friendly. *Non-alcoholic drinks included.*

Price	€190-€270. Singles from €160. Minimum 2 nights.
Rooms	9 doubles.
Meals	Light lunch, from €15. Dinner, 4 courses, €38. Wine from €12. Restaurant 4km.
Closed	November-February.
Directions	A1 Rome-Florence exit Perugia onto E45; exit Fratta Todina. On for 7km, left for Spineta, thro' Spineta; house on right after vineyard, up track behind gates.

Paola Maria & Stefano Zocchi
Via Clausura 17, Fraz. Spineta,
06054 Fratta Todina

Tel	+39 0758 745183
Email	info@lapalazzettadelvescovo.it
Web	www.lapalazzettadelvescovo.com

Casale Campodoro

This restored 18th-century building has been embellished inside with style and a quirky humour: imagine an Indonesian hippo's head over a fireplace and a plastic goose as a lamp. Piero, a gentle, humorous and intelligent man, lives here with warm-hearted Carolina, four cats, some geese, a pony and three daft, friendly and boisterous dogs. In one shower room, a muscular plaster-cast juts out of the wall as a towel rail; elsewhere, scary Scottish grandmother's clothes – lace interwoven with scarab beetles – have been framed. By the pool are plastic yellow Philippe Starck sofa and chairs; on the walls, religious icons. The garden sits on an Umbrian hillside and has little steps leading to hidden corners and a large aviary whose birds escape and return at night. There are lovely views across to an old abbey, and other, more edible delights: warm, fresh, homemade bread and tasty jams for breakfast. Once a week, guests get together for dinner with everyone contributing a national dish. If you like animals and don't mind the odd bit of peeling paint, this is a kind, joyously individual and eccentric place.

Price	€70-€80. Apts €80-€110 (€500-€700 per week).
Rooms	3 + 3: 3 doubles. 3 apts: 2 for 3, 1 for 5.
Meals	Breakfast €4 for self-caterers. Restaurants 2km.
Closed	Rarely.
Directions	From Perugia-Cesena exit Massa Martana (316) to Foligno/Bastaro; left to San Terenziano; 1km; right to Viepri; 100m, track on left; 1st on right.

Carolina Bonanno
Fraz. Viepri 106,
06056 Massa Martana

Mobile	+39 333 3875740
Email	info@casalecampodoro.com
Web	www.casalecampodoro.it

La Licina

Just beyond the outskirts of Spoleto you find yourself in winding leafy country lanes. And there is La Licina, tucked into a fold of the hills, a mini 'borgo' at the end of the track. Friendly open Lodovico and Francesca live in the main house, guests live in the ochre-washed stables a pace away. Ginestra, on the ground floor, may be where the horses slept but you wouldn't know it now, though the brick inner arch and the chunky beams remain. This simple, spotless, open-plan space opens to its own grassy garden with a round table, a barbecue and gentle green views. Tartufo, which lies above, is similarly comfortable, with slightly more workspace in its kitchen and a step away from its own elevated, furnished patio with pretty views. Lots to love: a pool, pines and hosts who give you figs, plums and pears from their garden, and all the local info you desire. The position is fantastic: you are walking distance from civilised Spoleto, and a three-minute stroll through the olive groves to a pizzeria... life in the slow lane, so pat the neighbours' donkeys on the way! *Minimum stay two nights.*

Price	€600-€1,000 per week.
Rooms	2 apartments: 1 for 4, 1 for 4-5.
Meals	Restaurants within walking distance.
Closed	8-20 January.
Directions	Sent on booking.

Ludovico Angelini Rota
Loc. La Licina 9,
06049 Spoleto

Tel	+39 0743 49323
Mobile	+39 349 5834907
Email	info@lalicina.it
Web	www.lalicina.it

Le Terre di Poreta – Borgo della Marmotta

No one fuses the past with the present so perfectly as the Italians. This venerable 150-hectare estate, in the family since 1673, lies in a landscape of beauty and tranquillity. Approach through olive groves with valley views, wash up at a *borgo* in the hamlet of Poreta. The square, the stables, the sheepfold, the granary, the mill – all have been exquisitely revived. Two friendly dogs and owner Filippo, tall, languid and charming, live in the villa up on the hill and welcome you on board. The Borgo exudes exclusivity yet feels unexpectedly relaxed. Imagine exposed stones and rustic rafters, colourwashed walls in muted earth tones, elegant rugs on terracotta floors, four-posters draped in soft cotton, upholstered bedheads, ancient doors, a sunken bath tub like a Turkish hamman: these are spaces to linger in. With a dining room and a multi-sofa'd 'salotto', a sauna, a kitchen for cookery courses and a trio of pools, it's a resort of the classiest kind. They're into Slow Food here and breakfasts are plentiful, served under the pergola in summer. Good value, too.

Price	€120-€180. Apts €180-€260 (€820-€1,140 per week).
Rooms	11 + 7: 7 doubles, 4 twins/doubles. 7 apartments: 6 for 2-4, 1 for 4.
Meals	Breakfast €10 for self-caterers. Dinner €30 & lunch €18 (on request). Restaurant 2km.
Closed	Easter & Christmas.
Directions	A1 exit Orte dir. Terni/Spoleto. After Spoleto, dir. Foligno. 2nd exit for Poreta S. Giacomo. Follow signs to Poreta/Le Terre di Poreta.

Filippo Montani Fargna
Poreta 74,
06049 Spoleto

Tel	+39 0743 274137
Email	info@leterrediporeta.it
Web	www.leterrediporeta.it

Le Terre di Poreta – Villa della Genga

Up near Pope Leone XII's ex-hunting lodge (the Fargna family home) are five solid estate buildings, homes of rustic sophistication and rare beauty. First La Colombaia, its brick staircase leading to a bedroom in the tower, a wonder of ancient beams and arches, doves' perches and niches. Then Il Grottone, whose cave-like living room wall stands in stark contrast to its fabulous ultra-chic décor. From Gli Ziri a glass door faces the sunsets; the roof garden of Casa Nello pulls the outside in. And everywhere: sumptuous fabrics, hand-made tiles, beautiful antiques, elegant lighting, and glorious kitchens that combine Italian modernity with rustic ceramics: ancient and modern go hand in hand. The estate produces organic beans, chickpeas, lentils and olive oil – note the enticing hand-made soaps – and the swimming pool is chemical-free. What to do? Learn to prune olives, help in the harvest, go truffle hunting, enjoy the family's restaurant nearby. Lovely hilltop Spoleto has its summer music festival and Assisi its Basilica di San Francesco; linger a while after the crowds have gone home.

Price	€750-€1,950 per week.
Rooms	5 houses: 3 for 4, 1 for 6, 1 for 10.
Meals	Breakfast €10. Restaurant 2km.
Closed	Easter & Christmas.
Directions	A1 exit Orte dir. Terni/Spoleto. After Spoleto, dir. Foligno. 2nd exit for Poreta S. Giacomo. Follow signs to Poreta/Le Terre di Poreta.

Filippo Montani Fargna
Poreta 74,
06049 Spoleto

Tel +39 0743 274137
Email info@leterrediporeta.it
Web www.leterrediporeta.it

Pianciano

The old borgo buildings (some 16th century) are now self-contained apartments; come for deep delicious comfort on a working, self-sufficient estate. Wander down the terraced orchards to a huge pick-your-own vegetable garden overlooking a sauna and sleek pool – and tables and chairs under a vine canopy, an idyllic setting for lunch. Beyond are olive groves, vineyards and pastures – space galore to explore. Lavender-scented bedrooms are touched with elegant details: jade-coloured vases arranged just so, divine hand-detailed linen, old doors mounted as headboards, antique frames holding romantic paintings. Neutral coloured throws complement beamed ceilings, terracotta floors and sturdy wooden pieces, bookshelves hold handsome tomes, framed copies of old letters and antique architectural plans dot walls. High-ceilinged sitting rooms and a cavernous dining room hewn from the hillside provide heart-warming living space; knock-out views across the valley mean you'll keep the curtains open. Visit the wonderful little villages of the Valnerina, fall in love with this magical place. *Ask about pizza nights.*

Price	€750-€1,600 per week.
Rooms	3 apartments for 6-8.
Meals	Breakfast €10. Chef available, by arrangement. Restaurant nearby.
Closed	Never.
Directions	Exit Eggi-San Giacomo from SS; right at lights, then right dir. Passo d'Acera. At Tamoil garage straight on, reach 6km milestone, on for 300m, then right at sharp bend onto dirt road. Through gate Pianciano (please close behind you) and on for 200m to estate.

Claudia Bachetoni
Loc. Silvignano,
06049 Spoleto

Tel +39 0743 521535
Email pianciano@pianciano.it
Web www.pianciano.it

Casa del Cinguettio

A winding road leads up into the hills and the rewards on arrival are great. Tucked out of sight from the village street, beneath a medieval castle, this beautifully restored barn appears to hang on to the side of the hill – and the views, from pool and terrace over the Spoleto valley, are stupendous. A night swim almost leaves you feeling suspended in space! As for the recently refurbished, split-level interiors, they combine traditional, solid, cave-like Umbrian architecture with funky modern touches. Slabs of wood from the wall make a glass-bannistered staircase, there are cream marble floors, a glass-topped dining table, a groovy, steep-stepped mezzanine area where children can sleep, state of the art showers; the contrasts and colours are gorgeous. Ethnic spreads, an oriental rug and a corner fireplace add warmth to the sitting room on cool evenings in, while the fully kitted kitchen leads onto a barbecue terrace for lazy lunches under the olives trees. Herbs scent the air. The hills are laced with walking and riding paths, the area is rich with history, Assisi is a short drive. *Parking for two cars.*

Price	£950-£1,900 per week.
Rooms	House for 6-8.
Meals	Restaurants 2km.
Closed	Rarely.
Directions	Sent on booking.

Berenice Anderson
06042 Campello Alto

Tel +44 (0)1865 553244
Mobile +44 (0)7713 638627
Email bma161@hotmail.com
Web www.casadelcinguettio.com

I Mandorli Agriturismo

I Mandorli is aptly named: there's at least one almond tree outside each apartment. The blossom in February is stunning and, in summer, masses of greenery shades the old *casa padronale*. Once the centre of a 200-hectare estate, the shepherd's house and the olive mill in particular are fascinating reminders of days gone by. Mama Wanda is passionate about the whole, lovely, rambling place and will show you around, embellishing everything you see with stories about its history. Widowed, she manages the remaining 47 hectares, apartments and rooms, *and* cooks, aided by her three charming daughters: home-grown produce and excellent gnocchi every Thursday. Bedrooms are sweet, simple affairs with new wrought-iron beds and pale patchwork quilts; small bathrooms are spotless. Children will love the wooden slide and seesaw, the old pathways and steps on this shallow hillside, the new pool – wonderful to return to after cultural outings to Assisi and Spoleto. This is olive oil country so make sure you go home with a few bottles of the best. *Laundry facilities: small charge.*

Price	€45-€90 (€300-€650 per week). Apts €70-€150 (€400-€700 per week).
Rooms	3 + 3: 1 twin/double, 2 triples. 3 apts: 1 for 2, 2 for 4.
Meals	Breakfast €5 for self-caterers. Restaurants 500m.
Closed	Rarely.
Directions	SS3 exit Trevi-Montefalco for Bovara; signed from main road.

Famiglia di Zappelli Cardarelli
Loc. Fondaccio 6,
06039 Bovara di Trevi

Tel	+39 0742 78669
Mobile	+39 333 498309
Email	info@agriturismoimandorli.com
Web	www.agriturismoimandorli.com

Villa di Monte Solare

A hushed, stylish, country retreat in a perfect Umbrian setting. This noble villa hotel, encircled by a formal walled garden, has uniformed staff, elegant rooms and a superior restaurant. The grounds, which include the little chapel of Santa Lucia and a small maze, envelop the hotel in calm. Big bedrooms in pale ice-cream colours are lovingly tended, full of local fabric and craftsmanship. The public rooms have kept their charm, their painted cornices and friezes, huge fireplaces, ancient terracotta floors. The restaurant, a gorgeous beamed room with a roaring fire in winter, seats bedroom capacity, so non-residents may only book if guests are dining out. Cappuccino from a bar machine at breakfast; at dinner, superb designer food and a choice 380 wines. The owners live for this place and eat with guests every night, the mood is refined and jackets are usually worn, though not insisted upon. In the old glass *limonaia* is a luxurious beauty spa, for guests only. There are bikes to rent, pools to swim, even concerts and talks on Umbrian history. The view stretches out in every direction. A pampering place.

Ethical Collection: Environment; Food. See page 419 for details.

Price	€200-€240. Single €130-€145. Suites €300-€450.
Rooms	25: 14 doubles, 1 single, 10 suites.
Meals	Lunch €45-€65. Dinner with wine, €45-€65. Restaurant 4km.
Closed	Never.
Directions	Exit A1 at Chiusi-Chianciano; right to Chiusi; right for Città della Pieve; signs for Perugia, wall on left; left for Perugia-Tavernelle (SS220); 1km after Tavernelle, left for Colle S. Paolo. 4km to Villa.

Rosemarie & Filippo Iannarone
Via Montali 7, Colle San Paolo,
06068 Tavernelle di Panicale

Tel	+39 0758 32376
Email	info@villamontesolare.com
Web	www.villamontesolare.com

Villa Lemura

Live like an aristocrat but without the pomp or circumstance. This 18th-century building, once the country villa of Umbrian nobility, has an opulent but faded grandeur. It is home to delightful, friendly Emma, Luca and family, so don't be surprised to find a bicycle propped against the gracious pillars of the entrance hall. The bedrooms will make you gasp – frescoed ceilings, richly tiled floors, Murano chandeliers – yet it all feels charmingly lived-in. Furniture is a comfortable mixture of antiques and brocante finds. The high-ceilinged, elegant bedrooms might include an antique French bed, a chaise longue or a painted ceramic stove. Most have frescoes, one has a private terrace. Sink into sofas in the ballroom-sized salon, browse through a book in the library, have breakfast on the terrace above the Italian garden. Dinner can be arranged – or you may rustle up your own in the delightful orangery. Lake Trasimeno, Perugia and Assisi wait to be discovered; or find a quiet spot in the villa's shady garden of delights – mossy statues, fountains, olive grove, terraced pool and views.

Price	€120-€150. Whole house on request.
Rooms	7: 3 doubles, 1 twin, 1 triple; 1 double, 1 twin sharing bath.
Meals	Dinner €30 (min. 8), on request. Wine from €10. Restaurant 1km.
Closed	Occasionally.
Directions	From A1 exit Chiusi for Perugia; exit Perugia/Magione (not Panicale); signs to Panicale; thro' Macchie & Colgiordano (not up to Panicale); left to Lemura, Villa 1st on left.

Emma Mesenzio
Via Le Mura 1,
06064 Panicale

Tel +39 0758 37134
Email villalemura@alice.it
Web www.villalemura.com

Mazzarelli 2

On the edge of a truly tiny village is a century-old house in an engaging, organically-run garden. A vineyard too, olive groves and a charming pool that's yours all day – in one compact, beautiful, untamed acre. Annie and her husband moved from Scotland to create a characterful Italian home with pictures on every wall; you couldn't hope to meet nicer people. Once in that lovely garden – look out for the two dear little dogs – head up the stone steps to classic but eclectic B&B bedroom, finished with a designer's touch. Breakfast on eggs from their hens and local sausages, out on the deck with rich hill views – or around the table in an adorable kitchen with an Aga. The guests' living room is inviting with its plump library of books, chandelier and gorgeous artwork. You can also self-cater, in an apartment downstairs with exposed stone walls, an elegant white bed and a comfy blue and white living room. If you feel your inner artist emerging, head off to Annie's studio – or explore the medieval Tuscan towns and Lake Trasimeno. That is, if you can bear to leave this perfect little world! We loved it.

Price	€100. Apt €110 (€590-€690 per week).
Rooms	1 + 1: 1 double. 1 apt for 2.
Meals	Restaurants 2km.
Closed	Rarely.
Directions	Sent on booking.

Annie Robertson
06060 Paciano

Tel	+39 0758 30441
Email	anniebr50@gmail.com
Web	www.justfortwoitaly.co.uk

Villa Aureli

Little has changed since the Villa was built in the 18th century and became the country house of the Serègo Alighieri family 100 years later. The ornamental plasterwork, floor tiles and decorative shutters reflect its noble past, it is known to all the locals and is full of precious and historic treasures (walled up by a perspicacious housekeeper during the Occupation) which inspire the interest, attention and care of Signor Sperello. The house in fact has its origins in the 16th century, and the grounds are suitably formal – overgrown here, tamed there, with lemon trees in amazing 18th-century pots in the *limonaia* and a swimming pool created from an irrigation tank. The apartments are big and beautiful, the one on the second floor the largest and grandest, with balconies and views. Floors have mellow old tiles, ceilings are high and raftered, bedrooms are delightfully faded. You are a step away from the village, so can walk to the few shops and bar. A quietly impressive retreat, wonderfully peaceful – and special. *Min. stay one week in high season; two nights in low season.*

Price	€700-€1,500 per week.
Rooms	4 apartments: 1 for 4, 1 for 4-8, 1 for 5, 1 for 6.
Meals	Occasional dinner with wine, €36. Restaurant 2km.
Closed	Never.
Directions	From A1, exit Valdichiana for Perugia, exit Madonna Alta towards Città della Pieve. At square, sign for Bagnaia; on left after 200m. Alternatively, go to centre of Castel del Piano and ask.

Sperello di Serègo Alighieri
Via Luigi Cirenei 70,
06132 Castel del Piano
Mobile +39 340 6459061
Email villa.aureli@libero.it
Web www.villaaureli.it

Brigolante Guest Apartments

In the foothills of St Francis' beloved Mount Subasio, the 16th-century stone farmhouse has been thoughtfully restored by Stefano and Rebecca. She is American and came to Italy to study, he is an architectural land surveyor; here was the perfect project. The apartments feel private but you can always chat over a homemade aperitif with the other guests in the garden. Rooms are light, airy and stylishly simple, combining grandmother's furniture with Rebecca's kind touches: a rustic basket of delicacies from the farm (wine, eggs, salami, prosciutto, honey, olive oil, homemade jam), handmade soap and bags of lavender by the bath. Pretty lace curtains flutter at the window, kitchens are well-equipped, and laundry facilities are available. This is a farm with animals on children can enjoy pigs, cows and chickens. Feel free to pluck whatever you like from the vegetable garden – red peppers, fat tomatoes, huge lettuces. Warm, lively, outgoing and with two young children of their own, your hosts set the tone: a charming place, and bliss for families and walkers. *Minimum stay one week in high season.*

Price	€275-€550 per week.
Rooms	3 apartments: 1 for 2, 2 for 2-4.
Meals	Restaurant 1km.
Closed	Rarely.
Directions	Assisi ring road to Porta Perlici, then towards Gualdo Tadino, 6km. Right, signed Brigolante. Over 1st bridge, right, over 2nd wooden bridge, up hill 500m, right at 1st gravel road.

Rebecca Winke Bagnoli
Via Costa di Trex 31,
06081 Assisi

Tel +39 0758 02250
Email info@brigolante.com
Web www.brigolante.com

Romantik Hotel Le Silve & Agriturismo

The setting, deep in the heart of the Umbrian hills, takes your breath away. It's as beautiful and as peaceful as Shangri-La – so remote you'd do well to fill up with petrol before leaving Spello or Assisi. The medieval buildings have been beautifully restored and the whole place breathes an air of tranquillity and exclusivity. Superb, generous-sized bedrooms have stone walls, exquisite terracotta floors, beautiful furniture, old mirrors and (a rarity, this!) proper reading lights. Bathrooms are similarly rustic with terracotta floors and delicious pampering extras. The apartments are spread across three converted farm buildings. We loved the restaurant, a brisk walk: intimate and inviting indoors and out. The produce is mostly organic, the bread is homemade, the cheeses, hams and salami are delectable. There's tennis and table tennis, an enormous new pool on the edge of the hill, a hydromassage and a sauna, and hectares of hills and woods in which to walk or ride: pick an estate horse. A delightful, friendly place, and popular – be sure to book well in advance. *Minimum stay two nights in apts.*

Price	Half-board €210-€300 for 2. Apartments €100 (€600 per week).
Rooms	20 + 13: 20 doubles. 13 apartments for 2-4.
Meals	Breakfast €10 for self-caterers. Dinner €40. Wine from €10. Restaurants 12km.
Closed	Hotel: November-March. Agriturismo: never.
Directions	Milan A1 exit Valdichiana for Perugia, then Assisi. Signs for Gualdo Tadino then Armenzano, km12; signs for hotel, 2km.

Ethical Collection: Community; Food. See page 419 for details.

Marco Sirignani
Loc. Armenzano,
06081 Assisi

Tel +39 0758 019000
Email info@lesilve.it
Web www.lesilve.it

Agriturismo Alla Madonna del Piatto

The road winds up and up through woods and off the track to a simple, centuries-old farmhouse in a hidden corner of Umbria. The position is stupendous. Views stretch over olive groves and forested hills to Assisi and its basilica, yet you are an easy distance from Perugia, Assisi, Spoleto. The old farmhouse was abandoned for decades until these Italian-Dutch owners fell in love with the view, then restored the building with sympathy and style, then replanted the olive groves. Bedrooms are airy, uncluttered, their country antiques mixed with Moroccan delights picked up on Letizia's travels; one room has a loo with a view. Lovely Litizia – a walking encyclopaedia of the area – joins you for breakfast (her own breads and jams) at mosaic-topped tables, in a fresh, modern space of white and rose walls, with sofa and open fire. Your hosts are approachable and share their home gladly. If you can tear yourself away from the terraces and their panoramas, there are walks, medieval hill towns and all of Umbria to explore. And be sure to dine at Il Pioppo!

Min. stay two nights; three in May & Sept. Ask about cookery courses.

Price	€90-€95.
Rooms	6: 5 twins/doubles, 1 family room for 3.
Meals	Restaurant 1km.
Closed	Beginning November-end March.
Directions	From Assisi SS147 for Perugia; after Ponte San Vittorino turn right, Via San Fortunato; uphill 6.5km; right; Via Petrata. Ask owner for detailed directions.

Letizia Mattiacci
Via Petrata 37, Pieve San Nicolo,
06081 Assisi

Tel	+39 0758 199050
Mobile	+39 328 7025297
Email	letizia.mattiacci@gmail.com
Web	www.incampagna.com

Casa Rosa

Once you've wrenched your gaze from pool-side panoramas over the forested flanks of Mount Subasio National Park, and had your senses tickled by the sweet orchestra of lavender, Russian sage and Mediterranean herbs that assail you – strategically planted to waft their perfumes into the apartments – let wonderful host Jennifer welcome you in. An expat artist whose mural and decorative work embellishes these homely, colourful, bohemian interiors, she will relate Elysian tales of living off the land and raising a family on the 17-acre farm estate. Antique kettles and pots, bunches of dried herbs suspended from ceilings, well-stocked wine racks and flora'n'fauna painted surrounds to mirrors and French windows, all lend themselves to a relaxed vibe, while an organic vegetable garden, and a yurt tucked away in the woods, add to the communal, convivial idyll. There's WiFi if you need it but it won't distract you from the views; lap them up from your balconied terrace. Better still, take the book of local walks provided, add a picnic, and head for the wooded hills. *Minimum stay one week.*

Price	€380-€1,150 per week.
Rooms	4 apartments for 2-5.
Meals	Dinner €20, on request. Community freezer stocked with meals. Restaurants 3km.
Closed	Rarely.
Directions	From Assisi road SS444 for Gualdo Todimo. After 6km right on Santa Maria Lignano. After 2.5km left for Casa Rosa. House 1km on right.

Jennifer Holmes
Santa Maria Lignano,
06081 Assisi

Tel +39 0758 02322
Email jennifer@casa-rosa.it
Web www.casa-rosa.it

Villa Rosa

The beautifully restored farmhouse looks out over fields and farms to the villages of Solomeo and Corciano, with Perugia in the distance. Distant church bells, the hum of a tractor, the bray of a donkey... yet you are five kilometres from the superstrada. You couldn't find a better spot from which to discover Tuscany and Umbria. Megan, who is Australian, and Lino are a helpful and hospitable couple, and will help you enjoy every aspect of your stay: hunt for truffles (or cashmere, in Solomeo!), book in for a twice-weekly cookery class with a chef from Perugia, take advantage of a personalised tour. There are three apartments here. For a family, the two-storey *casetta* at the end of the garden is perfect – a delightful mix of recycled beams and terracotta tiles, with open fire, air con, jacuzzi and perfect views. The flat on the ground floor of the farmhouse is similarly good – new bunk beds in the living area, cool in summer, a great terrace. There's a saltwater pool to cool you down, and the views are wonderful. *Minimum stay three nights in apartments.*

Price	Cottage €160-€180 (€600-€1,200 per week). Apts €80-€120 (€375-€750 per week).
Rooms	1 cottage for 6. 3 apartments: 1 for 2, 1 for 3, 1 for 4.
Meals	Breakfast €10. Restaurant 1km.
Closed	Rarely.
Directions	Exit Perugia-Bettolle at Corciano, for Castelvieto thro' village (via underpass & bridge) to shrine. Left & on to 2nd shrine; right uphill; house after couple of bends.

Megan & Lino Rialti
Voc. Docciolano 9, Montemelino, 06060 Magione

Tel	+39 0758 41814
Mobile	+39 329 6154531
Email	meglino@libero.it
Web	www.villarosaweb.com

San Lorenzo della Rabatta Agriturismo

Only 15 minutes from Perugia yet in another world, this medieval mountain-top hamlet is tucked into the wooded hills: a lovely setting. The restored houses congregate around a central gravel area filled with terracotta pots; walls are covered with ivy and roses. It's a good place to bring children – pleasant, practical – and you can meet other families over breakfast in the vast cantina. Note the interesting agricultural touches: rickety farm stools, a cattle stall converted into a seat, a wine barrel acting as a side table. One bed has a recycled gate for a bedhead and there are several draped four-posters. Living spaces are open-plan, sofas wear nylon stretch covers and gingham is much in evidence; most apartments have a fireplace and a basket of wood, and all is clean and spacious – though bathrooms are small and kitchens pretty basic. Outside, narrow steps neatly bordered with miniature roses take you down to the pool, and delicious views to the hills. There's also table tennis and a small play area for children in among the olive trees. Friendly Tanya pops by each day.

Price	€80-€120. Minimum 2 nights.
Rooms	8 apartments for 2-8.
Meals	Breakfast included 15 June-15 September. Dinner, 5 courses, €20 (served in your apartment).
Closed	January-February.
Directions	A1 south exit Valdichiana. From south exit Orte. E45 dir. Perugia exit Madonna Alta. Follow signs for Cenerente & S. Marco. At Cenerente right after church; signed.

Paola Cascini
Loc. Cenerente,
06134 Perugia

Mobile +39 331 6768889
Email info@sanlorenzodellarabatta.com
Web www.sanlorenzodellarabatta.com

Le Torri di Bagnara - Medieval Historic Villas

Contessa Giunta runs her empire with professionalism and pride. Hers is a magnificent estate midway between Florence and Rome, 1,500 acres of pastoral perfection with vast views, a pristine pool (bathing hats on, please!), an 11th-century abbey and tower, four castles, lakes and many terraces. It is a medieval framework for a modern holiday enterprise and you feel you're on top of the world. The abbey – a fully staffed, super-luxe villa with seven bedrooms and nine bathrooms – comes with billiard room, bar and fully equipped kitchen, fine antiques, air con, WiFi, and a delightful paved courtyard with a small church and bell tower. The views from every bedroom are wonderful. Four rustic but pretty apartments fill the tower, each on a different floor, some with barrow-vault ceilings and Romanesque windows. On the ground floor is a dining and sitting area for the sociable; outside, figs, peaches, olives, herbs and a shared laundry. Beyond: a botanic garden, a kitchen garden and that infinity pool. Cookery, wine tastings, free mountain bikes... Contessa Giunta has thought of everything. *Chef available. Bus stop 500m.*

Ethical Collection: Food.
See page 419 for details.

Price	Abbey €9,600-€14,400. Tower €4,500-€6,700. Prices per week. Minimum one week (Sat-Sat).
Rooms	Abbey for 15: 7 bedrooms; 9 bathrooms. Tower: 4 apts for 2-5 (rented only in conjunction with abbey).
Meals	Restaurants 2km.
Closed	November-March.
Directions	E45 exit Resina; north for Pieve San Quirico Bagnara; 4km, signed on left.

Zenaide Giunta
Strada della Bruna 8, Solfagnano,
06134 Perugia

Tel	+39 0755 792001
Email	info@letorridibagnara.it
Web	www.letorridibagnara.it

L'Ariete

Well-travelled Martina and Andreas from Vienna are full of love for their new venture: a restaurant with apartments (and two rooms) in Umbria. It's a 'casa padronale' plus outbuildings, above which teeters lovely Montone on its hill. The apartments are in the main house, spread over the first and second floors, most with a big open fireplace, all with a kitchenette or kitchen. Find original beams and terracotta floors, charming wrought-iron beds and antique chandeliers, embroidered white cotton and light-filled bathrooms that range from small to vast: there's a fresh and beautiful simplicity. The rustic restaurant in the old stables is the perfect setting for seasonal regional fare in Slow Food style, where ingredients are home-grown or from the local farms and the dishes are delicious Umbrian (with warm applestrudel for pudding if you're lucky); there's a grocer's shop, too. Montone is a joy to explore: atmospheric churches and cobbled squares, cafés, bars and a film festival in July. Wend your way back down the hill to a garden of sunflowers and birds, lawns mown by sheep and a charming pool. A gem!

Price	B&B €60-€100. Apts €400-€1,200 per week.
Rooms	2 + 4: 2 doubles (can interconnect). 4 apts: 3 for 2, 1 for 4.
Meals	Breakfast €7 for self-caterers. Dinner with wine, €20.
Closed	Rarely.
Directions	E45 exit Montone; 3km dir. Pietralunga on SP201.

Andreas Sax
06014 Montone Perugia
Tel +39 0759 306128
Email andreas@lariete.org
Web www.lariete.org

Podere Cardaneto

Warm, welcoming, enticing, a delight for the senses and with spell-binding views. The 14th-century look-out tower is the oldest part of this mellow stone podere; the house is for B&Bers, the barn apartments for self-caterers. To a backdrop of ancient beams and flagstone floors, intriguing arches, undulating walls and small deep-set windows (some framing views of Montone on the hill) is an elegant and inviting décor: a huge fireplace with a 16th-century fireback, mismatched sofas heaped with cushions, side tables here and there with magazines to browse, a collection of hats, books galore (vintage and new), a standard lamp of antlers… and fabulous idiosyncratic antiques: your hosts are in the trade in Milan. Cultured, gentle, quietly spoken, they are hugely accommodating to people's wants and needs, give you big beautiful bedrooms (one with a stand-alone bath), homemade cakes at breakfast and jams in season, and simple delicious dinners from the best quality produce. Classical music wafts in summer to pergolas entwined with wisteria and vines; seats are of wicker or wrought-iron. Irresistible, enchanting!

Price	€130-€180. Apt: from €600 for 2; from €2,500 for 8. Prices per week.
Rooms	6 + 1: 5 doubles, 1 twin. Apartment for 2-8.
Meals	Restaurants 1.5km.
Closed	Rarely.
Directions	Sent on booking.

Maurizio Munari
06014 Montone

Tel	+39 0759 306453
Mobile	+39 337 688137
Email	maurizio@cardaneto.it
Web	www.cardaneto.it

Casa delle Grazie

Skirt upwards around the edge of the lovely old town walls of Montone to find an ancient stone farmhouse and enthusiastic owners Aine and Fabio; two holiday homes form part of a long, low building opposite. La Stalla is single storey; La Torretta, in the middle, has two floors. All is new inside. Both apartments have open-plan living/kitchen areas with simple wooden tables, eco-heated floors, beamed ceilings and white walls. Bedrooms are simple and traditional, with pretty rose-pink quilts and good mattresses; the upstairs bedroom in La Torretta has the views, but all are bright and airy. Bathrooms are spacious with good big showers and warm biscuit coloured tiles. You have your own furnished garden area outside, for which privacy is provided by hedging and a trellis with roses. Supplies are left for breakfast on your first morning and the kitchen is stocked with the essentials. A further studio apartment near the farmhouse has one room with a basic kitchen area, a bedroom separated by blinds, and a big patio with views. Explore the area: the walks are sublime and there's a film festival in June.

Price: €85 (B&B Oct-Apr only). €400-€1,100 per week.
Rooms: La Stalla: 2 twins/doubles. La Torretta: 1 twin/double. La Rimessa: studio for 2.
Meals: Wednesday night barbecue, €25. Restaurants within walking distance.
Closed: Rarely.
Directions: Sent on booking.

Aine Browne and Fabio Urso
Via Case Sparse 19,
06014 Montone
Mobile +39 331 9862638
Email aine@casadellegrazie.com
Web www.casadellegrazie.com

La Preghiera Residenza d'Epoca

This glorious 12th-century monastery, hidden in a wooded valley near Gubbio and Cortona, was a pilgrim's resting place. The Tunstills, welcoming, well-travelled and cultured architect and interior designer, have restored it with English country-house flair and Italian attention to detail. The big sitting and dining rooms are elegantly scattered with sofas, paintings and antiques; there is a billiard room and a library. Bedrooms combine original features – beamed and raftered ceilings, terracotta floors, wooden shutters, exposed stone – with sophistications such as cotton and silk bed linen, handmade furniture, wardrobes with interior lights, marbled bathrooms. Outside are shady terraces, a sunken garden, a flower-filled loggia and a private chapel. So many tranquil spots in which to recharge batteries. Have breakfast on the terrace, tea by the pool, dine by candlelight on local boar and truffles. There are vintage bikes to borrow, horse riding and golf nearby, medieval hilltop towns to visit, lovely staff to look after you. You can even book a massage by the pool. *Ask about half-price deals.*

Price	€98-€230. Whole house on request.
Rooms	11 twins/doubles.
Meals	Dinner with wine, 4 courses, €50; by arrangement. Restaurant 1km.
Closed	December-February (open on request).
Directions	Exit E45 at Promano dir. Città di Castello; left at r'bout; next r'bout right thro' Trestina; right to Calzolaro; before bridge left to Vecchio Granaio; road bears right; along river, hotel on left, 300m.

Liliana & John Tunstill
Via del Refari,
06018 Calzolaro

Tel +39 0759 302428
Mobile +39 333 1855737
Email info@lapreghiera.com
Web www.lapreghiera.com

Villa Bastiola

Perhaps you cherish dreams of stumbling across an ancient casa, a pearl in the yawning landscapes of Umbria. Here, among a handful of neighbours, the former farmhouse Villa Bastiola invites you to your own little haven in the olive groves overlooking the Tiber valley. Outside, stone steps lead to a first-floor apartment: a laid-back living room with an ancient fireplace, giant beams, books and a cream leather sofa to to melt into. By contrast the bright kitchen-diner is in Shaker style with thick marble worktops and a welcome pack on arrival; whip up a Mediterranean meal to enjoy on your own private sunspot, or on the panoramic terrace. The cosy little double bedrooms are impeccably decked in Busatti bedding and fabrics, as luxuriant as the bathroom's slabs of honey-coloured travertine marble and the thick soft towels; lovely Sally Ann has a flair for the stylish side of rustic. This is an area adored by many, with delights cultural, rural and edible in all directions, layered views of distant hills and an occasional car to remind you of the outside world. And you can walk to a good little restaurant...

Price	From £400 per week. Minimum stay one week.
Rooms	Apartment for 4.
Meals	Restaurant 100m.
Closed	November-March.
Directions	Exit E45 Promano; follow for Trestina. After Trestina right for Calzolaro. Left in Calzolaro, up hill for 2km. Villa on right.

Sally Ann Marconi
Via Comunaglia 387,
06018 Calzolaro

Email info@villabastiola.com
Web www.villabastiola.com

La Cuccagna

A big, solid, traditional style farmhouse – meticulously restored after the Assisi earthquake – with chestnut windows, shutters, doors, and achingly beautiful panoramas across wooded hills, farmland, olive groves and the odd tower-topped hamlet; you feel on top of the world. Paved paths lead through old olive and cherry trees, lavender and herbs (plus a little veg patch for guests to raid) to a hammock, pergola and exquisitely sited infinity pool. The cowshed cottage is cosy, the bedrooms in the farmhouse are simple and spare, with their tiled floors, beamed ceilings, locally made fabrics and ceramics, and 'memory foam' mattresses to ensure deep sleep. Everywhere, lots of child-friendly space. Your lovely eco-conscious hosts Salvatore and Sarah ensure a special stay and think of every last detail: lavender bags, flowers, their own olive oil, truffle and asparagus foraging tips, local lore; pizza and pasta making (and eating), too. Sip Sal's homemade limoncellos over sublime sunsets on the terrace, gaze at the stars. And look forward to your discovery of this history steeped, culturally rich region.

Ethical Collection: Environment; Food.
See page 419 for details.

Price	€80-€110. Minimum 3 nights.
Rooms	4 + 1: 2 doubles, 2 twins/doubles. Cottage for 2-3.
Meals	Dinner €25. Restaurant 1.5km.
Closed	January to mid-March.
Directions	Sent on booking.

Salvatore & Sarah
Fraz. S. Cristina 22,
06024 Gubbio

Tel +39 0759 20317
Email info@lacuccagna.com
Web www.lacuccagna.com

Le Cinciallegre Agriturismo

This was once a tiny 13th-century hamlet on an ancient crossroads where local farmers met to buy and sell their produce. It's an incredibly peaceful spot, overlooking valley, meadows and woods, reached via a long, unmade road. English-speaking Fabrizio was an architect and his conversion of these old houses is inspired: all feels authentic and delightful. In the cool, beamed living room, comfy seats pull up around a 200-year-old wood-burning stove, there's rustic furniture and a fine old dresser. The simple, comfortable bedrooms, named after birds, have their own terrace areas and immaculate bathrooms. You can cook in the outhouse but Cristina is a wonderful chef serving real country food and Umbrian wines so you're likely to leave her to it. Fabrizio is a local expert and will point you in the direction of the most beautiful medieval towns and wonderful walking and, very importantly, knows when to avoid the crowds. This is a warm and hospitable place, looked after by a couple who are passionate about the environment, their lovely natural garden, and ten organic hectares of wildlife. Heaven for independent couples.

Price	€80-€100.
Rooms	7: 3 doubles, 1 single, 1 family room, 2 triples.
Meals	Dinner €30, on request. Guest kitchen.
Closed	October-March.
Directions	A1 exit Val di Chiana for Perugia & follow E45 to Cesena. Exit Umbertide Gubbio. Follow 219 for Gubbio. Signed from Mocaiana.

Fabrizio & Cristina de Robertis
Fraz. Pisciano,
06024 Gubbio

Tel +39 0759 255957
Mobile +39 340 8986953
Email cince@lecinciallegre.it
Web www.lecinciallegre.it

Locanda del Gallo

A restful, almost spiritual calm emanates from this wonderful home. In a medieval hamlet, the *locanda* has all the beams and antique tiles you could wish for. Light, airy rooms with pale limewashed walls are a perfect foil for the exquisite reclaimed doors and carved hardwood furniture from Bali and Indonesia; your charming hosts have picked up some fabulous pieces from far-off places and have given the house a colonial feel. Each bedroom is different, one almond with Italian country furniture, another white, with wicker and Provençal prints; some have carved four-poster beds. Bathrooms are gorgeous, with deep baths and walk-in, glass-doored showers. A stunning veranda wraps itself around the house: doze off in a wicker armchair, sip a drink at dusk as the sun melts into the valley. The pool is spectacular, like a mirage clinging to the side of the hill; and there's a huge lime tree. Jimmy the cook conjures up food rich in genuine flavours, with aromatic herbs and vegetables from the garden; he and his wife are part of the extended family. Paola and Erich are interesting, cultural and warm. *Minimum stay two nights. Spa.*

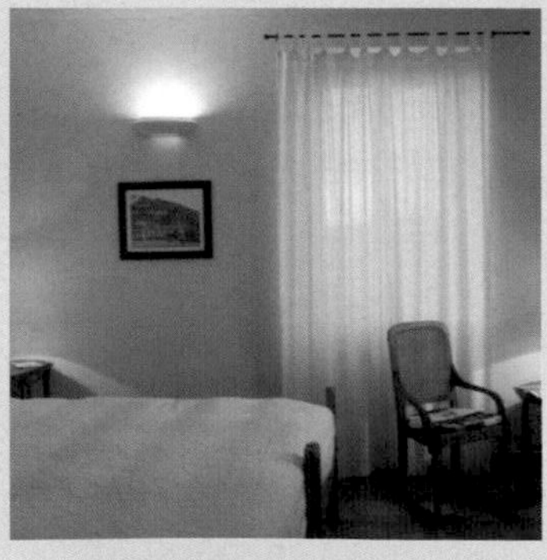

Ethical Collection: Environment; Food.
See page 419 for details.

Price	€140-€150. Suites €270-€290. Half-board €90-€100 p.p.
Rooms	9: 6 doubles, 3 suites for 4.
Meals	Lunch €12. Dinner €28. Wine from €10.
Closed	Rarely.
Directions	Exit E45 at Ponte Pattoli for Casa del Diavolo; for S. Cristina 8km. 1st left, 100m after La Dolce Vita restaurant; continue to Locanda.

Paola Moro & Erich Breuer
Loc. Santa Cristina,
06020 Gubbio

Tel	+39 0759 229912
Email	info@locandadelgallo.it
Web	www.locandadelgallo.it

Castello di Petroia

Brave the loops of the Gubbio-Assisi road to arrive at the castle at dusk. The front gate is locked, you ring to be let in; an eerie silence, the gates creak open. Inside, dim lighting, stone walls, a splendid austerity. Come morning, you will appreciate the vast-fireplaced magnificence of the place, and the terrace that catches the all-day sun. The restaurant is open to the public now and the food is something to write home about; dinner is candlelit, refined, and sociable when presided over by Carlo, your gracious tweed-clad host. Then it's up the stairs – some steep – to bedrooms with beeswax polished floors and shadowy corners, aristocratic furniture and elegant beds, the swishest with hydromassage baths. (Ask for bathside strawberries and cream for the ultimate romantic escape!). The castle is set on a hillock surrounded by pines in beautiful unpopulated countryside with a marked footpath running through it. Walk to Assisi – it takes a day – then taxi back. Or take the bus into Gubbio and the funicular into the hills: the views are stupendous. A privilege to come home to this 900-acre estate.

Price	€110-€170. Suites €170-€210.
Rooms	8: 4 doubles (1 in tower), 4 suites.
Meals	Dinner with wine, €30-€38. Restaurant 5km.
Closed	January-March.
Directions	S298 from Gubbio south for Assisi & Perugia. After Scritto, just before Biscina & Fratticiola, take stony road signed to Castello.

Carlo Sagrini
Scritto di Gubbio,
06020 Gubbio

Tel +39 0759 20287
Email info@petroia.it
Web www.petroia.it

Slow Life Umbria – Relais de Charme

You are met with a friendly handshake and a big smile. Bruno welcomes you to his 1600s farmstead, chic-ly restored and furnished with a sympathetic eye. Life is lived here according to the rhythm of the seasons and shared with family and guests on two beautifully tended hectares of land with undulating views. It's wholesome, rural and peaceful, luxurious too, with an infinity pool by the olive grove, shiatsu massage in your bedroom, and underfloor heating throughout: a place to truly unwind. The light airy restaurant has a 'living roof' topped with vegetation, the sitting room is soothing and inviting, the bedrooms are refreshingly understated. Outside are jasmine, lavender, wisteria, bamboo; inside, goose feather pillows and mattresses that mould to your shape, white oval basins and mosaic'd showers, and simple refined food created from local organic produce. Delicious breakfast is whenever and wherever you want it, and you can book into a cookery class or truffle-hunt all year round (bar July/August). If you must spread your wings, visit Perugia, all of 20 minutes away. Superb. *Minimum stay two nights.*

Price	€220-€240.
Rooms	12 doubles.
Meals	Dinner €45. Wine €15. Restaurants 4km.
Closed	Never.
Directions	Exit A1 at Magione, signs to Castel Rigone. Under dual carriageway, continue 1km. Right onto gravel road signed La Goga; after 1.5km, pink house on left; right for 1.5km. Left after 1km; on left.

Bruno Arcuri
Loc. Castel Rigone Campagna 32,
06065 Passignano sul Trasimeno

Tel +39 0758 44231
Email bruno.arcuri@slowlifeumbria.it
Web www.slowlifeumbria.it

Casa Panfili

A steep, bumpy approach – but the welcome more than makes up for it. As for the position, overlooking the wooded hills and olive groves of the Niccone valley, it is glorious. The farmhouse, once used for drying and storing tobacco (spot the old ventilation bricks in the walls), has been rescued from ruin and is now immaculate. Typically Italian rooms – white-painted walls, arches, terracotta floors – have been given the English treatment with masses of books and rugs, old wooden chests and delicate lace, prints and family photos. Beds have silky smooth sheets, spotless bathrooms are fragrant with fresh flowers, and Al and Betty (who were stationed in Naples for three years and decided they couldn't face returning to Whitehall) are generous, friendly hosts. They produce their own wine, olive oil and honey and Betty offers Italian cookery classes in her kitchen. Meals are at a dining table gleaming with cut glass and silver, or outside under a vine-covered pergola. The gardens are tranquil and pretty, the olive trees screen the pool from the house and the nightingales serenade you at night.

Price	€110-€130. Minimum 2 nights.
Rooms	3: 2 doubles, 1 twin.
Meals	Lunch €10. Dinner with wine, €30, book ahead. Restaurant 8km.
Closed	November-Easter.
Directions	Sent on booking.

Alastair & Betty Stuart
San Lorenzo di Bibbiano 14,
06010 San Leo Bastia

Tel	+39 0758 504244
Email	casafanfili@gmail.com
Web	www.casapanfili.com

La Molinella

Eat, sleep and dream in the little old watermill in the Umbrian hills – an enchanting bolthole for two. Though you can reach Perugia in under an hour it is fairly remote; but the hiking and riding are easy. Potted lavender, herbs and tidy vines are plentiful, and apple trees and a few olives up by the cool circular pool (all yours, with views)... the 'shabby chic' of the interior repeats itself outside so you barely notice where the gardens end and nature begins. Loveliest of all is the dappled veranda complete with daybed for outdoor R&R. Back inside, ceilings are low, floors are old wood or terracotta, beams are rustic, pale blue paintwork is deliberately worn, and the kitchen, with its antique marble-topped table and old-fashioned pellet stove in one corner, will make you giddy with delight. (It also has loads of workspace and a modern oven.) Owner Annie is here when guests arrive, lives nearby should you need her, and moves back in in winter! At the top is the snug bedroom with romantic bed and sweet white linen, below is a sitting room with deep sofa and open fire. Honeymoon heaven. *Minimum stay one week.*

Price	€995-€,1195 per week.
Rooms	House for 2-3.
Meals	Welcome pack on arrival. Restaurant 15-minute drive.
Closed	November-April.
Directions	From A1 exit Valdichiana/Betolle/Sinalunga dir. Perugia; stay on 75 bis carriageway to Tuoro exit. Follow signs for Tuoro, Umbertide, Lisciano Niccone and Mercatale. Thro' Mercatale, then small village Mengaccini; Annie will send directions from here on booking.

The Owner
Voc. La Molinella,
06010 San Leo Bastia

Mobile	+39 340 6349783
Email	lamolinella2012@googlemail.com

Casa San Gabriel

Enjoy David's wine on arrival, absorb the view of cultivated and wooded hills and unwind. Chrissie and David, warm, generous, thoughtful, bought the farmstead in a ruinous state and did it up it all up in under a year. The little 'houses', private but close, each with its own terrace, are suitable for singles, couples or families. For further space there's a living room in the main house with books and open fire. The restoration is sympathetic, unpretentious, delightful, the off-white décor and soft furnishings enhancing undulating beams and stone walls; the bathrooms are so lovely you could spend all day in them. Supplies are left for breakfast on your first morning and should last until you're ready to venture out. You may also pick produce from the vegetable gardens or feed a fluffy alpaca. David cooks on Tuesdays, and Thursday is pizza night – your chance to use an original wood-fired oven. Bliss to have Perugia so near by – a 20-minute drive – and to return to a pool with views down the valley all the way to Assisi, a bottle of chilled Orvieto by your side. *B&B option October-April only.*

Price	B&B: €85. Self-catering: €400-€1,150 per week.
Rooms	3 apartments: 1 for 2, 1 for 2-4, 1 for 4.
Meals	Breakfast on first day for self-caterers. Dinner €25 (Tues), pizza €15 (Thurs). Wine €10. Restaurant 5km.
Closed	Rarely.
Directions	E45, exit Pierantonio for Castle Antognolla; after 4.5km, left for Santa Caterina; 1.5km on white road.

Christina Todd & David Lang
CP No 29, V. Petrarca No 2,
06015 Pierantonio

Tel +39 0759 414219
Mobile +39 338 8916641
Email chrissie@casasangabriel.com
Web www.casasangabriel.com

Monte Valentino Agriturismo

On top of the world in Umbria, woods fall away, hills climb to snow-scattered heights. It's the perfect escape, the only route in a steep, winding, two-kilometre track. All around you lie 60 hectares of organically farmed land – mushrooms are gathered from the woods, cereals and vegetables from the fields, fruit from the trees, water from the spring. These new apartments are contemporary yet cosy and comfortable with simple wooden furniture, tiled floors and throws on striped sofas. All have small balconies and kitchens and clean, fresh shower rooms; two have access to beautifully designed brick terraces where the views sweep and soar away. Surrounded by deck chairs and olive trees, the pool is delightful. Fabrizia, who lives next door, is enthusiastic and charming with an engaging smile, and proud of her venture – meet her over a simple breakfast in her homely kitchen. This is perfect cycling terrain – if you're tough! You can also swim in the river, horse riding is six miles away, cookery lessons can be arranged and Nicola will give you archery lessons if you fancy something different. They are lovely people.

Price	€70-€80 (€450-€560 per week).
Rooms	4 apartments for 2-3.
Meals	Breakfast included. Restaurants 12km.
Closed	Never.
Directions	SS E45 Orte-Cesena exit Montone-Pietralunga; SP201 to Pietralunga. At km12, Carpini (before Pietralunga); right at x-roads, signed.

Fabrizia Gargano & Nicola Polchi
Loc. Monte Valentino,
06026 Pietralunga

Tel +39 0759 462092
Email info@montevalentino.it
Web www.montevalentino.it

Agriturismo Campara

In spring and summer you swim amongst irises and lilies. No salt, no chlorine in this 'bio lake', just lovely clear water, a small cascade and the odd friendly frog. Children adore it and the setting is sweet, 500 metres above sea level and never too hot. As you approach up a winding tarmac road the house suddenly appears above on the side of the hill. Delightful Margherita lives here with her artist husband, plus cats, hens, rabbits and children, growing their own olives, fruits and veg. If you ask, she will happily cook you dinner and bring it to the garden. You have a choice of three apartments here: Ninfea (upstairs) and Davina (down), twin homes in a peachy sixties' villa; and Ginestra, older, snugger, beamier, more characterful, attached to the farmhouse. All have patios or a terrace with views and all are really well furnished: find colourful rugs on spotless floors (lovely old terracotta ones in Ginestra), light cotton curtains at sturdy windows and well-dressed wrought-iron beds. Borrow rods for the lake, play on the swings or visit Cortona, Perugia, Arezzo for classic Umbrian magic.

Price	€430-€650 per week.
Rooms	3 apartments for 4.
Meals	Restaurant 4km.
Closed	Rarely.
Directions	Exit Orte on A1; dir. Terni E45, dir. Cesena; exit Promano. Left at r'bout, dir. Trestina. Over river Tevere, cont. to right, past bar Fuego, dir. Volterrano. On for 13km.

Margherita Cerrai
Voc. Campara 84, Loc. Volterrano,
06010 Città di Castello

Tel +39 0758 574136
Email info@campara.it
Web www.campara.it

La Buia

Twenty years ago, La Buia was in desperate need of a facelift. Who better to assign to the task than an artist and a garden designer? Now Richard and Lucie greet you with a glass of chilled prosecco and a delicious bruschetta: this is a wonderfully welcoming home. The views are gorgeous, the gardens are glorious and there's raw forest to roam. Choose between the charming bedroom with its own private entrance – all soothing blues and flowing mosquito net – and the even more romantic peachy-pink room upstairs (which has its own basin but shares a bathroom with the family). Or, if you're a group, self-cater in the recently renovated and stunningly furnished Tobacco Tower. Throughout, artist Lucie's paintings adorn the walls – almost outshone by the views from every window. Start the day slowly by savouring breakfast, a feast served under the arbour at a big antique table, and plan your day. For explorers, medieval towns are a short drive; for home bodies, there are the estate's three hectares. Return to a dip in the lovely pool, fringed by rosemary and lavender. Gorgeous. *Ask about truffle walks.*

Price	€85-€150. Tower €1,995-€2,500 per week.
Rooms	3 + 1: 2 doubles; 1 double, sharing family bathroom. Tower for 6.
Meals	Dinner, with wine, €35. Restaurants 5km.
Closed	Rarely.
Directions	A1 exit north Arezzo; follow signs for Città di Castello. In Monterchi, follow signs to Monte S. Maria Tiberina. Past Lippiano turning, up hill; right down hill into valley.

Richard & Lucie Shelbourne
Voc. La Buia 43,
06010 Lippiano

Tel +39 0758 502007
Mobile +39 338 8868397 or +39 334 2368887
Email richardshelbourne@virgilio.it
Web www.labuia.com

Marche and Molise

Locanda della Valle Nuova

In gentle, breeze-cooled hills, surrounded by ancient, protected oaks and on the road that leads to glorious Urbino, this 185-acre farm produces organic meat, vegetables and wine. It is an unusual, unexpectedly modern place whose owners have a special interest in horses and in the environment: solar panels for heating, photovoltaic panels for electricity. Savini and daughter Giulia – forces to be reckoned with! – make a professional team and cook delicious meals presented on white porcelain and terracotta. The breads, pastas and jams are homemade, the wines are local, the water is purified and de-chlorinated, the truffles are gathered from the woods nearby. The conversion has given La Locanda the feel of a discreet modern hotel, where perfectly turned sheets lie on perfect beds, and it's worth asking for one of the bigger rooms, preferably with a view. The riding school has a club house for horsey talk and showers; there are two outdoor arenas as well as lessons and hacks, and a fabulous pool. If you arrive at the airport after dark, Giulia kindly meets you to guide you back. *Minimum two nights; one week in apts.*

Ethical Collection: Environment; Food.
See page 419 for details.

Price	€112. Half-board €86 p.p. Apartments €680-€900 per week.
Rooms	6 + 2: 5 doubles, 1 twin. 2 apartments for 2-4.
Meals	Dinner €30 (twice a week). Wine from €9. Restaurant 2km.
Closed	Mid-November to May.
Directions	Exit Fano-Rome m'way at Acqualagna & Piobbico. Head towards Piobbico as far as Pole; right for Castellaro; on 3.5km, signed. Or, bus from Pesaro or Fano to Fermignano; owners will pick up.

Giulia Savini
La Cappella 14,
61033 Sagrata di Fermignano

Tel	+39 0722 330303
Email	info@vallenuova.it
Web	www.vallenuova.it

La Casetta

The pretty twin bedroom once housed the wood oven. La Casetta dates back to the 1700s and has been seamlessly extended by Peter and Richard – it is simple, unpretentious, charming. Separate from the main house, it faces the opposite way, with wonderful rolling views across farmland and to mountains. Bliss it is to spill into your own private garden with a pergola covered in roses and a fig tree to plunder; all this yours, and – beyond a leafy arch – box hedges guarding herbs and lavender. Back inside are peachy curtains and two checked sofas, an open fireplace and lovely low beams: a warm and inviting place to hole up in winter. The kitchen is proper country-style, a delight to work in, but if you wish to shed your chef's apron there are restaurants in Frontone – and medieval Cagli, three miles away. Urbino and Gubbio, sensational 'città d'arte', are a half-hour drive, and beaches not much further. Peter and Richard, who have written guides about Italy, have a big library of books for guests to borrow. Hard to imagine more generous – or good-humoured – hosts. *Minimum stay one week.*

Price	€780-€870 per week.
Rooms	Cottage for 4.
Meals	Restaurants 3km.
Closed	January-March.
Directions	A14 exit Fano. Follow Roma signs, exit Cagli Est & skirt town until traffic lights. Left over bridge on main road out of town. Pass restaurant Le Fontane, over bridge, left onto 'strada bianca.'

Richard Dixon & Peter Greene
San Cristoforo, Strada Santa Barbara 5,
61043 Cagli

Tel +39 0721 790215
Mobile +39 339 2411737
Email mail@le-marche.com
Web www.sancristoforo.info

La Pieve

It is spacious, arched and lofty; the former sacristy is a bedroom (serene, simple, charming) and the confessional still stands in a corner. La Pieve was a chapel that dates from the 1700s. Colours are warm, floors are modern tiled, the shower is roomy and there's so much space you each have your own sofa! It's cosy for winter (books to borrow; a wood-burning stove) and gorgeous in summer, with French windows opening to your own little garden with luscious views; sit out midst the lavender and raise a glass to the vines. Richard and Peter live and share this 'dolce vita' with their two gentle dogs on the other side of the metre-thick walls. Cultured and humorous, happy to lend you chicken-bricks or juniper berries, they are conscious of their guests' privacy but on hand if required. Come for wild flowers in May, river swims in summer, funghi and truffles in autumn (visit the truffle fair at Acqualagna) and the gutsy, restorative cuisine of the Marche all year round. Note the posters advertising the local 'sagra': a festival dedicated to a town's particular speciality – a foodie's delight. *Minimum stay one week.*

Price	€500-€630 per week.
Rooms	Chapel for 2.
Meals	Restaurants 3km.
Closed	January-March.
Directions	A14 exit Fano. Follow Roma signs, exit Cagli Est & skirt town until traffic lights. Left over bridge on main road out of town. Pass restaurant Le Fontane, over bridge, left onto 'strada bianca.'

Richard Dixon & Peter Greene
San Cristoforo, Strada Santa Barbara 5,
61043 Cagli

Tel	+39 0721 790215
Mobile	+39 339 2411737
Email	mail@le-marche.com
Web	www.sancristoforo.info

Villa Giulia

Place and people have extraordinary charm. Pines, cypress oaks and roses surround the Napoleonic villa, wisteria billows over the lemon house, the gardens merge into the family olive groves and an ancient wood. No formality, no fuss, just an easy, gracious and kind welcome from Anna, who moved lives with her youngest son. The villa was named after an indomitable great-aunt (the first woman to climb Mont Blanc!) and the family furniture is perfect for it – big wood-framed mirrors, stunning antiques – along with a candle burn on the mantelpiece left by the Nazis. Bedrooms, the best and most baronial in the villa, have shutters and old-fashioned metal beds; one noble bathroom has its own balcony, another is up a winding stair. The two suites in La Dependenza have kitchenettes while the apartments proper are divided between the Farmhouse and the Casa Piccola. Sitting rooms are grand but easy, dining room chairs are gay with red checks, summer breakfasts are taken at pink-clothed tables on a terrace whose views reach to the Adriatic (the beach is a mile away). Atmospheric, historic, beautiful, and good for all ages.

Price	€120-€260. Apartments €800-€1,800 per week.
Rooms	11 + 5: 6 doubles, 5 suites. 5 apartments for 3-6.
Meals	Breakfast €10 for self-caterers. Dinner €30-€50. Wine €8-€36. Restaurant 2km.
Closed	January-March.
Directions	SS16 from Fano for Pesaro, 3km north of Fano turn left; signed.

Anna Passi
Via di Villa Giulia, Loc. San Biagio 40,
61032 Fano

Tel	+39 0721 823159
Mobile	+39 347 0823935
Email	info@relaisvillagiulia.com
Web	www.relaisvillagiulia.com

Castello di Monterado

Orlando's great-great-grandfather bought the Castello, parts of which date from 1100. The renovation continues, and is glorious. Orlando and Kira, quietly spoken and charming, are deeply passionate about the family home whose exquisite revival has been achieved floor by floor. The Music Room is a living museum; its terrace overlooks the new, azure-blue, arc-shaped pool, a foil to the grand park and its ancient trees and, in the distance, the Caseno valley and the Adriatic. The Library combines vast armchairs with ancient tomes, there are frescoes on every wall and ceiling, antiques, works of art, chandeliers – the sheer beauty will thrill you. There's a lovely balcony for fresh-air breakfasts and a dining room for drearier mornings (overseen by Bacchus and Ariadne, of course). Bedrooms, all vast, all generously different, ooze splendour; cherubs chase each other across ceilings, beds are soberly but beautifully dressed, cupboards have been crafted from the cellar's barrels, one suite has its hydromassage bath positioned so you gaze on gardens as you soak. Very special, and good value.

Price €200.
Rooms 4 suites.
Meals Restaurants within walking distance.
Closed Never.
Directions A14 exit at Marotta, right for Pergola; after 7km left for Monterado. Signed.

Orlando & Kira Rodano
Piazza Roma 18,
60010 Monterado
Tel +39 0717 958395
Email info@castellodimonterado.it
Web www.castellodimonterado.it

Castello di Monterado - Apartments

Cut off from western Italy by the Apennines is Le Marche; peaceful, charming, undiscovered. At the top of a steep wooded hill is Monterado, a small medieval town of cobbled streets and fabulous views. Beyond is the sea. On a small square in town, opposite the Castle of Monterado is a solid old stone building housing six apartments with a contemporary and luxurious feel. One is on the ground floor, two are on the first and two are on the second; Anemone, the largest, spreads itself over two levels. Lofty walls are plastered white, floors are polished parquet, styling is minimalist, classy and sleek. Guests in the apartments can use the pool in the castle gardens. In the town are a handful of restaurants and shops, tennis courts and, in May, a hog roast festival to which locals flock; the region is the home of *porchetta*. If you want beach resorts with a Sixties feel, then head west for the resorts of Le Marche. After a day's touring, return to the peaceful garden of the Castello, with its cedar trees and scented roses and, beyond, a landscaped woodland with winding paths.

Price	€385-€700.
Rooms	6 apartments: 3 for 4, 2 for 5, 1 for 6.
Meals	Restaurants within walking distance.
Closed	Never.
Directions	A14 exit Marotta, dir. Pergola. After 7km left for Monterado; signed.

Orlando & Kira Rodano
Piazza Roma 26,
60010 Monterado

Tel +39 0717 958395
Email info@castellodimonterado.it
Web www.castellodimonterado.it

Caserma Carina Country House

Nothing is too much trouble for Lesley, whose easy-going vivacity makes this place a delight, while Dean gardens immaculately. Cots, toys, DVDs, a bottle of wine at the end of a journey, a welcoming smile – she and Dean provide it all. The apartments are immaculate, the gardens prettily landscaped, the pool has long views. A 15-minute walk down the hill from historic Mogliano (three restaurants, shops, banks and bars) is this magnificent 19th-century country house, its four new apartments spanning three floors. The unrestored part sits quietly, rustically alongside. Inside, all is new, inviting and spotlessly clean. Showers have cream tiles and white towels, kitchens are quietly luxurious, sofas gleam in brown leather, cushions add splashes of red, wooden furniture is stylish and new, indoor shutters cut out early morning light, and views are of rolling hills. You are in the heart of the lovely, unsung Le Marche, an easy drive from historic Macerata and not much further from the Adriatic coast. Couples love it, and families, too. A year-round treat. *Shared laundry. Wine tastings, cookery & art courses in low season.*

Price	£450-£950 per week.
Rooms	4 apartments: 1 for 2, 2 for 2-4, 1 for 4-5.
Meals	Restaurant 1km.
Closed	Rarely.
Directions	Sent on booking.

Lesley McMorran
Contrada Mossa 16,
62010 Mogliano

Tel	+39 0733 557990
Mobile	+39 334 8260695
Email	info@caserma-carina.co.uk
Web	www.caserma-carina.co.uk

Casa Nobile

From the ancient pink-brick'd town of Loro Piceno the road winds down to a beautifully restored farmhouse in idyllic countryside. It is a comfortable, spacious, well-proportioned house with an open ground-floor layout: a wide arch links the dining room to the high-raftered kitchen (with an extravagant stone sink), and opens to a wonderful terrace. Lovely to dine al fresco at the big glass-covered dining table or sink into deep armchairs, then to drift over to the glittering saltwater pool: super-smart, with Roman steps and loungers. A charming friend of the Canadian owners meets and greets; a cleaner pops by to change sheets and towels. Up the stairs, past the portrait of Giuseppe Verdi – rumour has it he once stayed – to three bedrooms with sprung mattresses, crisp linen, ceiling fans and gentle views. The master en suite has an open fire and dressing room, the twin is under the rafters. Walking sticks in the hall hint at the proximity of the Sibillini mountains. The less sporty will love Loro Piceno, a historian's delight and festival-home to sweet velvety Vino Cotto. *Weekly changeover: Saturday.*

Price	€1,800-€2,400 per week.
Rooms	House for 6-8.
Meals	Restaurants 1km.
Closed	End October-end March.
Directions	Sent on booking.

Margaret Rose
Contrada Salsaro Ete 49,
62020 Loro Piceno
Email mrose_1344@hotmail.com

Casa San Ruffino

In a land that venerates the 'bella figura', Claire and Ray Gorman, transplants from London, keep their rural B&B running on perfectly oiled wheels and a huge dose of style. The four smart guest rooms in their recently renovated 19th-century farmhouse are decorated in neutral tones in sympathy with clean white walls,beamed ceilings and beautiful old terracotta floors. Beds with crisp white linen, neatly folded fuzzy blankets and four lush pillows will cradle you to sleep, while pinch-me views from sparkling French windows will welcome you in the morning. Plan your day over homemade breads and cakes in the neat, chic breakfast room or outside at your own little garden table. The medieval towns of Montegiorgio and Fermo, and the Adriatic beaches, are a short drive. If, however, you can't tear yourself away from this glorious country spot, trot down the gravel path, past sweet-smelling lavender and perfectly potted lemon trees, to the pool, and take your fill of the rolling vineyard hills, the silvery olive groves and the distant snow-capped mountains. Who would not fall in love with this place?

Price	€115-€140.
Rooms	4 doubles. Child's bed available.
Meals	Restaurants 3km.
Closed	Rarely.
Directions	From Francavilla d'Ete dir. Montegiorgio, past Montegiorgio sign, blue street sign for Contrada Montese on right; next right after 500m, sign for house on corner points right. 1st house on left after 250m; dirt track to house, silver post box on left. Phone for detailed directions.

Ray & Claire Gorman
Contrada Montese 13,
63025 Montegiorgio

Tel	+39 0734 962753
Email	info@casasanruffino.com
Web	www.casasanruffino.com

Agriturismo Contrada Durano

Spend a few days at this tranquil agriturismo and you may never want to leave. The hillside farm, built in the late 18th century as a refuge for monks, has been lovingly restored by its generous, delightful and energetic owners: Englishman Jimmy and Italian Maria Concetta. No clutter, no fuss, just tiled floors, white walls, dark furniture. The bedrooms are simple and some are small, but the bar and sitting areas have masses of space. If you want a view – of olive groves, vineyards and perched villages – ask for rooms 1 or 2. There's dinner most evenings: Maria's food will make your heart sing – home-grown in their wonderful kitchen garden or local organic prosciutto, pecorino, their own bread and wine. As you feast your eyes on distant mountains from all three dining rooms you may ask yourself, why eat elsewhere? In spring and summer, walk through wild flowers up to the village of Smerillo. And do visit the 'cantina' and stock up with Durano bounty: olives, preserved apricots and beetroot, wines from Le Marche and homemade passata – an Italian summer in a bottle. *Minimum stay two nights; three in July/August.*

Price	€90-€110.
Rooms	7 doubles.
Meals	Dinner with wine, €38.
Closed	Rarely.
Directions	A14 Ancona-Bari exit Porto San Giorgio for Amandola, 38km. 10km after Servigliano, sign on left; house 2km off road.

Ethical Collection: Environment; Food.
See page 419 for details.

Maria Concetta Furnari
Contrada Durano,
63856 Smerillo

Tel +39 0734 786012
Email info@contradadurano.it
Web www.contradadurano.it

Villa in the Vineyards

Down the steep winding road from Montelparo – with a thrilling final lap to the house – is a haven of birdsong and tranquillity. This is a smart villa built in traditional style, constructed from 100% local materials and enviably eco: solar panels for hot water, top-notch heating and insulation, non-toxic varnishes and paints, and ionized water for the pool. There's an apartment upstairs, occupied in holiday times by the owners (charming, English, happy to provide occasional meals), a further apartment on the ground floor, and wonderful valley-of-vineyards views. White walls, terracotta tiles and freshly treated beams give interiors a refreshing feel – expect great comfort here. There are beautiful bathrooms and a super-duper kitchen, a dining table crafted from ash, a cream sofa topped with stylish cushions, and fine new wrought-iron beds. Whisk the children off to the sea (unspoilt Altidona) or visit one of Italy's loveliest cities, Ascoli Piceno, a half-hour drive. Or arrange a wine-tasting with a recommended grower, followed by a full-blown Marchegiano lunch cooked by his mother – fabulous!

Price	£560-£1,195 per week.
Rooms	Apartment for 2-6.
Meals	Home-cooked meals by arrangement. Restaurant 3km.
Closed	December-February.
Directions	Sent on booking.

Wendy Richardson
Contrada Celestiale 16,
65020 Montelparo

Tel +39 0734 788204
Email wendy@villainthevineyard.com
Web www.villainthevineyard.com

Vento di Rose B&B

House, orchards, breakfasts, roses, owners... in the foothills of Monterubbiano, ten minutes from the sea, these all add up to unexpected treasure. Your gentle, happy, delightful hosts, with a little English between them, fill the house with artistic flourishes and love doing B&B. Emanuela's sunny personality infuses everything; on the first night Emidio will take you to a local restaurant to see you don't get lost. The kitchen/breakfast room, exquisitely Italian, is all blues and creams, its lace tablecloth strewn with rose petals then laden with garden cherries, peaches, pears, fresh frittata of artichokes, mulberry fruit tarts, warm bread from Moresco – a different treat every day. Too much? Borrow a picnic basket and take some for lunch. Shady bowers are scented with roses, honeysuckle and jasmine; views are long; pillows carry sprigs of lavender at night. Bright airy bedrooms, each with a sitting area, have pale colourwashed walls and embroidered linen; and you're welcome to share the salone. A paradise of peace, hospitality and blissful breakfasts. *Hot tub in garden.*

Price	€90-€100.
Rooms	3: 1 double, 2 family rooms for 2-4.
Meals	Picnic available. Restaurants 3km.
Closed	January-February.
Directions	A14 exit Pedaso dir. Monterubbiamo. After 200m, left at lights; on SP85 for 7km. After Bar Giardino on left, cont. 2km. On right, signed.

Emidio di Ruscio
Via Canniccio 7 (Via Pozzetto),
63026 Monterubbiano

Tel +39 0734 59226
Mobile +39 348 7761166
Email ventodirose@libero.it
Web www.ventodirose.it

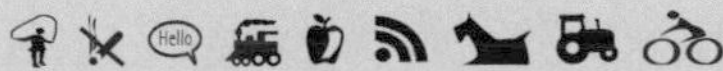

Relais del Colle

Patrizia has succeeded brilliantly in merging luxury with being green. Her home and B&B are on an eight-hectare biodynamic farm, so the wines you enjoy, the wheat that makes your delicious breads and pastas and the vegetables that beautify your plate are all home-grown. Not only is the food organic but the fluffy towels, bathrobes and bed linen are too; all are of organic cotton. Crisp, country-chic guest rooms, each with a piece of balcony or terrace, give a sweet nod to the past: white linen curtains made of antique fabric stitched by the former owner's grandmother; the occasional charming antique. Bathrooms are über-sleek. Relais del Colle may be off the beaten track but perfectionist Patrizia has thought of everything to keep you happy, including a romantic grotto with a huge hot tub, a massage room and a Turkish colour-therapy bath – heated with solar energy, of course – and an elegantly smart dining room for the restaurant. Come for the inviting bedrooms, the gorgeous setting, the vineyard rambles, the organic spa and the lovely, leisurely meals. Worth a very long weekend.

Ethical Collection: Environment; Food.
See page 419 for details.

Price	€75-€120. Triple €165-€195. Quadruple €210-€240.
Rooms	6: 4 doubles, 1 triple, 1 quadruple.
Meals	Lunch/dinner €30-€50 (Fri, Sat & Sun). Restaurant 3km.
Closed	Never.
Directions	A14 exit Grottammare; right after toll. Left at lights, on for 12km to S. Maria Goretti. Right at sign to village; after 10m sign to Trivio di Ripatransone. Up hill, left at stop sign. 450m, right; left after 200m on Contrada S. Greg; to end.

Patrizia Weiszflog
Trivio, Contrada S. Gregorio,
63038 Ripatransone

Tel	+39 0735 987003
Mobile	+39 335 215859
Email	info@relaisdelcolle.it
Web	www.relaisdelcolle.it

Casa Pazzi

You know there's fun in store when you spot the vintage Fiat 600 against the ancient stone walls. In renovating this 18th-century palazzo, the designers chose to introduce an unusually playful touch. The result is a series of apartments whose décor is whimsical but elegant, humorous but sophisticated... every room will make you smile. Carved painted headboards complement each apartment's theme – Palm, Garden, Orient – gorgeous curtains dress windows, bathrooms are bright and cheery, fittings are sleek and modern, and there are breathtaking views of the sea. You get swirls on bannisters and retro touches in kitchens – and big chandeliers. Whip up your own breakfast or request it from Noemi or Sabrine – professional, helpful hosts – and take it to tables under the young citrus trees on the verdant grassed terrace. Note, too, the oversized, flower-spilled urns. Grab one of the cute palazzo bikes for trips down the hill to some of Italy's cleanest beaches. Or zip around town: you're smack dab in the middle of it, beautifully elevated, behind private gates.

Price	€120-€150. Apartments €140-€280.
Rooms	1 + 4: 1 double. 4 apartments for 2-4.
Meals	Breakfast €15. Restaurant 50m.
Closed	Rarely.
Directions	Sent on booking.

Roberto Pazzi
Via Sotto le Mure 5,
63013 Grottammare

Tel	+39 0735 736617
Mobile	+39 331 5385546
Email	info@casapazzi.com
Web	www.casapazzi.com

Agriturismo Ramuse

Our inspector met two English guests who were returning to Ramuse for the 23rd time, so enamoured were they with Paolo and his mother's cooking. Sign up on a blackboard in the dining room if you will be staying for dinner – and why wouldn't you when the set menu sounds tantalising? Everything is produced on the farm or locally and Paolo's enthusiasm for his venture is intoxicating. In a former life, he would nip back and forth to London with a precious cargo of truffles to sell to top chefs (some of whom have stayed here – Gennaro Contaldo's cook book, *Gennaro's Italian Year*, includes a Ramuse recipe). Since then, he's been busy restoring his grandparents' old farm and creating a rustic haven: traditional interiors, stepped vine-clad terraces, a birdsong soundtrack and a super pool. Summer days lolling in hammocks by the stream after a lazy lunch would be sublime but so too would a visit in the autumn or winter for foraging trips and the prospect of returning to sausages cooking over the open fire! If you can bear to tear yourself away, the Sibillini mountains and the Adriatic coast are close.

Price	€560-€1,190 per week (Sat-Sat). Minimum 3 nights.
Rooms	2 + 2: 2 twins/doubles. 2 apartments for 4-6.
Meals	Dinner by arrangement, €18. Wine €8-€20. Restaurant 6km.
Closed	12 November–February.
Directions	Sent on booking.

Paolo Ciccioli
Loc. Casette 3,
63045 Force

Mobile	+39 328 6291859
Email	agriturismoramuse@gmail.com
Web	www.ramuse.it

Dimora del Prete di Belmonte

The old palace hides among the cobbled streets of the medieval centre – a gem once you step inside. Venafro, a Roman town, lies in the lovely valley of Monte Santa Croce, ringed by mountains. The first thrill is the enchanting internal garden with its lush banana palms and citrus trees, where a miscellany of Roman artefacts and olive presses lie scattered among tables and chairs. Next, a frescoed interior in an astonishing state of preservation; painted birds, family crests and *grotteschi* adorn the walls of the state rooms and entrance hall. Bedrooms are furnished in simple good taste, one with a big fireplace and a sleigh bed, another with chestnut country furniture, most with views. Shower rooms are small – bar one, which has a bath. Dorothy is a wonderful hostess and has fantastic local knowledge; she and her son are a great team. They also run an organic farm with 1,000 olive trees (many of them over 400 years old), vines, walnut-trees and sheep. An area and a palace rich in content – and relaxed, delicious dinners do full justice to the setting. Breakfasts are as good. *Easy access by train.*

Price	€120. Suite €150. Apartment €500 per week (€200 for weekend).
Rooms	5 + 1: 4 doubles, 1 suite. Apartment for 2-4.
Meals	Breakfast €10 for self-caterers. Lunch/dinner with wine, €30.
Closed	Rarely.
Directions	Leave A1 Rome-Naples motorway at S. Vittore from north; follow signs for Venafro, Isernia and Campobasso. The Palace is easy to find in the historical centre of Venafro.

Ethical Collection: Food.
See page 419 for details.

Dorothy Volpe del Prete
Via Cristo 49,
86079 Venafro

Tel	+39 0865 900159
Email	info@dimoradelprete.it
Web	www.dimoradelprete.it

Lazio

Casa in Trastevere

Down a quiet back street, seconds from the lush botanic gardens, minutes from the bars, restaurants, boutiques and alleyways of the old quarter of Trastevere, this apartment is perfect for anyone fortunate enough to be planning more than a fleeting trip to Rome. The area, though residential, has a great buzz at night and is fascinating to discover. Signora Nicolini, once a specialist restorer, has furnished this sunny first-floor flat as if it were her own home. She has kept the original 19th-century tan and black terrazzo floor and has added contemporary touches: a cream sofa, an all-white kitchen (no oven but a microwave), kilims and modern art. You have a large open-plan living/dining room with screened kitchen, a double and a twin bedroom, each with a white bathroom, and an extra sofabed. All is bright, light and airy with pretty window boxes, and a charming big bedroom with a hand-quilted bedspread. Marta is a delight and does her best to ensure you go home with happy memories. Put your feet up after a long day, pour yourself a glass of wine... then set off to explore some more of this magical city.

Price	€150-€200.
Rooms	1 apartment for 2-6: 1 double, 1 twin, 1 double sofabed; 2 shower rooms.
Meals	Restaurants nearby.
Closed	Rarely.
Directions	From Ponte Sisto cross Piazza Trilussa. Right into Via della Lungara, left into Via dei Riari, right into Vicolo della Penitenza. From Termini bus line H. From Trastevere station, bus No. 8.

Marta Nicolini
Vicolo della Penitenza 19,
00165 Rome

Email info@casatrevi.it
Web www.casaintrastevere.it

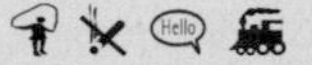

Casa in Trastevere No.2

Wend your way through Trastevere's buzzing streets, past old palazzi to a quiet alley leading to the Aurelian walls of Rome. Just before the ancient stone, spy a more modern – 15th-century! – rose-clad building. Fold back the wooden doors with a whoosh to the 21st century: a swooping space of white and glass, lofty beams and brick. All is light and city-chic, from sisal mats on shiny floors to modern lights illuminating violet sofabeds and Marta's abstract photos. Behind thick glass, a pristine kitchen. Bedrooms contrast bright white walls with streaks of brick; peep out over pretty window boxes to a convent. The all-white bathroom is just as modern, with a rectangular sink, mosaic shower and glinting spotlights. Trastevere hums with life: organic food shops, trendy boutiques, bars and restaurants – but its shady squares are far from touristy and you may find yourself chatting with locals over an aperitivo. Peek into the (very) old church of Santa Maria, or that of Cecilia, patron saint of musicians. Warm, cultured Marta will tell you of local events. The Vatican is a 20-minute walk – and then there's all of Rome.

Price	€150-€200. Minimum 4 nights.
Rooms	Apartment for 4-6 (1 double, 1 twin, 2 single sofabeds).
Meals	Restaurant 100m.
Closed	Never.
Directions	Sent on booking.

Marta Nicolini
Vicolo Moroni 12,
00165 Rome

Email info@casatrevi.it
Web www.casaintrastevere.it

Buonanotte Garibaldi

Cross the Tiber into maze-like Travestere. Turn right for boisterous bars, left for cobblestoned tranquillity. Here lies a place that is small and special – an artistic find behind solid green doors. Fashion and textiles designer Luisa, as welcoming as can be, has transformed her studio and home into a vibrant three-bedroom B&B. Built around a beautiful sun-dappled courtyard, it is a showcase for her creations. Two bedrooms, Orange and Green, are on the ground floor opening to the courtyard (orange trees and magnolias, a marvel in spring) while Blue is above with its own big terrace, heaven for honeymooners. Walls are clean and minimalist, bathrooms mosaic'd and sparkling; splashes of colour come from hand-painted organza. Yours to retire to – a winter treat – is a salon with stylish settees and books on art and Rome. Charming staff, friendly and discreet, serve breakfast at an oval dining table surrounded by silk panels: fresh fruits, breads, meats, eggs how you like them, lavender shortbread, baked peaches; a wonder. All this in Rome's old heart – and Luisa's lovable dog, Tinto.

Price	€220-€280.
Rooms	3 twins/doubles.
Meals	Restaurants within walking distance.
Closed	January-15 February; 15-30 August.
Directions	Off Via Garibaldi in Trastevere.

Luisa Longo
Via Garibaldi 83,
00153 Rome
Tel +39 0658 330733
Email info@buonanottegaribaldi.com
Web www.buonanottegaribaldi.com

Guest House Arco de' Tolomei

Up the sweep of the dark communal wooden staircase into another world, a fascinating little B&B in the peaceful old Jewish quarter of Trastevere. The house has been in Marco's family for 200 years and those sedate gentlemen on the blue walls are just some of the previous inhabitants. Marco and his wife Gianna, great travellers and anglophiles, have filled the family home with bits and pieces from their journeys abroad. Floor to ceiling shelves heave under the weight of books in the red drawing room, gorgeous pieces of art and sculpture beautify walls and tables, and floors are laid with exquisite parquet; there's plenty of dark wood and every square inch gleams. The convivial oval dining table awaits guests eager to sample Gianna's lavish breakfasts. Bedrooms, reached through a guest sitting room, have bold flowers – pinks, reds, yellows – or pinstripes on the walls, a backdrop to handsome bedsteads and great little bathrooms, while the best have miniature staircases up to private terraces with views that roll down over the terracotta patchwork of Trastevere's tiny terracotta roofs and fascinating web of streets.

Price	€160-€220.
Rooms	6: 3 twins/doubles, 3 triples.
Meals	Restaurants 50m.
Closed	Never.
Directions	From Ciampino airport to Trastevere train station; line H to Piazza Sonnino, then Via della Lungaretta to Piazza in Piscinula.

Marco Fè d'Ostiani
Via dell'Arco de' Tolomei 27,
00153 Rome

Tel +39 0658 320819
Email info@bbarcodeitolomei.com
Web www.bbarcodeitolomei.com

Hotel San Francesco

Trastevere – Rome's stylish and bohemian quarter – is at its best on a sleepy Sunday morning when the flea market unfurls and the smell of spicy *porchetta* infuses the air. But first, enjoy a generous Italian breakfast (forget about toast, indulge in cakes), served by ever-friendly staff in a long, light room that overlooks a 15th-century cloister complete with friar, garden and hens... Built in 1926 as a training school for missionaries, this young hotel runs on well-oiled wheels. There's a black and white tiled sitting room with black leather armchairs, big white lilies and a piano. And there's a stylishly furnished roof garden with canvas parasols and views to the Vatican; gorgeous by day, ravishing by night. Marble stairs lead to carpeted corridors off which feed small, comfortable bedrooms – lined curtains at double-glazed windows, fabulous bathrooms, garden views at the back. Pop into the Santa Cecilia next door for a peep at Bellini's *Madonna*, stroll to the sights across the river, rent a bike. Not truly central – you'll be using the odd taxi – but a very pleasant launching pad for discovering the city.

Price	€69-€310.
Rooms	24 doubles.
Meals	Restaurants nearby.
Closed	Never.
Directions	From Termini station, bus No. 75, 44 or line H. Airport train to Travestere (35 mins).

Daniele Frontoni
Via Jacopa de' Settesoli 7,
00153 Rome

Tel	+39 0658 300051
Email	info@hotelsanfrancesco.net
Web	www.hotelsanfrancesco.net

Villa Giulia Suites

Up above bustling bars and hooting vespas, this is peaceful: the odd car passing, the odd screech from a free-ranging parrot! On one of the Eternal City's seven hills: fresh air and pretty buildings, cobbles and umbrella pines, and fabulous views across the rooftops of Rome. Enter a large palazzo dating back to the 1940s, trip down a short flight of stairs, step into a small light lobby off which three apartments lie. Rosso is the largest, Verde the smallest and Marrone is the one with the bath. Marrone also connects with Verde through a bookshelf/door in the dressing room... Each is stylish and modern, bright and inviting: a window seat here, a carved headboard there, elegant little kitchens and thick luxurious curtains. Best of all, each apartment has its own pretty outside seating area just below the big spreading garden; there's a gazebo for aperitivi, a proper barbecue, a veg plot from which you can choose herbs. The delightful Mila settles you in, then it's off to discover Testaccio, Trastevere, the Colosseum – and, round the corner, Gregorian chant in the Church of Sant'Anselmo all'Aventino.

Price	€140-€240 (€980-€1,680 per week). Minimum 3 nights.
Rooms	3 apartments for 2-4 (each with extra sofabed). 2 apts interconnect.
Meals	Restaurants within walking distance.
Closed	Rarely.
Directions	Metro: line B from Termini to Circo Massimo; then 10-min walk. From Ostiense station: bus 715 or 175 to Via delle Terme Deciane.

Anna Passi
Via Marcella 2,
00153 Rome

Tel +39 0721 823159
Mobile +39 347 0823935
Email info@relaisvillagiulia.com
Web www.villagiuliaroma.com

B&B di Piazza Vittorio

A marquis built this Cuban-style palazzo in the 1880s and Alessandra's fifth-floor B&B retains its noble sense of style. A former journalist, she has turned her energy and enthusiasm to this spacious, airy apartment, where light floods through large windows and family antiques rest on pale wooden floors. All is classic, calm, cool, and white predominates. Suite G has two romantic rooms linked by an arched doorway, one with a sofabed, desk and windows catching the morning sun over via Machiavelli. Koko's has shelves of travel books, chess, family mementoes. Single travellers like Magnolia with its French double bed and antique desk; it shares a bathroom with Alessandra. She'll bring continental breakfast to your door or serve up in the modern little kitchen and, if you wish, wrap a lunch panini for later. Best is the position, in cosmopolitan Esquilino – highest hill in Rome. You're 500 metres from the Colosseum and a few steps from humming Piazza Vittorio for restaurants and delis. Alessandra is a mine of information and quirky ideas, from a city tour in a classic convertible to a trip down the Tiber.

Price	€94-€154. Single €72-€122. Suite €126-€206 for 3; €158-€258 for 4. Minimum 2 nights.
Rooms	3: 1 twin/double, 1 suite for 2-4; 1 single sharing bathroom.
Meals	Packed lunch available on request. Restaurants nearby.
Closed	Rarely.
Directions	Sent on booking.

Alessandra Daveri
Via Machiavelli 60,
00185 Rome

Tel	+39 0645 502561
Mobile	+39 340 8605321
Email	info@bebdipiazzavittorio.com
Web	www.bebdipiazzavittorio.com

Caesar House Romane

A calm, comfortable and welcoming oasis above the Roman din. The Forum can be glimpsed from one window, elegant cafés, shops and restaurants lie below, the Colosseum is a five-minute stroll. Take the lift to the second floor of the ancient palazzo, grand reception doors open to a bright, welcoming space. Charming, stylish sisters Giulia and Simona run things together with the help of Grandmama: a family affair. Bedrooms, named after celebrated *italiani*, have warm-red floors, heavy curtains in maroon or blue, matching sofas and quilted covers, a choice of blankets or duvets, vestibules to keep luggage out of the way and every modern thing: air con, minibar, internet, safe, satellite TV. You breakfast in your room – it's big enough – or in the pretty dining room with its tables draped in cream linen and modern art dotted here and there. There's even a gym for those who have surplus energy after a long day's sightseeing among the city's ancient ruins. The service here is exemplary – maps, guided tours, airport pick up, babysitting, theatre booking, bike hire. It's thoroughly professional, and personal too.

Price	€140-€230. Singles €120-€200. Extra bed €20.
Rooms	6: 4 doubles, 2 twins.
Meals	Restaurants nearby.
Closed	Never.
Directions	Metro: line B from Termini station to Cavour, then 5-minute walk or bus No. 74 or 40 down Via Cavour.

Giulia & Simona Barela
Via Cavour 310,
00184 Rome

Tel +39 0667 92674
Email info@caesarhouse.com
Web www.caesarhouse.com

Relais Teatro Argentina

Five-star service with family charm and the elegance of a vintage palazzo – the best of all worlds in central Rome. This boutique hotel, run by gentle Paolo and his niece Carlotta, is steps from Largo Argentina's ruined temples and the spot where Julius Caesar met his fate, an easy walk from the Campo dei Fiori fruit and veg market, the glorious Pantheon and Rome's backstreet art galleries. Ring the bell at the imposing doorway and ascend the pale marble stairs to the warm red reception. Gilt-framed mirrors and chandeliers give a taste of what's to come in palatial bedrooms: wallpapers of pale green willow or rose-pink, king-size beds and parquet floors, antique tables, long draped curtains and gleaming windows. Bathrooms are shiny-new and modern. All is refined and restful, a grand hideaway for a special stay. Fresh pastries, fruit and Italian coffee arrive on a breakfast trolley; no bar/lounge, but you can take a drink out to the little terrace overlooking Rome's rooftops. Paolo and Carlotta are like your personal concierge (but much more friendly!), arranging transport, guides, opera tickets and more.

Price	€143-€265.
Rooms	6: 1 double, 3 twins/doubles, 2 triples.
Meals	Restaurants nearby.
Closed	Rarely.
Directions	Sent on booking.

Carlotta Fè d'Ostiani
Via del Sudario 35,
00186 Rome

Tel +39 0698 931617
Email info@relaisteatroargentina.com
Web www.relaisteatroargentina.com

Casa Trevi I & II

A hop, skip and a jump from Italy's most famous fountain, here be treasure. Find yourself in an astonishingly peaceful courtyard, all olive trees, scented oranges and a fountain inhabited by small turtles. On three sides are 17th-century buildings in yellows, ochres and reds; on the fourth, a modern monstrosity. You're in Rome's most vibrant heart yet not a sound squeezes in from outside. The apartments (Trevi II, the smaller, is an all-in-one studio), on the ground floor of one of the old buildings, open directly off the courtyard. Interiors are bright, soothing and minimalist in the loveliest way: white walls and terracotta, glass shelving and concealed lighting, a mix of modern and brocante finds. There are no windows as such but the double glazed doors let in plenty of light. Hobs and fridges are provided in the airy, white kitchens but serious cooking is not catered for (who wants to cook in Rome?). Shower rooms are gorgeous. Marta could not be sweeter, and the security – a big plus – is excellent, with a porter and security camera in the main entrance. Good value for central Rome. *Minimum stay four nights.*

Price	€120-€200.
Rooms	2 apartments: 1 for 2-3, 1 for 2-4.
Meals	Restaurants nearby.
Closed	Rarely.
Directions	Sent on booking; no parking in pedestrianised area. 10-minute taxi from Termini station. Metro: Piazza Barberini.

Marta Nicolini
Via in Arcione 98,
00187 Rome

Mobile	+39 335 6205768
Email	info@casatrevi.it
Web	www.casatrevi.it

Casa Trevi III

This, too, is five minutes from the Trevi Fountain (most breathtaking by night) but in a separate street from Casas Trevi I and II. Marta – full of warmth, a busy bee – has waved her stylish wand again and created a desirable place to stay. She employed one of Rome's top restoration experts to bring ceiling beams and terracotta floors back to life – and the result? Old Rome meets new. Take the tiny lift to the third floor and into an open-plan sitting, dining and kitchen area – black, white, grey, chic, with a polished wooden floor. A discarded shutter for a frame, an antique door for a bedhead, air con to keep you cool. The white-raftered twin and double rooms share a sparkling, 21st-century shower in beige marble. Modigliani prints beautify cream walls, sliding mirrored doors reflect the light and the cleanly, cleverly separate spaces, silk cushions sprinkle the sofa, shutters are painted dove-grey. Never mind the tourists and the street vendors, Rome lies at your feet. And you have the unassuming Trattoria della Stampa, where the locals go, in the very same street. *Minimum stay four nights.*

Price	€140-€200.
Rooms	Apartment for 3-5.
Meals	Restaurants nearby.
Closed	Never.
Directions	No cars in pedestrianised area; 10-minute taxi from Termini station. Metro: Piazza Barberini. Directions on booking.

Marta Nicolini
Via dei Maroniti 7,
00187 Rome

Mobile +39 335 6205768
Email info@casatrevi.it
Web www.casatrevi.it

Hotel Modigliani

There's a sense of anticipation the moment you enter the marble hall, with its deep, pale sofas and fresh flowers – Marco's wide smile and infectious enthusiasm reinforce the feeling. This is an unusual, delightful place, hidden down a side street just five minutes' walk from the Spanish Steps and Via Veneto. The house belonged to Marco's father, and Marco and Giulia (he a writer, she a musician) have turned it into the perfect small hotel. Marble floors and white walls are a dramatic setting for black-and-white photos taken by Marco, their starkness softened by luxuriant plants. The bread oven of the 1700s has become a dining room – all vaulted ceilings, whitewashed walls, cherrywood tables, fabulous photos. Bedrooms are fresh and elegant; some have balconies and wonderful views, all have small, perfect bathrooms. There's a lovely new sitting room and bar for guests to use. The whole place has a sweet, stylish air, it's unusually quiet for the centre of the city and there's a patio scented with jasmine. Marco and Giulia will tell you about Rome's secret corners – or grab a copy of Marco's new guide and discover Rome for yourselves.

Price	€90-€205. Suites €208-€340. Family suite €330-€440. Apartments €200-€250.
Rooms	25: 20 twins/doubles, 2 suites, 1 family suite for 4-6, 2 apartments: 1 for 3, 1 for 6.
Meals	Restaurant 10m.
Closed	Never.
Directions	Metro: line A, 2nd stop Piazza Barberini. 5-minute walk from Spanish Steps.

Giulia & Marco di Tillo
Via della Purificazione 42,
00187 Rome

Tel	+39 0642 815226
Email	info@hotelmodigliani.com
Web	www.hotelmodigliani.com

Quod Libet

Have breakfast in bed in this zany-bright B&B, high in a 19th-century palazzo near the Vatican. Gianluca and Consolata deliver a tray piled with eggs and fresh bread from the gorgeous-smelling bakery downstairs – and if you don't fancy crumbs in the sheets, each big bright double room has space for a table and chairs. Shiny-new bedrooms are themed by season – spring rose-pink, summery yellow, frosty blue-grey – and overlook a wide plane tree-lined viale leading to the river. Families will choose the chocolatey red of Autunno, with its sofabed, bath and windows over a quiet inner courtyard. Canvas paintings are by Gianluca, owner, artist and computer whizz; he and Consolata will share a welcome drink and tips on the best local markets, restaurants, nightlife. Best of all, it's a five-minute walk to Saint Peter's and the Vatican Museums, perfect for early tours before the crowds. Ottaviano-San Pietro metro station is a block away and you're a pleasant 30-minute stroll to most of Rome's delights. A superb addition to Rome's B&Bs: as fresh, bright and cheerful as its owners. *Parking €4 per day.*

Price €70-€220. Singles €60-€100.
Rooms 4 doubles (1 with extra sofabed).
Meals Restaurants within walking distance.
Closed Rarely.
Directions Sent on booking.

Consolata Sodaro
Via Barletta 29,
00192 Rome
Tel +39 347 1222642
Mobile +39 347 3355160
Email info@quodlibetroma.com
Web www.quodlibetroma.com

Casa Mary

Seasonal fruits in the hamper, Roman ruins all over the place, heavenly views from wherever you stand. Welcome to a fabulous house built into the hillside in the park of Campo Soriano. The once-derelict farmhouse, surrounded by figs, lemons, lavender and 400 olive trees, has been revived by its English owner – beautifully. Inside all is fresh, uncluttered and Italian, with terracotta floors and soft colours and walls a metre thick (keeping you cool in summer). The bedrooms are delightful, the bathrooms are en suite and the kitchen, rustic-contemporary and very well equipped, opens to the terraced gardens; help yourself to herbs. Further provisions are a 15-minute drive away, in the wonderful market at Terracina; you're close to a good supermarket, too. Bliss to dine on the terrace, in the shade of the olive tree by day, under the stars by night. History buffs can visit the Cistercian Abbey at Fossanova – a must-see – while families will head off for the beaches at Sperlonga (itself enchanting) and Sabaudia; the house information booklet is a boon. Then there's Pompeii, Naples, Rome… a treat. *Minimum stay one week.*

Price	€1,000-€1,500 per week.
Rooms	House for 8 (4 twins/doubles).
Meals	Restaurants 15-minute drive.
Closed	December-March.
Directions	Sent on booking.

Mary Tucker
Via Campo Soriano Snc,
04010 Cascano
Email marytucker0609@aol.com

Azienda Agrituristica Sant'Ilario sul Farfa

Friendly, for families, no frills, and an hour from Rome by car. The little farm sits high on one of the steeply terraced hills above the river Farfa: no wonder the views are incredible. As for the approach along a steep tarmac track, it is marked by that typically Italian juxtaposition of swish modern gates and an olive tree of great antiquity. Susanna is a creative hostess whose dinners – delivered on request, from organic farm produce – are brilliant value. The aspect of the place is rather ranch-like, with bedrooms in two single-storey farm buildings, white with wooden shutters. Bedrooms are snug and wood-panelled with some fine antique bedheads, white walls and showers. The two apartments in the main house have small kitchens for simple meals: great for families. A pleasing tangle of trellises extends across the garden – more farmyard than formal. Take a dip in the pool or the river, knock a ball around the football pitch or court (tennis 100m), book into yoga or an olive (or grape) harvesting weekend. There are painting classes for grown-ups, cookery and craft classes for children. Little ones love it.

Price	€80. Half-board €55-€60. Apartment €480-€880 per week.
Rooms	6 + 3: 2 doubles, 4 family rooms. 3 apts: 1 for 3, 1 for 4, 1 for 5-6.
Meals	Dinner/Sunday lunch with wine, €25. Restaurants 2km.
Closed	Rarely.
Directions	From SS4 Rome-Rieti exit to Osteria Nuova dir. Poggio Nativo. Just after Monte S. Maria sharp left onto Via Sant'Ilario signed to Sant'Ilario sul Farfa.

Susanna Serafini
Via Sant'Ilario,
02030 Poggio Nativo

Tel +39 0765 872410
Email info@santilariosulfarfa.it
Web www.santilariosulfarfa.it

La Torretta

Casperia is a joyful, characterful, car-free maze of steepish streets in the Sabine hills. La Torretta has the dreamiest views from its terrace, and easy interior spaces that have been wonderfully designed by architect Roberto. A huge ground-floor sitting room with beautiful frescoes around the cornicing welcomes you… an old stone fireplace, modern sofas and chairs, books, paintings, piano. The upper room – opening onto that terrace – is a stunning, vaulted, contemporary living space with an open stainless-steel kitchen and views through skylights to the church tower and valley. Maureen, warm-hearted and hospitable, is passionate about the region and its food. She arranges cookery courses and will cook (on request) using the best olive oil and whatever is in season – mushrooms, truffles, wild boar. Whitewashed, high-ceilinged bedrooms are charming in their simplicity; beds are made and towels changed regularly; bathrooms are a treat. Don't worry about having to leave your car in the square below the town: Roberto has a buggy for luggage. Fine breakfasts, too – among the best in Italy!

Price	€90. Single €70. Family room €150.
Rooms	7: 5 doubles, 1 single, 1 family room (2 connecting rooms) for 4.
Meals	Dinner with wine, €30, by arrangement. Restaurant 100m.
Closed	Rarely.
Directions	From north, A1 exit Ponzano Soratte towards Poggio Mirteto. Continue on SS657 for 5km to T-junc. Left on SS313 to Cantalupo towards Casperia.

Roberto & Maureen Scheda
Via G. Mazzini 7,
02041 Casperia

Tel	+39 0765 63202
Mobile	+39 338 1451859
Email	latorretta@tiscali.it
Web	www.latorrettabandb.com

La Locanda della Chiocciola

The perfect place to unwind after Rome. Maria Cristina and Roberto have turned a 15th-century stone farmstead in the Tiber valley – 'The House of the Snail' – into an entrancing small hotel and restaurant where you are welcomed by glowing floors, mellow furniture and the intoxicating smell of beeswax. Gardens full of flowering shrubs and peaceful paths are set in 25 hectares of woods, olive groves and orchards, and there's a delicious pool. A fine staircase sweeps up to the bedrooms, each with its name painted on the door: 'Mimosa', 'Coccinella', 'Ciclamine'... These are arresting rooms – large, refined, elegant and cool – with wrought-iron beds and fine bathrooms. Terracotta tiles contrast with pale walls and lovely fabrics, family antiques with elegant modern furniture or pieces that your hosts have collected on their travels. They're a charming young couple, warm, smiling, thoughtful, proud of what they have created. The food is delicious and the spa (hammam, sauna, jacuzzi), soothing and sprinkled with candles, is a delight. Discover the region's hidden gems and return to sleep in serenity.

Price	€140-€170. Half-board €105-€120 p.p.
Rooms	8: 3 doubles, 2 suites, 1 family room, 2 triples.
Meals	Dinner €35. Wine from €10. Menu à la carte also available.
Closed	Mid-December to mid-January.
Directions	Exit autostrada at Orte for Orte Town. Before Orte, dir. Penna in Teverina. After 2.5km, sign for La Chiocciola on left.

Roberto & Maria Cristina de Fonseca Pimentel
Seripola, 01028 Orte

Tel	+39 0761 402734
Email	info@lachiocciola.net
Web	www.lachiocciola.net

Locanda Settimo Cielo

Bounce down the track through olives and orchards to the vine-smothered arbour, park up and enter an exotic oasis of rusticity and peace. Built in the early 19th century to house the estate's sharecroppers, this sturdy farmhouse sits grandly atop a cliff of tuff surrounded by elms, pines and splendid views of forested, wildlife-stuffed hills. A stroll down stepped paths cut into the rock and tunnelled fruit trees reveals a secluded, deck-fringed pool, while a fabulous covered patio terrace with solid tables and chairs provides lovely outdoor space. Interiors are gorgeous, rustic and reminiscent of a safari lodge: massive hand-carved beds and tables; looming wardrobes; framed African tapestries. Ambient lighting and an enormous fireplace illuminate a high-ceilinged, decadently comfortable sitting room – heaven – while lovely Francesca's breakfasts of homemade breads and juices harvested from the estate set you up for a day's hiking in the hills, touring the vineyards or visiting mediaeval villages. Or simply stay put and nod off to the birdsong with a book.

Price	B&B €130. Whole house €6,000 per week.
Rooms	9: 5 doubles, 3 triples, 1 quadruple. Whole house available (sleeps 23).
Meals	Occasional dinner with wine, €30. Restaurant 3km.
Closed	End October-April (open Christmas and New Year).
Directions	From A1 exit Orvieto; follow signs to Todi then to Lubriano. Stay on street until Strada Sterrata Locanda Santa Caterina N. Dal 28 al 34. Left; on to B&B.

Francesca Anghileri
Loc. Santa Caterina 28,
01020 Lubriano

Tel +39 0761 780451
Email info@settimocieloagriturismo.com
Web www.settimocieloagriturismo.com

Casale Giommetta

The tap water is as fresh as a Norwegian mountain spring! So say the owners, charming Scandinavians who have upped sticks and moved to this wonderful Etruscan-steeped region. Ten minutes away is Bolsena, Italy's largest lake; swim, fish, windsurf, catch a boat to the island in the middle. (The town too is worth a visit, for ramparts, ruins and marvellous views.) Smiling Eva and her family were all involved in this restoration, of a 1700s farmhouse that once housed 30 souls with the animals on the ground floor. They've spruced it up wonderfully but kept the rustic walls; now it feels spacious, airy and inviting with a homely Norwegian feel: note the red and white check fabrics and the hand-painted furniture, much of it constructed by Eva. Every family room is huge: sitting room with deep chairs, grand piano, open fire; dining room with chunky rafters and two tables; kitchen with crockery and cutlery for scores of people! Fat quilts top new beds; windows open to field views; mountains and woods lie beyond. All is immaculate outside and in, and that includes the lovely big pool.

Price	€3,750-€5,000 per week. Shorter breaks out of season.
Rooms	House for 14 (5 doubles, 1 children's room for 4; 6 bathrooms).
Meals	Meals from €15, on request. Restaurants 4km.
Closed	Rarely.
Directions	A1 exit Orvieto. Follow signs to Bolsena & Montefiascone on s.71. Then s.74 to Castel Giorgio, thro' town; after dairy & sharp bend, left onto a 'strada bianca' for 1km.

Eva Groth
Voc. Madonna 12,
01020 San Lorenzo Nuovo

Tel	+39 339 8271641
Mobile	+47 918 68808
Email	evagroth@live.no

Giommetta - La Stalla

Approach across open fields and through electric gates to pull up in front of a long low farmhouse and be greeted by Eva, warm and effusive. Your home is the Porcellaio, the old piggery, a single-storey building perfectly restored and surrounded by springy lawn. Floors are tiled, walls are chunky, rafters are slopey and ceilings unexpectedly high. Expect a charming rusticity combined with luxury, and cushions and curtains – some simple checked, others flowery – made by Norwegian Eva. The dining room and sitting room (traditional striped sofas, warm burgundy lampshades) are linked by a galley-style kitchen; bathrooms, one white, the other mushroom, have warm toasty floors. Outside is a big open garden with young bushes and trees, a sandpit, a play area and a swing, a super pizza oven and a serious grill, and one big lovely communal pool. Young families could spend the whole holiday here without budging an inch. But budge you must: this is on the border of Tuscany and Umbria and Orvieto is a delight, a Renaissance hilltop city with Slow status (no cars) reached by funicular railway.

Price	€2,500-€3,750 per week. Min. one week in high season.
Rooms	House for 6-8 (2 doubles, 1 bunk room for 2; 3 bathrooms).
Meals	Meals from €15, on request. Restaurants 4km.
Closed	Rarely.
Directions	A1 exit Orvieto. Follow signs to Bolsena & Montefiascone on s.71. Then s.74 to Castel Giorgio, thro' town; after dairy & sharp bend, left onto a 'strada bianca' for 1km.

Eva Groth
Voc. Madonna 12,
01020 San Lorenzo Nuovo

Tel +39 339 8271641
Mobile +47 918 68808
Email evagroth@live.no

Villa Felceto

In a landscape rich with wild flowers, hares and deer is an immaculate renovation of an abandoned farmhouse, furnished in elegant English style. Who would guess downstairs' bedrooms, kitchen, dining room and den once housed shepherd and sheep? Now they glow with pale travertine worktops and cupboards in olive green, distinctive wallpapers and Persian rugs, cosy armchairs and stylish showers. In baronial contrast is the lofty drawing room upstairs, all majestic rafters and sweeping terracotta, books and games, family antiques and old English oils. Also a second kitchen, and a second dining space, making this big old house just perfect for two families. French windows open to a vine-covered pergola and a dining terrace with views west to Monte Amiata – and sunsets! Wherever you look, the views are 360 degrees: perched on a knoll one can see for miles. Take a dip in the pool that waits serenely below; gather salads and veg for your supper; listen to the doves, follow the swallows. Sleepy Trevinano has two good restaurants, medieval San Casciano has Etruscan thermal baths that open to the sky.

Price	Whole house €1,000-€4,750 per week. B&B €110-€130 per night.
Rooms	House for 13 (5 twins/doubles, 1 family room for 3). Also available for B&B.
Meals	Dinner with wine, from €30. By arrangement. Restaurants 2km.
Closed	Rarely.
Directions	Exit A1 at Fabbro or Chiusi, signed San Casciano dei Bagni. Thro' town, signs to Trevinano. Before Trevinano, 300m after Tuscany/Lazio border, left to Podere Felceto (signed).

Francesco Rosso
Trevinano, Acquapendente,
01021 Viterbo

Mobile +39 328 4491393
Email info@lecollinedeisogni.it
Web www.lecollinedeisogni.it

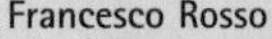

Campania

Masseria Giosole Agriturismo

A wonderful place for families. Sixty hectares of olives and fruit trees – help yourself! – a children's playground, a stunning pool, free bikes, tennis and a relaxed, no-rules atmosphere. Children scamper safely, parents flop around lazily... occasionally ambling off via the orchards to the river with just the birds for company. The di Maglianos, a handsome lively couple whose family have farmed here for three centuries, have created a place that reflects their gracious, easy-going nature. Rooms in the sprawling, peachy coloured *masseria* are large and airy with terracotta or wooden floors, high beamed ceilings and pale washed walls, and lightly sprinkled family antiques. Colourful textiles add dash. Bedrooms, some with a garden terrace, are uncluttered and restful, their bathrooms small but spotless. Nearby are ancient churches and palazzi in Capua, the Royal Palace at Caserta, and Naples and Pompeii are under an hour's drive. Come back to a delicious meal of local dishes – home-produced, naturally – dining around the fire in winter, in the garden in summer. *Minimum stay two nights.*

Price	€86-€120. Suites €110-€150. Apartment €90-€125.
Rooms	5 + 1: 3 doubles, 2 suites for 2-4. Apartment for 2-4.
Meals	Breakfast €8 for self-caterers. Dinner €25, by arrangement. Restaurants 1km.
Closed	Rarely.
Directions	A1 Rome-Naples exit Capua. Follow signs for Capua and Agriturismo Masseria Giosole for 7km. Past San Giuseppe church on right; after 500m, right. On for 1.5km; signed.

Barone Alessandro & Baronessa Francesca Pasca di Magliano
Via Giardini 31,
81043 Capua

Tel	+39 0823 961108
Email	info@masseriagiosole.com
Web	www.masseriagiosole.com

Il Cortile Agriturismo

Special place, special people, and, behind the plain brown door, a verdant surprise. Off the suburban street is a stunning flagged courtyard rich in jasmine and oranges – ravishing in spring. Now this historic villa, built as a summer retreat for Arturo's forebears, offers two sober, uncluttered and charming B&B rooms, one facing the courtyard with its own secluded entrance, the other in a building just beyond the garden gates. This is a delightful two-bedroom family suite with views onto the lush and lovely garden of Il Cortile. Dutch Sijtsken is charming and thoughtful, serves delicious meals in the vaulted cellar – a stunningly atmospheric dining room – and is aided in her enterprise by daughters Giovanna (trainee sommelier) and Alessandra (dessert chef extraordinaire). As for the 'giardinello delle delizie' – the 'little garden of delights' – it is far from small; indeed weddings are held here in the summer, in among the date palms and the magnolias, the glistening roses and the camellia. Find a deckchair and dream. The family delight in sharing their table and their home with guests – wonderful.

Price	€70-€75. €110 for 3. €120 for 4.
Rooms	2: 1 family room for 3, 1 suite for 2-4.
Meals	Dinner €25. Wine from €5.
Closed	Never.
Directions	From Rome or Naples: m'way to Bari exit Nola. Follow signs to Cimitile & Cicciano. House 10-minute drive from m'way.

Sijtsken, Giovanna & Alessandra Nucci
Via Roma 43,
80033 Cicciano

Tel	+39 0818 248897
Email	info@agriturismoilcortile.com
Web	www.agriturismoilcortile.com

Luna Caprese

A five-minute stroll from Naples' romantic waterfront, this fourth-floor palazzo apartment, reached via a smart central courtyard, is tucked away in charmingly posh Chiaia. The feeling is one of refined 19th-century elegance and your friendly, time-generous host Arnaldo has a passion for art: a lavish collection of paintings, photos and sculptures adorn this sophisticated apartment. The snazzy reception recalls a gentleman's club: high ceilings, wooden floors, beautiful rugs, Neapolitan furniture; deep, comfy sofas everywhere, soft lighting, fine paintings, sculptures and floor-to-ceiling books. Restful colours – beige, wine, terracotta, cream – add to the feeling of elegance and a genteel way of life – with every modern luxury added. Bedrooms are spacious and light, with fine cotton sheets, old style bedsteads, terracotta floors and private balconies. Arnaldo's love of Naples is infectious, so take advantage of his local knowledge and of tours to the Aeolian Isles. Note you are wonderfully placed for the Via Morelli and its fabulous antiques – browse or buy!

Price	€110-€125. Singles €85-€95.
Rooms	6: 3 doubles, 3 twins/doubles.
Meals	Restaurants within walking distance.
Closed	Rarely.
Directions	Sent on booking.

Arnaldo Cotugno
Via Chiatamone 7,
80121 Naples

Tel	+39 0817 646383
Email	info@lunacaprese.net
Web	www.lunacaprese.net

La Murena Bed & Breakfast

Views from the rooftop terrace stretch to chestnut forests and the Gulf of Naples below. Here, high on the slopes of Vesuvius, the peace is palpable and the air cool and pure. Giovanni and his son live on the ground floor of this modern house and you have the option of self-catering (shops are very near) or B&B. The three bedrooms, kitchen and huge terrace are upstairs, and guests are welcome to share Giovanni's living room below; this is where he serves a delicious breakfast of peaches, apricots and oranges from the garden, cheeses and homemade jams. There's also a large outside area for children to romp in. The big, light and airy bedrooms are very traditional – beds may be of wrought iron, writing desks are antique with marble tops and floor tiles are patterned blue. The kitchen, too, is well equipped and prettily tiled, there's blue glassware in a sea-blue cupboard, a white-clothed table and no shortage of mod cons. A dream for lovers of archaeological sites – Herculaneum, Pompeii, Torre Annunziata, Boscoreale – and Naples is a short train ride away. *Minimum stay three nights. Airport pick up.*

Price	B&B €80. Singles €60. Whole house €240 (€1,500 per week).
Rooms	3: 2 doubles, 1 triple.
Meals	Restaurants nearby.
Closed	Rarely.
Directions	From autostrada Napoli-Pompei-Salerno exit Torre del Greco; follow signs for Il Vesuvio (via Osservatorio).

Giovanni Scognamiglio
Via Osservatorio 10,
80056 Herculaneum

Tel	+39 0817 779819
Email	lamurena@lamurena.it
Web	www.lamurena.it

www.istockphoto.com/Anton-Marlot

Casa di Zasta

Visions of ancient stones burnished by the gleaming intensity of the southern Italian sun, tables groaning with local artisan cheeses, hand-rolled pasta, prosciutto, figs and focaccia set in a charmingly rustic fashion beneath silvery-leaved olives, the heady scent of luscious lemons as they ripen in the citrus groves that stretch to the glittering blue Mediterranean, a landscape of vivid scarlet as far as the eye can see, a happy band of characterful farm workers laying their intensely flavoured plum tomatoes to dry in the searing heat: all this and more is available a few miles up the road. But for less fussy types on a tight budget, there's not much to beat a stay at the legendary Casa di Zasta. Okay, it's yet to have a front door or a roof, or rooms, or plumbing, or parking, but you're are in Italy now, the home of the Slow Movement and these things take time; Rome wasn't built in a day you know. The previous occupants left under a bit of a cloud but don't let that put you off… it was around 2,000 years ago after all! The owner is holding out for an EU subsidy for vital repair work; he'll be lucky.

Price	Only a Roman knows.
Rooms	1 dormitorium with en suite thermae.
Meals	The occasional bacchanalian feast.
Closed	No, open to the skies.
Directions	Plumes of billowing smoke will guide you.

www.istockphoto.com/franckreporter

Signor V. Suvio
01234 Pompeii
Tel XIVLM XXXC
Web www.casadizasta.it

Villa Giusso

An intriguing place, and quite a challenge to reach, but once there you fall into the staggering view – and know why you came. Originally a monastery (1600s), it stands high on a promontory overlooking the bay of Naples and the Sorrento coast. The whole place could be a Fellini film setting. After an effusive welcome from Erminia, Giovanna and the rest of the Giusso family, you will settle into your rooms – romantic with vintage iron beds, quirky antique furnishings and old paintings. Two are in the old monks' quarters, the others overlook the courtyard where a couple of friendly dogs welcome you. The sitting rooms include a wonderful salon (wisely roped off) full of collapsing antique sofas and heirlooms. Dinner, biodynamically home-grown and delicious, is served at a vast communal table in the vaulted, ancient-tiled kitchen – an occasion to relish. At breakfast of fruit, fresh ricotta and homemade cakes, plan an exciting day in Naples, to return to a blissfully peaceful stroll through the estate's vines and olive groves then a glass of homemade walnut liqueur on the terrace – with that view. *Minimum stay two nights.*

Price	€90-€130.
Rooms	7: 5 doubles, 1 suite for 4; 1 double with separate bath.
Meals	Dinner €28 (except Mondays). Restaurants 2km.
Closed	November-Palm Sunday.
Directions	A3 Napoli-Salerno exit Castellammare di Stabia; signs for Sorrento. At Seiano, after Moon Valley Hotel, left for M. Faito; cont. for 4.6km, right after Arola sign, follow signs to Astapiana Villa Giusso.

Famiglia Giusso Rispoli
Via Camaldoli 51, Astapiana,
Loc. Arola, 80069 Vico Equense

Tel	+39 0818 024392
Mobile	+39 329 1150475
Email	astapiana@tin.it
Web	www.astapiana.com

Agriturismo La Ginestra

There is a fresh, rustic feel to this farmhouse, and its position, 680m above sea level, is incredible. From the terraces, plunging views stretch in two directions: the Bay of Naples and the Bay of Salerno. The hills behind hold more delights, particularly for serious walkers: the 'Sentieri degli Dei' is a stone's throw away; some of the paths, especially those down to Positano, are vertiginous and tough. The four delightful families who own La Ginestra will happily organise guided nature walks (the younger generation speak English); they are also passionate about their co-operative farm and its organic status. All the farm's produce – nuts, honey, vegetables, olive oil – is sold from a little cottage, and served in the restaurant, too, where delicious Sorrento dishes arrive at check-clothed tables for contented Italians. Sunday lunch is a joyous affair. This is quite a tribute to La Ginestra as it is not the easiest place to reach – though not so inaccessible that the local bus can't make it up the hill. Bedrooms and shower rooms are charming and mostly a good size, some with their own terrace. Tremendous value.

Price	Half-board €45 p.p. Full-board €55 p.p. Singles half-board €60. Singles full-board €65.
Rooms	7 doubles/triples.
Meals	Half-board or full-board only.
Closed	Never.
Directions	A3 exit Castellammare di Stabia; SS145 coast road to Vico Equense; SS269 to Raffaele Bosco; at Moiano-Ticciano follow road to Santa Maria del Castello.

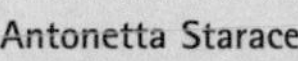

Antonetta Starace
Via Tessa 2, Santa Maria del Castello,
80060 Moiano di Vico Equense

Tel +39 0818 023211
Email info@laginestra.org
Web www.laginestra.org

Azienda Agricola Le Tore Agriturismo

Vittoria is a vibrant presence and knows almost every inch of this wonderful coastline – its paths, its hill-perched villages, its secret corners. She sells award-winning organic olive oil, vinegar, preserves, nuts and lemons on her terraced five hectares. The cocks crow at dawn, distant dogs bark in the early hours and fireflies glimmer at night in the lemon groves. It's rural, the sort of place where you want to get up while there's still dew on the vegetables. The names of the bedrooms reflect their conversion from old farm buildings – 'Stalla', 'Fienile', 'Balcone' – and are simply but solidly furnished. We are told by those who stay that dinners are abundant and delicious, so do eat in, and get to meet Vittoria and your fellow guests. Breakfast is taken at your own table under the pergola, and may include raspberries, apple tart and fresh fruit juices. You must descend to coast level to buy your postcards, but this is a great spot from which to explore, and to walk – the CAI 'Alta via di Lattari' footpath is nearby. Le Tore is heaven to return to after a day's sightseeing, with views of the sea. *Ask about weddings.*

Ethical Collection: Community; Food.
See page 419 for details.

Price	€90. Apartment €700-€1,000 per week.
Rooms	6 + 1: 4 doubles, 1 twin, 1 family room for 4. Apartment for 6.
Meals	Dinner €25, by arrangement. Restaurant 5-minute walk.
Closed	November-Palm Sunday (apartment available all year).
Directions	A3 Naples-Palermo, exit Castellammare di Stabia for Positano. At x-roads for Positano, by restaurant Teresinella, sign for Sant'Agata; 7km, left on Via Pontone; 1km.

Vittoria Brancaccio
Via Pontone 43, Sant'Agata sui due Golfi,
80064 Massa Lubrense

Tel +39 0818 080637
Mobile +39 333 9866691
Email info@letore.com
Web www.letore.com

Hotel Villa San Michele

Unashamedly romantic! Stone steps tumble down from terrace to terrace past lemon trees, palms, bougainvillea and scented jasmine to the rocks below, and a dip in the deep blue sea. It's a treat to stay in this small, intimate, family-run hotel, with heart-stopping views and easy-going Nicola and his smiley staff to minister to you. It may stand at an apparently busy road junction but its hanging gardens and bedrooms all turn towards the sea and you live in perfect peace. The hotel building is at the top – light, airy, cool; almost every room has a balcony or terrace; you are lulled to sleep by the lapping of the sea. Cool floors are tiled in classic Amalfi style or white; beds have patterned bedcovers, shower rooms are clean. It is all charming and unpretentious, from the white plastic tables to the stripey deckchairs where you can gaze on the sea and watch the ferries slip by towards Positano or Capri. Delectable aromas waft from a cheerful kitchen where Signora is chef; the menu is short and just right. Atrani and Amalfi are walkable, though traffic is heavy in summer; for the weary, a bus stops at the hotel.

Price	€100-€170.
Rooms	12 doubles.
Meals	Dinner €28. Wine from €15. June-Sept half-board only. Restaurants 500m.
Closed	7 January-14 February; 7 November-25 December.
Directions	A3 to Salerno exit Vietri sul Mare; follow signs to Amalfi; hotel 1km before Amalfi on left. Discuss parking on booking.

Nicola Dipino
SS163 Costiera Amalfitana,
Via Carusiello 2, 84010 Ravello
Tel +39 0898 72237
Email smichele@starnet.it
Web www.hotel-villasanmichele.it

Villa en Rose

Get a feel here of what life must have been like before roads came to these hillsides; this is a place for walkers. And for some of the most stupendous views in Italy; you are halfway between Minori and Ravello on a marked footpath that was once a mule trail. In fact, the only way to get here is on foot, with about 15 minutes' worth of steps down from the closest road. (Lugging provisions up here could be a challenge in bad weather.) The open-plan apartment is modern-functional not aesthetic, and spotless; its bedroom is in an alcove off the sitting room, its views from arched windows are a glory and you are surrounded by terraced lemon groves. It feels a world away from the crowds down on the coast, and the secluded little pool means you are not obliged to climb miles down to the beach. The second, much smaller apartment is on the owner's floor above, with no sitting space as such: very basic. If you don't feel like cooking, hot-foot it up to the main square in ravishing Ravello; heaps of restaurants to choose from. Don't miss the glorious gardens of the Villas Rufolo and Cimbrone. *Air conditioning extra.*

Price	From €104. Minimum 3 nights.
Rooms	2 apartments: 1 for 2-4 (+ sofabed), 1 for 2-3.
Meals	Breakfast €6. Restaurants 3km.
Closed	Rarely.
Directions	Details on booking. Valeria will meet you in Ravello.

Valeria Civale
Via Torretta a Marmorata 22,
84010 Ravello

Tel	+39 0898 57661
Email	valeriacivale@yahoo.it
Web	www.villaenrose.com

Boccaccio B&B

Between the post office and the hardware shop, climb the marble staircase, step into your room and your heart will skip a beat. Just the other side of the busy road, one thousand feet below, is the dizzying curve of the Bay of Salerno. Vineyards, lemon groves, white houses, all cling to the steep valley sides in apparent defiance of gravity; it is almost impossible to pull yourself away from the view. And all four rooms have it. Boccaccio is a family affair; grandmother had these rooms and the family still live on the upper floor. Bonaventura and his family have refurbished the house in a cleancut, understated modern style that has the virtue of simplicity (as does the breakfast): beech wood furniture, crisp bed linen, sleek lighting and sunny, hand-painted Vietri floor tiles. Bathrooms are spotless, with all necessary fittings. Two minutes from Ravello's picture-perfect piazza (a tourist trap in season), and the Rufolo and Cimbrone gardens, Boccaccio's position is enviable. Your host worked 35 years in the film industry, and appears still to be very busy in the village. *Discounted parking: book ahead.*

Price	€75-€95.
Rooms	4 twins/doubles.
Meals	Restaurants 100m.
Closed	Rarely.
Directions	2-min walk from central pedestrian square of Ravello.

Bonaventura Fraulo
G. Boccaccio 19,
84010 Ravello

Tel	+39 0898 57194
Email	infoboccaccio@hotmail.com
Web	www.boccaccioravello.com

Agriturismo Biologico Barone Antonio Negri

Monica's grandfather, the Barone Antonio, was a much-loved mayor and the piazza named in his honour is a fine place for an evening passeggiata amongst the locals. The farm has been in the family for 150 years, but it's only once you pass the high gates and approach the house that you appreciate the beautiful far-reaching views toward Salerno – and the sunsets are divine. Positioned on various levels, each of the good-sized and individually decorated Provençal style rooms, some sporting modern frescoes, keeps its original tiles and surveys nine hectares of nut, fruit and olive trees and vines; enjoy a morning stroll before cooling off in the pool. The exuberant Monica offers cookery classes using regional ingredients, and dinner on the terrace (or in the restaurant) is delicious: local mozzarella, just-picked tomatoes, chicken cooked to grandmother's recipe, and always, a dessert extravaganza. It's wonderful being high and cool and within easy reach of the Amalfi coast, but for children it's the farm animals who steal the show; everyone loves the donkey Serafina who has her own knowing call for Monica.

Price	€90-€110. Singles €80-€100. Half-board €140-€160.
Rooms	5: 2 doubles, 2 twins/doubles, 1 family room for 2-4.
Meals	Dinner with wine, €25. Restaurants 5-minute walk.
Closed	Rarely.
Directions	Sent on booking.

Monica Negri
Via Teggiano 8, Gaiano di Fisciano,
84084 Salerno

Tel	+39 0899 58561
Mobile	+39 335 6852140
Email	info@agrinegri.it
Web	www.agrinegri.it

Borgoriccio

All the pleasures of a Slow holiday in Italy. A quiet hilltop village in the Cilento National Park; a beautiful big house hugged by olives, figs, flowers; a local restaurant (special deal for guests) serving regional wines; a 'via verde' through the stunning scenery of upper and lower Torchiara. Angela has rebuilt an old family home in a traditional style. Casa Bassa (the old olive press) has country-style suites in the landscape's warm browns and bright yellow-greens. Casa Alta (on the terrace above) holds more bedrooms, a large, fire-warmed sitting room, a small library, a dining room with country antiques, a small tower for reading and reflection. Outside, a swimming pool simmers in southern Italian sunshine, a jacuzzi bubbles and gardens sprawl; views stretch over Cilento's forested hills. Feisty Angela knows the area's best spots while Michaela looks after guests with homemade cakes, fresh juice and a warm smile. It's a 20-minute drive to Agropoli for blue flag beaches and the ferry to Positano; if you prefer sightseeing to sunbathing, Pompeii is within reach. Enchanting, carefree, delightfully Slow.

Price	€90-€120. Singles €80-€110. Suites: €180-€210 for 3, €200-€230 for 4.
Rooms	6: 4 doubles, 2 suites: 1 for 3, 1 for 4.
Meals	Restaurants 5-minute walk.
Closed	Rarely.
Directions	Sent on booking.

Angela Riccio
Strada Provinciale 86, nº 56,
84076 Torchiara

Tel +39 0974 831554
Email info@borgoriccio.com
Web www.borgoriccio.com

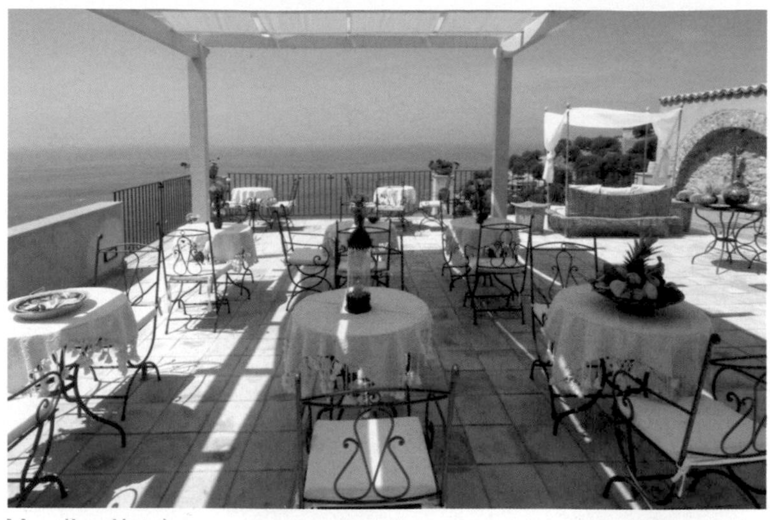

Marulivo Hotel

Cool – in both senses of the word. Metre-thick walls give the whole place that delicious damp-ancient smell, a constant reminder that you are staying in a 14th-century monastery. Architect Lea, and Massimo, lovely people, have revived the ruin after 100 years of abandonment. Open to the elements, its topsy-turvy layout is intriguing, the kind of place that cries out to be explored the moment you duck under the archway. Gorgeous bedrooms have exposed brickwork, terracotta floors, balconies and super beds with curly-whirly headboards – and heaps of individual touches: dividing the bedrooms of one suite is the 'window' of a confessional unearthed during the restoration. The terraces, the numerous steps and the blue views will leave you giddy; sink into a cushioned wicker sofa and toast the beauty with a lovely glass of the local greco. This is a place that won't play on your eco conscience either; they've won awards for their green efforts. Potter around exquisite, car-free Pisciotta, scramble down through the olive groves to the harbour, visit the famous grottos. New to us, but a favourite already.

Price	€70-€160. Suites €130-€200. Cottages & house €290-€1,500 per week. Min. 2 nights in cottages.
Rooms	11 + 4: 9 doubles, 2 suites. House for 5. 3 cottages for 2-6.
Meals	Breakfast €7.50 for self-caterers. Restaurant 40m.
Closed	November-February.
Directions	From Naples A3 Salerno-Reggio Calabria exit Battipaglia; SS dir. Agropoli-Sapri exit Poderia; follow signs to Palinuro, then Pisciotta; in Pisciotta off Piazza Pinto.

Lea Pinto
Via Castello,
84066 Pisciotta

Tel	+39 0974 973792
Email	info@marulivohotel.it
Web	www.marulivohotel.it

Calabria, Basilicata and Puglia

Il Giardino di Iti Agriturismo

The farm, peaceful, remote and five minutes from the Ionian sea, has been in the family for three centuries. A massive arched doorway leads to a courtyard and vast enclosed garden, with rabbits for the children; pigs, goats and cats, too. The large, cool bedrooms have been simply and prettily decorated. Ask for one that opens directly off the courtyard, its big old fireplace (lit in winter) and brick-paved floors intact. Each room has a wall painting of one of the farm's crops, and is correspondingly named: 'Lemon', 'Peach', 'Sunflower', 'Grape'. The bathrooms are old-fashioned but charming, the apartment kitchens basic. Courses are held here on regional cooking; weaving, too. If neither appeals, revel in the atmosphere and the gastronomic delights, and atone for the calories later. (On warm nights you eat in the little walled garden; at night, the lemon and orange trees glow from little lights tucked into their branches.) There's a host of activities on offer in the area, and, of course, heaps of history. Signora is gentle and charming. You'll be sad to leave.

Price	Half-board €45-€55 p.p. Full-board €55-€65 p.p.
Rooms	12 + 2: 10 family rooms; 2 doubles sharing bath. 2 apartments for 3-4.
Meals	Half-board or full-board only. Wine from €10. Limited self-catering in apts.
Closed	Never.
Directions	A3 Salerno-Reggio Calabria exit Sibari. Rossano road (SS106) to Contrada Amica, then towards Paludi.

Francesca Cherubini
Contrada Amica,
87068 Rossano

Tel +39 0983 64508
Email info@giardinoiti.it
Web www.giardinoiti.it

L'Orto di Lucania

Relish this organic family farm in an unspoilt region of Italy – and the delicious food that Fulvio and his brother grow using time-honoured methods: tomatoes, artichokes, rare red aubergines... Much turns up on your dinner plate, for the restaurant serves farm-fresh meals by the fire in a big old barn, or on the terrace among gnarled olives. Bubbly multilingual Cinzia (Fulvio's wife) takes care of the smattering of smart white bungalows, set among meandering paths on shrubby lawns. Apartments have full kitchens, terrace doors and open fires; B&B guests get a homemade, home-grown feast for breakfast. And you can buy farm produce in the shop: olive oil, fruit jams, honey... Swim up an appetite in the large parasol-ringed pool, borrow a bike or arrange horse riding nearby: this area of Basilicata, on the Puglian border, is an undiscovered delight with heaps to see and do. Visit ancient Matera, famed for Sassi cave dwellings and rock chapels, and sweet Montescaglioso with its Benedictine monastery and 15th-century castle. Or head through Puglia to Ionian beaches. Great value for a special farm stay.

Price	€80-€90. Suite €90-€100. Apts €100-€120. Minimum 2 nights.
Rooms	3 + 7: 2 doubles, 1 suite for 2-4. 7 apts: 6 for 2-4, 1 for 2-5.
Meals	Breakfast €5. Dinner €25. Wine from €5. Restaurants 10-min drive.
Closed	Rarely.
Directions	Sent on booking.

Fulvio & Cinzia Spada
Contrada Dogana,
75024 Montescaglioso

Tel +39 0835 202195
Email info@ortodilucania.it
Web www.ortodilucania.it

San Teodoro Nuovo Agriturismo

A haven in a green sea of citrus and olive groves. Bougainvillea disguises the lower half of the delightful Marchesa's old rose-tinted mansion; shutters peep from above. Maria is ever-present, loves meeting her guests and is always on hand, on her working farm redolent with family history. Rent an apartment furnished with family antiques in a wing, or choose one of four a stroll away, in the old stables where the restaurant is housed. The spacious gardens are beautifully maintained and the rooms are large and light, some with vaulted ceilings, all elegantly and charmingly furnished; and they have small parterre gardens. Make the most of the range of Basilicata cuisine here; breakfasts and candlelit dinners are extremely good, the vegetarian choices are excellent and you may wish to book into a cookery class. Follow the routes taken by 18th-century travellers, visit workshops devoted to reproducing classical antiques, jog, cycle, walk, return to a dip in the swimming pool. You are a ten-minute drive from white sands and the Ionian Sea, golf courses are nearby, archaeological sites abound. *Popular wedding venue.*

Price	€120-€140 (€840-€980 per week). Half-board €85-€95 p.p. Min. stay 2 nights.
Rooms	9 apartments for 2, 4 or 6.
Meals	Dinner with wine, €25-€30, by arrangement. Restaurant 4km.
Closed	Never.
Directions	Sent on booking.

Maria Xenia d'Oria
Loc. Marconia,
75015 Pisticci

Tel +39 0835 470042
Mobile +39 338 5698116
Email doria@santeodoronuovo.com
Web www.santeodoronuovo.com

Foresteria Illicini

Come for the views of the tiny islands of Matrela and Santojanni, the caves and rocky coves, the water lapping at the beach. This bewitching place could be a set for *The Tempest*. Guglielmo's father bought the whole spectacular promontory and surrounding land with olive trees, holm oaks and myrtles 50 years ago; they spent every family holiday here. Now Guglielmo, a gentle architect, and his wife Diane have turned it into a deliciously unmanicured resort. Foreigners have barely discovered the area so, apart from two weeks in August, the five-acre park, the two small beaches and the large pool are beautifully peaceful (the restaurant only opens in August). Wrought iron furnishes garden and terrace (a festival of flowers in June) but the view is the thing. The small breakfast room also overlooks the sea. The bedrooms are housed in little cottages just a few yards back from the shoreline, each with a deckchair'd terrace and a view of the sea. Each is neatly and simply furnished, with tiled floors, comfortable beds and a spotless bathroom. The sunsets are exceptional. Good value, great for families.

Price	€70-€130. Half-board for 2 €180-€200 (August only).
Rooms	11: 8 doubles, 1 single, 2 family rooms for 3-4.
Meals	Lunch €15-€30 (July-August only). Wine from €10. Restaurants 5-min. drive.
Closed	Mid-October to mid-May.
Directions	From A3, exit Lagonegro nord. SS585, exit Maratea sud. SS18 to Maratea, left at km 236.7.

Guglielmo & Diane Rivetti
Loc. Illicini,
85046 Maratea

Tel +39 0973 879028
Email staff@illicini.it
Web www.illicini.it

Villa Cheta Elite

Villa Cheta Elite is a gracious Art Nouveau villa a drive up the coastal road, embraced by a terraced garden of winding paths, tropical trees, scented plants – and views so lovely they'll have you rooted to the spot. Relax in the shade of the gardens, or cross the road and take the lift down for a swim in the clear green waters below. (Then, if you prefer, clamber back up: there are 165 steps!). Bedrooms are classic Italian, all antiques and fine fabrics, marble floors, large windows and plenty of light; the loveliest have a view of the sea. The public rooms, with ornate cornices and mouldings, are exquisitely furnished with good paintings and portraits of previous occupants. There's also a small sitting room, and a library where you can bone up on the history of the region. Breakfast is outstanding, dinner is delicious and the restaurant is fabulous, with its Murano glass chandeliers and embroidered linen. In summer you dine on the terrace, beneath starry skies and moon. You may even hear nightingales sing. Stefania and Piero are delightful hosts, their staff courteous and kind. *Daily hotel shuttle to coast.*

Price	€144-€280. Half-board €204-€364 for 2.
Rooms	20 doubles.
Meals	Lunch/dinner €38-€45. Wine €22. Restaurants 1km.
Closed	November-Palm Sunday.
Directions	From A3 exit Lagonegro-Maratea; 10km, SS104 right to Sapri. In Sapri left onto coast road for Maratea. Villa 9km along coast, above road on left.

Stefania Aquadro
Via Nazionale,
85041 Acquafredda di Maratea

Tel +39 0973 878134
Email info@villacheta.it
Web www.villacheta.it

La Chiusa delle More

The Italians flock here in August but foreigners have not yet discovered Peschici, so come out of season when the lovely beaches and fresh-fish restaurants are idyllically uncrowded and you can watch the fishermen sort their catch on the front. Francesco and Antonella's 16th-century farmhouse is 500 metres from the sea: park under an ancient olive tree and climb up to the reception terrace whence to drink in the views. On another terrace, teak loungers flank a sparkling pool and the air is scented with citrus. The B&B rooms, some in the main house, some in an attractive separate building, are light, cool and simply furnished, with good little shower rooms. Family rooms have ladders up to childrens' mezzanines. Your hosts, a delightful pair, vibrant and full of fun, have five hectares of olive groves and a big kitchen garden. The olive oil and vegetables supply their restaurant and the food is divine – hard not to love the typically Puglian dishes and the local wines. Breakfast on the terrace is a treat too, a wonderful start to a day among the splendours of the Gargano National Park. Fabulous for walkers.

Price €160-€240.
Rooms 10: 4 doubles. Cottage: 4 doubles, 2 family rooms for 4.
Meals Dinner €30. Wine €5-€50.
Closed October-April.
Directions Sent on booking.

Francesco & Antonella Martucci
Loc. Padula,
71010 Peschici

Mobile +39 347 0577272
Email lachiusadellemore@libero.it
Web www.lachiusadellemore.it

Cefalicchio Country House

In 1901 the Rossi brothers built a present for their mother: a grandiose country house, an extension of their almond farm. Their descendants developed this into a successful biodynamic winery; now it is also a beautiful place to stay. The architecture is unusual for this area; rather than simple and rustic it is romantic and grand, with a zigzagging external staircase. The first floor houses two spectacular suites, with museum-worthy antiques and floor-to-ceiling windows; the gloriously tiled original kitchen is used for cooking lessons. The second floor contains 'loft' guest rooms, simpler but just as elegant, pale-walled and furnished with polished wood. There are also two characterful apartments, one on the ground floor with tall arched ceilings, the other, ideal for families, next to the tree-framed pool. Wine lovers will adore it, but there's plenty for everyone, with the rambling grounds, the remote setting, the impressive restaurant and the rustic-chic spa: indulge in wine-based therapies – not drinking, but bathing. Lovely young Katrin and Livio look after you well. *Ask about gourmet weekends.*

Ethical Collection: Environment; Food. See page 419 for details.

Price	€120. Suites €180-€280. Apartments €180-€270.
Rooms	7 + 2: 5 doubles, 2 suites. 2 apartments for 2-4.
Meals	Dinner €33.
Closed	January-February.
Directions	Milan-Taranto (A14) or Naples-Bari (A16) to Canosa di Puglia exit; thro' Canosa to state road 98 (now regional road 6), then provincial road 143; follow signs for Cefalicchio (3km).

Livio & Kathrin Colapinto
Contrada Cefalicchio, SP143,
70053 Canosa di Puglia

Tel +39 0883 642123
Email info@cefalicchio.it
Web www.cefalicchio.com

Lama di Luna - Biomasseria Agriturismo

The sister of Pietro's great-grandmother lived here until 1820; Pietro bought the farm in 1990, then discovered the family connection. It was "meant to be". Lama di Luna is the most integrated organic farm in Italy: 200 hectares of olives and wines, 40 solar panels for heat and hot water, beds facing north, feng shui-style. Petro, who lives here with his family, is young, lively, charming, passionate about the environment and this supremely serene place. The farm goes back 300 years and wraps its dazzling white self around a vast courtyard with a central bread oven, its 40 chimney pots "telling the story" of the many farm workers that once lived here. Each bedroom, complete with fireplace and small window, once housed an entire family. Pietro searched high and low for the beds, the natural latex mattresses, the reclaimed wood for the doors. There's a library for reading and a veranda for sunsets and stars, and views that reach over flat farmland as far as the eye can see. Breakfast here on homemade cakes and jams, orchard fruits, local cheeses. Remote, relaxing, memorable. *New pool.*

Price	€140-€160. Suites €230-€300. Extra bed €40.
Rooms	11: 9 twins/doubles, 2 suites for 3-4.
Meals	Dinner with wine, €25. Restaurants 3km.
Closed	Never.
Directions	A14 exit Canosa di Puglia; right for Monervino Murge, Canosa-Andria, turn off for Montegrosso. After Montegrosso, 3.5km dir. Minervino; on left.

Ethical Collection: Environment; Food.
See page 419 for details.

Pietro Petroni
Loc. Montegrosso,
70031 Andria

Tel	+39 0883 569505
Mobile	+39 328 0117375
Email	info@lamadiluna.com
Web	www.lamadiluna.com

Masseria Serra dell'Isola

Spirits may fall as you lose your way down tiny lanes in a featureless landscape... no matter. Rita's smile as she scoops you up to guide you home brings instant cheer. Step over the threshold of the somewhat gaunt white *masseria* and you'll feel even better. The great hall with its uneven stone floor was once part of an olive mill (see where the presses used to stand) and, like the rest of the house, is filled with portraits and antiques with stories to tell. The light, gracious bedrooms are named after the women who once occupied them – Donnas Angelina, Ritella, Annina – and the elegant old beds bear new mattresses. The house has been in the family since 1726 and Rita is passionately proud of her heritage. You're welcome to browse through her impressive library of history books; she'll also gladly tell you about less well-known local places to visit. She organises courses, too, in art, antiques, restoration, cookery; dine by candlelight and you'll sample ancient family recipes and liqueurs from the time the Bourbons reigned in southern Italy. Unusual and authentic. *Minimum stay two nights.*

Price	B&B €130. Whole house €3,300-€3,900 per week.
Rooms	6: 4 doubles, 2 twins/doubles.
Meals	Dinner, 3 courses, €35-€40. Wine €12-€18.
Closed	Rarely.
Directions	SS16 Bari-Brindisi exit Mola-Rutigliano, dir. Mola. When you reach bridge call Rita to come & guide you.

Rita Guastamacchia
S.P 165 Mola, Conversano n.35,
70042 Mola di Bari

Mobile +39 349 5311256
Email info@masseriaserradellisola.it
Web www.masseriaserradellisola.it

Masseria Due Torri

At this graceful masseria expect immaculate rooms and heart-warming service from Elizabeth and Douglas. Their big country house has two bedrooms and a self-catering apartment on the ground floor; they live upstairs. The B&B rooms are inviting with chintz curtains, wrought-iron chairs and pretty eiderdowns on comfy mattresses, while the apartment has a charming sitting room with a high arched ceiling and original beams, three sofas, a pristine kitchen. There's a further kitchen on the ground floor, where a sumptuous breakfast is served in warm weather you eat at a canopied table outside, surrounded by lush and lovely gardens. There are six hectares here of olives (they produce their own oil), figs, prickly pears, garden flowers, wild flowers – green fingers are at work. The pool is nearby, with sunbeds, hammock and a bamboo-shaded picnic area alongside. In the grounds too is a new-build self-catering villa with its own access road and an arty modern décor. Books, magazines, outdoor games, indoor games, DVDs, a taxi service to and from local restaurants… it's all here.

Price	€80-110. Apt €540-€900. Villa €940-€2,100.
Rooms	2 + 2: 1 double, 1 twin/double. Extra bed/cot available. Apartment for 4-5. Villa for 8.
Meals	Breakfast €10 for self-caterers. Wine from €5. Restaurants 1km.
Closed	Rarely.
Directions	From Monopoli SP114 dir. Conversano; right after 3km at refuse bin. Masseria 200m on right.

Elizabeth & Douglas Manuel
Contrada Due Torri 187,
70043 Monopoli

Tel	+39 0802 146007
Email	info@masseria2torri.com
Web	www.masseria2torri.com

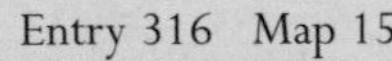

Valle Rita

Here is a rambling but beautifully maintained organic estate where citrus groves, ubiquitous olives, grapes for the table and swathes of seasonal fruit and veg flourish. Families and couples will flourish too – happily whiling away a week dipping in and out of the prickly pear-fringed pool, playing tennis and ping pong or borrowing bikes and shooting around the tracks of the estate. So much heat-drenched activity will surely warrant a lazy lunch on the terrace of the super restaurant with its seasonal, home-grown delights and wines from the owners' other estate in Basilicata – locals flock in too (always a good sign). There are pleasant enough rooms for B&B while a series of traditional one-storey apartments and houses with little gardens and barbecue areas for DIY-ers dot the estate (note: from 2012 all prices will include breakfast). The owners don't live on site but manager Giorgio is hugely helpful and weekly film nights and occasional jazz evenings in the old stables sound like fun. No need to be nonplussed by the slightly featureless landscape en route: breathe a sigh of relief at your lucky find.

Price	€69-€89 for 2 (€400-€700 p.w.); €89-€129 for 3 (€550-€850 p.w.); €129-€149 for 5 (€750-€1,300 p.w.).
Rooms	8 apartments: 2 for 2, 5 for 3, 1 for 5.
Meals	Lunch/dinner €25. Restaurants 10km.
Closed	Mid-November to mid-March.
Directions	Sent on booking.

Giorgio Ribaudo
Contrada Girifalco,
74013 Ginosa

Tel +39 0998 271824
Email info@vallerita.it
Web www.vallerita.it

Masseria Iazzo Scagno

An intriguing, calming, earthy place, tucked away in gentle countryside behind magnificent dry stone walls, not easy to find... but worth it! When Crescenzio and Annamaria chanced upon the semi-ruined, overgrown masseria – a Sleeping Beauty moment – they dreamed of creating the stylish country bolthole it is today. Cuddle by candlelight in a pointy-hatted trullo or lounge by the fire in a vast light-filled salon complete with quirky straw bale seats. Bedrooms line up in the old stables: breathe deeply amid soft-toned fabrics, stone and natural wood, step out to a shady terrace. There are dappled shower rooms, space for a child's bed, no TV to jar the peace. Self-catering apartments are open-plan, with four-posters and jacuzzi baths. Rise early to swim lengths in the saltwater pool, or laze around it on mattresses draped in flowing white gauze. Then breakfast on home-laid eggs in the shade of the spreading oak. Visit Martina Franca for good food and shops, Grottaglie for famed ceramics, white-walled Ostuni for festivals and beaches. Your hosts – with waggy dog Carlo – couldn't be kinder.

Price	€110-€150. Apartments €125-€180. Minimum 3 nights.
Rooms	7 + 3: 6 doubles, 1 family room for 4. 3 apartments for 2-4.
Meals	Restaurant 4km.
Closed	Rarely.
Directions	Sent on booking.

Crescenzio Marzano
Via Monti del Duca 307,
74015 Martina Franca

Tel +39 0802 144522
Email info@iazzoscagno.it
Web www.iazzoscagno.it/en

Masseria Alchimia

The masseria, a whitewashed, history-steeped, 350-year-old building – once with a watchtower – lies at the end of a cypress-lined drive and, at first glance, looks a little stark: a hint of the contemporary aesthetic to come. Not far from the main road, yet peaceful, eco-friendly and surrounded by seven acres of olive and fruit trees with sitting areas dotted around – some with a sea view – there's a sense of stillness. True design mag material: the building is unadorned, with clean, square lines despite its age, and part of it (the Romantic studio suite, ask for it) is new but blends seamlessly. Bright, well-lit studios and suites filled with designer classics – Panton chairs, Man Ray mirrors, lots of Eames, Starck, etc – are, like Swiss owner Caroline, cool, chic and urbane. There are concrete floors and perfect kitchenettes; imagine whites, greys, black-and-white photos and flashes of colour, say a purple or yellow chair, all beautifully timed. Each room has a sun terrace and there are private beaches guests can make use of on request. A sophisticated break from the rustic Pugliese norm.

Price	€75-€235. Minimum stay 3 nights; one week in August.
Rooms	8 studios/family suites for 2-4.
Meals	Restaurants 1km.
Closed	Never.
Directions	Bari-Brindisi SS16; from south exit Taranto; follow signs for Masseria Alchimia 1km dir. Adriatic coast.

Caroline Groszer
Contrada Fascianello,
72015 Fasano

Mobile +39 335 6094647
Email info@masseria-alchimia.it
Web www.masseria-alchimia.it

Masseria La Rascina

A charming country house – with charming hosts and staff – five minutes from the Adriatic's sandy coast: an elegant base if you enjoy birdsong and beach. Its peachy stone walls rise from immaculate lawns ringed by olives, palms, figs. Inside breathes Leonie's light-touch style: Mediterranean hues, world ornaments, beautiful dried flowers in spacious communal rooms. On the vast chandelier'd veranda, settle on sofas and sweep your gaze across the horizon: a stunning breakfast spot. Or lounge – all day if you wish – by the deep, inviting pool. Bedrooms sprinkle the house, with three off a cool inner court, others across the lawn. All are beautiful: lemon walls, four-posters draped in voile, a terrace for the evening aperitif. Families may prefer more homely self-catering apartments so pick up ingredients in Rosamarina or fine-dine in Ostuni, just minutes away. You can horse ride, hire bikes, hit the beach, snorkel in a nature sanctuary, tour the Valle d'Itria, join in summer festivals... the area teems with activity. Back at the house, with lovely Leonie, Paolo and the dogs, all is peaceful and refined.

Price	€100-€140. Apts €110-€240. Prices per night. Minimum 2 nights (7 in apts).
Rooms	6 + 4: 6 doubles. 4 apartments: 3 for 2, 1 for 4.
Meals	Breakfast €10 for self-caterers. Restaurants 2km.
Closed	November-Easter.
Directions	Sent on booking.

Leonie Jansen Schiroli
Strada Provinciale 19, Rosamarina,
72017 Ostuni

Mobile +39 338 4331573
Email larascina@inwind.it
Web www.larascina.it

Villa Cervarolo

A trulli house, marooned in rolling countryside dotted by fruit and olive trees – a beautiful Puglian blend of ancient vernacular and minimalist modern. A surprising find at the end of an unpaved track, this is a designer dream: exquisitely chic, sublimely inviting. The living spaces are open plan. Via the unobtrusively swish kitchen (modish appliances, Smeg fridge) you enter the sitting room, with DVDs (no TV: no signal!) and built-in sofa. Beyond, a study with a dusky pink chaise longue. Bedrooms are a serene marriage of gleaming linen, sheepskin rugs, pale velvet cushions, cool polished cement. Bathrooms ooze style, one with a tub with views: gaze on the garden as you soak. A beach-style pool (unheated) is an invitation to laze, with its outdoor 'room' alongside: relax on the cushioned swing seat, recline on Moroccan kilims, cook up a storm in the outdoor kitchen, dine at table hewn out of rock. If you don't feel like cooking you can always employ a chef, and other treats can be arranged, from yoga to massage. Make sure you find time to explore the lovely wine villages of Valle d'Itria. *Minimum one week.*

Price	£2,000-£3,360 per week.
Rooms	House for 6 (2 doubles, 1 twin/double).
Meals	Welcome pack with wine. Restaurants 7km.
Closed	December-February
Directions	Sent on booking.

The Owner
Ostuni

Mobile +44 (0)7771 713070
Email info@homeinpuglia.com
Web www.homeinpuglia.com

Masseria Impisi

Hidden but not hard to find, close to lovely hilltop Ostuni, is a 15th-century masseria and two inspirational new builds. Artistic, friendly David and Leonie have lived in Italy for 20 years and in Puglia for five; his sculptures dot the grounds, her mosaics shine like jewels. There's art in the bedrooms too; simple, tranquil spaces with cool Trani stone underfoot, they are havens on a hot day. The apartment is in the old gatehouse, its door washed in blue, its kitchen/dining area serene. All the bedrooms are quietly stylish, their walls white plaster or creamy stone, their bed frames made by David. None are huge but they open onto a colonnaded area, creating a feeling of space. Wet rooms have tiles that echo the Trani stone; towels are white and pristine. Wake to hot rolls and homemade jams, local cheeses and fruits from the garden, served above an olive mill that dates to the 10th century. The semi-wild grounds are filled with Pampas grass, cacti, olive trees, shady corners and a gorgeous natural pool; ancient cisterns still harvest rainwater. Bikes to borrow, boules to play, a beach a mile away... heaven in Puglia.

Price	€85-€105. Minimum 2 nights in B&B. Gate house €560-€900 per week.
Rooms	4 + 1: 1 double, 3 twins/doubles. Gate house for 2.
Meals	Restaurants 2.5km.
Closed	November-February.
Directions	Exit Gorgognolo on SS379 (E55). Take road parallel to SS, dir. Brindisi. 500m right at traffic island; left-hand narrow road 3km. Signed on left just before railway bridge. Detailed directions on booking.

Leonie Whitton & David Westby
Il Collegio, Contrada Impisi,
72017 Ostuni
Mobile +39 340 3602352
Email info@ilcollegio.com
Web www.ilcollegio.com

Masseria Il Frantoio Agriturismo

So many ravishing things! An old, white house clear-cut against a blue sky, mysterious gardens, the scent of jasmine – and private beaches five kilometres away. Armando and Rosalba spent a year restoring this 17th-century house (built over a sixth-century oil press) after abandoning city life. Inside – sheer delight. A series of beautiful rooms, ranging from fairytale (a froth of lace and toile) to endearingly simple (madras bedcovers and old desks) to formal (antique armoires and doughty gilt frames)... a gloriously eclectic mix. Dinner is equally marvellous – put your name down. Rosalba specialises in Puglian dishes accompanied by good local wines; Armando rings the courtyard bell at 8.30: the feast begins, either in the arched dining room or outside in the candlelit courtyard. It will linger in your memory – as will other details: an exterior white stone stairway climbing to a bedroom, an arched doorway swathed in wisteria. Armando is deeply passionate about his totally organic *masseria*, surrounded by olive groves and with a view of the sea; Silvana is on hand ensuring you bask in comfort. *Min. two nights in August.*

Ethical Collection: Community; Food.
See page 419 for details.

Price	€139-€269; children €39-€69. Apartment €319-€389.
Rooms	8 + 1: 3 doubles, 2 triples, 3 family rooms. Apartment for 2-4.
Meals	Dinner with wine, €59, by arrangement. Children €34. Supper €44. Restaurant 5km.
Closed	Never.
Directions	Bari airport, E55 exit Pezze di Greco dir. Ostuni. On SS16, look for Ostuni km874 sign. Right into drive.

Silvana Caramia
SS 16km 874,
72017 Ostuni

Tel	+39 0831 330276
Email	prenota@masseriailfrantoio.it
Web	www.masseriailfrantoio.it

B&B Masseria Piccola

It is a simple, unsophisticated village place – and utterly endearing. Who could fail to be enchanted by the round walls, the conical roofs, the charming little rooms? These trulli were built a century ago by Nicola's great-grandfather (he paid the equivalent of one euro for the site); now they have been converted into one delightful, good-value, B&B. The 'little farm' is in a quiet side street in Casalini di Cisternino, with a terrace at the front and a patch of garden behind. A wicker sofa and chairs welcome you in the hall. Snug, spotless bedrooms have pale walls and stone arches and are furnished with country antiques; beds are very comfortable, shower rooms are well-equipped and breakfast is at the big table in the kitchen or out under the flowers on the terrace. Nicola, young, busy, charming, looks after his guests well and will point you to a choice of decent restaurants five minutes' walk away – or possibly do an unpretentious supper on his wicker-chaired terrace. The town is nothing special but Cisternino, with its lively weekly market, is well worth the visit. Perfect for the young at heart.

Price	€80. Half-board €20 extra p.p.
Rooms	5: 3 doubles, 1 single, 1 child's single.
Meals	Wine from €8. Restaurant 1km.
Closed	Rarely.
Directions	A14 Bari-Lecce exit Cisternino-Ostuni, then SP7 & SP9.

Ethical Collection: Food.
See page 419 for details.

Nicola Fanelli
Via Masseria Piccola 56,
72014 Casalini di Cisternino

Tel +39 0804 449668
Mobile +39 334 7662408
Email info@masseriapiccola.it
Web www.masseriapiccola.it

Trullo Giardino

Grapes droop lazily over the terrace, peach and plum trees melt into Apulian countryside, the pool invites a cool dip... this is a glorious Italian getaway, with friendly owners next door to make you feel in famiglia. Trulli are unique to the quiet Itria valley at the top of Italy's heel, and this 19th-century trullo is typical, its chunky walls topped by five conical roofs like magicians' hats. Inside is doll's house-pretty, a warren of softly lit white walls, local tiles and low arches. Find a log fire, a stencilled dresser, a wooden dining table, a compact kitchen. Quirky antiques – candlesticks, ceramics, a typewriter – peek from nooks and crannies. Duck into two plain bedrooms, with little windows, pictures, a tiny shared shower room. It's cosy, yes, but much of the time you're outside. A lazy barbecue on the terrace, a snooze by the shady cedar, a splash in the shallow child-friendly pool... why not ask Michele and Mimma to cook breakfast or dinner, or fire up the pizza oven? They know the best local markets, the best joints in Cisternino town, and the best spots on the Adriatic coast – a short drive away.

Price	€650-€1,500 per week.
Rooms	House for 4 (1 double, 1 twin/double).
Meals	Dinner on request. Restaurants 3km.
Closed	January.
Directions	From Cisternino on Via Locorotondo (SP134), after 2.5 km turn right before Bari/Brindisi sign. After 200m on left.

Cosima Vita Semeraro
Contrada Calongo 25,
72014 Cisternino

Mobile +39 328 5470038
Email palumbo.2007@libero.it
Web www.trullogiardino.com

Vivificante

Vivacious Jane Shaw is a potter, textile designer and former teacher, who gives tailormade courses in her workshop. She has carried out extensive works on her house, at the heart of which is a delightful little trullo... it's a lovely vibrant place in which to live and work. There are just two rooms in the guest wing (let to one party) with a private bathroom between. The bedrooms are charming – terracotta floors, a Deco bed from Naples, her daughter's artwork, garden views – and have a happy, homely feel. Guests are also free to relax in Jane's large sitting room with its sofas and wood-burner. You breakfast – lavishly – in the wonderfully lofty kitchen, with three skylights and a wall of wood-framed glass. This overlooks the garden, a work in progress... so far Jane has planted oranges and lemons alongside 40 established olive trees, a goat-shaped piece of driftwood and a small hexagonal plunge pool for bobbing about. There's also an outdoor eating area, all mismatched wooden furniture and lanterns – lovely. *Ask about pottery, textile & cookery workshops. Wired internet access.*

Price	€95. Minimum 2 nights.
Rooms	2: 1 double, 1 twin/double, sharing bath.
Meals	Dinner €20. Restaurants 2km.
Closed	Never.
Directions	From Ceglie Messapica SP23 'Fedele Grande'. After 4km right at x-roads; 1st house on left.

Jane Shaw
Tratturo delle Vache 1, Contrada Circiello, 72013 Ceglie Messapica

Tel +39 0831 380987
Email vivificante@rocketmail.com
Web www.vivificante.com

Ethical Collection: Environment; Community. See page 419 for details.

Trullo Solari

At the end of a bumpy unpaved lane, three conical trulli framed by pine, olive and fruit trees: a delightful sight. Inside is just as good, open plan with a dining area and a compact, fully equipped kitchen. But it's the sitting room that dazzles, with its eight-metre wall of glass overlooking the pool. Fold the doors back in summer and merge your living space with the beautiful outside. This is a fabulously renovated house and you can really spread out. You get four big whitewashed bedrooms, simply furnished and served by sleek bathrooms. There's a terrace attached to the master bedroom, a rooftop sundeck, and an outdoors dining area with a barbecue and a pizza oven. There are a couple of other trulli in sight, but that doesn't stop you feeling private and remote. The lovely laid-back owners live nearby, leave you a luxurious welcome pack and lend you a pre-programmed Tom Tom so you don't get lost finding their recommended places! They're keen greenies – solar-fired underfloor heating, ecological products – and will help you plant a tree of your choice to reduce your carbon footprint. We loved it all.

Ethical Collection: Environment.
See page 419 for details.

Price	£1,200-£3,600 per week.
Rooms	House for 8 (2 doubles, 2 twins/doubles).
Meals	Restaurant 500m.
Closed	Never.
Directions	2km from Ceglie Messapica. Directions on booking.

Cathy & Keith Upton
Contrada Petrelli,
72013 Ceglie Messapica

Tel +39 0831 342153
Email cathyupton@hotmail.it
Web www.trullosolari.com

Villa Magnolia

Off the road to Brindisi, yet refreshingly peaceful and calm, is a dusky pink 'villa nobile' fronted by two magnificent palms. Owners Lesley and Ron, hands-on, talented and thoughtful, welcome you with a glass of prosecco to a pretty pergola; they live in a house to the side. The villa itself has four bedrooms opening to a central 'salotto', beautifully decorated in an apricot finish and furnished with charming auction finds; a wonderful tapestry hangs on one wall. Each bedroom is light, lofty, luxurious, with polished antiques on old patina'd floors, and super-stylish bathrooms with big wet rooms and stone walls; one has its own patio behind a sweet jasmine hedge. Ron is the designer-builder, Lesley the cook, concocting jams from the estate's fruits and using olive branches for the outdoor oven: don't miss once-weekly pizza night. Straight Roman roads whisk you to the beach (5km), or Ostuni – summer festivals aplenty. Then back to gardens and grounds, almond, olive and citrus trees and a Romanesque saltwater pool, exquisitely lit for night swims. *Free cookery classes April/May & Sept/Oct. Bottle of wine on arrival.*

Price	€110-€160. Min. stay 2-3 nights, according to season.
Rooms	4 doubles.
Meals	Once weekly pizza night: 3 courses with wine, €25. Restaurants 2km.
Closed	November-March.
Directions	Sent on booking.

Ron & Lesley Simon
Contrada Argentieri, Serranova,
72012 Carovigno

Tel +39 0831 989215
Email info@villamagnoliaitaly.com
Web www.villamagnoliaitaly.com

Masseria Varano

Wine and olive oil from the estate, local bread, pasta and cheese – the generous welcome sets the tone for your stay. Victoria and Giuseppe, an Anglo-Italian couple, combine the best of English and Italian hospitality – gentle, warm, easy – reflected in their handsome pale-stone and green-shuttered *masseria*. The apartments, each with private entrance and terrace, are in the main house and two cottages (one has spiral stairs to the second bedroom). The largest has a fleet of French windows and its own superb, view-rich terrace. Elegant and airy, with creamy tiled floors, white walls and handsome chestnut fittings, rooms are decorated with modern furniture and old family pieces. Dotted with family photographs, Victoria's paintings, pretty fabrics and objects collected from travels, there's a gentle country-house feel, a home from home. Kitchens are light and modern, equipped to please the serious cook. Masses to do: beaches, Gallipoli, the harbours of Tricase and Santa Maria di Leuca... or just enjoy the pretty walled gardens and the pool. The owners are happy to leave you alone or chat over a glass of wine.

Price	€400-€1,400 per week.
Rooms	4 apartments: 1 for 2, 3 for 2-4.
Meals	Restaurant 4km.
Closed	November-Easter.
Directions	M'way Brindisi-Lecce, take Tangenziale (ring road) west of Lecce, exit 13 dir. Gallipoli; exit Taurisano. After 3km, before slow down sign overhead, left onto Via Trappeto di Varano. Left at x-roads; follow road to estate with high walls, 2nd set of double gates with intercom.

Giuseppe & Victoria Lopez y Royo di Taurisano
Contrada Varano, 73056 Taurisano

Tel	+39 0833 623216
Mobile	+39 348 5151391
Email	lopezyroyo@hotmail.com
Web	www.masseriainsalento.com

Palazzo Bacile di Castiglione

The palazzo's 16th-century walls dominate Spongano's Piazza Bacile; behind is a secret oasis. The charming *barone* and his English wife offer you a choice of apartments for couples or families, and B&B for groups; the history is interesting, the comforts seductive. On the first floor, a series of large terraces and four bedrooms open off a vaulted baronial hall – beige check sofas, an open fire (replete with home-grown cones and logs), a grand piano. Expect choice fabrics and new four-posters, pink, yellow or marble bathrooms, wardrobes dwarfed by lofty ceilings, kitchens for cooks. The outbuildings at the end of the long garden are similarly swish: olive wood tables, big lamps, framed engravings, books and CDs; kitchens reveal the owners' passion. (They are also keen greens, saving energy, going solar and composting madly.) The garden is lovely, all orange trees and wisteria, secluded walkways and corners, old pillars and impressive pool; at twilight, scops owls chime like bells. Beyond lie the baroque splendours of Lecce, Gallipoli and Otranto – and the coast. Borrow the bikes! *Minimum stay four nights.*

Price	€900-€2,770 per week.
Rooms	7 apartments: 2 for 2, 3 for 4, 1 for 6, 1 for 8.
Meals	Restaurant 500m.
Closed	Never.
Directions	SS16 dir. Maglie/S M di Leuca; pass Maglie, then SS275 to Leuca until signs for Spongano on left.

Ethical Collection: Environment.
See page 419 for details.

Sarah & Alessandro Bacile di Castiglione
73038 Spongano
Tel +39 0832 351131
Mobile +39 349 8329308
Email albadica@hotmail.com
Web www.palazzobacile.it

La Macchiola

The courtyard walls drip with creepers and geraniums; in front, across a little road, is a verdant citrus grove worth resting in. All this is part of a vibrant working farm. La Macchiola, a 17th-century *azienda agricola*, is devoted to the production of organic olive oil (massages available) and Anna's family make some of Puglia's finest oils. Go through the massive gates and the Moorish-arch portico and you will leave the narrow and unremarkable streets of Spongano village to enter a white-gravelled, white-walled courtyard dotted with elegant wrought-iron tables and chairs. Off the courtyard, ground-floor apartments have been carefully converted into a series of airy, old-style rooms. Walls are colourwashed warm yellow and soft blue, sleeping areas are separated by fabric screens, ceilings are lofty and vaulted. One apartment for two has a dining space squeezed into an ancient fireplace, bathrooms have pretty mosaic mirrors, most of the kitchenettes are tiny. There's a vast roof terrace *marmellata* and cakes for breakfast in an impressive stone-vaulted room. Beaches are a short drive.

Price	€80-€100. Apartments €570-€1,500 per week. Min. 3 nights.
Rooms	4 + 5: 4 doubles. 5 apartments for 2, 3 or 4.
Meals	Breakfast €6 for self-caterers. Restaurants 300m.
Closed	9 January-16 March; 5 November-22 December
Directions	Sent on booking.

Anna Addario-Chieco
Via Congregazione 53/57,
73038 Spongano

Tel +39 0836 945023
Mobile +39 339 5451307
Email lamacchiola@libero.it
Web www.lamacchiola.it

Sicily and Sardinia

Hotel Signum

Leave the car and Sicily behind. Salina may not be as famous as some of her glamorous Aeolian neighbours (though *Il Postino* was filmed here) but is all the more peaceful for that. The friendly, unassuming hotel sits so quietly at the end of a narrow lane you'd hardly guess it was there. Dine on a shaded terracotta terrace with chunky tile-topped tables, colourful iron and wicker chairs; gaze out over lemon trees to the glistening sea. Traditional dishes and local ingredients are the norm. Then wind along the labyrinth of paths, where plants flow and tumble, to a simple and striking bedroom: cool pale walls, pretty antiques, a wrought-iron bed, good linen; starched lace flutters at the windows. The island architecture is typically low and unobtrusive and Clara and Michele (Luca's parents) have let the hotel grow organically as they've bought and converted farm buildings. The result is a beautiful, relaxing space where, even at busy times, you feel as if you are one of a handful of guests. Snooze on a shady veranda, take a dip in the infinity pool – that view again – or clamber down the path to a quiet pebbly cove.

Price	€130-€400.
Rooms	30: 28 doubles, 2 singles.
Meals	Dinner à la carte, €35-€70. Wine from €18.
Closed	Mid-November to mid-March.
Directions	By boat or hydrofoil from Naples, Palermo, Messina & Reggio Calabria. If you want to leave your car, there are garages in Milazzo.

Luca Caruso
Via Scalo 15, Malfa,
98050 Salina, Aeolian Islands

Tel +39 0909 844222
Email info@hotelsignum.it
Web www.hotelsignum.it

La Locanda del Postino

No surprise this was the setting for the film *Il Postino*. The tiny settlement of Pollara sits in a natural amphitheatre of a valley, rising steeply on three sides before opening onto the warm blue of the Mediterranean – and mesmerising views of further islands. From the port, you drive up through 14km of Salina's coastal woodland and vineyards, and wash up at the converted stone farmhouse. Once owned by a priest, built into the hillside, it's a perfect place to catch the sunsets, especially from your own terrace, slung in a colourful hammock. There's a friendly informal feel, as you help yourself to Sicilian breakfasts of homemade cakes, croissants and jams, and later, regional dishes, al fresco with a glass of full-bodied house wine. A giant old wine press tells of hard yet good living, while the bedrooms are unpretentious affairs of terracotta tiles, walls pale yellow and white, and decorative wrought-iron beds. Amelia and her husband carefully restored the building and remain hands-on owners; Amelia also writes novels. In the visitor's book one guest writes: 'a special place where the soul is reborn.'

Price	€120-€260.
Rooms	10: 6 twins/doubles, 4 family rooms.
Meals	Dinner with wine, €30.
Closed	November-April.
Directions	Sent on booking.

Mauro Leva
Via Leni 10, Pollara, Malfa Salina,
98050 Aeolian Islands

Tel +39 0909 843958
Email info@lalocandadelpostino.it
Web www.lalocandadelpostino.it

Green Manors

Your hosts spotted the remote and dilapidated 1600s manor house years ago; it has been theatrically, gloriously, revived. Bedrooms, some with terraces, are part baroque, part contemporary: rich colours, tiled floors, Sicilian patchwork, laced linen, family antiques, flowers. Tapestries and paintings are illuminated by chandeliers, tapered candles stand in silver candelabra; bathrooms come with huge baths or showers, delicately scented homemade soaps and waffle towels. Chris, Paolo and Pierangela have also been busy establishing their bio-dynamic orchard and you reap the rewards at breakfast, alongside silver cutlery and antique napkins. The homemade jams are divine – cherry, apricot, ginger; the juices are freshly squeezed. Languid dinners are totally delicious, served outside behind a curtain of shimmering plants, or by the huge fireplace when the weather is cooler. There's a wooden cabin in the olive groves (with outside kitchen and bathroom); a lush tropical park with peacocks and ponies; a deep pool. Expect occasional summer concerts beneath the mulberry tree, and the distant chimes of Castroreale's churches.

Ethical Collection: Environment; Community; Food. See page 419 for details.

Price	€100-€180. Cabin €80 (summer only). Cottage €200-€260. Min. stay two nights.
Rooms	9 + 2: 5 doubles, 1 single, 3 suites. 1 cabin for 2, 1 cottage for 4-6.
Meals	Dinner €35. Wine €10-€60. Restaurants 1km.
Closed	Rarely.
Directions	Messina-Palermo, exit Barcellona dir. SS113 Palermo; immed. before Terme bridge, sharp left. Signed.

Pierangela & Chris Jannelli Christiaens
Borgo Porticato,
98053 Castroreale

Tel	+39 0909 746515
Mobile	+39 338 4340917
Email	info@greenmanors.it
Web	www.greenmanors.it

Santa Marina

In the historic centre of hilltop Castroreale – 500 souls, a scattering of restaurants, 26 churches – is a noble palazzo behind whose doors three apartments lie, each steeped in aristocratic character. Cobalt blues and soft ochres, thick walls and arched windows, personal possessions and inherited antiques – no designer could dream up such an atmosphere. Although divided into three, the house has the feeling of a family home, thanks to owner Pierangela, gracious and gregarious, who settles you in (be sure to book a meal at her hotel, the legendary Green Manors). Kitchens and dining rooms vary in size but not in style, bedrooms glory in grand four-posters, a Greek column makes a stunning coffee table and one shower stands in a small square marble pool, originally intended as a bath! The top apartment has a terrace, a small forest of pot plants with views; the bottom apartment stays super-cool in summer. You are a short drive from the beaches and Milazzo, launch pad for the Eolie Isles, and the surroundings are beautiful: lush valley, wooded mountain, distant sea.

Price	€980-€1,400 per week.
Rooms	3 apartments: 2 for 2, 1 for 3. Minimum stay one week.
Meals	Breakfast €15. Restaurants within walking distance.
Closed	Rarely.
Directions	Sent on booking.

Pierangela & Chris Jannelli Christiaens
98053 Castroreale
Tel +39 0909 746515
Mobile +39 338 4340917
Email info@greenmanors.it
Web www.greenmanors.it

Quattro Venti

From the roof terrace is a breathtaking view, of the valley flanked by farmland and woods, and in the distance, the sea. The house stands high, and the hillside opposite has small villages tucked into its folds, one of which is unspoilt Castroreale, all cobbles, churches and bars; you feel remote, but the village is ten minutes away. This is a modernist, minimalist structure of steel, wood, white concrete and slate, an uplifting and luxurious holiday home, a lovely place to rent with friends. There's a sitting room with a huge stone fireplace for winter logs, and a kitchen with a marble island, beautifully equipped. Bedrooms are airy and light, with black slate tiles on the floors and polished sleigh beds with snazzy covers. The end wall of one room is a sliding window onto a terrace with views. Bathrooms are ultra-chic, with delicious Italian tiles and floor-to-ceiling linen curtains; two bedrooms have the tub in the room itself. All feels brand new and the garden is yet young, but there's plenty of safe space for children to run around in. Milazzo, departure point for the Eolie isles, is a short drive.

Price	€1,700-€4,000 per week. Minimum stay one week.
Rooms	House for 7 (3 doubles, 1 single).
Meals	Breakfast €15. Restaurants 10-minute drive.
Closed	Rarely.
Directions	Sent on booking.

Pierangela & Chris Jannelli Christiaens
98053 Castroreale

Tel +39 0909 746515
Mobile +39 338 4340917
Email info@greenmanors.it
Web www.greenmanors.it

Casa Turchetti

Turn back the clock a hundred or so years and you would have heard Puccini or Vivaldi resounding from deep within this 19th-century townhouse. The music academy is no more, but Casa Turchetti has not let go of its musical past: you'll spot the little lyre, the B&B's motif, dotted all over the place. Cheerful hosts Pino and Francesca are understandably proud of their restoration and will be as hands on or off as you want. Big bedrooms are elegant and supremely comfortable: soft yellow walls, generous red swags at balconied windows, marble floors that sparkle, embroidered white linen on antique beds. Bathrooms are designed for serious grooming; you'll want to spend far longer than necessary in here, wrapped in a fluffy towel or relaxed under a rain shower. Breakfasts are a talking point – the guest book is heaped with praise. Catch your breath on the rooftop terrace: the Greek amphitheatre to your left, smouldering Etna to your right, the uninterrupted sweep of blue straight ahead, the hum of Taormina just below. All without having to step foot outside the door. *Minimum stay four nights.*

Price	€200-€250. Suites €350-€450.
Rooms	6: 3 doubles, 1 twin, 2 suites: 1 for 2, 1 for 4.
Meals	Restaurants within walking distance.
Closed	November-20 March.
Directions	In "centro storico".

Pino & Francesca Lombardo
Salita dei Gracchi 18/20, 98039
Taormina

Tel	+39 0942 625013
Email	info@casaturchetti.com
Web	www.casaturchetti.com

Le Case del Principe

This vast walled estate with an impressive 17th-century palazzo in an ocean of citrus trees lives up to its name; your host Gabriele is a prince. Overlooking a vineyard, across a labyrinth of pot-holed tracks linking the various parts, are a villa and five converted farm buildings. The villa, with its own garden and gazebo-covered terrace with tiled banquettes, has a 12-seater dining room with lacquered cane ceiling, a living room with an open fire and formal bedrooms with large beds, all quirkily decorated with unusual period pieces. The terraced row of single-storey cottages, backing onto a quiet road, have hedged-off terraces, cotto floors, neat kitchens, mezzanine bedrooms for children (with ladders) and pretty, traditional bathrooms tiled top-to-toe in blues and whites. Tucked away in the formal garden, a rose-smothered, thyme-scented pergola provides shady recess and a discreet pool with sleek recliners has a good view of the smoking volcano. Taormina with all its cultural hot spots, and Etna with all of hers (lava flows are visible during eruptions) are a short drive, as are the beaches.

Price	€400-€5,500 per week.
Rooms	5 cottages for 2, 4 or 6. Villa for 10.
Meals	Dinner with wine, for groups only, €40. Restaurant 2km.
Closed	Never.
Directions	Sent on booking.

Principe Alliata di Villafranca
Tenuta Alliata,
98039 Taormina

Mobile	+39 349 7880906
Email	info@lecasedelprincipe.it
Web	www.lecasedelprincipe.it

Hotel Villa Schuler

Late in the 19th century, Sig. Schuler's great-grandfather travelled by coach from Germany and built his house high above the Ionian Sea. He built on a grand scale and he chose the site well: the views of the Bay of Naxos and Mount Etna are gorgeous. When he died in 1905, Great Grandmama decided to let out some rooms and the villa has been a hotel ever since. Though restored and brought up to date, it still has an old, elegant charm and a relaxed, peaceful atmosphere. Lavish organic breakfasts are served in the chandelier'd breakfast room or out on the terrace. Bedrooms vary; some have beautifully tiled floors, antique furniture and stone balconies; the more modern top-floor suites sport beamed ceilings and large terraces. All come with organic bed linen, jacuzzi showers heated by solar panels, heating from biomass – it's all super-eco – and views to gardens or sea. Hidden away behind a stone arch, in subtropical gardens scented with jasmine, is a delightful, very private little apartment; a path from here leads all the way to the town's pedestrianised Corso Umberto. *Minimum two nights mid/high season.*

Price	€99-€212. Apartment €258 for 2; €400 for 4.
Rooms	26 + 1: 17 doubles, 5 suites, 4 triples. Apt for 2-4.
Meals	Breakfast for self-caterers included. Restaurants 100m (special prices for Hotel Villa Schuler guests).
Closed	Mid-November to February.
Directions	A18 exit Taormina; 3km; at 'Lumbi' car park into 'Monte Tauro' tunnel; around 'Porta Catania' car park to Piazza S. Antonio; right at P.O. into Via Pietro Rizzo; right into Via Roma.

Christine Voss & Gerhard Schuler
Piazzetta Bastione, Via Roma,
98039 Taormina

Tel +39 0942 23481
Email info@hotelvillaschuler.com
Web www.hotelvillaschuler.com

Ethical Collection: Environment.
See page 419 for details.

Villa Carlotta

There's a pretty, peaceful village above (Castelmola), a private beach below (Lido Stockholm), and a roof terrace that catches the sea breezes. It's a joy to have breakfast up here, looking out to Mount Etna. The setting is perfect, the hotel is comfortable, the staff are attentive and friendly – this must be one of the best-loved hotels in Sicily. It's an aristocratic 19th-century villa with 15th-century pretensions, renovated in modern style with theatrical flourishes. Breakfast chairs are dressed in pleated linen, dove-grey sofas face glassy tables that mirror the sea, bedrooms trumpet generous beds and swagged curtains, a square blue pool sinks into a lush garden and shaded loungers line up on two sides. Here a barman serves stylish drinks on silver platters – magical at night. No indoor sitting space but an exotic bar in the Roman catacombs (there's a perfectly preserved Roman road in the garden, too); no restaurant either, but plenty in clifftop Taormina, a stroll away, or a hotel shuttle. It's a pretty little town but gets busy when the cruise ships are docked. Better by far to be chez Carlotta.

Price	€130-€300. Suites €200-€550.
Rooms	23: 7 doubles, 16 suites.
Meals	Lunch/dinner €20-€30. Wine €18-€40.
Closed	Mid-January to mid-February.
Directions	A18 exit Taormina. In town, left on Via Pirandello.

Andrea & Rosaria Quartucci
Via Pirandello 81,
98039 Taormina

Tel +39 0942 626058
Email info@villacarlotta.net
Web www.hotelvillacarlottataormina.com

Hotel Villa Ducale

The ebullient Dottor Quartucci and his family have restored their fine old village house with panache. Rosaria has travelled the world for ideas – her style is antique-Sicilian – and cherishes every guest. From the delicious little pastries at tea to the large umbrellas on loan, from the valet parking to the shuttle to the private beach, every detail has been considered. Now the big roofed terrace high on the hill has clear plastic walls – perfect for the wetter months – and distance lends enchantment to the view, so gaze on the sweep of five bays and looming Mount Etna as you breakfast on Sicilian specialities. This is Taormina, the chicest resort in Sicily, and rich in archaeology and architecture. Flowers are the keynote of this romantic little hotel: bunches in every room, pots placed like punctuation marks on the steps, private terraces romping with bougainvillea. Bedrooms, not large, are full of subtle detail, each with a luxurious shower room, bathrobes and slippers; warm old terracotta tiles carry family antiques and hand-painted wardrobes, and five of the suites are across the road. One of our favourites.

Price	€130-€250. Suites €250-€400.
Rooms	17: 11 doubles, 6 suites for 2-4.
Meals	Lunch/dinner €30-40. Wine €18-€45.
Closed	10 January-10 February.
Directions	From Taormina centre towards Castelmola; signed.

Andrea & Rosaria Quartucci
Via L. da Vinci 60,
98039 Taormina

Tel +39 0942 28153
Email info@villaducale.com
Web www.villaducale.com

La Casa di Pippinitto

The farm is small, delightful and organic, the coast is a short drive, and you can walk to simple cafés, restaurant and museum. But the real star here is Mount Etna, the largest active volcano in Europe. Come for organised treks to the crater, skiing in winter, walking the rest of the year. Back at the farm, delightfully hands on, is Cesare. His wife is a teacher; the family is multi-lingual and well-travelled. This is a lovely set up for a family stay, with gardens to run around in, hammocks slung between walnut trees, a guest kitchen in which to rustle up a meal, and two friendly labs to chase. You can also self-cater, in the characterful old casita dedicated to Pippinitto, the farmer who once lived here with his family and donkey. Expect new mattresses and good linen, en suite showers, wood-burning stoves; the décor, complimented by wonderful country beams and old terracotta, is simple, modern and comfortable throughout. As you'd expect, Cesare's breakfasts are plentiful and delicious – warm rolls, yogurts, home fruits, cakes and jams – served at separate wooden tables in a lovely airy room.

Price	€70-€80. Cottage €70-€80. Minimum stay 2 nights.
Rooms	4 + 1: 4 doubles. Cottage for 4-5.
Meals	Restaurants in village.
Closed	December-March.
Directions	Sent on booking.

Cesare Gulisano
Via Pennisi 44,
95010 Santa Venerina

Tel +39 0959 53314
Email info@lacasadipippinitto.it
Web www.lacasadipippinitto.it

Palmento la Rosa Agriturismo

A chunky ten-metre beam dominates the lofty living area, a reminder that Palmento la Rosa ('wine estate Rosa') once housed a wine press. Now it is a sophisticated estate – Franz loves his wines and has an excellent cellar – and a charming place to stay. Your stylish, lively, delightful hosts have swapped Paris for this green haven at the foot of Europe's most celebrated volcano, 700 metres above sea level (never too hot) and surrounded by acres of Etna vines, sharing their passion for life, culture, sunshine and good food with guests. Served at one big granite table on the terrace in summer, meals are fresh colourful Sicilian and desserts are magnificently baroque; wines are from Biondi and Benanti. There's a generosity of spirit here; high ceilings and sweeping chestnut floors, sprawling sofas, two fireplaces, original art and bedrooms flooded with light. Those on the ground floor open to palm trees and roses, those on the first have sea views. Trek in the National Park or climb the lower craters of Etna – cable cars can replace legs if need be – or dine simply at La Tana del Lupo in Pedara.

Price	€120-€160. Minimum 2 nights.
Rooms	4: 3 doubles, 1 twin.
Meals	Dinner €35-€45. Wine from €15. Restaurants 3km.
Closed	8 January-15 February.
Directions	Sent on booking.

Franz & Zora Hochreutener
Via Lorenzo Bolano 55,
75030 Pedara

Tel +39 0957 896206
Email info@palmentolarosa.com
Web www.palmentolarosa.com

Borgopetra

In the historic centre of Mascalucia, an exquisite revival of a 400-year-old manor house surrounded by orchards and gardens. Journalist Cristina left the high life in Milan to join Toto in the restoration of his family *borgo*. On the southern slopes of Mount Etna, self-contained yet unremote and ten kilometres from the sea, the luxurious apartments wrap themselves around a square courtyard brimful of cacti and jasmine. The attention to detail is exceptional, from the ergonomic beds to the soaps hand-made in Catania, from the Mascalucia olive oil in the kitchens to the thyme-infused honeys at breakfast. Stunning antique rubs shoulders with stylish modern: perhaps a chic red basin on an ancient terracotta floor, an old country wardrobe, a sleek chaise longue. Among apricot and orange trees and the pergola of an ancient vine is a cool pool; in the old marionette theatre, a massage room, gym, bar, and shelves crammed with Cristina's crime mysteries and board games. Cristina and Toto are the warmest pair you're ever likely to meet, in this oasis of beauty and peace. *Minimum stay two nights.*

Price	€125-€210.
Rooms	1 + 3: 1 suite. 1 apt for 2-3, 2 apts for 6.
Meals	Restaurant 300m.
Closed	Mid-November to end February.
Directions	15km from Catania; from m'way, exit Gravina-Etna. Detailed directions on booking.

Cristina Pauly
Via Teatro 9,
95030 Mascalucia

Tel +39 0957 277184
Mobile +39 333 8284930
Email info@borgopetra.it
Web www.borgopetra.it

Monteluce Country House

In deep country – four miles from sleepy baroque Noto (World Heritage site) and two from the beautiful Vendicari nature reserve – Monteluce is a jewel of design and warm-heartedness. Designer Imelda has created a wilderness bolthole from the grey urban north and loves to receive guests. As carefully as these two houses lie respectfully low among their 12 hectares of olive and citrus groves, their sense of space and style wrap you gently in colour, texture, excitement, and extreme Italian comfort. Brilliant, individually tiled bathrooms, fun stylish furniture, superb beds, fine detailing, nothing tacky, and each room with its own patio or garden – with spectacular views to the sea. If you are self-catering in one of the apartments, your kitchen will be a further delight of colour and style; beds may be on big generous mezzanines. Breakfast is a joy – fresh baking daily and wonderful Sicilian fruit salads, brought to a table overlooking the orange groves as Imelda entertains with her fascinating talk of north and south Sicilian life. *One hour from Catania Airport.*

Price	€150-€230. Apts €1,050-€1,400 per week.
Rooms	5 + 3: 4 doubles, 1 suite (with kitchenette). 3 apartments: 1 for 3, 2 for 2.
Meals	Breakfast €14 for self-caterers. Restaurant 3km.
Closed	B&B: November to mid-March.
Directions	M'way for Gela exit Noto, then Noto-Pachino-Villa Romana del Tellaro; left for Noto; at x-roads, left for Pachino Portopalo on SP19; at km5.5, right onto SP22 for Vaddeddi-Villa Romana del T; 2km, on right.

Imelda Rubiano
Contrada Vaddeddi, Villa Romana
del Tellaro, 96017 Noto
Mobile +39 335 6901871
Email info@monteluce.com
Web www.monteluce.com

Bed & Breakfast Villa Aurea

Once the family's summer house, Villa Aurea is now a gentle, friendly place to stay, thanks to the owner's son, Enrico, who has given up city hotels for this. His father shaped these surroundings, his architect's eye and his attention to detail ensuring the place feels calm, spacious and uncluttered; his mother bakes fabulous cakes and tarts and delivers a divine breakfast, enjoyed in the garden in summer. Cupboards blend discreetly into the walls, stylish shutters soften the Sicilian light and low round windows are designed to allow moonlight to play in the corridor. Bedrooms are minimalist with bright white walls and bold bedcovers. Upstairs rooms share a long terrace shaded by a huge carob tree; two rooms interconnect for families. Tiled bathrooms – some huge, with sea views – sparkle and use solar-heated water. A tree was planted to mark the birth of each of the three children and the garden is now luscious and filled with all kinds of tree: banana, orange, lemon, almond... you can idle in their shade, work up a steam on the tennis court, or cool off in the striped pool. *New hotel opened in Pozzallo, 5km.*

Price	€60-€110.
Rooms	7 doubles.
Meals	Restaurants 2km.
Closed	Rarely.
Directions	Motorway Siracusa-Gela, exit Rosolini. SP46 Ispica-Pozzallo for Pozzallo, house 4km. Signed.

Francesco Caruso
Contrada Senna,
97014 Ispica

Tel +39 0932 956575
Email villa.aurea@gmail.com
Web www.marenostrumpozzallo.it/villaaurea

Torre Marabino

Arrow slits for sea views remain – but with the bandits gone by 1868, Baron di Belmonte turned the thick walls of this coastal watchtower into a holiday retreat. Today it feels almost English, as oak, ash and poplar mix with figs, lemons and prickly pears. Manicured lawns are punctuated by palm and magnificent olive trees, while the pool and children's play area are discreetly tucked away. There's plenty of space to wander, picking tomatoes, exploring polytunnels of organic produce, and touring the olive groves and vineyards of this working farm. Inside, divergent living and dining rooms are elegant and comfortable beneath their high ceilings: deep pink furnishings here, the carved side of an old Sicilian cart there – a lovely authentic touch. All seven bedrooms divide onto mezzanine floors reached by staircases with wrought-iron railings, and the kitchenettes are perfect for picnic-making. Food matters here: even the locals come for homemade pasta, local sausage, fish of the day... Salvo is a tremendously proud restaurateur. For anything else, delightful Francesco and Simona are at hand. Heart-warming.

Price	€110-€180.
Rooms	7 doubles, all with kitchenette.
Meals	Half board €30 p.p. Wine €14-€30.
Closed	End January to early February.
Directions	Sent on booking.

Francesco Pluchinotta
C. da Marabino C.P. 19,
97014 Ispica

Tel +39 0932 795060
Email info@torremarabino.com
Web www.torremarabino.com

Nacalino Agriturismo

Concetta and Fillippo have bags of enthusiasm for their agriturismo, their food (it's exceptional), their children, and their eventful lives. They've been doing B&B in this pretty area of southern Sicily for over a decade now but there's no sign of their slowing down; everything is done with Sicilian energy, humour and flair. Simple bedrooms in the old stables border a grassy square with tables and chairs so you can sit out in the sun, while the rooms above the restaurant are more elegant, with high ceilings and polished chests at the foot of handsome beds. Dinner is a fabulous regional experience and everything is home-produced, from the olive oils to the wines. It's a great spot for families too – children will enjoy getting to know the friendly donkeys, and there's a communal sitting room stuffed with books and games for dreary days. The sea isn't far; Modica is a half-hour drive. Little English is spoken here but you'll leave with new friendships made – even if you haven't managed to exchange a single word in the same language! *Owners also have self-catering apartments 5km away.*

Price	€70-€130.
Rooms	12: 3 twins/doubles, 2 triples, 7 family rooms: 4 for 3, 3 for 4.
Meals	Dinner with wine, €25.
Closed	Rarely.
Directions	From Catania, m'way SR-Gela exit Rosolini; dir. Ispica, then Modica, then signs to Ragusa on SS115. Left for Marina di Modica after 7km, then right for Contrada Nacalino; on for 1.8km.

Filippo & Concetta Colombo
Contrada Nacalino, sn,
97015 Modica

Tel	+39 0932 779022
Mobile	+39 338 1611135
Email	info@nacalinoagriturismo.it
Web	www.nacalinoagriturismo.it

Palazzo Failla Hotel

Straddling a busy corner in spire-embellished Modica (there are dozens of churches on your doorstep) is this grand old hotel. Hemmed in by a lively café bar on one side, and its Michelin-starred restaurant on the other, the place buzzes with locals and tourists. The very smart exterior, with its red-carpeted stone steps and handsome red awnings, belies the atmosphere inside: informal, relaxed and friendly. Cheerful staff welcome you through sparkling glass doors and whisk you up wide stairs, through a beautiful old room with original floor-to-ceiling wood panelling, and into opulent bedrooms. Polished marble floors are decorated in exquisite geometric patterns; cherubs dance across high frescoed ceilings; and beautiful antiques from all corners of Italy pose against sumptuously papered walls. Chandeliers, gilt-framed paintings, rich embroidered bed linen: it's fabulous. Further rooms are found off a lovely sunlit courtyard a minute's walk from the main hotel. Have breakfast in the café, supper in the restaurant, and spend every hour in between exploring this beautiful town.

Price	€69-€169. Single €69-€169. Triple €99-€199. Quadruple €119-€219.
Rooms	10: 6 twins/doubles, 2 singles, 1 triple, 1 quadruple.
Meals	Restaurant next door. Wine €3-€12.
Closed	Never.
Directions	From Ragusa, 12km, 1st exit Modica Alta. Hotel is 300m after Duomo di San Giorgio, Piazza S. Teresa.

Paolo Failla
Via Blandini 5,
97015 Modica

Tel +39 0932 941059
Email info@palazzofailla.it
Web www.palazzofailla.it

Anime a Sud

In Modica's baroque heart is a small 19th-century townhouse in which history and modernity magically combine. It has been remodelled by artist and eco engineer Luca – zero-impact energy applies and feng shui principles shine. Off a narrow, broad-stepped alley to a solid wood front door, and a friendly housekeeper invites you in and shows you the ropes. Find a cool, calm, unexpectedly spacious interior, bright with natural colours and bold canvases, polished cement floors and wrought-iron banisters… and stylish candle lanterns for bedrooms, balcony and terrace. The double is off the open-plan living room while the family room is up some steps and opens to a big dining terrace, replete with lemon trees in pots and a roofscape that twinkles at night. White and chocolate brown linen enfolds simple wrought-iron bedsteads, there are antique floor tiles and painted wooden shutters, and bathrooms small but perfectly formed. Modica has endless fiestas and a jazz festival in July; lovely beaches are 20 minutes away. The serenity nourishes the soul. *Ask about Sicilian cookery courses & wine tours.*

Price	€910-€1,260 per week. Minimum stay 3 nights.
Rooms	House for 5 (1 double, 1 family room for 3).
Meals	Restaurants nearby.
Closed	Never.
Directions	Sent on booking.

Luca Giannini
Via S. Lucia 9,
97015 Modica Alta
Mobile +39 338 9275393
Email info@animeasud.it
Web www.animeasud.it

Tenuta Cammarana

Deep in Sicilian countryside, wrought-iron gates lead to a rare delight: a rich green lawn framed by rambling roses and scented plants. This gorgeous country house, built in 1778, remains in the family; so does impeccable taste. Arrive to vaulted stone ceilings that create elegant cocoons in which to unpack and unwind. Classic, understated furnishings have charming touches such as old lace tablecloths, warm rugs and fine china, while bedrooms are modest but modern, with small spotless bathrooms and delicious local soaps. One room opens to its own shaded piece of garden. At the heart of this baroque golden triangle, Roman mosaics, beautiful towns and stunning woodlands are yours to unravel; you could also hire horses from next door's farm and ride to the coast – or picnic in a valley grove. If asked, Giuseppe will make you exquisite dinner using recipes from his aristocratic roots, focusing on ricotta, milk, vegetables and herbs from the farm, matched by excellent wines. Stroll along flagstones, admire the views, relax beneath star-dusted skies. A stunningly lovely place – one for the grown-ups!

Price	€120-€200.
Rooms	3: 2 doubles, 1 suite.
Meals	Dinner on request.
Closed	Rarely.
Directions	Sent on booking.

Giuseppe Pulvirenti
Contrada Cammarana sn,
97100 Ragusa

Tel	+39 0932 616158
Mobile	+39 339 8196562
Email	info@tenutacammarana.it
Web	www.tenutacammarana.it

Fattoria Mosè Agriturismo

The town creeps ever up towards the Agnello olive groves but the imposing house still stands proudly on the hill, protecting its private chapel and a blissfully informal family interior. In the main house, high, cool rooms have superb original floor tiles, antiques and family mementos. The B&B room is plainer, has an old-fashioned idiosyncratic bathroom and olive-grove views. Breakfast is in a huge, shutter-shaded dining room or on the terrace, the dumb-waiter laden with homemade jams served on silver. Three generations still work this farm where Chiara's family used to come to escape Palermo's summer heat; she runs cookery courses and all ages are invited to join in the olive harvest. The stables, now six airy modern apartments, have high, pine-clad ceilings, contemporary fabrics and good little kitchens, plain white walls, no pretensions. Most have their own terrace, all spill onto the lovely plant-packed courtyard (with barbecue), and there are Chiara's olive oils, almonds and fruits and vegetables to buy. The 'Valley of the Temples' is a short and hugely worthwhile drive. You may never want to leave.

Ethical Collection: Food.
See page 419 for details.

Price	€100. Apts €500 for 2; €800 for 4; €1,100 for 6. Apt prices per week. Min. 2 nights.
Rooms	1 + 6: 1 double. 6 apartments for 2, 4 or 6.
Meals	Breakfast €8 for self-caterers. Dinner with wine €25, by arrangement. Restaurants 2km.
Closed	7 Jan-March; November-22 December.
Directions	From Agrigento SS115 for Gela-Siracusa. At end of Villaggio Mosè road (past supermarkets, houses) left at sign for Fattoria Mosè; signed.

Chiara Agnello
Via M. Pascal 4,
92100 Villaggio Mosé

Tel	+39 0922 606115
Email	info@fattoriamose.com
Web	www.fattoriamose.com

Agriturismo Sillitti

Drive through rolling farmland, up past the almond and olive groves, until you can climb no further. This is it: stunning 360 degree views over the island and, on a clear day, Mount Etna in the distance. Silvia's family have farmed for generations. She's passionately organic – grows olives, almonds, wheat, vegetables – and loves to share both recipes and kitchen garden. The farmhouse is new, its apartments bright and simple, furnished in unfussy style with cream floor tiles, modern pine and colourful fabrics. Open-plan living areas include tiny kitchens for rustling up simple meals. Rooms won't win design prizes but are spotless and airy and have superlative views. Silvia and Bruno (a doctor in nearby Caltanissetta) are open and welcoming; you'll be won over by their warmth and her cooking. Breakfast on homemade bread, cakes and jams; dinner is a feast of Sicilian dishes. A great spot from which to explore the island – castles, temples, Palermo, Taormina – or enjoy the views from the lovely large garden, with pool, terrace and shady pavilion. Space, peace, delightful people. *Minimum stay two nights.*

Price	€80-€90. Apartments €500-€1,000 per week.
Rooms	5 + 3: 5 doubles. 3 apartments for 2-5.
Meals	Dinner with wine, €25. Restaurants 5km.
Closed	Rarely.
Directions	From Catania or Palermo A19 exit Caltanissetta onto SS640. Cont. on SS640 past Caltanissetta dir. Agrigento. After 10km exit for Serradifalco/Roccella. Stop here and phone Silvia.

Ethical Collection: Food.
See page 419 for details.

Silvia Sillitti
Contrada Grotta d'Acqua,
93100 Caltanissetta

Tel +39 0934 930733
Mobile +39 338 7634601
Email info@sillitti.it
Web www.sillitti.it

Villa Mimosa

Near the breathtaking temples of the Greek city of Selinunte, among umbrella pines, orange trees and olive groves, is Villa Mimosa. The great thing is you can self-cater here and do B&B – Jackie will deliver irresistible warm bread each morning. Three of her apartments stretch along the back and open onto a long pergola-shaded terrace and a garden – bright with poppies in spring. The fourth apartment is on the first floor, with a balcony. Each is open plan, with a simple shower room and a kitchenette, homely spaces traditionally furnished with chunky carved Sicilian armchairs, high antique beds, good linen. If you dine with Jackie, it's outside on the terrace on her side of the house, or in her *salotto* on cool evenings. She's lived in Sicily for years (and has managed to collect a goodly number of friendly cats and dogs along the way) so follow her priceless suggestions on what to do. The main road that passes close transports you to ancient temples, medieval towns, nature reserves and beautiful beaches. A favourite with our readers. *Email erratic: please always give a contact telephone number.*

Price	€70-€100. Apts €400-€600 per week. €10 extra for one night stays.
Rooms	4 apartments: 3 studio apts for 2-3, 1 apt for 2-3.
Meals	Dinner, 3 courses with wine, €35-€40. Restaurants 2km.
Closed	Rarely.
Directions	From Agrigento SS115 to very end, exit Castelvetrano. At end of slip-road sharp right; 2nd entrance on left.

Jackie Sirimanne
La Rocchetta, Selinunte,
91022 Castelvetrano

Tel	+39 0924 44583
Mobile	+39 338 1387388
Email	j.sirimanne@virgilio.it
Web	www.aboutsicily.net

La Casa di Argo

A delight to find B&B in the fishermen's quarter, bright with bobbing boats, still unposh, still unspoiled. Nice and peaceful too: there are no through roads and the sea is on three sides. Slip into the hall of this 1900s block – past Enzo's bike and canoe – then up a narrow stone stair to the flat on the first floor. Warm generous Enzo, ex lecturer in tourism, lives with his much-loved dog – Argo! To the right are the two guest bedrooms; to the left, a small living area and a strikingly colourful terrace; find a couple of sunloungers, bright flowers, a potted olive, objets trouvés. This is where Enzo brings you a breakfast of fresh breads, great coffee, exotic jams. Steps continue to a larger terrace bright with Tunisian tiles, and up to a small secluded patio from which you can gaze on the Egadi isles: a pretty spot for a glass of wine and a snooze. The two bedrooms, not large but interesting and original, have firm beds, decorative antique floor tiles and domed ceilings. Trapani's once neglected baroque centre is rich with churches, museums, restaurants and shops; the beaches are sandy and gorgeous.

Price	€60-€70. Minimum stay 3 nights.
Rooms	2 doubles.
Meals	Restaurants within walking distance.
Closed	November-January
Directions	Sent on booking.

Vincenzo Lo Coco
Via Baracche 17,
91100 Trapani

Tel +39 0923 360323
Mobile +39 333 9500424
Email enzolococo@libero.it

Zarbo di Mare

A simple stone-built house, slap on the sea, on a beautiful stretch of coast to the north-west tip of the island. Sun worshippers can follow the progress of the rays by moving from terrace to terrace through the day; those who prefer the shade will be just as happy. A vine-clad courtyard behind is a lovely place to take breakfast; for lunch, move to the large shady terrace with a barbecue; take dinner on the front terrace looking out to sea. Inside: two bedrooms, one double, one twin, an open-plan sitting room with an open fire (there's heating to keep you cosy), and a pine-and-white kitchen. Below the house are steps down to a private swimming platform, perfect for confident swimmers; the sea is deep, and great for snorkelling. Families with small children should swim from the beach at San Vito, where the water is shallow. There are some lovely things to see in this part of Sicily; visit the extraordinary Greek temple at Segesta, standing gravely and peacefully at the head of the valley. You're just three miles from St Vito, for shops, festivals, bars. *Contact number is in Belgium. Bikes for hire in village.*

Price	€750-€900 per week. Shorter breaks in low season.
Rooms	House for 2-4.
Meals	Restaurant 4km.
Closed	7 July-25 August.
Directions	Approx. 120km from Palermo airport. M'way to Trapani, exit Castellammare del Golfo. Coast road SS187 to Trapani. San Vito clearly signed. House 5km after village.

Barbara Yates
Contrada Zarbo di Mare 37,
91010 San Vito Lo Capo
Mobile +32 (0)474 984899
Email barbara.yates@belgacom.net

Chez Jasmine

Such a pretty, peaceful little place, reached through a private courtyard and up steps splashed with flowers. Jasmine stands away from tourist bustle in a 10th-century courtyard in the old Arab quarter; you are enveloped in the history of handsome Palermo yet all you hear are the birds. Irish-turned-Sicilian, the delightful Mary lives round the corner, leaves fresh breakfast in your kitchen, is involved in conservation, and can keep you entertained for hours with her insights into local mores. Her vertical, newly renovated 'doll's house' is adorable and the layout's fun. You step up to the bedroom on the first floor, then up to the little living area, then up again to the rooftop terrace. The bathroom is cute, the bedroom has its own wicker sofa and the living room has a lovely lived-in feel – plenty of books and well-chosen fabrics and furniture. Finally, an iron spiral leads to that leafy terrace, an oasis shaded by bamboo blinds, bliss for breakfast or a pre-dinner drink. Kalsart, a feast of music, art and many talents, makes summer evenings in La Kalsa especially pleasurable.

Price	€100-€130 per night. Minimum 3 nights.
Rooms	House for 2-4.
Meals	Restaurants on doorstep.
Closed	Rarely.
Directions	From port road in Palermo go towards La Kalsa; at Piazza Kalsa, right; house to left of Chiesa della Pietà.

Mary Goggin
Vicolo dei Nassaiuoli 15,
90133 Palermo

Tel +39 0916 164268
Mobile +39 338 6325192
Email info@chezjasmine.biz
Web www.chezjasmine.biz

Palazzo Cannata

The stone escutcheon over the door justifies the palatial name, the tenderly scruffy yard inside tells today's humbler tale. One of the most exuberantly, generously hospitable men you could hope to meet, Carmelo inhabits the top of the former bishop's palace; from the big plant-packed terrace your gaze plunges into the grand Palazzo dei Normani; Palermo's domes are beyond, all the treasures are within walking distance (and quite a bit of the traffic). The flat is as full of eclectic interest as Carmelo's captivating mixed-lingo conversation. He teaches mechanics, with deep commitment, and breathes a passion for dance and music. Everywhere are paintings and photographs, bits of furniture and cabinets of mementoes, yet there's space for everything to make sense. One could explore the details for hours, the madonnas in the high-bedded double room, the painted beds in the triple... A fount of insight into his home town, eco-conscious Carmelo will tell you all about it, and his eco-shop recycling project, too. After the pastry breakfast he has prepared before going to work, set out to discover his fascinating city.

Ethical Collection: Environment.
See page 419 for details.

Price	€80-€90.
Rooms	2: 1 double, 1 triple, sharing bath.
Meals	Restaurants nearby.
Closed	Rarely.
Directions	In Palermo, from Palazzo dei Normanni; left down small street off Via del Bastione.

Carmelo Sardegna
Vicolo Cannata 5,
90134 Palermo

Tel +39 0916 519269
Email sardegnacarmelo@hotmail.com

Le Terrazze

Don't tell! This is one of Palermo's sweetest secrets. Down one of the few quiet streets of this vibrant city, Le Terraze is hard to find (harder still to book into: advance bookings only). But as you climb its five plant-filled terraces, each level revealing yet more fine rooftop views, you know it's been worth it. Set in a 16th-century palazzo, this calm and gracious apartment opens up into lofty sunlit rooms bedecked in antiques, ceramics and paintings, all of which tell of a wealthy family history. During the renovation, Sicilian-born Giovanni and Magda made two remarkable discoveries: a stunning painted wooden ceiling in the sitting room, and fragments of frescoes in the grand, traditional bedrooms. Elegance is de rigeur here, even when sitting down to breakfast. Whether on the shaded terrace or in the dining room, lace table cloths, heirloom silver and fine china add distinction to pastries, fruits and jams. What better way to begin a day of cultural exploration? Then end it with a gentle 'passeggiata' towards dinner in one of the many local restaurants.

Price	€110. Singles €80. Quadruple €160.
Rooms	2: 1 double, 1 quadruple.
Meals	Restaurants nearby.
Closed	Rarely.
Directions	Sent on booking.

Giovanni & Magda Rizzo
Via Pietro Novelli 14,
90134 Palermo

Tel +39 0916 520866
Email leterrazze_palermo@yahoo.it
Web www.leterrazzebb.it

Palazzo Prestipino

A two minutes' walk from the station but a world away from its hustle and bustle, this is a cool, elegant refuge. Duck down a side street and into the courtyard sandwiched between a chic bar and a sushi restaurant (recommended by the palazzo owners), and take the wide marble stair to one of six beautiful apartments. This is no sterile conversion kitted out on the cheap but a considered restoration. The 18th-century building with fabulous vaulted ceilings was once covered in colourful and ornate frescos; many have been uncovered and restored and now sit successfully alongside the muted hues of designer furniture and state-of-the-art fittings – perhaps rather more suited to families with older children than gelato-toting tots! If you are inclined to cook, a cupboard at one end of your sunny sitting room opens to reveal the kitchen area so live like a Palermo local and pick up supplies from the wildly lively Ballarò market: it's close by. Charming young caretaker Lycia, justifiably proud of the new apartments in her charge, will be on hand with help and advice. *Ask about parking.*

Price	€80-€200 (€500-€800 per week).
Rooms	1 apartment for 2-5 (1 double, 1 double sofabed, 1 single sofabed).
Meals	Restaurants on doorstep.
Closed	Rarely.
Directions	Sent on booking.

The Owner
Via San Nicolò all'Albergheria 4,
90134 Palermo

Mobile	+39 338 6994011
Email	lyciat@libero.it
Web	www.palazzoprestipino.it

Casa Margaret

Stay in one of three freshly converted stone houses perched thrillingly on top of a hill. Reached by a rough wiggling track (be warned!), surrounded by ancient gnarled olive groves, each is filled with gorgeous bits and pieces from the owners' travels. Margherita, the highest, feels relaxed and laid back: a large covered terrace, wooden ceilings, stone floors, colourful objets old and new, sofas by the open fire. There's a glass-topped dining table and a mod-conned kitchen, and comfy bedrooms with hand-painted details. Rosita, above a main road, is the largest house, stylish yet cosy, with lots of bare stone and tiles, an iron candelabra in a snazzy dining room, and a children's bedroom under the rafters. Bianca, dinky and cute, has a peek-over wrought-iron mezzanine to the living room below, lined with lovely pottery and characterful tomes. All have barbecue terraces for the views: a glorious panorama of snow-capped mountains and sea. Far enough apart for privacy they are close enough for friends to enjoy. There's a swimming pool on site – a bit of a hike – and acres of ancient olive estate to roam wild in.

Price	€625-€2,215 per week.
Rooms	3 cottages: 1 for 2, 1 for 4, 1 for 5.
Meals	Restaurant 2km.
Closed	Rarely.
Directions	A29 for Palermo; A19 for Messina-Catania; 50km to x-roads, dir. Catania. 1st exit for "Buonfornello-Piano Zucchi-Sito Archeologico Imera". SS113 for Messina; 4.6km, right for Campofelice; road 9 to Madonie (SP9) for Collesano. After Campofelice stay on road; 2km 1st gate, right.

Margherita Carducci Artenisio
Km 4 della strada provinciale 9, Pizzillo, 90016 Collesano

Tel	+39 0916 199221
Email	info@casamargaret.it
Web	www.casamargaret.it

Casa Serena

Deep in hazelnut country is a white minimalist house with sliding glass doors and stupendous views. The mountain soars above, the valley plunges below, the peace is profound and walkers are in heaven: you have the beech woods of the Madonie National Park to explore. Walker or sybarite, you will be supremely comfortable in this perfectly insulated home. Downstairs is fully open-plan, all sweeping polished concrete floors and lofty white walls, with urban-sleek living areas and super-duper kitchen wrapped around a central sculptural stair. Expect cutting-edge LED lighting and abstract paintings on the walls, top-notch furnishings and fittings, and a white and grey palette with accents of fuchsia, violet and red – a strong stark personal style. For your entertainment are music, TV, board games and a wood-burning stove – no need to worry if you get snowed in! For summer: a four-acre garden, generous terraces on two sides, a sloping orchard behind, a barbecue and a plunge pool. As for civilisation, it's no distance at all: the unspoilt hilltop town of Polizzi Generosa is under three miles.

Price	£1,000-£1,500 per week. Minimum one week: May-September.
Rooms	House for 6.
Meals	Restaurants 4km.
Closed	Rarely.
Directions	Sent on booking.

Carl Gardner & Sylvie Pierce
90028 Polizzi Generosa

Tel +44 (0)20 7724 8543
Mobile +44 (0)7967 158206
Email carl@csglightingdesign.com

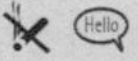

Ca' La Somara Agriturismo

A short drive to stunning bays, a far cry from the fleshpots of Costa Smeralda, Ca' La Somara's white buildings stand out against the wooded hills and crags of Gallura. As you'd expect from the name, donkeys feature here – they're one of Laura's passions. A vivacious ex-architect, she has converted the stables with charm and flair. Welcome to a serene, Moroccan oasis around a lovely central courtyard smothered in bouganvillea, hibiscus, plumbago, guarding a Turkish bath, a hay bath, a sauna, a yoga room, a massage room and a gym. Bedrooms, small and rustic-stylish, have floors of coloured cement or painted boards, Sardinian bedcovers, zingy hand-painted tiles, and lamps, rugs, objects from their travels. Visit the pretty village of San Pantaleo, an artists' community just up the hill, return to cushioned benches in the garden or hessian hammocks in the paddock, and views of the valley and its windswept cork oaks. Dinner is fresh Mediterranean, served with Sardinian wines and enjoyed at the convivial table. It's all deliciously restful and undemanding – and there's a fabulous pool.

Price	€58-€136.
Rooms	9 doubles.
Meals	Dinner €20. Guest kitchen.
Closed	Rarely.
Directions	From Olbia, S125 dir. Arzachena. Look out for track on right, signed San Pantaleo; through village, dir. Porto Cervo. Signed at bottom of hill on right.

Alberto & Laura Lagattolla
Loc. Sarra Balestra,
07021 Arzachena

Tel +39 0789 98969
Email info@calasomara.it
Web www.calasomara.it

La Vignaredda - Residenza d'Epoca

Twenty minutes from northern Sardinia's sandy beaches, in a mountain village famed for weaving, an 18th-century family house to make you feel at home. It's set in a tree-filled garden near the village museum, bright geraniums spilling from cast-iron balconies against a tall stone façade. Inside has a country feel with big fires, terracotta tiles and local rugs, and walls of chunky granite hewn from nearby hills. But there's period elegance in the antique chests, ornate lamps, carved mirrors and white walls of the family apartments; these come with kitchenettes and balconies for sunset drinks. Views tumble over cork oaks and rocky outcrops, and a maze of boulders in 'Moon Valley' below. Milan-based owner Maria Cristina may greet you in summer; otherwise gentle Maria Teresa serves breakfast, if you are doing B&B, by the shady porch or fire. The village's high position gives cool relief from Sardinian summers, but there's a terrace for soaking up sun. Aggius is an intriguing village with tapestry, carpets, gold filigree, hot springs, horse riding and quiet, star-filled nights.

Price	€80-€110. Apts €420-€885 per week.
Rooms	2 + 4: 2 doubles. 4 apartments: 3 for 2, 1 for 4.
Meals	Breakfast €10-€15. Restaurant 100m.
Closed	Rarely.
Directions	Sent on booking.

Maria Cristina Zara
Via Gallura 14,
07020 Aggius Olbia-Tempio

Tel +39 0796 20818
Mobile +39 335 8018240
Email info@lavignaredda.com
Web www.lavignaredda.com

Li Licci

Not so long ago, this tranquil place was inaccessible among immense rocks and cork oaks. Deserted after the death of Gianmichele's grandfather, it was rescued by Jane and Gianmichele in 1985. Then they began entertaining friends. English-born Jane is an inspired cook of Sardinian food and they eventually created a delightful restaurant, now under an excellent Moroccan chef who uses home-grown, organic produce – pecorino, ricotta, salamis, hams, preserves, liqueurs – to prepare well-reputed traditional and local food. And they have added four immaculate, simple, white-painted bedrooms, each with a shower. Jane looks after guests as she would like to be looked after herself, so staying here is like being in the home of a relaxed and hospitable friend. Li Licci has its own wells, producing the most delicious clear water, and a 2,000-year-old olive tree. Breakfast is outside in summer, overlooking the oak woods and hills of Gallura, or by the fire in the converted stables in winter: either way, a superb start to a day's walking, climbing or sailing... or lazing on the north coast beaches. *Minimum stay two nights.*

Price	€100. Half-board €65-€75 p.p.
Rooms	4: 2 doubles, 1 twin, 1 family room for 4.
Meals	Dinner with wine, €30-€40.
Closed	October-March.
Directions	Through S. Antonio to r'bout, then dir. Olbia. After 3.5km, right at sign. From Olbia Airport dir. Palau exit S. Mariedda-Tempio. 2km after Priatu, left at sign.

Agri Mar
Via Capo d'Orso 35,
07020 Palau

Tel	+39 0796 651149
Email	info@lilicci.com
Web	www.lilicci.com

Stazzo Chivoni

Cordiality, tranquillity, simplicity, at the end of a long winding road. Built in 1850, modernised in 2003, the plain granite 'stazzu gallurese' still keeps its reed-woven ceiling, its corner fireplace, its little windows: there's no artifice here. This charming Milanese couple swapped the city for nature and beaches (eight miles off), lone cattle grazing, peasant foods and homemade wines: life in the slow lane. He is a garden designer and has created an ornamental and a vegetable garden in harmony with the landscape; she is a translator. They give you your own bright sitting room with a rustic bohemian décor – vine branches and sea shells, a comfortable sofa, a simple table and chairs – off which is a sweet bedroom with soothing colours and polished cement floor. The bathroom has a bath with a curtain and a washing machine; all is spotless, frill-free. Breakfasts, in contrast, are sumptuous: yogurts, fruits, pastries, cakes, quiches, cheeses, eggs and cold cuts, brought to the pergola in summer. Discover a hinterland of cork oaks and wild olives, return to a hammock slung between the trees.

Price	€60-€70. Minimum stay 2 nights.
Rooms	1 double.
Meals	Restaurant 5km.
Closed	Rarely.
Directions	From Alghero dir. Sassari, then Tempio. In Tempio, left at lights, then SS133 dir. Palau. At km 24 of route SS133 left to Chessa. On for 2.5km; B&B signed.

Leo Rescigno
07020 Luogosanto
Mobile +39 328 6914505
Email bbsardinia@gmail.com
Web www.bbsardinia.it

Villa Las Tronas Hotel & Spa

It could be the setting for an Agatha Christie whodunnit (Hercule Poirot perhaps?): a crenellated, late 19th-century hotel dramatically set on a rocky spit jutting into the sea, though far more five-star-deluxe than the sleuth's usual haunts. The outer walls, gate and entry phone give the requisite aloof feeling, the atmosphere within is hushed and formal. Originally owned by a Piemontese count, it was bought by the present owners in the 1950s and they take huge pride in the place. The big reception rooms and bedrooms – formal, ornate, immaculate – have a curiously muted, old-fashioned air, while the new, high-ceilinged bathrooms are vibrant with modern fittings and green and blue mosaic tiles. On all sides, windows look down at fingers of rock pointing accusingly into azure Sardinian waters. There's a little lawned garden and a swimming pool, and a restaurant area poised just above the rocks; it's delightful to dine to the music the waves below. Close by is the pretty, interesting old quarter of Alghero, and there are fabulous beaches and good restaurants along the coast. *New wellness centre with indoor pool.*

Price	€200-€470. Suites €425-€2,200.
Rooms	24: 18 doubles, 6 suites.
Meals	Dinner à la carte. Wine from €25.
Closed	Never.
Directions	Leave Alghero, signs for Bosa/ Lungomare. Hotel on right.

Vito La Spina
Lungomare Valencia 1,
07041 Alghero

Tel +39 0799 81818
Email info@hvlt.com
Web www.hvlt.com

Su Dandaru

A totter down a cobbled alley in Bosa's impossibly quaint old town brings you to a prettily painted 1700s house with a red and yellow exterior. In contrast to the lovely old arches, the wooden beams, the stone floors is a fresh and imaginative décor. Four bedrooms are spread over three floors. The first, earth themed, is warmly hued and cosy with a big wrought-iron bed. The second, inspired by the river, is in greens and yellows, with linen curtains and a basket-weave bed; off the room, just before the bathroom, is a small room with a single bed. The third room, the suite, is all sea blues and greens, with a French armoire and antique lace curtains. Charming and inviting one and all, with small but perfectly formed bathrooms. Above is a sitting room with a comfy sofa, and a big roof terrace with views up to the medieval castle, down to the rooftops of Sa Costa; lovely for an evening under the stars. Or a chilled chianti after a day's boating on the river or lazing on the beach. You breakfast in an Italian café and can dine anywhere in town, perhaps at the owner's own little place, by the river under the palms.

Price	€50-€125. Single from €35. Minimum 2 nights in high season.
Rooms	4: 1 double, 1 family room; 1 double, 1 single sharing bathroom.
Meals	Restaurants within walking distance.
Closed	Rarely.
Directions	Coast road from Alghero to Bosa. In Bosa, left into town. Follow road, veer left, then 1st right, straight to end to r'bout/square. Park here; B&B is a 2-minute walk.

Giacomo Forte
Via del Pozzo 25,
Bosa

Mobile	+39 347 9680120
Email	info@sardiniabandb.com
Web	www.sardiniabandb.com

Hotel Su Gologone

The white buildings of Hotel Su Gologone stand among ancient vineyards and olive groves at the foot of towering Supramonte. Lavender and rosemary scent the valley. The hotel began life in the 1960s as a simple restaurant serving simple Sardinian dishes – roast suckling pig, wild boar sausages, ice cream with thyme honey; it is now known throughout Europe. Run by the founders' daughter, committed Sardinian Giovanna, it employs only local chefs and has a brilliant mountain-view terrace. In this remote wilderness region of the island this is an elegant and magical place, super-friendly despite its size, and only 30 minutes from the coast and wonderful beaches. Juniper-beamed bedrooms have intriguing arches and alcoves and lots of local crafts and art: embroidered cushions, Sardinian fabrics, original paintings, ceramics and sculpture. There's a new group of local crafts shops, too. Browse through a book about the island from the library, curl up in one of many cosy corners; hiking can be arranged; the pool is fed by cold spring water, there's a spa, a hot tub outside... A real treat. *Book in advance May-September.*

Price	Half-board €210-€320 for 2.
Rooms	69: 54 twins/doubles, 15 suites.
Meals	Half-board only. Wine from €10. Restaurant 8km.
Closed	Rarely.
Directions	From Oliena towards Dorgali. Right at sign for Su Gologone; hotel on right.

Luigi Crisponi
Loc. Su Gologone,
08025 Oliena

Tel	+39 0784 287512
Email	gologone@tin.it
Web	www.sugologone.it

The Ethical Collection is made up of places going the extra mile, and taking the steps that most people have not yet taken, in one or more of the following areas:

• **Environment** Those making great efforts to reduce the environmental impact of their Special Place. We expect more than energy-saving light bulbs and recycling – in this part of the Collection you might find owners who make their own natural cleaning products, properties with solar hot water and biomass boilers, the odd green roof and a good measure of green elbow grease.

• **Community** Given to owners who use their property to play a positive role in their local and wider community. For example, by making a contribution from every guest's bill to a local fund, or running pond-dipping courses for local school children on their farm.

• **Food** Awarded to owners who make a real effort to source local or organic food, or to grow their own. We look for those who have gone out of their way to strike up relationships with local producers or to seek out organic suppliers. It is easier for an owner on a farm to produce their own eggs than for someone in the middle of a city, so we take this into account.

How it works

To become part of our Ethical Collection owners fill in a detailed questionnaire asking demanding questions about their activities in the chosen areas.

We then review each questionnaire carefully before deciding whether or not to give the award(s). The final decision is subjective; it is based not only on whether an owner ticks 'yes' to a question but also on the detailed explanation that accompanies each 'yes' or 'no' answer.

We have not checked out the claims of owners before making our decisions, but we do trust them to be honest. We are only human, as are they, so please let us know if you think we have made any mistakes.

Ethical Collection in this book

A list of the places in our Ethical Collection is shown below, by entry number.

Environment

3 • 9 • 35 • 41 • 49 • 83 • 110 • 155 • 161 • 168 • 175 • 181 • 190 • 204 • 229 • 245 • 247 • 256 • 265 • 268 • 313 • 314 • 326 • 327 • 330 • 334 • 339 • 358

Community

83 • 160 • 177 • 234 • 300 • 323 • 326 • 334

Food

5 • 31 • 35 • 38 • 46 • 49 • 83 • 93 • 96 • 123 • 124 • 135 • 143 • 160 • 161 • 168 • 169 • 175 • 177 • 178 • 180 • 181 • 190 • 204 • 229 • 234 • 239 • 245 • 247 • 256 • 265 • 268 • 271 • 300 • 313 • 314 • 323 • 324 • 334 • 352 • 353

Ethical Collection online

There is stacks more information on our website, www.sawdays.co.uk/about_us_ethical_collection/faq/

For many years Alastair Sawday Publishing has been 'greening' the business in different ways. Our aim is to reduce our environmental footprint as far as possible and with almost everything we do we have environmental implications in mind. In recognition of our efforts we won a Business Commitment to the Environment Award in 2005, a Queen's Award for Enterprise in the Sustainable Development category in 2006, and the Independent Publishers Guild Environmental Award in 2008.

The buildings

Beautiful as they were, our old offices leaked heat, used electricity to heat water and rooms, flooded spaces with light to illuminate one person, and were not ours to alter.

So in 2005 we created our own eco offices by converting some old barns to create a low-emissions building. Heating and lighting the building, which houses over 30 employees, now produces only 0.28 tonnes of carbon dioxide per year – a reduction of 35%. Not bad when you compare this with the six tonnes emitted by the average UK household. We achieved this through a variety of innovative and energy-saving building techniques, some of which are described below.

Insulation By laying insulating board 90mm thick immediately under the roof tiles and on the floor, and lining the inside of the building with plastic sheeting, we are now insulated even for Arctic weather, and almost totally air-tight.

Heating We installed a wood pellet boiler from Austria in order to be largely fossil-fuel free. The heat is conveyed by water to all corners of the building via an underfloor system.

Water We installed a 6,000-litre tank to collect rainwater from the roofs. This is pumped back, via an ultra-violet filter, to lavatories, shower and basins. There are also two solar thermal panels on the roof providing heat to the one hot-water cylinder.

Lighting We have a mix of low-energy lighting – task lighting and up lighting – and have installed three sun pipes.

Electricity Our electricity has long come from the Good Energy Company and is 100% renewable.

Photo left: Tom Germain
Photo right: Jackie King

Materials Virtually all materials are non-toxic or natural, and our carpets are made from (80%) Herdwick sheep wool from National Trust farms in the Lake District.

Doors and windows Outside doors and new windows are wooden, double-glazed and beautifully constructed in Norway. Old windows have been double-glazed.

More greenery

Besides having a building we are proud of, and which is pretty impressive visually, too, we work in a number of other ways to reduce the company's overall environmental footprint.

- office travel is logged as part of a carbon sequestration programme, and money for compensatory tree planting donated to SCAD in India for a tree-planting and development project
- we avoid flying and take the train for business trips wherever possible
- car sharing and the use of a company pool car are part of company policy, with recycled cooking oil used in one car and LPG in the other
- organic and Fair Trade basic provisions are used in the staff kitchen and organic and/or local food is provided by the company at all in-house events
- green cleaning products are used throughout
- kitchen waste is composted on our allotment
- the allotment is part of a community garden – alongside which we keep a small family of pigs and hens

However, becoming 'green' is a journey and, although we began long before most companies, we realise we still have a long way to go.

1 Friuli-Venezia Giulia

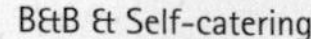

B&B & Self-catering 2

3 Agriturismo La Faula

4 An exuberant miscellany of dogs, donkeys and peacocks on a modern, working farm where rural laissez-faire and modern commerce happily mingle. La Faula has been in Luca's family for years; he and Paul, young and dynamic, abandoned the city to find themselves working harder than ever. Yet they put as much thought and energy into their guests as into the wine business and farm. The house stands in gentle countryside at the base of the Julian Alps – a big, comfortable home, and each bedroom delightful. Furniture is old, bathrooms new. There is a bistro-style restaurant where wonderful home-reared produce is served (free-range veal, beef, chicken, lamb, just-picked vegetables and fruits); on summer nights there may be a barbecue. An enormous old pergola provides dappled shade during the day; sit and dream awhile with a glass of estate wine or aqua vita. Or wander round the vineyard and *cantina*, watch the wine-making in progress, practice your skills with a golf club on the residents' driving range, cool off in the river, visit the beaches of the Adriatic. Perfect for families. *Minimum stay two nights.*

Price	€80. Apartments €455 per week.	5
Rooms	9 + 4: 9 twins/doubles. 4 studio apartments for 2-4.	6
Meals	Lunch/dinner €19. Wine €10. Restaurant 500m.	7
Closed	16 September-14 March.	8
Directions	A23 exit Udine Nord dir. Tarvisio/ Tricesimo. From SS13 Pontebbana dir. Povoletto-Cividale. At r'bout, right dir. Povoletto. At Ravosa, pass Trattoria Al Sole on left; right after 20m. Signed.	9

10 Ethical Collection: Environment; Community; Food. See page 419 for details.

Paul Mackay & Luca Colautti
Via Faula 5, Ravosa di Povoletto,
33040 Udine

Mobile +39 334 3996734
Web www.faula.com

11 Entry 83 Map 5 12